THE POETICAL WORKS

OF

ALEXANDER POPE

EDITED

WITH NOTES AND INTRODUCTORY MEMOIR

BY

ADOLPHUS WILLIAM WARD, M.A., Litt.D.

FROM THE GLOBE EDITION
REVISED AND ENLARGED

VOL. II

WILDSIDE PRESS

SATIRES.

[THE Satires of Pope, which form the fourth volume of Warburton's edition, were published very nearly in the order in which they stand, viz. —

First Satire of Second Book of Horace	.		.		.	.	.	1733
Second " " "		.	.		.	1734 (written 1732)		
Epistle to Dr. Arbuthnot (Prologue to Satires)				.	.	.		1735
Donne's Satires Versified.	.	.	.	.	.	.	.	1735

First Epistle of First Book of Horace . . . . .
Sixth " " " . . . . . } 1737
First " Second " . . . . .
Second " " " . . . . .

One Thousand Seven Hundred and Thirty-eight } 1738
(Epilogue to Satires, Dialogues I. and II.)

They originated in a happy suggestion of Bolingbroke's, made to Pope on a visit to the latter in the winter of 1732, at the time when the composition of the *Essay on Man* was interrupted by a slight attack of fever which confined the poet to his room for a few days. Bolingbroke, happening to take up a Horace and to light on the First Satire of the Second Book, was struck by its applicability to the position of Pope, and recommended him to translate it into English. This Pope accomplished in a morning or two; and the success of the first attempt led him to repeat the experiment until to his surprise he found he had reproduced more than a third of the Latin poet's Satires and Epistles in an English dress.

Even the Imitations of Horace proper are something very different from mere free translations of paraphrases; the Prologue and Epilogue are independent satires, the former in the form of an Epistle, the latter in that of Dialogues; and the Versified Satires of Dr. Donne, written by Pope (as he informs us) several years before their publication, were merely retouched with allusions which make them to a certain degree harmonise with the rest of the series. It will therefore be most convenient to prefix to the Prologue, the Imitations and the Epilogue independently, such remarks as are suggested by the characters of each; and to distinguish from all these the paraphrase of Donne's Satires. The common characteristics of the entire group need little demonstration. In versification and diction generally, these Satires are Pope's master-pieces. The spirit which dictated them is the same : a strong and not unworthy self-consciousness, combined with a relentless desire to damage the reputation of all to whom the poet was opposed on public or on private grounds. It would be unjust to attribute to personal spleen and personal animosity the whole of Pope's scathing invective; a zeal for public morality accompanies a genuine respect for individual merit; but no private enemy of the poet's, no political opponent of his friends, has a chance

T   273

of candid and fair treatment. Even Sir Robert Walpole is only incidentally recognized as not wholly without virtues, because he had once conferred a personal favour upon Pope; even Addison's moral purity only meets with recognition because the quarrel between him and Pope was at an end with the death of the former. The endless egotism of Pope, and the standard by which in the end he measured his opinion of others, accordingly deprive him of the right to be esteemed a moralist in these his most brilliant efforts; and notwithstanding his deprecation of the term, he can only be regarded, with reference to them, as a wit.]

EPISTLE TO DR. ARBUTHNOT.

ADVERTISEMENT.

To the first publication of this *Epistle*.

THIS paper is a sort of bill of complaint, begun many years since, and drawn up by snatches, as the several occasions offered. I had no thoughts of publishing it, till it pleased some Persons of Rank and Fortune (the Authors of *Verses to the Imitator of Horace*, and of an *Epistle to a Doctor of Divinity from a Nobleman at Hampton Court*)[1] to attack, in a very extraordinary manner, not only my Writings (of which, being public, the Public is judge) but my *Person, Morals*, and *Family*, whereof, to those who know me not, a truer information may be requisite. Being divided between the necessity to say something of *myself*, and my own laziness to undertake so awkward a task, I thought it the shortest way to put the last hand to this Epistle. If it have any thing pleasing, it will be that by which I am most desirous to please, the *Truth* and the *Sentiment;* and if any thing offensive, it will be only to those I am least sorry to offend, *the vicious* or *the ungenerous*.

Many will know their own pictures in it, there being not a circumstance but what is true; but I have, for the most part, spared their *Names*, and they may escape being laughed at, if they please.

I would have some of them know, it was owing to the request of the learned and candid Friend to whom it is inscribed, that I make not as free use of theirs as they have done of mine. However, I shall have this advantage, and honour, on my side, that whereas, by their proceeding, any abuse may be directed at any man, no injury can possibly be done by mine, since a nameless character can never be found out, but by its *truth* and *likeness*. P.

[Parts of this poem, and notably the famous passage relating to Addison, had been written many years previously and published as fragments. But there is no trace of disjointedness in this, one of the most finished of Pope's compositions, which may be almost regarded in the light of a poetical apology *pro vitâ*, and an attempt for ever to silence the most notable of the poet's detractors. It was appropriately addressed to the most generally esteemed member of Pope's circle of friends and literary associates — one who in the last letter which he wrote to Pope (Arbuthnot died about a month after the publication of the *Epistle*) expressed his belief, that since their first acquaintance there had not been 'any of those little suspicions or jealousies that often affect the sincerest friendships;' and his certainty that there had been none such on his own side. Pope was about this time in need of the support of such approval as the judgment of his friends as well as his own self-consciousness could bestow, to support him in the tempest which he had raised not only by his *Dunciad* among the small fry of his literary enemies, but by his first Imitations of Horace among former friends, such as Lady Mary Wortley Montagu and Lord Hervey (see note to v. 305). The Epistle, singularly perfect and rounded in form is, notwithstanding its fragmentary origin, of the highest interest from an ethical as well as a literary point of view; nor is it possible to forbear from admiring its lofty conclusion, where that Resignation is upheld to which in actual life it was never given to the poet to attain.]

---

[1] [Of these squibs the former was said to be a joint production of Lady Mary Wortley Montagu and Lord Hervey; the latter was written by Hervey alone. See Carruthers's *Life of Pope*, ch. VIII.]

EPISTLE TO DR. ARBUTHNOT,[1]

BEING THE

PROLOGUE TO THE SATIRES.

P.   SHUT, shut the door, good John![2] fatigu'd, I said,
      Tie up the knocker, say I 'm sick, I 'm dead.
The Dog-star rages![3] nay 't is past a doubt,
All Bedlam, or Parnassus, is let out:
Fire in each eye, and papers in each hand,   5
They rave, recite, and madden round the land.
   What walls can guard me, or what shade can hide?
They pierce my thickets, thro' my Grot they glide;
By land, by water, they renew the charge;
They stop the chariot, and they board the barge.   10
No place is sacred, not the Church is free;
Ev'n Sunday shines no Sabbath-day to me;
Then from the Mint[4] walks forth the Man of rhyme,
Happy to catch me just at Dinner-time.
   Is there a Parson, much bemus'd in beer,[5]   15
A maudlin Poetess, a rhyming Peer,
A Clerk, foredoom'd his father's soul to cross,
Who pens a Stanza, when he should *engross?*
Is there, who, lock'd from ink and paper, scrawls
With desp'rate charcoal[6] round his darken'd walls?[7]   20

[1] [John Arbuthnot (born in 1675, died in 1735) besides being a most distinguished member of his profession, the medical, was eminent as a mathematician and a classical scholar. As a politician he was firmly attached to the Tory party, and with Swift became a member of the October Club, established in 1710 by Oxford, Bolingbroke and their political and literary friends. He was also a member of the Scriblerus Club, and to him is attributed the chief share in the famous treatise of M.S. *on the Art of Sinking in Poetry*, which was published in the Miscellanies of Pope and Swift. *The History of John Bull, the Art of Political Lying* and other *jeux d'esprit* of the same kind, were Arbuthnot's own. On the accession of George I. Arbuthnot was deprived of his post as Physician extraordinary at Court. Of Pope's sentiments towards Arbuthnot this Epistle offers the best testimony; Swift said of him that ' he has more wit than we all have; and more humanity than wit.']

[2] *Shut, shut the door, good John!*] John Searl, his old and faithful servant: whom he has remembered, under that character, in his Will. *Warburton.*

[3] [See Pers. Sat. III. v. 5. Several touches in the Epistle appear to be derived from the same Satire.]

[4] *Mint.*] A place to which insolvent debtors retired, to enjoy an illegal protection, which they were there suffered to afford one another, from the persecution of their creditors. *Warburton.*

[5] Some lines in this Epistle had been used in a letter to Thomson [the author of the *Seasons*] when he was in Italy, and transferred from him to Arbuthnot, which naturally displeased the former, though they lived always on terms of civility and friendship: and Pope earnestly exerted himself, and used all his interest to promote the success of Thomson's *Agamemnon*. *Warton.* [The readers of the *Seasons* will remember the poet's tribute to the virtues of the 'brown October' in *Autumn*.]

[6] The idea is from Boileau's *Art of Poetry* — ' charbonner les murailles.' *Bowles.*

[7] After v. 20 in the MS.,
' Is there a Bard in durance? turn them free,
With all their brandish'd reams they run to me:
Is there a Prentice, having seen two plays,
Who would do something in his Sempstress' praise.'   *Warburton.*

All fly to Twit'nam,[1] and in humble strain
Apply to me, to keep them mad or vain.
Arthur,[2] whose giddy son neglects the Laws,
Imputes to me and my damn'd works the cause:
Poor Cornus sees his frantic wife elope,   25
And curses Wit, and Poetry, and Pope.
    Friend to my Life! (which did not you prolong,
The world had wanted many an idle song)[3]
What *Drop* or *Nostrum* can this plague remove?
Or which must end me, a Fool's wrath or love?   30
A dire dilemma! either way I 'm sped,
If foes, they write, if friends, they read me dead.
Seiz'd and tied down to judge,[4] how wretched I!
Who can't be silent, and who will not lie.
To laugh, were want of goodness and of grace,   35
And to be grave, exceeds all Pow'r of face.
I sit with sad civility, I read
With honest anguish, and an aching head;
And drop at last, but in unwilling ears,
This saving counsel, "Keep your piece nine years."[5]   40
    "Nine years!" cries he, who high in Drury-lane,
Lull'd by soft Zephyrs thro' the broken pane,
Rhymes ere he wakes,[6] and prints before *Term* ends,
Oblig'd by hunger, and request of friends:
"The piece, you think, is incorrect? why, take it,   45
I 'm all submission, what you 'd have it, make it."
    Three things another's modest wishes bound,
My Friendship, and a Prologue,[7] and ten pound.
    Pitholeon sends to me: "You know his Grace,
I want a Patron; ask him for a Place."   50
'Pitholeon [8] libell'd me,' — "but here 's a letter
Informs you, Sir, 't was when he knew no better.

---

[1] [As to Pope's Villa at Twickenham, or 'Twitenham' as he preferred to write the name, see *Introductory Memoir*, p. xxxiv.]

[2] *Arthur*,] Arthur Moore, a leading politician of Queen Anne's time, who had raised himself by ability and unscrupulousness to place and power. His son James Moore (afterwards James Moore-Smythe), a small placeman and poetaster, and an acquaintance of the Blount family, became a noted object of Pope's scorn. See above all the famous description of the 'Phantom' in the *Dunciad*, bk. II. vv. 35-50, and cf. *Lines to Martha Blount*, in *Miscellaneous Poems*.]

[3] [Compare the charming dedication of Thackeray's *Pendennis*.]

[4] *Seiz'd and tied down to judge*,] Alluding to the scene in [Wycherley's] *Plain-Dealer*, where *Oldfox* gags, and ties down the Widow to hear his *well-penn'd stanzas. Warburton.* Rather from Horace; *vide* his Druso. *Warton.* [Hor. *Sat.* Bk. I. *S.* III. v. 86.]

[5] [Hor. *de Arte Poet*, v. 388.]

[6] *Rhymes ere he wakes*,] A pleasant allusion to those words of Milton,

    Dictates to me slumb'ring, or inspires
    Easy my unpremeditated Verse.
                                    Warburton.

[7] [A service commonly rendered by popular authors of that age to their less successful brethren. Pope wrote a Prologue to a play acted for the benefit of his ancient enemy Dennis in 1733. See *Miscellaneous Poems*.]

[8] *Pitholeon*] The name taken from a foolish Poet of Rhodes, who pretended much to *Greek*. Schol. in Horat. l. i. Dr. Bentley pretends, that this Pitholeon libelled Cæsar also. See notes on Hor. Sat. 10 *lib*. i. P.

POPE'S VILLA AT TWICKENHAM.

Dare you refuse him? Curll[1] invites to dine,
He 'll write a *Journal*,[2] or he 'll turn Divine."
  Bless me! a packet.— "'T is a stranger sues,   55
A Virgin Tragedy, an Orphan Muse."[3]
If I dislike it, " Furies, death and rage!"
If I approve, " Commend it to the Stage."
There (thank my stars) my whole Commission ends,
The Play'rs and I are, luckily, no friends,[4]   60
Fir'd that the house reject him, "'Sdeath I 'll print it,
And shame the fools —— Your Int'rest, Sir, with Lintot!"[5]
' Lintot, dull rogue! will think your price too much : '
" Not, Sir, if you revise it, and retouch."
All my demurs but double his Attacks;   65
At last he whispers, "Do; and we go snacks."[6]
Glad of a quarrel, straight I clap the door,
Sir, let me see your works and you no more.
  'T is sung,[7] when Midas' Ears began to spring,
(Midas, a sacred person and a king)   70
His very Minister who spy'd them first,
(Some say his Queen)[8] was forc'd to speak, or burst.
And is not mine, my friend, a sorer case,
When ev'ry coxcomb perks them in my face?
A. Good friend, forbear! you deal in dang'rous things.   75
I 'd never name Queens, Ministers, or Kings;
Keep close to Ears, and those let asses prick;
'T is nothing— P. Nothing? if they bite and kick?
Out with it, DUNCIAD! let the secret pass,
That secret to each fool, that he 's an Ass:[9]   80
The truth once told (and wherefore should we lie?)
The Queen of Midas slept, and so may I.
  You think this cruel? take it for a rule,
No creature smarts so little as a fool.
Let peals of laughter, Codrus! round thee break,   85
Thou unconcern'd canst hear the mighty crack :
Pit, Box, and gall'ry in convulsions hurl'd,
Thou stand'st unshook amidst a bursting world.[10]

---

[1] [Edmund Curll the bookseller. — See *Introductory Memoir*, p. xxxii.]

[2] Meaning the *London Journal;* a paper in favour of Sir R. Walpole's ministry. *Warton.*

[3] Alludes to a tragedy called the *Virgin Queen*, by Mr. R. Barford, published 1729, who displeased Pope by daring to adopt the machinery of his Sylphs in an heroi-comical poem called *the Assembly*. (1726.) *Warton.*

[4] Ver. 60 in the former Ed.
' Cibber and I are luckily no friends.'
                Warburton.
[Pope's own dramatic effort *Three Hours after Marriage* had been deservedly damned in 1717; whence the origin of his quarrel with Colley Cibber.]

[5] [Bernard Lintot, who began to publish for Pope in 1712.]

[6] [i.e. go shares. *Snack* or *snap* is properly a hastily snatched bit of food.]

[7] [Pers. *Sat.* I. 120.]

[8] *Queen*] The story is told, by some, of his Barber, but by *Chaucer* of his Queen. See Wife of Bath's Tale in Dryden's Fables. P.

[9] [Some ' false' editions of the Dunciad having an owl in their frontispiece, like the original edition, the next true edition, to distinguish it, fixed in its stead an ass laden with authors.]

[10] Alluding to *Horace*. [Od. III. 3.]
    Si fractus illabatur orbis,
      Impavidum ferient ruinæ. P.
[' The mighty crack,' as Warton points out, is

Who shames a Scribbler? break one cobweb thro',
He spins the slight, self-pleasing thread anew: 90
Destroy his fib or sophistry, in vain,
The creature 's at his dirty work again,
Thron'd in the centre of his thin designs,
Proud of a vast extent of flimsy lines!
Whom have I hurt? has Poet yet, or Peer,   95
Lost the arch'd eye-brow, or Parnassian sneer?
And has not Colley still his Lord, and whore?
His Butchers [1] Henley, his free-masons Moore? [2]
Does not one table Bavius still admit?
Still to one Bishop Philips seem a wit? [3]   100
Still Sappho— A. Hold! for God's sake — you 'll offend,
No Names! — be calm! — learn prudence of a friend!
I too could write, and I am twice as tall;
But foes like these— P. One Flatt'rer 's worse than all.
Of all mad creatures, if the learn'd are right,   105
It is the slaver kills, and not the bite.
A fool quite angry is quite innocent:
Alas! 't is ten times worse when they *repent.*
    One dedicates in high heroic prose,
And ridicules beyond a hundred foes: 110
One from all Grubstreet will my fame defend,
And more abusive, calls himself my friend.
This prints my *Letters*,[4] that expects a bribe,
And others roar aloud, "Subscribe, subscribe."
    There are, who to my person pay their court: 115
I cough like *Horace*, and, tho' lean, am short,
Ammon's great son one shoulder had too high,
Such *Ovid's* nose, and "Sir! you have an Eye"[5] —
Go on, obliging creatures, make me see
All that disgrac'd my Betters, met in me.   120
Say for my comfort, languishing in bed,
"Just so immortal *Maro* held his head:"
And when I die, be sure you let me know
Great *Homer* died three thousand years ago.[6]

Addison's phrase in his version of the ode, ridiculed by Martinus Scriblerus.]

[1] [Henley, see *Dunciad*, III. 199 and foll.] His oratory was among the *butchers* in Newport Market and Butcher Row. *Bowles.*]

[2] *free-masons Moore ?*] He was of this society, and frequently headed their processions.
                                                Warburton.

[3] Boulter, afterwards Primate of all Ireland, was Ambrose Philips' great friend and patron. *Bowles.* [Ambrose, or namby-pamby, Philips, whose Pastorals were published in the same Miscellany as those of Pope, and with whom the latter quarrelled. He became M. P. for Armagh through the influence of his patron.]

[4] [Some of Pope's letters to Cromwell had been surreptitiously printed by Curll in 1726.]

[5] *Sir! you have an Eye*] It is remarkable that amongst these compliments on his infirmities and deformities, he mentions his *eye*, which was fine, sharp, and piercing. It was done to intimate that flattery was as odious to him when there was some ground for commendation as when there was none. *Warburton.*

[6] After v. 124 in the MS.

' But, Friend, this shape, which You and Curl *
    admire,
Came not from Ammon's son, but from my
    Sire: †
And for my head, if you 'll the truth excuse,
I had it from my Mother,‖ not the Muse.
Happy, if he, in whom these frailties join'd,
Had heir'd as well the virtues of the mind.'
    * Curl set up his head for a sign. † His

Why did I write? what sin to me unknown   125
Dipt me in ink, my parents', or my own?
As yet a child, nor yet a fool to fame,[1]
I lisp'd in numbers, for the numbers came.[2]
I left no calling for this idle trade,
No duty broke, no father disobey'd.[8]   130
The Muse but serv'd to ease some friend, not Wife,
To help me thro' this long disease, my Life,
To second, ARBUTHNOT! thy Art and Care,
And teach the Being you preserv'd, to bear.
   But why then publish? *Granville* the polite,[4]   135
And knowing *Walsh*,[5] would tell me I could write;
Well-natur'd *Garth*[6] inflam'd with early praise;
And *Congreve*[7] lov'd, and *Swift* endur'd my lays;
The courtly *Talbot*,[8] *Somers*,[9] *Sheffield*,[10] read;
Ev'n mitred *Rochester*[11] would nod the head,   140
And *St. John's*[12] self (great *Dryden's* friends before)
With open arms receiv'd one Poet more.
Happy my studies, when by these approv'd!
Happier their author, when by these belov'd!
From these the world will judge of men and books,   145
Not from the *Burnets, Oldmixons,* and *Cookes.*[13]
   Soft were my numbers; who could take offence,
While pure Description held the place of Sense?

Father was crooked. || His Mother was much afflicted with headaches. *Warburton.*

[1] [See *Introductory Memoir* p. xlvi.]

[2] From Ovid [*Trist.* bk. IV. *El.* x. vv. 25–6.] *Warton.*

[8] *No father disobey'd.*] When Mr. Pope was yet a Child, his Father, though no Poet, would set him to make English verses. He was pretty difficult to please, and would often send the boy back to new turn them. When they were to his mind, he took great pleasure in them, and would say, *These are good rhymes.* *Warburton.*

[4] [See note to p. 12.]

[5] [See note to p. 10.]

[6] [See note to p. 14.]

[7] [William Congreve (born 1669, died 1728,) the author of the *Mourning Bride* and many famous comedies, was one of those who encouraged Pope's earliest efforts.]

[8] *Talbot, &c.*] All these were Patrons or Admirers of Mr. *Dryden;* tho' a scandalous libel against him entitled, *Dryden's Satyr to his Muse*, has been printed in the name of the Lord *Somers*, of which he was wholly ignorant.

These are the persons to whose account the author charges the publication of his first pieces: persons with whom he was conversant (and he adds beloved) at 16 or 17 years of age; an early period for such acquaintance. The catalogue

might be made yet more illustrious, had he not confined it to that time when he writ the *Pastorals* and *Windsor Forest*, on which he passes a sort of censure in the lines following,
> *While pure Description held the place of Sense, &c.* P.

[*Talbot.* See Pope's note to *Epilogue to Satires*, Dial. II. v. 79.]

[9] [*Somers.* See Pope's note *ib.* v. 77.]

[10] [*Sheffield.* See note to *Essay on Criticism*, v. 724.]

[11] [Atterbury bishop of Rochester. See note to Epitaph XIII.]

[12] [See note to p. 192.]

[13] *Burnets, &c.*] Authors of secret and scandalous History. P.

Burnets, Oldmixons, and Cookes.] By no means Authors of the same class, though the violence of party might hurry them into the same mistakes. But if the first offended this way, it was only through an honest warmth of temper, that allowed too little to an excellent understanding. The other two, with very bad heads, had hearts still worse. P.

[Gilbert Burnet bishop of Salisbury, the author of the *History of My own Times from the Restoration to the Peace of Utrecht* (which Swift annotated in the spirit of Pope's reference), died in 1715; Oldmixon, see *Dunciad*, II. vv. 282, foll.; and Cooke, see *ib.* II. 138 and notes.]

Like gentle *Fanny's* was my flow'ry theme,
A painted mistress, or a purling stream.[1]   **150**
Yet then did *Gildon*[2] draw his venal quill ; —
I wish'd the man a dinner, and sat still.
Yet then did *Dennis*[3] rave in furious fret ;
I never answer'd, — I was not in debt.
If want provok'd, or madness made them print,   **155**
I wag'd no war with *Bedlam* or the *Mint*.[4]
   Did some more sober Critic come abroad ;
If wrong, I smil'd ; if right, I kiss'd the rod.
Pains, reading, study, are their just pretence,
And all they want is spirit, taste, and sense.   **160**
Commas and points they set exactly right,
And 't were a sin to rob them of their mite.
Yet ne'er one sprig of laurel grac'd these ribalds,
From slashing *Bentley*[5] down to pidling *Tibalds* :[6]
Each wight, who reads not, and but scans and spells, **165**
Each Word-catcher, that lives on syllables,
Ev'n such small Critics some regard may claim,
Preserv'd in *Milton's* or in *Shakespeare's* name.[7]
Pretty! in amber to observe the forms
Of hairs, or straws, or dirt, or grubs, or worms![8]   **170**
The things, we know, are neither rich nor rare,
But wonder how the devil they got there.
   Were others angry : I excus'd them too ;
Well might they rage, I gave them but their due.
A man's true merit 't is not hard to find ;   **175**
But each man's secret standard in his mind,
That Casting-weight pride adds to emptiness,
This, who can gratify? for who can *guess ?*
The Bard whom pilfer'd Pastorals renown,
Who turns a Persian tale for half a Crown,[9]   **180**
Just writes to make his barrenness appear,

---

[1] Meaning the *Rape of the Lock*, and *Windsor Forest. Warburton. A painted meadow &c.* is a verse of Mr. Addison. P.

[2] [Charles Gildon, a converted Roman Catholic, of whom Warburton says in a note to *Dunciad*, I. 296, that ' he signalised himself as a critic, having written some very bad plays ; abused Pope very scandalously in an anonymous pamphlet of the Life of Mr. Wycherly, and in other pamphlets.' See also *Dunciad*, III. 173.]

[3] [See *Essay on Criticism*, vv. 270, 586 ; and *Dunciad, passim*.]

[4] [Cf. *ante*, v. 13.]

[5] [Dr. Richard Bentley. See *Dunciad*, IV. 201.]

[6] [As to Theobald, see Introduction to *Dunciad*.]

[7] Bentley's edition of *Paradise Lost*, which appeared in 1732, was at once the last and the

least worthy effort of his critical prowess ; as to Theobald's Shakspere, it was an honest and not wholly unsuccessful piece of work, and a better edition than Pope's own. Bentley's Milton is better characterised in *Imitations of Horace*, I. Ep. of II. Bk. vv. 103-4.]

[8] [Warburton has a characteristic note on this passage, referring with unconscious irony to his own edition of Shakspere — the edition which pointed the best of Foote's jests, when he compared a chimney-sweep on a noble steed to ' Warburton on Shakspere.']

[9] [Ambrose Philips, v. *ante* v. 100. Philips translated the *Persian Tales*, as well as two ' Olympioniques' of Pindar, and other Greek poems. His Pastorals brought him ' renown' at the hands of Gildon, who in his *Art of Poetry* ranked him with Theocritus and Vergil.]

And strains, from hard-bound brains, eight lines a year;
He, who still wanting, tho' he lives on theft,
Steals much, spends little, yet has nothing left: [1]
And He, who now to sense, now nonsense leaning,   185
Means not, but blunders round about a meaning: [2]
And He, whose fustian 's so sublimely bad,
It is not Poetry, but prose run mad: [3]
All these, my modest Satire bade *translate*,[4]
And own'd that nine such Poets made a *Tate*.[5]   190
How did they fume, and stamp, and roar, and chafe!
And swear, not ADDISON himself was safe.

Peace to all such! but were there One whose fires [6]
True Genius kindles, and fair Fame inspires;
Blest with each talent and each art to please,   195
And born to write, converse, and live with ease:
Should such a man, too fond to rule alone,[7]
Bear, like the Turk, no brother near the throne.
View him with scornful, yet with jealous eyes,
And hate for arts that caus'd himself to rise;   200
Damn with faint praise, assent with civil leer,
And without sneering, teach the rest to sneer;
Willing to wound, and yet afraid to strike,
Just hint a fault, and hesitate dislike;
Alike reserv'd to blame, or to commend,   205
A tim'rous foe, and a suspicious friend;
Dreading ev'n fools, by Flatterers besieg'd,
And so obliging, that he ne'er oblig'd; [8]
Like *Cato*, give his little Senate laws,
And sit attentive to his own applause;   210
While Wits and Templars ev'ry sentence raise,

---

[1] *Steals much, spends little, yet has nothing left:*] A fine improvement of this line of Boileau,

Qui toujours emprunt, et jamais ne gagne rien.   *Warburton.*

[2] *Means not, but blunders round about a meaning:*] A case common both to *Poets* and *Critics* of a certain order; only with this difference, that the *Poet* writes himself out of his *own meaning;* and the *Critic* never gets into *another man's.* Yet both keep going on, and *blundering round about* their subject, as benighted people are wont to do, who seek for an entrance which they cannot find.

[3] A verse of Dr. Evans. *Wilkes.*

[4] *All these, my modest Satire bade translate,*] See their works, in the Translations of classical books by several *hands*.

[5] [Nahum Tate, compendiously described by the late Prof. Craik as ' the author of the worst alterations of Shakspere, the worst version of

the psalms of David, and the worst continuation of a great poem (Absalom and Achitophel) extant.']

[6] For an account of Pope's relations with Addison see *Introductory Memoir*, p. xv. f. The sentiments and imagery in Pope's letter to Craggs of July 15th 1715 were embodied in the [above] character of Atticus . . . which appears to have been first printed in 1723 (in a collection of poems called *Cytherea* published by Curll), then included by Pope in the *Miscellanies* of 1727, and finally, after undergoing revision, engrafted into the Epistle to Arbuthnot, published in 1735. *Carruthers.*

[7] This image is originally Denham's. *Johnson.*

[8] After v. 208 in the MS.
' Who, if two Wits on rival themes contest,
Approves of each, but likes the worst the best.'
Alluding to Mr. P.'s and Tickell's Translation of the first Book of the Iliad. *Warburton.*

And wonder with a foolish face of praise : ——
Who but must laugh, if such a man there be?
Who would not weep, if ATTICUS [1] were he?
What tho' my Name stood rubric on the walls   215
Or plaister'd posts, with claps, in capitals?
Or smoking forth, a hundred hawkers' load,
On wings of winds came flying all abroad? [2]
I sought no homage from the Race that write ;
I kept, like *Asian* Monarchs, from their sight :   220
Poems I heeded (now be-rhym'd so long)
No more than thou, great GEORGE! a birth-day song.
I ne'er with wits or witlings pass'd my days,
To spread about the itch of verse and praise ;
Nor like a puppy, daggled [3] thro' the town,   225
To fetch and carry sing-song up and down ;
Nor at Rehearsals sweat, and mouth'd, and cry'd,
With handkerchief and orange at my side ;
But sick of fops, and poetry, and prate,
To *Bufo* left the whole *Castalian* state.   230
   Proud as *Apollo* on his forked hill,
Sat full-blown *Bufo*, puff'd by ev'ry quill ; [4]
Fed with soft Dedication all day long,
Horace and he went hand in hand in song. [5]
His Library (where busts of Poets dead   235
And a true *Pindar* stood without a head,) [6]
Receiv'd of wits an undistinguish'd race,
Who first his judgment ask'd, and then a place :
Much they extoll'd his pictures, much his seat,
And flatter'd ev'ry day, and some days eat :   240
Till grown more frugal in his riper days,
He paid some bards with port, and some with praise ;

[1] [This famous couplet first stood thus :
' Who would not smile if such a man there be ?
Who would not laugh if ADDISON were he?'
Then,
' Who would not grieve if such a man there be ?
Who would not laugh if ADDISON were he?'
                    Johnson.]
It was a great falsehood, which some of the
Libels reported, that this Character was written
after the Gentleman's death ; which see refuted
in the Testimonies prefixed to the *Dunciad.*
But the occasion of writing it was such as he
would not make public out of regard to his
memory : and all that could further be done
was to omit the name, in the Edition of his
Works. P.

[2] *On wings of winds came flying all
abroad ?*] Hopkins, in the civth Psalm, P.

[3] [To *daggle* is to run through the mire.
Hence Swift's epithet *daggle-tail.*]

[4] [Roscoe has shown that this cannot refer to

Lord Halifax, whom Warton understood to be
alluded to. Lord H. had died as far back as
1715, and is mentioned with respect (as he de-
served) by Pope (to whom he had even offered
a pension) in the *Epilogue to the Satires*, Dial.
II. v. 77. Halifax was on terms of civility with
Dryden, although he with Prior burlesqued the
Hind and Panther ; and though he ' helped to
bury' the poet, he had in no sense ' helped to
starve.' him. The personal reference remains
obscure.]

[5] After v. 234 in the MS.
' To Bards reciting he vouchsaf'd a nod,
And snuff'd their incense like a gracious god.'
                    Warburton.

[6] — *a true Pindar stood without a head*]
Ridicules the affectation of Antiquaries, who
frequently exhibit the headless *Trunks* and
Terms of Statues, for Plato, Homer, Pindar,
&c. Vide *Fulv. Ursin. &c.* P.

To some a dry rehearsal was assign'd,
And others (harder still) he paid in kind.
Dryden alone (what wonder?) came not nigh,   245
Dryden alone escap'd this judging eye:
But still the *Great* have kindness in reserve,
He help'd to bury whom he help'd to starve.[1]
  May some choice patron bless each gray goose quill!
May ev'ry *Bavius* have his *Bufo* still!   250
So, when a Statesman wants a day's defence,
Or Envy holds a whole week's war with Sense,
Or simple price for flatt'ry makes demands,
May dunce by dunce be whistled off my hands!
Blest be the *Great!* for those they take away,   255
And those they left me; for they left me GAY;[2]
Left me to see neglected Genius bloom,
Neglected die, and tell it on his tomb:
Of all thy blameless life the sole return
My Verse, and QUEENSB'RY weeping o'er thy urn.   260
  Oh let me live my own, and die so too!
(To live and die is all I have to do:)
Maintain a Poet's dignity and ease,
And see what friends, and read what books I please;
Above a Patron, tho' I condescend   265
Sometimes to call a minister my friend.
I was not born for Courts or great affairs;
I pay my debts, believe, and say my pray'rs;
Can sleep without a Poem in my head;
Nor know, if *Dennis* be alive or dead.[3]   270
  Why am I ask'd what next shall see the light?
Heav'ns! was I born for nothing but to write?
Has Life no joys for me? or, (to be grave)
Have I no friend to serve, no soul to save?
"I found him close with *Swift*"—'Indeed? no doubt,   275
(Cries prating *Balbus*) 'something will come out.'

---

[1] *— help'd to bury*] Mr. *Dryden*, after having liv'd in exigencies, had a magnificent Funeral bestowed upon him by the contribution of several persons of quality. P.

[2] [John Gay (born in 1688) was one of Pope's dearest friends; and when he died, Dec. 4th 1732, was mourned by the former, in a letter to Swift, as one who must have achieved happiness 'if innocence and integrity can deserve it.' To what extent the genius of Gay was neglected, may appear from the following statement made by Pope himself to Spence: 'He dangled for twenty years about a court, and at last was offered to be made usher to the young princess. Secretary Craggs made G. a present of stock in the South-Sea year; and he was once worth £20,000; but lost it all again. He got about £500 by the first *Beggar's Opera*, and £1100 or £1200 by the Second. He was negligent and a bad manager. Latterly, the Duke of Queensbury took his money into his keeping, and let him only have what was necessary out of it; and, as he lived with them, he could not have occasion for much. He died worth upwards of £3000.' As to the Duchess of Queensbury see *Moral Essays*, II. v. 193.]

[3] After v. 270 in the MS.
' Friendships from youth I sought, and seek them still:
Fame, like the wind, may breathe where'er it will.
The World I knew, but made it not my School,
And in a course of flatt'ry liv'd no fool.'

'T is all in vain, deny it as I will.
'No, such a Genius never can lie still;'
And then for mine obligingly mistakes
The first Lampoon Sir *Will.*[1] or *Bubo*[2] makes.   280
Poor guiltless I! and can I choose but smile,
When ev'ry Coxcomb knows me by my *Style?*[3]
  Curst be the verse, how well soe'er it flow,[4]
That tends to make one worthy man my foe,
Give Virtue scandal, Innocence a fear,   285
Or from the soft-eyed Virgin steal a tear.
But he who hurts a harmless neighbour's peace,
Insults fall'n worth, or Beauty in distress,
Who loves a Lie, lame Slander helps about,
Who writes a Libel, or who copies out: 290
That Fop, whose pride affects a patron's name,
Yet absent, wounds an author's honest fame:
Who can *your* merit *selfishly* approve,
And show the *sense* of it without the *love*;
Who has the vanity to call you friend,   295
Yet wants the honour, injur'd, to defend;
Who tells whate'er you think, whate'er you say,
And, if he lie not, must at least betray:
Who to the *Dean*, and *silver bell* can swear,[5]
And sees at *Canons* what was never there;   300
Who reads, but with a lust to misapply,
Make Satire a Lampoon, and Fiction, Lie.
A lash like mine no honest man shall dread,
But all such babbling blockheads in his stead.
  Let *Sporus* tremble[6] —   A. What? that thing of silk,   305

---

[1] Sir William Yonge. *Bowles.* ['A man whose fluency and readiness of speech amounted to a fault, and were often urged as a reproach, and of whom Sir Robert Walpole himself always said that nothing but Y.'s character could keep down his parts, and nothing but his parts support his character.' *Lord Stanhope.* He was a supporter of Walpole's.]

[2] Bubb Doddington, afterwards Lord Melcombe, the author of a well known Diary and the confidential adviser of Frederick Prince of Wales. He is a character typical in many respects of his age; utterly unconscientious and cheerfully blind to his unconscientiousness; and a liberal rather than discriminating patron of literary men. He died in 1762.]

[3] After v. 282 in the MS.

'P. What if I sing Augustus, great and good?
A. You did so lately, was it understood?
P. Be nice no more, but, with a mouth profound,
As rumbling D—s * or a Norfolk hound;
  * [Dennis.]   † [See *Dunciad*, bk. ii. v. 315.]

With GEORGE and FRED'RIC roughen every verse,
Then smooth up all, and CAROLINE rehearse.
A. No — the high talk to lift up Kings to Gods
Leave to Court-sermons, and to birth-day Odes.
On themes like these, superior far to thine,
Let laurell'd Cibber, and great Arnal † shine.
P. Why write at all? — A. Yes, silence if you keep,
The Town, the Court, the Wits, the Dunces weep.'

                                        Warburton.

[4] [Contrast with the self-complacency of Pope Dryden's noble lines of self-reproach in the *Elegy on Anne Killigrew.*]

[5] *Who to the Dean, and silver bell, &c.*] Meaning the man who would have persuaded the Duke of Chandos that Mr. P. meant him in those circumstances ridiculed in the Epistle on *Taste.* See Mr. Pope's Letter to the Earl of Burlington concerning this matter. P. [See note on *Moral Essays*, Ep. i. v. 54.]

[6] [The original of this famous portrait was

Sporus, that mere white curd of Ass's milk?[1]
Satire or sense, alas! can *Sporus* feel?
Who breaks a butterfly upon a wheel?
P.   Yet let me flap this bug with gilded wings,
This painted child of dirt, that stinks and stings;   310
Whose buzz the witty and the fair annoys,
Yet wit ne'er tastes, and beauty ne'er enjoys:
So well-bred spaniels civilly delight
In mumbling of the game they dare not bite.
Eternal smiles his emptiness betray,   315
As shallow streams run dimpling all the way.
Whether in florid impotence he speaks,
And, as the prompter breathes, the puppet squeaks;
Or at the ear of *Eve*, familiar Toad,[2]
Half froth,[3] half venom, spits himself abroad,   320
In puns, or politics, or tales, or lies,
Or spite, or smut, or rhymes, or blasphemies.
His wit all see-saw, between *that* and *this*,   ⎫
Now high, now low, now master up, now miss,   ⎬
And he himself one vile Antithesis.[4]   ⎭   325
Amphibious thing! that acting either part,

John Lord Hervey, eldest surviving son of the Earl of Bristol and author of the *Memoirs of the Reign of George II.* At an early age he became a great favourite at the court of the Prince and Princess of Wales at Richmond, where Pope and his literary friends enjoyed high favour. He married Miss Lepell, whom Pope himself greatly admired. Afterwards he attached himself to Walpole's party and was appointed Vice Chamberlain to the King (George II.). Ultimately he attained to the office of Lord Privy Seal; and after Walpole's fall continued to take an active part in politics, notwithstanding his miserable health, till his death in 1743. The cause of his estrangement from Pope remains obscure; but the first public offence was given by Pope, in allusions in his *Miscellanies* (1727) and the first edition of the *Dunciad* (1728). Then in 1734 appeared the Imitation of the 2nd Satire of the 1st Bk. of Horace, where Lord Hervey was twice attacked under the sobriquet of Lord Fanny, and his friend Lady Mary Wortley Montagu was even more venomously aspersed. They retorted in verse and prose; and Pope wrote his prose *Letter to a noble Lord.* The character of *Sporus* followed in 1734; and another attack in the satire, originally called (*Epilogue to the Satires*) 1738 brought out a poem *The Difference between Verbal and Practical Virtue exemplified*, &c. by Lord H. The original hints for all the insinuations and insults introduced by Pope into the character of Sporus are, according to Mr. Croker, to be found in Pulte-

ney's *Reply* to a pamphlet against himself and Bolingbroke (1731) which he attributed to H. The *Reply* brought about a duel. Mr. Croker can find no evidence for the report that the rupture between Pope and Lady Mary was due to the 'rivalry' between himself and Hervey 'in her good graces.'] In the first edition, Pope had the name 'Paris' instead of 'Sporus.' *Bowles.*

[1] [Lady M. W. M. humorously divided the world into 'men, women and Herveys.' As to his whiteness cf. *Dunciad*, IV. 104. His miserable health necessitated a peculiar diet.]

[2] See Milton, Book IV. P. [In the first edition Pope explained this allusion by reference to a passage in Lady M. W. M.'s lampoon against himself.]

[3] *Half froth*,] Alluding to those *frothy* excretions, called by the people, *Toad-spits*, seen in summer-time hanging upon plants, and emitted by young insects which lie hid in the midst of them, for their preservation, while in their helpless state. *Warburton.* [Goethe's *Mephistophiles* is 'an abortion of mud and fire.']

[4] The only trait perhaps of the whole [character of Sporus] that is not either false or overcharged, is Hervey's love for *antithesis*, which Pulteney had already ridiculed. . . . His parliamentary speeches were, as Warton says, very far above '*florid impotence;*' but they were in favour of the Ministry, and that was sufficiently offensive to Pope.' *Croker, Lord Hervey's Memoirs, Biogr. Notice.*

The trifling head or the corrupted heart,
Fop at the toilet, flatt'rer at the board,
Now trips a Lady, and now struts a Lord.
Eve's tempter thus the Rabbins have exprest,   330
A Cherub's face, a reptile all the rest;
Beauty that shocks you, parts that none will trust;
Wit that can creep, and pride that licks the dust.
　　Not Fortune's worshipper, nor fashion's fool,
Not Lucre's madman, nor Ambition's tool,   335
Not proud, nor servile; — be one Poet's praise,
That, if he pleas'd, he pleas'd by manly ways:
That Flatt'ry, ev'n to Kings, he held a shame,
And thought a Lie in verse or prose the same.
That not in Fancy's maze he wander'd long,   340
But stoop'd to Truth,[1] and moraliz'd his song:[2]
That not for Fame, but Virtue's better end,
He stood the furious foe, the timid friend,
The damning critic, half approving wit,
The coxcomb hit, or fearing to be hit;   345
Laugh'd at the loss of friends he never had,
The dull, the proud, the wicked, and the mad;
The distant threats of vengeance on his head,
The blow unfelt, the tear he never shed;
The tale reviv'd, the lie so oft o'erthrown,[3]   350
Th' imputed trash, and dulness not his own;[4]
The morals blacken'd when the writings scape,
The libell'd person, and the pictur'd shape;
Abuse, on all he lov'd, or lov'd him, spread,[5]
A friend in exile, or a father, dead;   355
The whisper, that to greatness still too near,
Perhaps, yet vibrates on his Sov'reign's ear:-
Welcome for thee, fair *Virtue!* all the past;
For thee, fair Virtue! welcome ev'n the *last!*
　　A. But why insult the poor, affront the great?   360
　　P. A knave 's a knave, to me, in ev'ry state:
Alike my scorn, if he succeed or fail,
Sporus at court, or *Japhet* in a jail,
A hireling scribbler, or a hireling peer,

---

[1] *But stoop'd to Truth,*] The term is from falconry; and the allusion to one of those untamed birds of spirit, which sometimes wantons at large in airy circles before it regards, or *stoops to,* its prey. *Warburton.*

[2] [i.e. made his poetry *Moral,* in both senses of the term.]

[3] *the lie so oft o'erthrown*] As, that he received subscriptions for Shakespear, that he set his name to Mr. Broome's verses, &c. which, tho' publicly disproved were nevertheless shamelessly repeated in the Libels, and even in that called *the Nobleman's Epistle.* P.

[4] *Th' imputed trash,*] Such as profane *Psalms, Court-Poems,* and other scandalous things, printed in his Name by Curll and others. P.

[5] *Abuse, on all he lov'd, or lov'd him, spread,*] Namely on the Duke of Buckingham, the Earl of Burlington, Lord Bathurst, Lord Bolingbroke, Bishop Atterbury, Dr. Swift, Dr. Arbuthnot, Mr. Gay, his Friends, his Parents, and his very Nurse, aspersed in printed papers, by James Moore, G. Ducket, L. Welsted, Tho. Bentley, and other obscure persons. P.

Knight of the post[1] corrupt, or of the shire;   365
If on a Pillory, or near a Throne,
He gain his Prince's ear, or lose his own.
   Yet soft by nature, more a dupe than wit,[2]
Sappho can tell you how this man was bit;
This dreaded Sat'rist *Dennis* will confess   370
Foe to his pride, but friend to his distress:[3]
So humble, he has knock'd at *Tibbald's* door,
Has drunk with *Cibber*, nay has rhym'd for *Moore*.
Full ten years slander'd, did he once reply?[4]
Three thousand suns went down on *Welsted's* lie.[5]   375
To please a Mistress one aspers'd his life;
He lash'd him not, but let her be his wife.
Let *Budgel* charge low *Grubstreet* on his quill,[6]
And write whate'er he pleas'd, except his Will;[7]
Let the two *Curlls* of Town and Court, abuse   380
His father, mother, body, soul, and muse.[8]

[1] ['Like Knights o' th' Post, and falsely charge
Upon themselves what others forge.'
Hudibras, Part I. Canto I.
The so-called 'Knights of the Post' stood about the sheriff's pillars near the courts, in readiness to swear anything for pay. See R. Bell's note *ad loc.*]

[2] Ver. 368 in the MS.
'Once, and but once, his heedless youth was bit.
And lik'd that dang'rous thing, a female wit:
Safe as he thought, tho' all the prudent chid;
He writ no Libels, but my Lady did:
Great odds in am'rous or poetic game,
Where Woman's is the sin, and Man's the shame.'
[Again alluding to Lady Mary.]

[3] [V. *ante*, note to v. 48.]

[4] *ten years*] It was so long after many libels before the Author of the Dunciad published that poem, till when, he never writ a word in answer to the many scurrilities and falsehoods concerning him. P.

[5] *Welsted's lie.*] This man had the impudence to tell in print, that Mr. P. had occasioned a *Lady's death*, and to name a person he never heard of. He also publish'd that he libell'd the Duke of Chandos; with whom (it was added) that he had lived in familiarity, and received from him a present of *five hundred pounds*: the falsehood of both which is known to his Grace. Mr. P. never received any present farther than the subscription for Homer, from him, or from *Any great Man* whatsoever. P [Compare *Dunciad*, II. vv. 207–210.]

[6] *Let Budgel*] Budgel, in a weekly pamphlet called the *Bee*, bestowed much abuse on him, in the imagination that he writ some things about the *Last Will* of Dr. *Tindal*, in the *Grub-street*

Journal; a Paper wherein he never had the least hand, direction, or supervisal, nor the least knowledge of its Author. P. [He reappears in the *Dunciad*, II. v. 397.]

[7] *except his Will;*] Alluding to Tindal's Will: by which, and other indirect practices, Budgell, to the exclusion of the next heir, a nephew, got to himself almost the whole fortune of a man entirely unrelated to him. P. [Budgel was believed to have forged a will purporting to be by Dr. Matthew Tindal, the author of *Christianity as old as the Creation.*]

[8] *His father, mother, &c.*] In some of Curll's and other pamphlets, Mr. Pope's father was said to be a Mechanic, a Hatter, a Farmer, nay a Bankrupt. But, what is stranger, a *Nobleman* (if such a Reflection could be thought to come from a Nobleman) had dropt an allusion to that pitiful untruth, in a paper called an *Epistle to a Doctor of Divinity:* And the following line,

Hard as thy Heart, and as thy Birth obscure,

had fallen from a like *Courtly* pen, in certain *Verses to the Imitator of Horace.* Mr. Pope's Father was of a Gentleman's Family in Oxfordshire, the head of which was the Earl of Downe, whose sole Heiress married the Earl of Lindsey. His mother was the daughter of William Turnor, Esq. of York: she had three brothers, one of whom was killed, another died in the service of King Charles; the eldest following his fortunes, and becoming a general officer in Spain, left her what estate remained after the sequestrations and forfeitures of her family — Mr. Pope died in 1717, aged 75; she in 1733, aged 93, a very few weeks after this poem was finished. The following inscription was placed by their son on their

Yet why? that Father held it for a rule,
It was a sin to call our neighbour fool:
That harmless Mother thought no wife a whore:
Hear this, and spare his family, *James Moore!*   385
Unspotted names, and memorable long!
If there be force in Virtue, or in Song.
   Of gentle blood (part shed in Honour's cause,
While yet in *Britain* Honour had applause)
Each parent sprung [1] — A. What fortune, pray ? — P. Their own,
And better got, than *Bestia's* from the throne. [2]   391
Born to no Pride, inheriting no Strife,
Nor marrying Discord in a noble wife, [3]
Stranger to civil and religious rage,
The good man walk'd innoxious thro' his age.   395
Nor Courts he saw, no suits would ever try,
Nor dar'd an Oath, nor hazarded a Lie. [4]
Un-learn'd, he knew no schoolman's subtle art,
No language, but the language of the heart.
By Nature honest, by Experience wise,   400
Healthy by temp'rance, and by exercise;
His life, tho' long, to sickness past unknown,
His death was instant, and without a groan.
O grant me, thus to live, and thus to die!
Who sprung from Kings shall know less joy than I. [5]   405
   O Friend! may each domestic bliss be thine!
Be no unpleasing Melancholy mine:
Me. let the tender office long engage,
To rock the cradle of reposing Age,
With lenient arts extend a Mother's breath,   410
Make Languor smile, and smooth the bed of Death,
Explore the thought, explain the asking eye,
And keep a while one parent from the sky!
On cares like these if length of days attend,
May Heav'n, to bless those days, preserve my friend,   415
Preserve him social, cheerful, and serene,

Monument in the parish of Twickenham, in Middlesex.

D. O. M.

ALEXANDRO . POPE . VIRO . INNOCVO . PROBO . PIO .
QVI . VIXIT . ANNOS . LXXV . OB . MDCCXVII .
ET . EDITHAE . CONIVGI . INCVLPABILI .
PIENTISSIMAE . QVAE . VIXIT . ANNOS .
XCIII . OB . MDCCXXXIII .
PARENTIBVS . BENEMERENTIBVS . FILIVS . FECIT .
ET . SIBI . P.

[1] [See *Introductory Memoir*, p. viii.]

[2] [L. Calpurnius Bestia, who here seems to signify the Duke of Marlborough, was a Roman proconsul, bribed by Jugurtha into a dishonour-able peace.] [Crocker says the elder Horace Walpole is meant. *Am. Ed.*]

[3] Alluding to Addison's marriage with the Countess of Warwick, and Dryden's with Lady Elizabeth Howard. *Carruthers.*

[4] He was a nonjuror, and would not take the oath of· allegiance or supremacy, or the oath against the Pope. *Bowles.*

[5] After v. 405 in the MS.

' And of myself, too, something must I say?
Take then this verse, the trifle of a day.
And if it live, it lives but to commend
The man whose heart has ne'er forgot a Friend,
Or head, an Author: Critic, yet polite
And friend to Learning, yet too wise to write.'

QUEEN ANNE.

And just as rich as when he serv'd a QUEEN.[1]
A. Whether that blessing be deny'd or giv'n,
Thus far was right, the rest belongs to Heav'n.

————•oˆ•ĝˆoo————

SATIRES AND EPISTLES OF HORACE IMITATED.

ADVERTISEMENT.

THE Occasion of publishing these *Imitations* was the clamour raised on some of my *Epistles.* An Answer from *Horace* was both more full, and of more Dignity, than any I could have made in my own person; and the Example of much greater Freedom in so eminent a Divine as Dr. *Donne,* seem'd a proof with what indignation and contempt a Christian may treat Vice or Folly, in ever so low, or ever so high a Station. Both these Authors were acceptable to the *Princes* and *Ministers* under whom they lived. The Satires of Dr. *Donne* I versified, at the desire of the Earl of *Oxford* while he was Lord Treasurer, and of the Duke of *Shrewsbury* who had been Secretary of State; neither of whom look'd upon a Satire on Vicious Courts as any Reflection on those they serv'd in. And indeed there is not in the world a greater error, than that which Fools are so apt to fall into, and Knaves with good reason to encourage, the mistaking a *Satirist* for a *Libeller;* whereas to a *true Satirist* nothing is so odious as a *Libeller,* for the same reason as to a man truly *virtuous* nothing is so hateful as a *Hypocrite.*

Uni æquus Virtuti atque ejus Amicis. P.

[' Whoever,' says Warburton, 'expects a *paraphrase* of Horace, or a faithful copy of his genius, or manner of writing in these *Imitations,* will be much disappointed. Our author uses the Roman poet for little more than his canvas; and if the old design or colouring chance to suit his purpose, it is well; if not, he employs his own, without scruple or ceremony.' 'He deem'd it more modest,' felicitously adds the same authority, 'to give the name of Imitations to his Satires, than, like Despreaux' [Boileau], 'to give the name of Satires to Imitations.' 'In two large columns,' wrote a less kindly critic, from whom impartiality could hardly be expected, Lady Mary Wortley Montagu (alluding to the juxtaposition of the Latin and English texts), —

> ' In two large columns, on thy motley page
> Where Roman wit is strip'd with English rage;
> Where ribaldry to satire makes pretence,
> And modern scandal rolls with ancient sense:
> Whilst on one side we see how Horace thought
> And on the other how he never wrote:
> Who can believe, who views the bad and good,
> That the dull copyist better understood
> That spirit he pretends to imitate,
> Than heretofore the Greek he did translate; '

proceeded, from this pleasant allusion to Pope's Homer, to explain the moral obliquities of her detractor by his defects of person, birth and nature. It was not to be expected that Sappho would sing the praises of these Imitations; and the question

---

[1] *And just as rich as when he serv'd a Queen.*] An honest compliment to his Friend's real and unaffected disinterestedness, when he was the favourite Physician of Queen Anne.
Warburton.

U

remains, to what species of composition they belong, and what rank they hold among efforts of that species.

They are not Translations; neither of the close nor of the loose kind, and are therefore at once removed from comparison even with Dryden's magnificent versions, splendid in their very faults, of Juvenal. Nor do they properly bear the name of Imitations; for an Imitation of an earlier author is an attempt to produce a poem in his style and manner, though not necessarily on the same subject. Thomson's *Castle of Indolence* is an Imitation of Spenser; Johnson's *London* is an Imitation of Boileau, or, indeed, of Oldham and of Pope himself. But Pope differs quite sufficiently in manner and style from Horace to place his so-called 'Imitations' out of the category to which they assume to belong. They are rather Adaptations, or as Warburton has correctly suggested, Parodies; in other words, they take as much of the ancient form as suits the purposes of the modern poet, they occasionally cling closely to its outlines, occasionally desert them altogether. It was the form which came most readily, and originally almost accidentally, to Pope's hands; and which he justly thought himself free to use in his own way. The example of the First Epistle of the Second Book will best illustrate these remarks. In Pope's 'Imitation' the original is here turned upside down, and what in Horace is a panegyric, in the English poem becomes a covert satire. As Pope meant to suggest that George II. was a parody on Augustus, so his Epistle is a parody on, and not an imitation of, the Latin poem.

It is therefore obvious that any comparison or contrast between the Latin and English poets, interesting and suggestive as it doubtless is from other points of view, is idle with reference to the relation between these 'Imitations' and their 'originals.' Warburton is true to his self-imposed task of vindicating the Christian orthodoxy of Pope, in pointing out, ever and anon, passages where the latter has substituted for the Epicurean heresies of the genial Roman turns of thought more becoming the friend of an embryo bishop. Horace designed his Satires and Epistles as humorous sketches of society, seasoned with such personal allusions as appeared necessary to enliven his pictures, or as suggested themselves to a ready wit which can never teach a lesson without applying it. What with him was ornament, with Pope was purpose. Whatever may have been the philosophical system with which Warburton laboured so hard to credit him, the centre of that system was Pope; nor were his friends and foes so much introduced into these Imitations to point morals, as the morals preached to introduce his friends and foes, and himself.

The ease with which Pope moved in a form which imposed no restraint on his wit, makes these 'Imitations' the most enjoyable of all his productions. He closed the last Dialogue of the 'Epilogue' with an announcement of his resolution never to publish any more poems of the kind. Yet it was at the time (1741) when he was meditating a new Dunciad that he informed Lord Marchmont that 'uneasy desire of fame' and 'keen resentment of injuries' were 'both asleep together'; and even if we regard as spurious the fragment of an unpublished Satire entitled '1740,' found among his papers by Bolingbroke, and full of personal allusions to 'Bub,' and 'Hervey' and others, we may remain in doubt, whether had he lived he would or could have adhered to his determination. But he had done enough to establish himself as the unapproached master of personal satire in a poetic form; and to damn a multitude of victims, helpless against the strokes of genius, to everlasting fame.]

THE FIRST SATIRE

OF THE

SECOND BOOK OF HORACE.

SATIRE I.

TO MR. FORTESCUE.[1]

[First published in 1733 under the title of *Dialogue between Alexander Pope, of Twickenham, on the one part, and the learned counsel on the other.* In Horace's Satire the interlocutors are the poet and G. Trebatius Testa, the friend of Cæsar and of Cicero (among whose correspondents he appears). It forms a kind of introduction to Horace's Second Book of Satires.]

P.   THERE are, (I scarce can think it, but am told,)
      There are, to whom my Satire seems too bold :
Scarce to wise Peter complaisant enough,
And something said of Chartres much too rough.
The lines are weak, another's pleas'd to say,   5
Lord Fanny [2] spins a thousand such a day.
Tim'rous by nature, of the Rich in awe,
I come to Counsel learned in the Law :
You 'll give me, like a friend both sage and free,
Advice ; and (as you use) without a Fee.   10
    F.   I 'd write no more.
                    P.   Not write? but then I think,
And for my soul I cannot sleep a wink.
I nod in company, I wake at night,
Fools rush into my head, and so I write.
    F.   You could not do a worse thing for your life.   15
Why, if the nights seem tedious, — take a Wife :
Or rather truly, if your point be rest,
Lettuce and cowslip-wine ; *Probatum est.*
But talk with Celsus,[3] Celsus will advise
Hartshorn,[4] or something that shall close your eyes.   20
Or, if you needs must write, write Cæsar's Praise,
You 'll gain at least a *Knighthood*, or the *Bays*.
    P.   What? like Sir Richard, rumbling, rough, and fierce,[5]
With Arms, and George, and Brunswick crowd the verse,
Rend with tremendous sound your ears asunder,   25
With Gun, Drum, Trumpet, Blunderbuss, and Thunder?
Or nobly wild, with Budgel's fire and force,[6]

---

[1] [The Hon. W. Fortescue, an intimate friend and a frequent associate and correspondent of the poet's, and a schoolfellow of Gay's. He afterwards became one of the Barons of the Exchequer, and ultimately Master of the Rolls.]

[2] [Lord Hervey.]

[3] [i.e. any physician of note.]

[4] *Hartshorn*] This was intended as a pleasantry on the novelty of the prescription. *Warburton.* [Given by Dr. Hollins Fortescue's physician. *Am. Ed.*]

[5] [Sir Richard Blackmore.]

[6] [Budgel; see *Epistle to Arbuthnot*, v. 378.]

Paint Angels trembling round his falling Horse? [1]
   F. Then all your Muse's softer art display,
Let CAROLINA smooth the tuneful lay, [2]   30
Lull with AMELIA'S [3] liquid name the Nine,
And sweetly flow thro' all the Royal Line.
   P. Alas! few verses touch their nicer ear;
They scarce can bear their *Laureate* twice a year; [4]
And justly CÆSAR scorns the Poet's lays: 35
It is to *History* he trusts for Praise. [5]
   F. Better be Cibber, I 'll maintain it still,
Than ridicule all Taste, blaspheme Quadrille,
Abuse the City's best good men in metre,
And laugh at Peers that put their trust in Peter.   40
Ev'n those you touch not, hate you.
                  P. What should ail them? [6]
   F. A hundred smart in Timon and in Balaam: [7]
The fewer still you name, you wound the more;
Bond is but one, but Harpax is a score.
   P. Each mortal has his pleasure: none deny   45
Scarsdale his bottle, Darty his Ham-pie; [8]
Ridotta [9] sips and dances, till she see
The doubling Lustres dance as fast as she;
F— loves the Senate, [10] Hockley-hole [11] his brother,
Like in all else, as one Egg to another.   50
I love to pour out all my self, as plain
As downright SHIPPEN, [12] or as old Montaigne:

[1] *falling Horse?*] The Horse on which his Majesty charged at the battle of Oudenarde; when the Pretender, and the Princes of the blood of France, fled before him. *Warburton.*

[2] [Caroline of Brandenburg-Anspach, the Queen of George II. She became a frequent object of Pope's sarcasms, after George II. on his accession had retained Walpole and the Whigs in office.]

[3] [Princess Amelia, the second daughter of George II. She died unmarried in 1759.]

[4] [Colley Cibber; see Introductory Remarks to *Dunciad.*]

[5] [The House of Brunswick was however particularly unfortunate in this respect.]

[6] *What should ail them?*] Horace hints at *one* reason, *that each fears his own turn may be next;* his imitator gives *another*, and with more art, a reason which insinuates, that his very lenity, in using feigned names, increases the number of his Enemies.

[7] [See *Moral Essays*, Ep. IV. vv. 99-176, and Ep. III. vv. 339-402.]

[8] *Darty his Ham-pie;*] This Lover of Ham-pie own'd the fidelity of the poet's pencil; and said, he had done justice to his taste: but that if, instead of *Ham-pie*, he had given him *Sweet-*

pie, he never could have pardoned him. *Warburton.* Lyttelton in his *Dialogues of the Dead*, has introduced Darteneuf, bitterly lamenting his ill-fortune in having died before turtle-feasts were known in England. *Warton.* [Lord Scarsdale and Charles Dartique-nave, or Dartineuf, were noted epicures. The latter was in office as Paymaster of the Works; and the poet, Robert Dodsley, was his footman. Carruthers cites a paper written by him in the *Tatler*, No. 252, on the cheerful use of wine. Gay speaks of him as a ' grave joker.']

[9] [Ridotta; from Ridotto, the fashionable Italian term for an assembly.]

[10] Most likely Henry Fox, first Lord Holland, alluded to in *Epil. to Satires*, Dial. I. v. 71. The ' brother' is Stephen Fox, afterwards Lord Ilchester. *Carruthers.*

[11] [The bear-garden at Hockley-in-the-Hole is described in the *Spectator*, No. 436. Cf. *Dunciad*, Bk. I. v. 326.]

[12] William Shippen, an outspoken politician and a Jacobite, who was sent to the Tower in 1718. According to Coxe, he used to say of himself and Sir Robert Walpole: ' Robin and I are two honest men; though he is for King George, and I for King James.']

In them, as certain to be lov'd as seen,
The Soul stood forth, nor kept a thought within ;
In me what spots (for spots I have) appear,   55
Will prove at least the medium must be clear.
In this impartial glass, my Muse intends
Fair to expose myself, my foes, my friends ;
Publish the present age ; but where my text
Is Vice too high, reserve it for the next :   60
My foes shall wish my Life a longer date,
And ev'ry friend the less lament my fate.
My head and heart thus flowing thro' my quill,
Verse-man or Prose-man, term me which you will,
Papist or Protestant, or both between,[1]   65
Like good Erasmus in an honest Mean,
In moderation placing all my glory,
While Tories call me Whig, and Whigs a Tory.
    Satire 's my weapon, but I 'm too discreet
To run a muck, and tilt at all I meet ;   70
I only wear it in a land of Hectors,
Thieves, Supercargoes, Sharpers, and Directors.
Save but our *Army!* and let Jove encrust
Swords, pikes, and guns, with everlasting rust!
Peace is my dear delight — not FLEURY'S more :[2]   75
But touch me, and no Minister so sore.
Whoe'er offends, at some unlucky time
Slides into verse, and hitches in a rhyme,[3]
Sacred to Ridicule his whole life long,
And the sad burthen of some merry song.   80
    Slander or Poison dread from Delia's rage,[4]
Hard words or hanging, if your Judge be Page.[5]
From furious Sappho scarce a milder fate,
P-x'd by her love, or libell'd by her hate.
Its proper pow'r to hurt, each creature feels ;   85
Bulls aim their horns, and Asses lift their heels ;
'T is a Bear's talent not to kick, but hug ;
And no man wonders he 's not stung by Pug.
So drink with Walters, or with Chartres eat,
They 'll never poison you, they 'll only cheat.   90
    Then, learned Sir! (to cut the matter short)
Whate'er my fate, — or well or ill at Court,
Whether Old age, with faint but cheerful ray,

---

[1] [As Warburton points out, a great improvement on Horace's 'Lucanus an Appulus, anceps,' &c. As to Pope's religious standpoint see *Introductory Memoir*, p. xxxiii.]

[2] [Cardinal Fleury, formerly tutor of King Louis XV., became Prime Minister of France in 1726, and held power till his death in 1743. He was able to maintain the pacific policy which he advocated till two years before that event.]

[3] Closely copied from Boileau. *Warton.*

[4] [A Miss Mackenzie died about this time, and was supposed to have been poisoned from jealousy.] The person alluded to was Lady D—ne. *Bowles.* [Mary Howard Countess of Deloraine, who died in 1744. See note to Lord Hervey's *Memoirs* by Croker, who ' has not discovered the grounds of the suspicion, but it was very prevalent.']

[5] [Judge Page ; cf. *Epil. to Sat.* Dial. II. v. 156.]

Attends to gild the Ev'ning of my day,
Or Death's black wing already be display'd,   95
To wrap me in the universal shade;
Whether the darken'd room [1] to muse invite,
Or whiten'd wall provoke the skew'r to write: [2]
In durance, exile, Bedlam or the Mint, [3] —
Like Lee[4] or Budgel, I will rhyme and print.   100
     F. Alas young man! your days can ne'er be long,
In flow'r of age you perish for a song!
Plums and Directors, Shylock and his Wife, [5]
Will club their Testers, [6] now, to take your life!
     P. What? arm'd for Virtue when I point the pen,   105
Brand the bold front of shameless guilty men;
Dash the proud Gamester in his gilded Car;
Bare the mean Heart that lurks beneath a *Star*;
Can there be wanting, to defend Her cause,
Lights of the Church, or Guardians of the Laws?   110
Could pension'd Boileau lash in honest strain
Flatt'rers and Bigots ev'n in Louis' reign? [7]
Could Laureate Dryden Pimp and Friar engage, [8]
Yet neither Charles nor James be in a rage?
And I not strip the gilding off a knave,   115
Unplac'd, unpension'd, [9] no man's heir, or slave?
I will, or perish in the gen'rous cause:
Hear this, and tremble! you, who 'scape the Laws.
Yes, while I live, no rich or noble knave
Shall walk the World, in credit, to his grave.   120
To VIRTUE ONLY and HER FRIENDS A FRIEND,
The World beside may murmur, or commend.
Know, all the distant din that world can keep,
Rolls o'er my Grotto, and but soothes my sleep.
There, my retreat the best Companions grace,   125
Chiefs out of war, and Statesmen out of place.
There ST. JOHN mingles with my friendly bowl

[1] *Whether the darken'd room — Or whiten'd wall —*] This is only a wanton joke upon the terms of his Original,
     Quisquis erit vitæ, scribam, color.
                              Warburton.
[2] [*the skewer,* i.e. the stilus, or pen.]

[3] [*the Mint.* See *Epistle to Arbuthnot,* v. 13, 156.]

[4] [Nathaniel Lee (born 1657, died 1692). This gifted but extravagant tragic poet, the author of the *Rival Queen,* went mad in 1684, but recovered his sanity. Some critics have discovered in his most famous tragedy signs of his malady; another has well remarked on this that if ' it be madness, there 's method in it.' There is real fire in Lee, besides a great deal of smoke.]

[5] [*Shylock and his Wife,* the Wortley Montagus. *Am. Ed.*]

[6] [*Testers,* sixpences. *Am. Ed.*]

[7] Boileau acted with much caution when he first published his *Lutrin* here alluded to, and endeavoured to cover and conceal his subject by a preface laying the scene at Bourges, not at Paris, for which it was intended. When in 1683 he threw off the mask, no offence was taken by the Canons whom he had ridiculed. From *Warton's* note. [Moreover, the ascendancy of bigotry and Mad. de Maintenon had not begun when Boileau wrote his famous satire; when they fully prevailed he retired from Court.]

[8] [In his *Spanish Friar.* But he soon atoned for that piece by *Absalom and Achitophel.*]

[9] [Pope declined the pension offered him by Lord Halifax early in George I.'s reign.]

The Feast of Reason and the Flow of Soul:
And HE, whose lightning pierc'd th' Iberian Lines,[1]
Now forms my Quincunx, and now ranks my Vines,   130
Or tames the Genius of the stubborn plain,
Almost as quickly as he conquer'd Spain.
  Envy must own, I live among the Great,[2]
No Pimp of Pleasure, and no Spy of State.
With eyes that pry not, tongue that ne'er repeats,   135
Fond to spread friendships, but to cover heats;
To help who want, to forward who excel;
This, all who know me, know; who love me, tell;
And who unknown defame me, let them be
Scribblers or Peers, alike are *Mob* to me.   140
This is my plea, on this I rest my cause —
What saith my Counsel, learned in the laws?
  F. Your Plea is good; but still I say, beware!
Laws are explain'd by Men — so have a care.
It stands on record, that in Richard's times   145
A man was hang'd for very honest rhymes.[8]
Consult the Statute: *quart*. I think, it is,
Edwardi sext. or *prim. et quint. Eliz.*
See *Libels, Satires* — here you have it — read.
  P. *Libels* and *Satires!* lawless things indeed!   150
But grave *Epistles*, bringing Vice to light,
Such as a King might read, a Bishop write;
Such as Sir ROBERT[4] would approve——
                               F. Indeed?
The Case is alter'd — you may then proceed;
In such a cause the Plaintiff will be hiss'd;   155
My Lords the Judges laugh, and you 're dismiss'd.[5]

[1] *And* HE, *whose lightning, etc.*] Charles Mordaunt Earl of Peterborough, who in the year 1705 took Barcelona, and in the winter following with only 280 horse and 900 foot enterprized and accomplished the Conquest of Valentia. P. [See Macaulay's captivating account of Peterborough in his Essay on the *War of Succession in Spain*.]

[2] *Envy must own, etc.*] Horace makes the point of honour to consist simply in his living familiarly with the Great,

Cum magnis vixisse invita fatebitur usque Invidia.

Our poet, more nobly, in his living with them on the footing of an honest man. He prided himself in this superiority, as appears from the following words, in a letter to Dr. Swift: "To have pleased great men, according to Horace, is a praise; but not to have flattered them, and yet not have displeased them, is a greater." *Let.* VII. *Jan.* 12, 1723.   *Warburton.*

[8] [Bowles reminds the reader of the mob in Julius Cæsar (Act III. Sc. 3), demanding that Cinna the poet should be torn 'for his bad verses.']

[4] [Walpole.]

[5] *Solventur risu tabulæ: tu missus abibis. Hor.*

THE SECOND SATIRE

OF THE

SECOND BOOK OF HORACE.

SATIRE II.

To Mr. Bethel.[1]

[In Horace's *Satire* the praise of temperance is laid in the mouth of Ofellus, a simple farmer with whom the poet had been acquainted from his boyhood.]

WHAT, and how great, the Virtue and the Art
 To live on little with a cheerful heart,
(A doctrine sage, but truly none of mine,)
Let 's talk, my friends, but talk before we dine.
Not when a gilt Buffet's reflected pride   5
Turns you from sound Philosophy aside ;
Not when from plate to plate your eyeballs roll,
And the brain dances to the mantling bowl.
 Hear BETHEL'S Sermon, one not vers'd in schools,
But strong in sense, and wise without the rules.   10
 Go work, hunt, exercise! (he thus began)
Then scorn a homely dinner, if you can.
Your wine lock'd up, your Butler stroll'd abroad,
Or fish deny'd (the river yet unthaw'd),
If then plain bread and milk will do the feat,   15
The pleasure lies in you, and not the meat.
 Preach as I please, I doubt our curious men
Will choose a pheasant still before a hen ;
Yet hens of Guinea full as good I hold,
Except you eat the feathers green and gold.   20
Of carps and mullets why prefer the great,
(Tho' cut in pieces ere my Lord can eat)
Yet for small Turbots such esteem profess?
–Because God made these large, the other less.
 Oldfield[2] with more than Harpy throat endued,   25
Cries " Send me, Gods! a whole Hog barbecued![3]
Oh blast it, South-winds! till a stench exhale
Rank as the ripeness of a rabbit's tail.
By what Criterion do ye eat, d' ye think,

---

[1] [Hugh Bethel, the 'blameless Bethel' of *Moral Essays*, Ep. v., a Yorkshire gentleman with whom Pope was intimate, and frequently corresponded. He was a close friend of Pope's dearest friends, the Blounts of Mapledurham. He died in 1748.]

[2] *Oldfield*] This eminent Glutton ran thro'
a fortune of fifteen hundred pounds a year in the simple luxury of good eating. *Warburton.*

[3] *Hog barbecued, etc.*] A West Indian term of gluttony, a hog roasted whole, stuffed with spice, and basted with Madeira wine. P. [How gross an antithesis to Charles Lamb's favourite delicate sucking-pig!]

If this is priz'd for sweetness, that for stink? 30
When the tir'd glutton labours thro' a treat,
He finds no relish in the sweetest meat,
He calls for something bitter, something sour,
And the rich feast concludes extremely poor :
Cheap eggs, and herbs, and olives still we see ; 35
Thus much is left of old Simplicity!
The Robin-red-breast till of late had rest,[1]
And children sacred held a Martin's nest,
Till Becca-ficos sold so dev'lish dear
To one that was, or would have been a Peer. 40
Let me extol a Cat, on oysters fed,
I 'll have a party at the Bedford-head ;[2]
Or ev'n to crack live Crawfish recommend ;
I 'd never doubt at Court to make a friend.
　　'T is yet in vain, I own, to make a pother 45
About one vice, and fall into the other :
Between Excess and Famine lies a mean ;
Plain, but not sordid ; tho' not splendid, clean.
　　Avidien,[3] or his Wife (no matter which,
For him you 'll call a dog, and her a bitch) 50
Sell their presented partridges, and fruits,
And humbly live on rabbits and on roots :
One half-pint bottle serves them both to dine,
And is at once their vinegar and wine.
But on some lucky day (as when they found 55
A lost Bank-bill, or heard their Son was drown'd)
At such a feast, old vinegar to spare,
Is what two souls so gen'rous cannot bear :
O'l, tho' it stink, they drop by drop impart,
But souse the cabbage with a bounteous heart. 60
　　He knows to live, who keeps the middle state,
And neither leans on this side, nor on that ;
Nor stops, for one bad cork, his butler's pay,
Swears, like Albutius, a good cook away ;
Nor lets, like Nævius, ev'ry error pass, 65
The musty wine, foul cloth, or greasy glass.
　　Now hear what blessings Temperance can bring :
(Thus said our friend, and what he said I sing,)
First Health : The stomach (cramm'd from ev'ry dish,
A tomb of boil'd and roast, and flesh and fish, 70
Where bile, and wind, and phlegm, and acid jar,
And all the man is one intestine war)
Remembers oft the School-boy's simple fare,

---

[1] [' Cet aimable oiseau se mange à la broche et en salmi.' *Almanach des Gourmands,* quoted in Mr. Hayward's Essay on the *Art of Dining.*]

[2] *Bedford-head ;*] A famous Eating-House. P. [In Covent-Garden.]

[3] Edward Wortley Montagu, the husband of Lady Mary. *Carruthers.* [Their son Edward, alluded to in v. 56, was a source of constant annoyance to both his parents ; and Lady M. speaks of ' the impossibility of his behaving as a rational creature.']

The temp'rate sleeps, and spirits light as air.
  How pale, each Worshipful and Rev'rend guest   75
Rise from a Clergy, or a City feast!
What life in all that ample body, say?
What heav'nly particle inspires the clay?
The Soul subsides, and wickedly inclines
To seem but mortal, ev'n in sound Divines.[1]   80
  On morning wings how active springs the Mind
That leaves the load of yesterday behind!
How easy ev'ry labour it pursues!
How coming to the Poet ev'ry Muse!
Not but we may exceed, some holy time,   85
Or tir'd in search of Truth, or search of Rhyme;
Ill health some just indulgence may engage,
And more the sickness of long life, Old age;
For fainting Age what cordial drop remains,
If our intemp'rate Youth the vessel drains?   90
  Our fathers prais'd rank ven'son. You suppose
Perhaps, young men! our fathers had no nose.
Not so: a Buck was then a week's repast,
And 't was their point, I ween, to make it last;
More pleas'd to keep it till their friends could come, 95
Than eat the sweetest by themselves at home.
Why had I not in those good times my birth,
Ere coxcomb-pies[2] or coxcombs were on earth?
  Unworthy he, the voice of Fame to hear,
That sweetest music to an honest ear;   100
(For 'faith, Lord Fanny![3] you are in the wrong,
The world's good word is better than a song)
Who has not learned, fresh sturgeon and ham-pie
Are no rewards for want, and infamy!
When Luxury has lick'd up all thy pelf,   105
Curs'd by thy neighbours, thy trustees, thyself,
To friends, to fortune, to mankind a shame,
Think how posterity will treat thy name;
And buy a rope, that future times may tell
Thou hast at least bestow'd one penny well.   110
  "Right," cries his Lordship, "for a rogue in need
"To have a Taste is insolence indeed:
"In me 't is noble, suits my birth and state,
"My wealth unwieldy, and my heap too great."
Then, like the Sun, let Bounty spread her ray,   115
And shine that superfluity away.
Oh Impudence of wealth! with all thy store,
How dar'st thou let one worthy man be poor?
Shall half the new-built churches round thee fall?
Make Quays, build Bridges, or repair White-hall: 120

---

[1] [Warburton remarks on the orthodox turn   [2] [A delicacy still in vogue at academical
given by Pope to the Epicureanism of Horace.]   feasts.]   [3] [Lord Hervey.]

Or to thy country let that heap be lent,
As M * * o's [1] was, but not at five per cent.
Who thinks that Fortune cannot change her mind,
Prepares a dreadful jest for all mankind.
And who stands safest? tell me, is it he   125
That spreads and swells in puff'd prosperity,
Or blest with little, whose preventing care
In peace provides fit arms against a war?
   Thus BETHEL spoke, who always speaks his thought,
And always thinks the very thing he ought: 130
His equal mind I copy what I can,
And, as I love, would imitate the Man.
In South-sea days not happier, when surmis'd
The Lord of Thousands, than if now *Excis'd*; [2]
In forest planted by a Father's hand, [3]   135
Than in five acres now of rented land.
Content with little, I can piddle here
On brocoli and mutton, round the year;
But ancient friends (tho' poor, or out of play)
That touch my bell, I cannot turn away.   140
'T is true, no Turbots dignify my boards,
But gudgeons, flounders, what my Thames affords:
To Hounslow-heath I point and Bansted-down, [4]
Thence comes your mutton, and these chicks my own:
From yon old walnut-tree a show'r shall fall;   145
And grapes, long ling'ring on my only wall,
And figs from standard and espalier join;
The dev'l is in you if you cannot dine:
Then cheerful healths [5] (your Mistress shall have place),
And, what 's more rare, a Poet shall say Grace.   150
   Fortune not much of humbling me can boast;
Tho' double tax'd, how little have I lost?
My Life's amusements have been just the same,
Before, and after, Standing Armies came. [6]
My lands are sold, my father's house is gone;   155
I 'll hire another's; is not that my own,
And yours, my friends? thro' whose free-opening gate
None comes too early, none departs too late;
(For I, who hold sage Homer's rule the best,

---

[1] [The Duchess of Marlborough.]

[2] [See notes to *Moral Essays*, Ep. III. vv. 115 and 118.]

[3] [Pope's father originally purchased twenty acres of land in the outskirts of Windsor Forest, which he sold in 1716. The sum which he left to his son was something under £4000. The 'five acres of rented land' are the Twickenham estate.]

[4] [Between Caterham and Epsom.]

[5] [Pope's economy in the matter of wine offends Dr. Johnson, himself in general no enemy of more liberal potations: 'When he had two guests in his house he would set at supper a single pint of wine upon the table, and having taken himself two small glasses would retire and say, "Gentlemen, I leave you to your wine."']

[6] [Practically, England has had a standing army since the time of Charles II.; legally, the existence of the army depends on the annual Mutiny-bills, of which the first was passed in 1689. From the first years of Walpole's administration, the army (independently of the Irish

Welcome the coming, speed the going guest).[1]   160
" Pray heav'n it last!" (cries SWIFT!) "as you go on;
" I wish to God this house had been your own:
" Pity! to build, without a son or wife:
" Why, you'll enjoy it only all your life."
Well, if the use be mine, can it concern one,[2]   165
Whether the name belong to Pope or Vernon?
What's *Property?* dear Swift! you see it alter
From you to me, from me to Peter Walter;
Or, in a mortgage, prove a Lawyer's share;
Or, in a jointure, vanish from the heir;[3]   170
Or in pure equity (the case not clear)
The Chanc'ry takes your rents for twenty year:
At best, it falls to some ungracious son,
Who cries, " My father's damn'd and all's my own."
Shades, that to BACON could retreat afford,[4]   175
Become the portion of a booby Lord;
And Hemsley, once proud Buckingham's delight,[5]
Slides to a Scriv'ner or a city Knight.
Let lands and houses have what Lords they will,
Let Us be fix'd, and our own masters still.   180

---

establishment) continued in ordinary times to number about 17,000 men; but even its virtual perpetuity was not acknowledged; and as late as 1732 Pulteney declared that he 'always had been, and always would be, against a standing army of any kind.' See Hallam, *Const. History*, chap. xvi.]

[1] From Hom. *Od.* Bk. xv. v. 74. *Warton.*

[2] *Well, if the use be mine, etc.*] In a letter to this Mr. Bethel, of March 20, 1743, he says, " My Landlady, Mrs. *Vernon,* being dead, this " Garden and House are offered me in sale; " and, I believe (together with the cottages on " each side my grass-plot next the Thames) will " come at about a thousand pounds. If I thought " any very particular friend would be pleased to " live in it after my death (for, as it is, it serves " all my purposes as well during life) I would " purchase it," &c. *Warburton.* [Pope never carried out this intention.] [Mrs. Vernon's estate of Twickenham Park had formerly belonged to Robert, Earl of Essex, who gave it to Sir Francis Bacon, who in turn sold it for £1800. Thence, says Crocker, it came into Lord Cardigan's family, who sold it to King

William, and he gave it to Lord Albemarle, who sold it to Mr. Vernon. *Am. Ed.*]

[3] *Or, in a jointure, vanish from the heir;*] The expression well describes the surprise an heir must be in, to find himself excluded by that Instrument which was made to secure his succession. For Butler humorously defines a *Jointure* to be·the act whereby Parents

'turn
Their Children's Tenants, ere they're born.'
Warburton.

[4] [Gorhambury, near St. Alban's, the seat of Lord Bacon, was at the time of his disgrace conveyed by him to his quondam secretary, Sir J. Meantys, whose heir sold it to Sir Harbottle Grimston, whose grandson left it to his nephew (Wm. Lucklyn, who took the name of Grimston), whose second son was in 1719 created Viscount Grimston. This is the ' booby lord' to whom Pope refers.]

[5] *proud Buckingham's etc.*] Villiers Duke of Buckingham. P. The estate of Helmsley was purchased [for £90,000] by Sir Charles Duncombe, Lord Mayor in 1709, who changed its name to Duncombe Park. *Carruthers.*

Cibber

THE FIRST EPISTLE

OF THE

FIRST BOOK OF HORACE.

EPISTLE I.

TO LORD BOLINGBROKE.[1]

[Horace's Epistle is addressed to Mæcenas; and explains the causes why he had relinquished lyrical poetry in order to study philosophy as an eclectic after the fashion of Aristippus. It then proceeds to show that true happiness depends upon virtue and wisdom, to which that study leads, and not upon the external comforts of life.]

ST. JOHN, whose love indulg'd my labours past,
Matures my present, and shall bound my last!
Why will you break the Sabbath of my days?[2]
Now sick alike of Envy and of Praise.
Public too long, ah let me hide my Age!   5
See, Modest Cibber now has left the Stage:[3]
Our Gen'rals now, retir'd to their Estates,
Hang their old Trophies o'er the Garden gates,[4]
In Life's cool Ev'ning satiate of Applause,
Nor fond of bleeding, ev'n in BRUNSWICK'S cause.[5]   10
  A Voice there is, that whispers in my ear,
('T is Reason's voice, which sometimes one can hear)
"Friend Pope! be prudent, let your Muse take breath,
"And never gallop Pegasus to death;
"Lest stiff, and stately, void of fire or force,   15
"You limp, like Blackmore on a Lord Mayor's horse."[6]
  Farewell then Verse, and Love, and ev'ry Toy,
The Rhymes and Rattles of the Man or Boy;
What right, what true, what fit we justly call,
Let this be all my care — for this is All: 20
To lay this harvest up, and hoard with haste
What ev'ry day will want, and most, the last.

---

[1] [Cf. note to *Essay on Man*, Ep. 1.]

[2] *Sabbath of my days?*] i.e. The 49th year, the age of the Author. *Warburton.* [1738.]

[3] [Colley Cibber retired from the stage after a histrionic career of more than 40 years in 1733; but returned in 1734 and did not make his 'positively last appearance' till 1745.]

[4] [Warburton compares *Moral Essays*, Ep. IV. v. 30. Pope is said by Warton to allude to the entrance of Lord Peterborough's Lawn at Bevismount near Southampton.]

[5] *Ev'n in Brunswick's cause.*] In the former Editions it was, *Britain's cause.* But

the terms are synonymous. *Warburton.* [Hardly always so in Pope's mouth.]

[6] *You limp, like Blackmore on a Lord Mayor's horse.*] The fame of this heavy Poet, however problematical elsewhere, was universally received in the City of London. His versification is here exactly described: stiff, and not strong; stately and yet dull, like the sober and slow-paced Animal generally employed to mount the Lord Mayor: and therefore here humorously opposed to Pegasus. P. [Blackmore was City Physician.]

But ask not, to what Doctors I apply?
Sworn to no Master, of no Sect am I:
As drives the storm, at any door I knock: 25
And house with Montaigne now, or now with Locke.[1]
Sometimes a Patriot, active in debate,
Mix with the World, and battle for the State,
Free as young Lyttelton, her Cause pursue,
Still true to Virtue, and as warm as true:[2]   30
Sometimes with Aristippus,[3] or St. Paul,
Indulge my candor, and grow all to all;
Back to my native Moderation slide,
And win my way by yielding to the tide.

 Long, as to him who works for debt, the day,   35
Long as the Night to her whose Love's away,
Long as the Year's dull circle seems to run,
When the brisk Minor pants for twenty-one:
So slow th' unprofitable moments roll,
That lock up all the Functions of my soul;   40
That keep me from myself; and still delay
Life's instant business to a future day:
That task, which as we follow, or despise,
The eldest is a fool, the youngest wise;
Which done, the poorest can no wants endure;[4]   45
And which not done, the richest must be poor.

 Late as it is, I put myself to school,
And feel some comfort, not to be a fool.
Weak tho' I am of limb, and short of sight,
Far from a Lynx, and not a Giant quite;   50
I'll do what Mead[5] and Cheselden[6] advise,
To keep these limbs, and to preserve these eyes.
Not to go back, is somewhat to advance,
And men must walk at least before they dance.

 Say, does thy blood rebel, thy bosom move   55
With wretched Av'rice, or as wretched Love?

---

[1] *And house with Montaigne now, and now
with Locke.*] i.e. Choose either an *active* or a
contemplative life, as is most fitted to the season
and circumstances. — For he regarded these
Writers as the best Schools to form a man for
the world; or to give him a knowledge of him-
self: *Montaigne* excelling in his observations
on social and civil life; and *Locke,* in develop-
ing the faculties, and explaining the operations
of the human mind. *Warburton.* [Pope ap-
pears to have read Locke at an early age; and
to have recurred to him in his later and equally
desultory philosophical studies.]

[2] [George Lord Lyttelton, author of the *Dia-
logues of the Dead,* besides poems (Pastorals)
and theological and historical works, was a cor-
respondent of Pope's.]

[3] Omnis Aristippum decuit color, et status, et

res. P. There is an impropriety and indeco-
rum, in joining the name of the most profligate
parasite of the Court of Dionysius with that of
an apostle. In a few lines before, the name of
Montaigne is not sufficiently contrasted by the
name of Locke. *Warton.*

[4] *can no wants endure;*] i.e. Can want
nothing. Badly expressed. *Warburton.*

[5] [Mead : v. *Moral Essays,* Ep. IV. v. 10.]

[6] [In answer to Swift's enquiry who ' this
Cheselden was, Pope informed him that C. was
' the most noted and most deserving man in the
whole profession of chirurgery and had saved the
lives of thousands' by his skill. There is an
amusing letter from Pope to Cheselden in Ros-
coe's Life *ad ann.* 1737; speaking of the cata-
ract to which v. 52 appears to allude.]

Know, there are Words, and Spells, which can control
Between the Fits this Fever of the soul :
Know, there are Rhymes, which fresh and fresh apply'd
Will cure the arrant'st Puppy of his Pride.   60
Be furious, envious, slothful, mad, or drunk,
Slave to a Wife, or Vassal to a Punk,
A Switz, a High-dutch, or a Low-dutch Bear;
All that we ask is but a patient Ear.
'T is the first Virtue, Vices to abhor ;   65
And the first Wisdom, to be Fool no more.
But to the world no bugbear is so great,
As want of figure, and a small Estate.
To either India see the Merchant fly,
Scar'd at the spectre of pale Poverty!   70
See him, with pains of body, pangs of soul,
Burn through the Tropic, freeze beneath the Pole!
Wilt thou do nothing for a nobler end,
Nothing, to make Philosophy thy friend?
To stop thy foolish views, thy long desires,   75
And ease thy heart of all that it admires?
  Here, Wisdom calls : " Seek Virtue first, be bold!
" As Gold to Silver, Virtue is to Gold." [1]
There, London's voice : " Get Money, Money still!
" And then let Virtue follow, if she will."   80
This, this the saving doctrine, preach'd to all,
From low St. James's up to high St. Paul ; [2]
From him whose quills stand quiver'd at his ear, [3]
To him who notches sticks at Westminster. [4]
  Barnard in spirit, sense, and truth abounds ; [5]   85
" Pray then, what wants he?"   Fourscore thousand pounds ;
A Pension, or such Harness for a slave
As Bug now has, and Dorimant would have. [6]
Barnard, thou art a Cit, with all thy worth ;
But Bug and D*l, their *Honours*, and so forth.   90
  Yet ev'ry child another song will sing :
" Virtue, brave boys! 't is Virtue makes a King."
True, conscious Honour is to feel no sin,
He 's arm'd without that 's innocent within ;
Be this thy Screen, and this thy wall of Brass ; [7]   95
Compar'd to this, a Minister's an Ass.
  And say, to which shall our applause belong,
This new Court jargon, or the good old song?

---

[1] [Warburton points that this line gives the meaning neither of Pope nor of the Horatian: ' Vilius est auro argentum, virtutibus aurum.']

[2] [Referring to the opposite schools of theology in favour at court and in the metropolitan Chapter.]

[3] [i.e. a scrivener with his pen in his ear.]

[4] [i.e. Exchequer tallies. *Warburton.*]

[5] [Sir John Barnard, a quaker who joined the Church of England, member for the City and a great financial authority in Walpole's era. He was Lord Mayor in 1738. Cf. *Epil. to Sat.* Dial. II. v. 99.]

[6] [These allusions here and in v. 112 remain unexplained.]   [*Bug* is stated by Croker to be the Duke of Kent, *Dorimant* (*Bestia* in original draught) old Horace Walpole, and D*l the young Earl of Deloraine. *Am. Ed.*]

[7] *Hic murus aheneus esto. Hor.*

The modern language of corrupted Peers,
Or what was spoke at CRESSY and POITIERS?   100
Who counsels best? who whispers, "Be but **great**,
"With Praise or Infamy leave that to fate;
"Get Place and Wealth, if possible, with grace;
"If not, by any means get Wealth and Place—"
For what? to have a Box where Eunuchs sing,[1]   105
And foremost in the Circle eye a King.
Or he, who bids thee face with steady view
Proud Fortune, and look shallow Greatness thro':
And, while he bids thee, sets th' Example too?
If such a doctrine, in St. James's air,   110
Shou'd chance to make the well-drest Rabble stare;
If honest S*z[2] take scandal at a Spark,
That less admires the Palace than the Park:
Faith I shall give the answer Reynard gave:
"I cannot like, dread Sir, your Royal Cave: 115
"Because I see, by all the tracks about,
"Full many a Beast goes in, but none come out."[3]
Adieu to Virtue, if you 're once a Slave:
Send her to Court, you send her to her grave.
    Well, if a King 's a Lion, at the least   120
The People are a many-headed Beast:
Can they direct what measures to pursue,
Who know themselves so little what to do?
Alike in nothing but one Lust of Gold,
Just half the land would buy, and half be sold: 125
Their Country's wealth our mightier Misers drain,[4]
Or cross, to plunder Provinces, the Main;
The rest, some farm the Poor-box,[5] some the Pews;
Some keep Assemblies, and would keep the Stews;
Some with fat Bucks on childless dotards fawn;   130
Some win rich Widows by their Chine and Brawn;[6]
While with the silent growth of ten per cent,
In dirt and darkness, hundreds stink content.
    Of all these ways, if each pursues his own,
Satire be kind, and let the wretch alone: 135
But shew me one who has it in his pow'r
To act consistent with himself an hour.
Sir Job sail'd forth, the ev'ning bright and still,
"No place on earth (he cry'd) like Greenwich hill!"

---

[1] [The Italian Opera, with singers like Senesino and Farinelli, and Cuzzoni and Faustina, was at the zenith of its reputation in London in the reign of George II.]

[2] [Augustus Schutz, who held court offices near the person of George II. both before and after his accession to the throne. *Carruthers.*]

[3] Quia me vestigia terrent
Omnia te adversum spectantia, nulla retrorsum. *Hor.* [from Aesop's well-known fable.]

[4] *Their Country's wealth our mightier Misers drain,*] The undertakers for advancing Loans to the Public on the funds. *Warburton.*

[5] Alluding most probably to a Society calling itself the 'Charitable Corporation;' by which thousands were cheated and ruined. *Bowles.* [V. Pope's note to *Moral Essays*, Ep. III. v. 100.]

[6] Probably satirising Lord Sydney Beauclerck, fifth son of the Duke of St. Albans, a handsome fortune hunter who finally secured Miss Norris and £60,000. *Courthope.*

Up starts a Palace ; lo, th' obedient base   140
Slopes at its foot, the woods its sides embrace,
The silver Thames reflects its marble face.
Now let some whimsy, or that dev'l within
Which guides all those who know not what they mean,
But give the Knight (or give his Lady) spleen ;   145
" Away, away ! take all your scaffolds down,
" For Snug 's the word : My dear! we 'll live in Town."
    At am'rous Flavio is the stocking thrown?
That very night he longs to lie alone.
The Fool, whose Wife elopes some thrice a quarter,   150
For matrimonial solace dies a martyr.
Did ever Proteus, Merlin, any witch,
Transform themselves so strangely as the Rich?
Well, but the Poor — The Poor have the same itch ;
They change their weekly Barber, weekly News,   155
Prefer a new Japanner to their shoes,
Discharge their Garrets, move their beds, and run
(They know not whither) in a Chaise and one ;
They hire their sculler, and when once aboard,
Grow sick, and damn the climate — like a Lord.   160
    You laugh, half Beau, half Sloven if I stand,
My wig all powder, and all snuff my band ;
You laugh, if coat and breeches strangely vary,
White gloves, and linen worthy Lady Mary!
But when no Prelate's Lawn with hair-shirt lin'd,   165
Is half so incoherent as my Mind,
When (each opinion with the next at strife,
One ebb and flow of follies all my life)
I plant, root up ; I build, and then confound,
Turn round to square, and square again to round ;   170
You never change one muscle of your face,
You think this Madness but a common case,
Nor once to Chanc'ry, nor to Hale[1] apply ;
Yet hang your lip, to see a Seam awry!
Careless how ill I with myself agree,   175 .
Kind to my dress, my figure, not to Me.
Is this my Guide, Philosopher, and Friend?[2]
This, he who loves me, and who ought to mend?
Who ought to make me (what he can, or none,)
That Man divine whom Wisdom calls her own ;   180
Great without Title, without Fortune bless'd ;
Rich ev'n when plunder'd, honour'd while oppress'd ;
Lov'd without youth, and follow'd without pow'r ;
At home, tho' exil'd ; free, tho' in the Tower ;
In short, that reas'ning, high, immortal Thing,   185
Just less than Jove, and much above a King,
Nay, half in heav'n — except (what 's mighty odd)
A Fit of Vapours clouds this Demi-God.

[1] Dr. Hale, of Lincoln's Inn Fields, a physician employed in cases of insanity. *Carruthers.*

[2] [The titles by which Pope addresses Bolingbroke in the *Essay on Man*, Ep. IV. v. 390.]

THE SIXTH EPISTLE

OF THE

FIRST BOOK OF HORACE.

EPISTLE VI.

TO MR. MURRAY.[1]

[Horace's Epistle, addressed to an otherwise unknown Numicius, is designed to prove that Virtue is the sole means of true happiness. The celebrated Nil Admirari which it preaches is the expression of the doctrine that the wonder or admiration which leads to desire destroys the peace of mind essential to a happy condition.]

" **N**OT to admire, is all the Art I know,[2]
" To make men happy, and to keep them so."
(Plain truth, dear MURRAY, needs no flow'rs of speech,
So take it in the very words of Creech.)[3]
  This Vault of Air, this congregated Ball,   5
Self-center'd Sun, and Stars that rise and fall,
There are, my Friend! whose philosophic eyes
Look thro', and trust the Ruler with his skies,
To him commit the hour, the day, the year,
And view this dreadful All without a fear.   10
Admire we then what Earth's low entrails hold,
Arabian shores, or Indian seas infold;
All the mad trade of Fools and Slaves for Gold?
Or Popularity? or Stars and Strings?
The Mob's applauses, or the gifts of Kings?   15
Say with what eyes we ought at Courts to gaze,
And pay the Great our homage of Amaze?
  If weak the pleasure that from these can spring,
The fear to want them is as weak a thing:
Whether we dread, or whether we desire,   20
In either case, believe me, we admire;
Whether we joy or grieve, the same the curse,

[1] [William Murray (a younger son of Lord Stormont) began his public career by appearing at the Bar of the House of Commons as one of the Counsel for the British American merchants aggrieved by the Spaniards in 1738, just after the date of Pope's Epistle. He became Solicitor-General in Lord Wilmington's Cabinet 1742; and ultimately rose to the Chief Justiceship and a barony, which was afterwards raised to an Earldom. It was he who gave judgment in the case of Wilkes, who presided at the trial of Horne Tooke, and who lived to have his house burnt over his head by the 'Protestant' rioters of 1780. He died in 1793, leaving behind him a lofty reputation, tempered by the memory of the humour for which he is praised by Pope. Murray had originally won the gratitude of the latter by his defence of the *Essay on Man* from the attacks of Crousaz.]

[2] Nil admirari prope res est una, Numici,
Solaque, quae possit facere et servare beatum.
                           Hor.

[3] *Creech.*] From whose Translation of Horace the two first lines are taken. P. [Richard Creech, whose celebrated translation of Lucretius first appeared in 1682 (his Horace in 1684).]

Surpris'd at better, or surpris'd at worse.
Thus good or bad, to one extreme betray
Th' unbalanc'd Mind, and snatch the Man away;   25
For Virtue's self may too much zeal be had;
The worst of Madmen is a Saint run mad.[1]
  Go then, and if you can, admire the state
Of beaming diamonds, and reflected plate;
Procure a TASTE to double the surprise,   30
And gaze on Parian Charms with learned eyes:
Be struck with bright Brocade, or Tyrian Dye,
Our Birth-day Nobles' splendid Livery.
If not so pleas'd, at Council-board rejoice,
To see their Judgments hang upon thy Voice;   35
From morn to night, at Senate, Rolls, and Hall,
Plead much, read more, dine late, or not at all.
But wherefore all this labour, all this strife?
For Fame, for Riches, for a noble Wife?
Shall One whom Nature, Learning, Birth, conspir'd   40
To form, not to admire but be admir'd,
Sigh, while his Chloe blind to Wit and Worth
Weds the rich Dulness of some Son of earth?
Yet Time ennobles, or degrades each Line;
It brighten'd *Craggs's*,[2] and may darken thine: 45
And what is Fame? the Meanest have their Day,
The Greatest can but blaze, and pass away.
Grac'd as thou art, with all the Pow'r of Words,
So known, so honour'd, at the House of Lords:[3]
Conspicuous Scene! another yet is nigh,   50
(More silent far) where Kings and Poets lie;
Where MURRAY (long enough his Country's pride)
Shall be no more than TULLY, or than HYDE![4]
  Rack'd with Sciatics, martyr'd with the Stone,
Will any mortal let himself alone?   55
See Ward by batter'd Beaux invited over,
And desp'rate Misery lays hold on Dover.[5]
The case is easier in the Mind's disease;
There all Men may be cur'd, whene'er they please.
Would ye be blest? despise low Joys, low Gains; }   60
Disdain whatever CORNBURY[6] disdains;
Be virtuous, and be happy for your pains.

---

[1] [Horace merely preaches the Μηδὲν ἄγαν in his lines:

Insani sapiens nomen ferat, aequus iniqui,
Ultra quam satis est virtutem si petat ipsam.]

[2] *Craggs's*,] (See note to Epitaph IV.) His father had been in a low situation; but, by industry and ability, got to be Postmaster-General and agent to the Duke of Marlborough. *Warton.*

[3] [A piece of bathos, says Mr. Hayward, thus parodied by Cibber:

'Persuasion tips his tongue whene'er he talks,
And he has chambers in the King's Bench walks.']

[4] [The great Lord Clarendon.]

[5] [*Ward* and *Dover:* celebrated for their quack medicines. *Roscoe.*]

[6] [Lord Cornbury, known as Lord Hyde [though he died before his father], great-grandson of the first Lord Clarendon, a young Tory nobleman of literary tastes, to whom Bolingbroke addressed his *Letters on History.* Of

But art thou one, whom new opinions sway,
One who believes as Tindal [1] leads the way,
Who Virtue and a Church alike disowns,   65
Thinks that but words, and this but brick and stones?
Fly then, on all the wings of wild desire,
Admire whate'er the maddest can admire.
Is Wealth thy passion? Hence! from Pole to Pole,
Where winds can carry, or where waves can roll,   70
For Indian spices, for Peruvian Gold,
Prevent the greedy, and out-bid the bold:
Advance thy golden Mountain to the skies;
On the broad base of fifty thousand rise,
Add one round hundred, and (if that's not fair)   75
Add fifty more, and bring it to a square.
For, mark th' advantage; just so many score
Will gain a Wife with half as many more,
Procure her Beauty, make that beauty chaste,
And then such Friends — as cannot fail to last.   80
A Man of wealth is dubb'd a Man of worth,[2]
Venus shall give him Form, and Anstis [3] Birth.
(Believe me, many a German Prince is worse,
Who proud of Pedigree, is poor of Purse.)
His Wealth brave Timon gloriously confounds;   85
Ask'd for a groat, he gives a hundred pounds;
Or if three Ladies like a luckless Play,[4]
Takes the whole House upon the Poet's Day.
Now, in such exigencies not to need,
Upon my word, you must be rich indeed;   90
A noble superfluity it craves,
Not for yourself, but for your Fools and Knaves;
Something, which for your Honour they may cheat,
And which it much becomes you to forget.
If Wealth alone then make and keep us blest,   95
Still, still be getting, never, never rest.
But if to Pow'r and Place your passion lie,
If in the Pomp of Life consist the joy;
Then hire a Slave, or (if you will) a Lord
To do the Honours, and to give the Word;   100
Tell at your Levee, as the Crowds approach,
To whom to nod, whom take into your Coach,
Whom honour with your hand: to make remarks,
Who rules in Cornwall, or who rules in Berks:

Lord C., says Mr. Macknight, 'even Horace Walpole spoke with enthusiasm.' He died in 1753. Carruthers points out that he refused a pension obtained for him by his brother-in-law, Lord Essex.]

[1] [Dr. Matthew Tindal, author of *Christianity as old as the Creation.*]

[2] *dubb'd a Man of worth,*] Alluding to the City Knighthoods, where wealth and worship go together. *Warburton.*

[3] *Anstis*, whom Pope often mentions, was Garter King of Arms. *Bowles.*

[4] *Or if three Ladies like a luckless Play,*] The common reader, I am sensible, will be always more solicitous about the names of these *three Ladies*, the unlucky *Play*, and every other

" This may be troublesome, is near the Chair;   105
" That makes three members, this can choose a May'r."
Instructed thus, you bow, embrace, protest, ⎫
Adopt him Son, or Cousin at the least,   ⎬
Then·turn about, and laugh at your own Jest. ⎭
  Or if your life be one continu'd Treat,   110
If to live well means nothing but to eat;
Up, up! cries Gluttony, 't is break of day,
Go drive the Deer and drag the finny prey;
With hounds and horns go hunt an Appetite —
So Russel did, but could not eat at night,   115
Call'd happy Dog! the Beggar at his door,
And envy'd Thirst and Hunger to the Poor.
  Or shall we ev'ry Decency confound,
Thro' Taverns, Stews, and Bagnio's take our round,
Go dine with Chartres, in each Vice out-do   120
K—l's lewd Cargo, or Ty—y's Crew,[1]
From Latian Syrens, French Circean Feasts,
Return well travell'd, and transform'd to Beasts,
Or for a Titled Punk, or foreign Flame,
Renounce our Country, and degrade our Name?   125
  If, after all, we must with Wilmot[2] own,
The Cordial Drop of Life is Love·alone,
And SWIFT cry wisely, " Vive la Bagatelle! "[3]
The Man that loves and laughs, must sure do well.
Adieu — if this advice appear the worst,   130
E'en take the Counsel which I gave you first:
Or better Precepts if you can impart,
Why do, I 'll follow them with all my heart.

THE FIRST EPISTLE

OF THE

SECOND BOOK OF HORACE.

ADVERTISEMENT.

THE Reflections of *Horace*, and the Judgments past in his Epistle to *Augustus*, seem'd so seasonable to the present Times, that I could not help applying them to the use of my own Country. The Author thought them considerable enough to address them to his Prince; whom he paints with all the great and good qualities of a Monarch,

trifling circumstance that attended this piece of gallantry, than for the explanation of our Author's sense, or the illustration of his poetry; even where he is most moral and sublime. But had it been in Mr. Pope's purpose to indulge so impertinent a curiosity, he had sought elsewhere for a commentator on his writings *Warburton.* Notwithstanding this remark of Dr. Warburton, I have taken some pains, though indeed in vain,

to ascertain who these ladies were, and what the play they patronized. It was once said to be Young's *Busiris. Warton.*

[1] Lords Kinnoul and Tyrawley, two ambassadors noted for wild immorality. *Carruthers.*

[2] [Earl of Rochester. See note on p. 184.]

[3] [Warburton, with sundry unnecessary remarks, quotes the following *dicta* of Swift's latter days: ' I choose ' (says he, in a Letter to

upon whom the Romans depended for the Increase of an *Absolute Empire*. But to make the Poem entirely English, I was willing to add one or two of those which contribute to the Happiness of a *Free People*, and are more consistent with the Welfare of *our Neighbours*.

This Epistle will show the learned World to have fallen into Two mistakes: one, that *Augustus was a Patron of Poets in general;* whereas he not only prohibited all but the Best Writers to name him, but recommended that Care even to the Civil Magistrate: *Admonebat Praetores, ne paterentur Nomen suum obsolefieri,* etc. The other, that this Piece was only a *general Discourse of Poetry;* whereas it was an *Apology for the Poets,* in order to render *Augustus* more their Patron. *Horace* here pleads the Cause of his Cotemporaries, first against the Taste of the *Town,* whose humour it was to magnify the Authors of the preceding Age; secondly against the *Court* and *Nobility,* who encouraged only the Writers for the Theatre; and lastly against the *Emperor* himself, who had conceived them of little Use to the Government. He shows (by a View of the Progress of Learning, and the Change of Taste among the Romans) that the Introduction of the Polite Arts of *Greece* had given the Writers of his Time great advantages over their Predecessors; that their *Morals* were much improved, and the Licence of those ancient Poets restrained: that *Satire* and *Comedy* were become more just and useful; that whatever extravagancies were left on the Stage, were owing to the *Ill Taste* of the *Nobility;* that Poets, under due Regulations, were in many respects useful to the *State,* and concludes, that it was upon them the *Emperor* himself must depend, for his Fame with Posterity.

We may farther learn from this Epistle, that *Horace* made his Court to this great Prince by writing with a decent Freedom toward him, with a just Contempt of his low Flatterers, and with a manly Regard to his own Character. P.

[The bland statements of the above Advertisement will not deceive the reader as to the ironical character of Pope's Epistle, which ranks among the most finished of his compositions. According to Suetonius (*Vita Hor.*) the origin of the Horatian Epistle (probably written only a year or two before the poet's death) was the expression by Augustus of a desire that Horace might address one of his Epistles to the Emperor himself. No such wish, we may feel sure, ever suggested itself in the bosom of King George II. Augustus was a real patron of literature, and in particular of dramatic poetry. Horace accordingly takes occasion to examine the development of Roman literature with special reference to this branch of it; and after dwelling on the prejudicial influence of the prevalent preference for the older poets, to show the evil effects of the love of spectacle upon the progress of the Roman drama. He concludes by directing the attention of the Emperor to the non-dramatic, and particularly the epic poets, and while recognising the grandeur of their task — the glorification of the deeds of heroes like Augustus himself — modestly declares his own incapacity to enter their ranks.

Pope addresses himself to a monarch who, since his accession to the throne in 1727, had done nothing, and intended to do nothing, to foster a literature for which, notwithstanding his intelligence, he lacked sympathy. The opposition, to which Pope was attached by personal friendships rather than by any distinct political creed, had pretended to found high hopes in this respect, as in all others, upon George Prince of Wales, when he was on bad terms with his father and the Walpole ministry. But he had speedily undeceived them as to the real object of their hopes; and 'Bob, the poet's foe' (as Swift nicknamed Sir Robert Walpole), remained in power. The slight attempts on the part of Queen Caroline to patronise literature and literary men were lost in the general apathy, amounting almost to dislike, with which both were regarded by King and Minister.

While therefore all the allusions to the King himself must be understood as distinctly ironical, the review of English literature which they introduce is only addressed to the King *because* he would take no interest in it. This review itself contains many criticisms of much sagacity and acuteness; it will be found that upon the whole Pope in his manhood adhered very much to the opinions which as a youth he had expressed in his *Essay on Criticism,* which should be carefully compared with the present Epistle. It is strange to find Pope charging his age with an undue preference for the old poets; the truth being that the period of a renaissance in this respect had hardly yet begun in English popular taste. The observations on the stage are fully borne out by contemporary accounts; Pope was to live to hail the appearance of Garrick as the advent of better days.]

EPISTLE I.

To Augustus.

WHILE you, great Patron of Mankind! sustain
 The balanc'd World, and open all the Main;[1]
Your Country, chief, in Arms abroad defend,[2]
At home, with Morals, Arts, and Laws amend;
How shall the Muse, from such a Monarch, steal   5
An hour, and not defraud the Public Weal?
 Edward and Henry, now the Boast of Fame,[3]
And virtuous Alfred, a more sacred Name,
After a Life of gen'rous Toils endur'd,
The Gaul subdu'd, or Property secur'd,   10
Ambition humbled, mighty Cities storm'd,
Or Laws establish'd, and the world reform'd;
Clos'd their long Glories, with a sigh, to find
Th' unwilling Gratitude of base mankind!
All human Virtue, to its latest breath,   15
Finds Envy never conquer'd but by Death.
The great Alcides, ev'ry Labour past,
Had still this Monster to subdue at last.
Sure fate of all, beneath whose rising ray,
Each star of meaner merit fades away!   20
Oppress'd we feel the beam directly beat,
Those Suns of Glory please not till they set.
 To thee, the World its present homage pays,
The Harvest early, but mature the praise:
Great Friend of LIBERTY! in *Kings* a Name   25
Above all Greek, above all Roman fame:[4]
Whose Word is Truth, as sacred and rever'd,
As Heav'n's own Oracles from Altars heard.
Wonder of Kings! like whom, to mortal eyes
None e'er has risen, and none e'er shall rise.   30
Just in one instance, be it yet confest

Mr. Pope) ' my Companions amongst those of the least consequence, and most compliance: I read the most trifling Books I can find: and whenever I write, it is upon the most trifling subjects.' And again, ' I love *La Bagatelle* better than ever. I am always writing bad prose or worse verses, either of rage or raillery,' etc. And again, in a letter to Mr. Gay: ' My rule is, *Vive la Bagatelle.*']

[1] At this time (1737) the Spanish depredations at sea were such, that there was an universal cry that the British flag had been insulted, and the English braved on their own element. ' Opening all the main' therefore, means that the King was so liberal as to leave it open to the Spaniards. *Bowles.*

[2] [This again ironically refers to the general cry for war after a long period of peace.]

[3] [These historical parallels or antitheta, substituted by Pope for Horace's safer names of Romulus, Bacchus and the Dioscuri, must be taken *quantum valeant.* The close of Edward III.'s reign offers a melancholy proof that a great man may outlive his own greatness; and Henry V. enjoyed a high popularity with his subjects to the day of his death, except of course with the Lollards.]

[4] Te nostris ducibus, te Graiis anteferendo.
           Hor.

Your People, Sir, are partial in the rest :
Foes to all living worth except your own,
And Advocates for folly dead and gone.
Authors, like coins, grow dear as they grow old ;   35
It is the rust we value, not the gold.
Chaucer's worst ribaldry is learn'd by rote,[1]
And beastly Skelton Heads of Houses quote :[2]
One likes no language but the Faery Queen ;
A Scot will fight for Christ's Kirk o' the Green ;[3]   40
And each true Briton is to Ben so civil,
He swears the Muses met him at the Devil.[4]
    Tho' justly Greece her eldest sons admires,
Why should not We be wiser than our sires ?
In ev'ry Public virtue we excel ;   45
We build, we paint, we sing, we dance as well,
And learned Athens to our art must stoop,
Could she behold us tumbling thro' a hoop.
    If Time improve our Wit as well as Wine,
Say at what age a Poet grows divine ?   50
Shall we, or shall we not, account him so,
Who died, perhaps, an hundred years ago?
End all dispute ; and fix the year precise
When British bards begin t' immortalize ?[5]
    "Who lasts a century can have no flaw,   55
"I hold that Wit a Classic, good in law."
    Suppose he wants a year, will you compound?
And shall we deem him Ancient, right and sound,
Or damn to all eternity at once,
At ninety-nine, a Modern and a Dunce?   60
    "We shall not quarrel for a year or two ;
"By courtesy of England,[6] he may do."
    Then by the rule that made the Horse-tail bear,[7]
I pluck out year by year, as hair by hair,
And melt down Ancients like a heap of snow :   65
While you to measure merits, look in Stowe,[8]
And estimating authors by the year,
Bestow a Garland only on a Bier.

---

[1] [Particularly when modernised.]

[2] *And beastly Skelton, etc.*] Skelton, Poet Laureate to Hen. VIII. a volume of whose verses has been lately reprinted, consisting almost wholly of ribaldry, obscenity, and scurrilous language. P. [John Skelton born about 1460, tutor to prince Henry (afterwards K. H. VIII.) and ultimately Rector of Diss in Norfolk, died in 1529. His English verse, which is chiefly satirical and in part directed against Wolsey, is by no means entirely what Pope's perfunctory epithets declare it to be.]

[3] *Christ's Kirk o' the Green ;*] A Ballad made by a King of Scotland. P. [James I.]

[4] *met him at the Devil*] The Devil Tavern, where Ben Jonson held his Poetical Club. P.

[5] [i.e. to be immortal.]

[6] [' Courtesy of England,' a legal term signifying the custom by which a widower holds during his lifetime the lands of which his wife was seized in fee, if she had issue by him born alive.]

[7] [The reference in Horace is to the so-called *Argumentatio Acervalis*, or *Sorites*, the purpose of which is to show that relative terms of measure admit of no precise definition.]

[8] [Stowe's *Annals of England* appear to have been first published in 1580.]

Shakespear [1] (whom you and ev'ry Play-house bill
Style the divine, the matchless, what you will)　　　　70
For gain, not glory, wing'd his roving flight,
And grew Immortal in his own despite.
Ben, old and poor, as little seem'd to heed
The Life to come, in ev'ry Poet's Creed.
Who now reads Cowley? if he pleases yet,　　　　75
His Moral pleases, not his pointed wit;
Forget his Epic, nay Pindaric Art; [2]
But still I love the language of his heart. [3]
　　"Yet surely, surely, these were famous men!
"What boy but hears the sayings of old Ben?　　　　80
"In all debates where Critics bear a part, [4]
"Not one but nods, and talks of Jonson's Art,
"Of Shakespear's Nature, and of Cowley's Wit;
"How Beaumont's judgment check'd what Fletcher [5] writ;
"How Shadwell [6] hasty, Wycherley [7] was slow; [8]　　　　85
"But for the Passions, Southern [9] sure and Rowe. [10]
"These, only these, support the crowded stage,
"From eldest Heywood [11] down to Cibber's age."
　　All this may be; the People's Voice is odd,
It is, and it is not, the voice of God.　　　　90
To Gammer Gurton [12] if it give the bays,

---

[1] *Shakespear*] Shakespear and Ben Jonson may truly be said not much to have thought of this Immortality, the one in many pieces composed in haste for the Stage; the other in his latter works in general, which Dryden call'd his *Dotages*. P.

[2] *Pindaric Art;*] which has much more merit than his Epic, but very unlike the Character, as well as Numbers of Pindar. P.

[3] [Compare p. 183.]

[4] *In all debates, etc.*] The Poet has here put the bald cant of women and boys into extreme fine verse. This is in strict imitation of his Original, where the same impertinent and gratuitous criticism is admirably ridiculed.

[5] [This common assumption should in its turn be checked by the consideration that out of 52 plays known as Beaumont and Fletcher's the former can only be proved to have had part in 17. Beaumont, though ten years younger than Fletcher, published plays before the latter.]

[6] [Thomas Shadwell, poet-laureate, the original of Dryden's *Mac Flecknoe*.]

[7] [Wycherley, see note to p. 20.]

[8] *Shadwell hasty, Wycherley was slow.*] Nothing was less true than this particular: But the whole paragraph has a mixture of Irony, and must not altogether be taken for Horace's own Judgment, only the common Chat of the pre-

tenders to Criticism; in some things right, in others, wrong; as he tells us in his answer,
Interdum vulgus rectum videt: est ubi peccat.
　　　　　　　　　　　　　　　　　　　　　　P.

— *hasty Shadwell and slow Wycherley*, is a line of Wilmot, Earl of Rochester: the sense of which seems to have been generally mistaken. It gives to each his epithet, not to design the *difference* of their talents, but the *number* of their productions. *Warburton.*

[9] [Thomas Southern (1660–1746), the author of the tragedy of *Oroonoko.*]

[10] [Rowe. See *Epitaph* v.]

[11] [Of John Heywood's 'Interludes,' which form a transition from the moral-plays to the regular drama, the earliest was probably written in the first quarter of the 16th century.]

[12] *Gammer Gurton*] A piece of very low humour, one of the first printed Plays in English, and therefore much valued by some Antiquaries. P. [Believed, on insufficient evidence, to have been written by Bishop Still. The oldest extant edition of this play is dated 1575; Udall's *Ralph Roister Doister* (of which a copy was first discovered in 1818) was certainly printed nine years previously; and, being founded on Plautus, is infinitely superior to *Gammer Gurton's Needle*, although the latter has a few touches of considerable humour and contains an excellent drinking-song.]

And yet deny the Careless Husband [1] praise,
Or say our Fathers never broke a rule;
Why then, I say, the Public is a fool.
But let them own, that greater Faults than we   95
They had, and greater Virtues, I'll agree.
Spenser himself affects the Obsolete,[2]
And Sidney's verse halts ill on Roman feet: [3]
Milton's strong pinion now not Heav'n can bound,
Now Serpent-like, in prose he sweeps the ground,   100
In Quibbles Angel and Archangel join,
And God the Father turns a School-divine.[4]
Not that I'd lop the Beauties from his book,
Like slashing Bentley with his desp'rate hook,[5]
Or damn all Shakespear, like th' affected Fool   105
At court, who hates whate'er he read at school.[6]
    But for the Wits of either Charles's days,
The Mob of Gentlemen who wrote with Ease;
Sprat,[8] Carew,[9] Sedley,[10] and a hundred more,
(Like twinkling stars the Miscellanies o'er)   110
One Simile, that solitary shines
In the dry desert of a thousand lines,
Or lengthen'd Thought that gleams through many a page,
Has sanctify'd whole poems for an age.
I lose my patience, and I own it too,   115
When works are censur'd, not as bad but new;
While if our Elders break all reason's laws,
These fools demand not pardon, but Applause.[11]
    On Avon's bank, where flow'rs eternal blow,
If I but ask, if any weed can grow;   120
One Tragic sentence if I dare deride
Which Betterton's [12] grave action dignify'd,

---

[1] [Cibber's *Careless Husband*, in which the character of Lord Foppington is taken from Vanbrugh, was first acted in 1704; and kept the stage throughout the century. Lady Betty Modish is a character in this comedy.]

[2] [Compare p. 179.]

[3] [In Bk. I. of Sir Philip Sidney's *Arcadia* are specimens of his English hexameters and pentameters as well as sapphics; in Bk. II. there is also an experiment in the metre of Anacreon, by no means unpleasant in its effect.]

[4] [*Paradise Lost*, Bk. III.]

[5] [Cf. *Epistle to Arbuthnot*, v. 168.]

[6] An indirect satire on Lord Hervey, in allusion to certain lines in his Epistle to a D.D. from a nobleman at Hampton Court. *Carruthers*.

[7] [Cf. *Essay on Criticism*, vv. 715 f.]

[8] [Thomas Sprat, Bishop of Rochester; who read James II.'s Declaration in Westminster Abbey and was arrested on a false charge of treason under William III. He was one of the earliest members of the Royal Society; and a popular writer of both prose and verse.]

[9] [Thomas Carew, a courtier of Charles II. and a charming lyrical poet, died in 1639.]

[10] [Sir Charles Sedley, the favourite poet of King Charles II., died in 1701. He was a boon-companion of the Earl of Rochester.]

[11] [Pope's edition of Shakspere was published in 1725. It was a failure as a speculation; and though it is not without merits, both in the preface (of which the general spirit is upon the whole creditable to Pope's appreciation of Shakspere's genius) and in the emendations (frequently very clever), yet it deservedly exposed Pope to the cavils of Theobald. See Introduction to *Dunciad*.]

[12] [This famous actor was an early friend of Pope's, a copy by whose hand of the actor's portrait by Kneller still exists at Lord Mansfield's seat at Caen Wood, Hampstead. An

Or well-mouth'd Booth[1] with emphasis proclaims,
(Tho' but, perhaps, a muster-roll of Names)[2]
How will our Fathers rise up in a rage,   125
And swear, all shame is lost in George's Age!
You 'd think no Fools disgrac'd the former reign,
Did not some grave Examples yet remain,
Who scorn a Lad should teach his father skill,
And, having once been wrong, will be so still.   130
He, who to seem more deep than you or I,
Extols old Bards, or Merlin's Prophecy,
Mistake him not; he envies, not admires,
And to debase the Sons, exalts the Sires.
Had ancient times conspir'd to disallow   135
What then was new, what had been ancient now?
Or what remain'd, so worthy to be read
By learned Critics, of the mighty Dead?
    In Days of Ease, when now the weary Sword
Was sheath'd, and *Luxury* with *Charles* restor'd;   140
In ev'ry taste of foreign Courts improv'd,
"All, by the King's Example, liv'd and lov'd."[3]
Then Peers grew proud in Horsemanship t' excel,[4]
Newmarket's Glory rose, as Britain's fell;[5]
The Soldier breath'd the Gallantries of France,   145
And ev'ry flow'ry Courtier writ Romance.
Then Marble. soften'd into life, grew warm:[6]
And yielding Metal flow'd to human form:
Lely on animated Canvas stole
The Sleepy Eye, that spoke the melting soul.[7]   150
No wonder then, when all was Love and sport,
The willing Muses were debauch'd at Court:
On each enervate string they taught the note[8]

account of his famous Benefit in April 7th, 1709, will be found in the *Tatler*. His 'grave action' was probably due in part to his large habit of body; yet he played an unusually wide range of characters, and according to Cibber was particularly great in Othello, Hamlet, Hotspur, Macbeth and Brutus. See Leigh Hunt's *The Town*.]

[1] [Barton Booth (who died in 1733) was an actor particularly celebrated for the excellence of his articulation. He was the original Cato in Addison's tragedy. Cf. v. 327.]

[2] *A muster-roll of Names*] An absurd custom of several Actors, to pronounce with emphasis the mere *Proper Names* of Greeks or Romans, which (as they call it) *fill the mouth* of the Player. P. [Like the 'Bombomachides Clutomestoridysarchides' of Plautus.]

[3] A verse of the Lord Lansdown. P.

[4] *in Horsemanship t' excel, And ev'ry flow'ry Courtier writ Romance.*] The Duke

of Newcastle's book of Horsemanship: the Romance of *Parthenissa*, by the Earl of Orrery, and most of the French Romances translated by *Persons of Quality*. P.

[5] [Newmarket, which became popular with the rise of horse-racing under James I., was a favourite resort of Charles II., whose palace there still stands.]

[6] [The two most eminent sculptors of the Restoration period were Cibber, a Dane, and Gibbons, a Dutchman.]

[7] [Sir Peter Lely, by birth a Westphalian, died in 1680, after accumulating a large fortune. Warton compares for the delightful expression, 'the sleepy eye,' an epigram of Antipater, 'which it is not probable Pope could have seen.']

[8] *On each enervate string, etc.*] The Siege of Rhodes by Sir William Davenant, the first Opera sung in England. P. [It was brought out in 1656.]

To pant, or tremble thro' an Eunuch's throat.
  But Britain, changeful as a Child at play,   155
Now calls in Princes, and now turns away.
Now Whig, now Tory, what we lov'd we hate;
Now all for Pleasure, now for Church and State;
Now for Prerogative, and now for Laws;
Effects unhappy from a Noble Cause.   160
  Time was, a sober Englishman would knock
His servants up, and rise by five o'clock,
Instruct his Family in ev'ry rule,
And send his Wife to church, his Son to school.
To worship like his Fathers, was his care;   165
To teach their frugal Virtues to his Heir;
To prove, that Luxury could never hold;
And place, on good Security, his Gold.
Now times are chang'd, and one Poetic Itch
Has seiz'd the Court and City, poor and rich: 170
Sons, Sires, and Grandsires, all will wear the bays,
Our Wives read Milton, and our Daughters Plays,
To Theatres, and to Rehearsals throng,
And all our Grace at table is a Song.
I, who so oft renounce the Muses, lie,   175
Not —'s self e'er tells more *Fibs* than I;
When sick of Muse, our follies we deplore,
And promise our best Friends to rhyme no more;
We wake next morning in a raging fit,
And call for pen and ink to show our Wit.   180
  He serv'd a 'Prenticeship, who sets up shop;
Ward try'd on Puppies, and the Poor, his Drop;[1]
Ev'n Radcliff's Doctors travel first to France,
Nor dare to practise till they 've learn'd to dance.[2]
Who builds a Bridge that never drove a pile?   185
(Should Ripley[3] venture, all the world would smile)
But those who cannot write, and those who can,
All rhyme, and scrawl, and scribble, to a man.
  Yet, Sir, reflect, the mischief is not great;
These Madmen never hurt the Church or State: 190
Sometimes the Folly benefits Mankind;
And rarely Av'rice taints the tuneful mind.
Allow him but his plaything of a Pen,
He ne'er rebels, or plots, like other men:
Flight of Cashiers,[4] or Mobs, he 'll never mind;   195

---

[1] *Ward.*] A famous Empiric, whose Pill and Drop had several surprizing effects, and were one of the principal subjects of writing and conversation at this time. P.

[2] *Ev'n Radcliff's Doctors travel first to France, Nor dare to practise till they 've learn'd to dance.*] By no means an insinuation as if these travelling Doctors had misspent their time. *Radcliff* had sent them on a medicinal mission, to examine the produce of each Country, and see in what it might be made subservient to the art of healing. The native commodity of France is DANCING. SCRIBL.

[3] [Cf. Pope's note to *Moral Essays*, Ep. IV. v. 18.]

[4] [Bowles cites Coxe's *Memoirs of Sir R. Walpole* for an account of the flight of Knight, the cashier of the South Sea Company.]

DEAN SWIFT.

And knows no losses while the Muse is kind.
To cheat a Friend, or Ward, he leaves to Peter;[1]
The good man heaps up nothing but mere metre,
Enjoys his Garden and his book in quiet;
And then — a perfect Hermit in his diet.   200
  Of little use the Man you may suppose,
Who says in verse what others say in prose;
Yet let me show, a Poet 's of some weight,
And (tho' no Soldier) useful to the State.[2]
What will a Child learn sooner than a Song?   205
What better teach a Foreigner the tongue?
What 's long or short, each accent where to place,
And speak in public with some sort of grace?
I scarce can think him such a worthless thing,
Unless he praise some Monster of a King;   210
Or Virtue, or Religion turn to sport,
To please a lewd or unbelieving Court.
Unhappy Dryden! — In all Charles's days,
Roscommon only boasts unspotted bays;[3]
And in our own (excuse some Courtly stains)[4]   215
No whiter page than Addison remains.
He, from the taste obscene reclaims our youth,
And sets the Passions on the side of Truth,
Forms the soft bosom with the gentlest art,
And pours each human Virtue in the heart.   220
Let Ireland tell how Wit upheld her cause,
Her Trade supported, and supplied her Laws;
And leave on SWIFT this grateful verse engrav'd:
'The Rights a Court attack'd, a Poet sav'd.'[5]
Behold the hand that wrought a Nation's cure,   225

---

[1] [Conjectured by Bowles to refer to the cheating of Mr. George Pitt, in the management of his estates, by Peter Walter.]

[2] *And (tho' no Soldier)*] Horace had not acquitted himself much to his credit in this capacity (*non bene relicta parmula*) in the battle of Philippi. It is manifest he alludes to himself, in this whole account of a Poet's character; but with an intermixture of irony: *Vixit siliquis et pane secundo* has a relation to his Epicurism; *Os tenerum pueri*, is ridicule: The nobler office of a Poet follows, *Torquet ab obscœnis — Mox etiam pectus Recte facta refert, etc.* which the Imitator has apply'd where he thinks it more due than to himself. He hopes to be pardon'd, if, as he is sincerely inclined to praise what deserves to be praised, he arraigns what deserves to be arraigned, in the 210, 211, and 212th Verses. P.

[3] [V. *Essay on Criticism*, v. 726.]

[4] [Warburton explains this as specially referring to the opening lines of Addison's poem *To*

H. R. H. the Princess of Wales, in which A. claims merit for his tragedy of *Cato*, as purposely written to oppose the schemes of a faction, after he had previously assured Pope that the play was composed with no party views.]

[5] [The first of Swift's pamphlets in defence of the independence of Irish trade was published in 1720; the *Drapier's Letters* (written to oppose the patent of coining copper halfpence to be current in Ireland, granted to William Wood through the influence of the Duchess of Kendal, favourite of George I.) appeared in 1723. Swift thus writes to Pope (May 31st, 1737), after reading the above tribute: 'Your admirers here, I mean every man of taste, affect to be certain that the profession of friendship to me will not suffer you to be thought a flatterer. My happiness is that you are too far engaged, and in spite of you the ages to come will celebrate me, and know you were a friend who loved and esteemed me, although I died the object of Court and Party hatred.']

Stretch'd to relieve the Idiot and the Poor,[1]
Proud Vice to brand, or injur'd Worth adorn,
And stretch the Ray to Ages yet unborn.
Not but there are, who merit other palms;
Hopkins and Sternhold glad the heart with Psalms:[2]   230
The Boys and Girls whom charity maintains,
Implore your help in these pathetic strains:
How could Devotion touch the country pews,
Unless the Gods bestow'd a proper Muse?
Verse cheers their leisure, Verse assists their work,   235
Verse prays for Peace, or sings down Pope and Turk.
The silenc'd Preacher yields to potent strain,
And feels that grace his pray'r besought in vain;
The blessing thrills thro' all the lab'ring throng,
And Heav'n is won by Violence of Song,   240
   Our rural Ancestors, with little blest,
Patient of labour when the end was rest,
Indulg'd the day that hous'd their annual grain,
With feasts, and off'rings, and a thankful strain:
The joy their wives, their sons, and servants share,   245
Ease of their toil, and part'ners of their care:
The laugh, the jest, attendants on the bowl,
Smooth'd ev'ry brow, and open'd ev'ry soul:
With growing years the pleasing Licence grew,
And Taunts alternate innocently flew.   250
But Times corrupt, and Nature, ill-inclin'd,
Produc'd the point that left a sting behind;
Till friend with friend, and families at strife,
Triumphant Malice rag'd thro' private life.
Who felt the wrong, or fear'd it, took th' alarm,   255
Appeal'd to Law, and Justice lent her arm.
At length, by wholesome dread of statutes bound,[3]
The Poets learn'd to please, and not to wound:
Most warp'd to Flatt'ry's side; but some, more nice,
Preserv'd the freedom, and forbore the vice.   260
Hence Satire rose, that just the medium hit,
And heals with Morals what it hurts with Wit.
   We conquer'd France, but felt our Captive's charms;
Her Arts victorious triumph'd o'er our Arms;
Britain to soft refinements less a foe,   265
Wit grew polite, and Numbers learn'd to flow.
Waller was smooth;[4] but Dryden taught to join

---

[1] *the Idiot and the Poor.*] A foundation for
the maintenance of Idiots, and a Fund for assist-
ing the Poor, by lending small sums of money
on demand. P.

[2] [The time-honoured version of the Psalms
by Thomas Sternhold, a courtier of King Edward
. VI., and John Hopkins, a Suffolk schoolmaster,
in which they were assisted by others, was first

published as a complete collection in 1562. The
germ of this amusing passage will be found in
Pope's letter to Swift of Oct. 15, 1725.]

[3] [There is no direct historical allusion in
this; the law of libel was still very indefinite
even in Pope's times.]

[4] *Waller was smooth;*] Mr. Waller, about
this time with the Earl of Dorset, Mr. Godol-

The varying verse, the full-resounding line,
The long majestic March, and Energy divine.[1]
Tho' still some traces of our rustic vein   270
And splay-foot verse, remain'd, and will remain.
Late, very late, correctness grew our care,
When the tir'd Nation breath'd from civil war.
Exact Racine. and Corneille's noble fire,
Show'd us that France had something to admire.   275
Not but the Tragic spirit was our own,
And full in Shakespear, fair in Otway shone : [2]
But Otway fail'd to polish or refine,
And fluent Shakespear scarce effac'd a line.[3]
Ev'n copious Dryden wanted, or forgot,[4]   280
The last and greatest Art, the Art to blot.
Some doubt, if equal pains, or equal fire
The humbler Muse of Comedy require.
But in known Images of life, I guess
The labour greater, as th' indulgence less.   285
Observe how seldom ev'n the best succeed :
Tell me if Congreve's Fools are Fools indeed?[5]
What pert, low Dialogue has Farquhar writ![6]
How Van wants grace, who never wanted wit![7]
The stage how loosely does Astræa tread,[8]   290
Who fairly puts all Characters to bed!
And idle Cibber, how he breaks the laws,
To make poor Pinky eat with vast applause![9]

phin, and others, translated the Pompey of
Corneille; and the more correct French Poets
began to be in reputation. P.
   [1] [Cf. *Essay on Criticism*, vv. 358–384.]
   [2] [Racine, the younger of the two great French
tragedians, was more frequently translated by
the English dramatists of the Restoration than
Corneille; although Hallam is doubtless right in
agreeing with Sir Walter Scott that the unnat-
ural dialogue which prevailed in the English
tragedies of that age was derived from baser
models than these, viz. the French romances
referred to *ante*, v. 145. The pathetic Otway
(1651-1685) was indeed among the translators
and adapters of Racine; but his *Venice Pre-
served* and *Orphan*, on which his fame rests,
were, as dramatic pieces, original.]
   [3] [I remember the players often mentioned it
as an honour to S., that in his writings, what-
soever he penned, he never blotted out a line.
My answer hath been, 'Would he had blotted
out a thousand.' Ben Jonson's *Discoveries*.]
   [4] *Ev'n copious Dryden*] *copious* aggravated
the fault. For when a writer has great stores,
he is inexcusable not to discharge the easy task
of choosing from the best. *Warburton*.

   [5] ['Another fault which often may befal,
Is, when the wit of some great poet shall
So overflow, that is, be none at all
That ev'n his fools speak sense, as if possessed,
And each by inspiration breaks his jest.'
Sheffield, Duke of Buckinghamshire, *Essay on
Poetry*.]
   [6] [George Farquhar (1678-1707), the author
of *Sir Harry Wildair* and the *Beaux' Strat-
agem*.]
   [7] [John Vanbrugh (1672-1726), author of the
Relapse, and architect of Blenheim. His come-
dies, though offensive on the ground mentioned
by Pope, are perhaps healthier in feeling than
those of any of his contemporaries.]
   [8] *Astræa*] A Name taken by Mrs. Behn,
Authoress of several obscene Plays, etc. P.
[Mrs. Aphra Behn owed her popularity not only
to her sins, but to a wonderful knack of contriv-
ing ingenious stage-situations which must arouse
the envy of modern sensational playwrights.
Astræa is the title of a French romance by
Honoré d'Urfé, published in 1610.]
   [9] [*Poor Pinky* is the popular low comedian,
William Pinkethman, of whose face some writers,
according to Cibber, made a livelihood; and

But fill their purse, our Poet's work is done,
Alike to them, by Pathos or by Pun.   295
   O you! whom Vanity's light bark conveys
On Fame's mad voyage by the wind of praise,
With what a shifting gale your course you ply,
For ever sunk too low, or borne too high!
Who pants for glory finds but short repose,   300
A breath revives him, or a breath o'erthrows.
Farewell the stage! if just as thrives the play,
The silly bard grows fat, or falls away.
   There still remains, to mortify a Wit,
The many-headed Monster of the Pit: 305
A senseless, worthless, and unhonour'd crowd;
Who, to disturb their betters mighty proud,
Clatt'ring their sticks before ten lines are spoke,
Call for the Farce, the Bear, or the Black-joke.[1]
What dear delight to Britons Farce affords!   310
Ever the taste of Mobs, but now of Lords;
(Taste, that eternal wanderer, which flies
From heads to ears, and now from ears to eyes.)[2]
The play stands still; damn action and discourse,
Back fly the scenes, and enter foot and horse;   315
Pageants on Pageants, in long order drawn,
Peers, Heralds, Bishops, Ermine, Gold and Lawn;
The Champion too! and, to complete the jest,
Old Edward's Armour beams on Cibber's breast.[3]
With laughter sure Democritus had died,   320
Had he beheld an Audience gape so wide.
Let Bear or Elephant be e'er so white,
The people, sure, the people are the sight!
Ah luckless Poet! stretch thy lungs and roar,
That Bear or Elephant shall heed thee more;   325
While all its throats the Gallery extends,
And all the Thunder of the Pit ascends!
Loud as the Wolves, on Orcas' stormy steep,[4]
Howl to the roarings of the Northern deep.
Such is the shout, the long-applauding note,   330

concerning whom the *Tatler* 'informs posterity,' among other things, that 'he devours a cold chicken with great applause' (in the character of Harlequin). See Geneste's *History of the Stage*, III. pp. 136–9.]

[1] [i.e. the black-pudding.]

[2] *From heads to ears, and now from ears to eyes.*] From *Plays* to *Operas*, and from Operas to *Pantomimes. Warburton.* [Pantomimes were brought into the full blaze of public favour by Rich, manager of Covent Garden, in 1723; and Cibber, at Drury Lane, was obliged to produce the same kind of entertainment in self-defence.]

[3] *Old Edward's Armour beams on Cibber's breast.*] The Coronation of Henry VIII. and Queen Anne Boleyn, in which the Playhouses vied with each other to represent all the pomp of a Coronation. In this noble contention, the Armour of one of the Kings of England was borrowed from the Tower, to dress the Champion. P. [This spectacle was brought out in 1727, in consequence of the coronation of George II., and ran for 40 nights.]

[4] *Orcas' stormy steep.*] The farthest Northern Promontory of Scotland, opposite to the Orcades. P.

At Quin's [1] high plume, or Oldfield's [2] petticoat;
Or when from Court a birth-day suit bestow'd,
Sinks the lost Actor in the tawdry load.
Booth enters — hark! the Universal peal!
" But has he spoken?" Not a syllable.   335
What shook the stage, and made the People stare?
Cato's long Wig, flow'r'd gown, and lacquer'd chair.
   Yet lest you think I rally more than teach,
Or praise malignly Arts I cannot reach,
Let me for once presume t' instruct the times,   340
To know the Poet from the Man of rhymes:
'T is he, who gives my breast a thousand pains,
Can make me feel each Passion that he feigns;
Enrage, compose, with more than magic Art,
With Pity, and with Terror, tear my heart;   345
And snatch me, o'er the earth, or thro' the air,
To Thebes, to Athens, when he will, and where.
   But not this part of the Poetic state
Alone, deserves the favour of the Great;
Think of those Authors, Sir, who would rely   350
More on a Reader's sense, than Gazer's eye.
Or who shall wander where the Muses sing?
Who climb their mountain, or who taste their spring?
How shall we fill a Library with Wit,[3]
When Merlin's Cave is half unfurnish'd yet? [4]   355
   My Liege! why Writers little claim your thought,
I guess; and, with their leave, will tell the fault:
We Poets are (upon a Poet's word)
Of all mankind, the creatures most absurd:
The season, when to come, and when to go,   360
To sing, or cease to sing, we never know;
And if we will recite nine hours in ten,
You lose your patience, just like other men.
Then too we hurt ourselves, when to defend
A single verse, we quarrel with a friend;   365
Repeat unask'd; lament, the Wit's too fine
For vulgar eyes, and point out ev'ry line.
But most, when straining with too weak a wing,
We needs will write Epistles to the King;
And from the moment we oblige the town,   370
Expect a place, or pension from the Crown;
Or dubb'd Historians, by express command,
T' enroll your Triumphs o'er the seas and land,[5]

---

[1] [The famous tragic actor whose popularity was at its height at the time of Garrick's first appearance. See the celebrated character of him in Churchill's *Rosciad*. He died in 1766.]

[2] [Mrs. Oldfield, who died in 1730; the most popular comic actress of her age.]

[3] *a Library*] *Munus Appoline dignum.* The Palatine Library then building by Augustus. P.

[4] *Merlin's Cave*] A Building in the Royal Gardens of Richmond, where is a small, but choice Collection of Books. P.

[5] [The office of Historiographer Royal was frequently united to that of Poet Laureate.]

Be call'd to Court to plan some work divine,
As once for LOUIS, Boileau and Racine.   375
  Yet think, great Sir! (so many Virtues shown)
Ah think, what Poet best may make them known?
Or choose at least some Minister of Grace,
Fit to bestow the Laureate's weighty place.[1]
  Charles, to late times to be transmitted fair,   380
Assign'd his figure to Bernini's care;[2]
And great Nassau[3] to Kneller's hand decreed
To fix him graceful on the bounding Steed;
So well in paint and stone they judg'd of merit:
But Kings in Wit may want discerning Spirit.   385
The Hero William, and the Martyr Charles,
One knighted Blackmore, and one pension'd Quarles;[4]
Which made old Ben, and surly Dennis swear,
"No Lord 's anointed, but a Russian Bear."
  Not with such majesty, such bold relief,   390
The Forms august, of King, or conqu'ring Chief,
E'er swell'd on marble; as in verse have shin'd
(In polish'd verse) the Manners and the Mind.
Oh! could I mount on the Mæonian wing,
Your Arms, your Actions, your repose to sing!   395
What seas you travers'd, and what fields you fought!
Your Country's Peace, how oft, how deeply bought![5]
How barb'rous rage subsided at your word,
And Nations wonder'd while they dropp'd the sword!
How, when you nodded, o'er the land and deep,   400
Peace stole her wing, and wrapt the world in sleep;
'Till earth's extremes your mediation own,
And Asia's Tyrants tremble at your Throne —
But Verse, alas! your Majesty disdains;
And I 'm not us'd to Panegyric strains: 405
The Zeal of Fools offends at any time,
But most of all, the Zeal of Fools in rhyme.
Besides, a fate attends on all I write,
That when I aim at praise, they say I bite.
A vile Encomium doubly ridicules: 410
There 's nothing blackens like the ink of fools.
If true, a woeful likeness; and if lies,
" Praise undeserv'd is scandal in disguise : "[6]
Well may he blush, who gives it, or receives;

---

[1] Warton quotes Johnson's epigram on the laureateship of Colley Cibber:

' Augustus still survives in Maro's strain,
And Spenser's verse prolongs Eliza's reign;
Great George's acts let tuneful Cibber sing;
For nature formed the poet for the king.'

[2] [The Italian sculptor, Bernini, whose roccoco works fill St. Peter's at Rome.]

[3] [King William III.]

[4] [Francis Quarles, the author of the *Em-blems*, died in 1644. Pope has done this ingenious member of the religious section of the Fantastic school great injustice in ranking him on a level with Blackmore.]

[5] [Ironical allusions to the pacific policy of George II.'s minister Walpole.]

[6] [From an anonymous poem, 'The Celebrated Beauties,' published in Tonson's *Miscellany* in 1709. *Carruthers.*

And when I flatter, let my dirty leaves   415
(Like Journals, Odes, and such forgotton things
As Eusden,[1] Philips,[2] Settle,[3] writ of Kings)
Clothe spice, line trunks, or, flutt'ring in a row,
Befringe the rails of Bedlam and Soho.

THE SECOND EPISTLE

OF

THE SECOND BOOK OF HORACE.

Ludentis speciem dabit, et torquebitur.   HOR. [v. 124.]

[Horace's Epistle is addressed to Julius Florus, an officer attached to the person of
Tiberius in a military expedition abroad. Pope's Epistle, which like the Horatian
treats the subject chiefly from a personal point of view, has much biographical value.]

DEAR Colnel,[4] COBHAM'S and your country's Friend!
You love a Verse, take such as I can send.
A Frenchman comes, presents you with his Boy,
Bows and begins — "This Lad, Sir, is of Blois:[5]
"Observe his shape how clean! his locks how curl'd!   5
"My only son, I'd have him see the world:
"His French is pure; his Voice too — you shall hear.
"Sir, he's your slave, for twenty pound a year.
"Mere wax as yet, you fashion him with ease,
"Your Barber, Cook, Upholst'rer, what you please: 10
"A perfect genius at an Opera-song —
"To say too much, might do my honour wrong.
"Take him with all his virtues, on my word;
"His whole ambition was to serve a Lord:
"But, Sir, to you, with what would I not part?   15
"Tho' faith, I fear, 't will break his Mother's heart.
"Once (and but once) I caught him in a lie,
"And then, unwhipp'd, he had the grace to cry:
"The fault he has I fairly shall reveal,   •
"(Could you o'erlook but that) it is to steal."   20
    If, after this, you took the graceless lad,
Could you complain, my Friend, he prov'd so bad?
Faith, in such case, if you should prosecute,

---

[1] [Laurence Eusden, poet laureate under
Charles II. Cf. *Dunciad*, I. v. 104.]

[2] [Ambrose Philips, among other offences,
perpetrated an Ode in honour of Walpole.]

[3] [Elkanah Settle, the city-poet and the Doeg
of *Absalom and Achitophel*.]

[4] Colonel Cotterell, of Rousham near Oxford,
the descendant of Sir Charles Cotterell, who, at
the desire of Charles I., translated Davila into

English. *Warton.* [Courthope says "Warton
must be wrong altogether or in part"; and
suggests Pope's friend James Dormer, Colonel
of the first troop of Horse Grenadier Guards.
Am. Ed.]

[5] *This Lad, Sir, is of Blois:*] A Town in
Beauce, where the French tongue is spoken in
great purity. *Warburton.*

I think Sir Godfrey [1] should decide the suit;
Who sent the Thief that stole the Cash away,   25
And punish'd him that put it in his way.
  Consider then, and judge me in this light;
I told you when I went, I could not write;
You said the same, and are you discontent
With Laws, to which you gave your own assent?   30
Nay worse, to ask for Verse at such a time!
D' ye think me good for nothing but to rhyme?
  In ANNA's Wars, a Soldier poor and old
Had dearly earn'd a little purse of gold;
Tir'd with a tedious march, one luckless night,   35
He slept, poor dog! and lost it, to a doit.
This put the man in such a desp'rate mind,   ⎫
Between revenge, and grief, and hunger join'd ⎬
Against the foe, himself, and all mankind,   ⎭
He leap'd the trenches, scal'd a Castle-wall,   40
Tore down a Standard, took the Fort and all.
"Prodigious well;" his great Commander cry'd,
Gave him much praise, and some reward beside.
Next pleas'd his Excellence a town to batter:
(Its name I know not, and its no great matter)   45
"Go on, my Friend (he cry'd), see yonder walls!
"Advance and conquer! go where glory calls!
"More honours, more rewards, attend the brave."
Don't you remember what reply he gave?
"D' ye think me, noble Gen'ral, such a Sot?   50
"Let him take Castles who has ne'er a groat." ·
  Bred up at home, full early I begun [2]
To read in Greek the wrath of Peleus' son.
Besides, my Father taught me from a lad,
The better art to know the good from bad: 55
(And little sure imported to remove,
To hunt for Truth in Maudlin's learned grove.) [3]
But knottier points we knew not half so well,
Depriv'd us soon of our paternal Cell;
And certain Laws, [4] by suff'rers thought unjust,   60
Deny'd all posts of profit or of trust:
Hopes after hopes of pious Papists fail'd,
While mighty WILLIAM's thund'ring arm prevail'd,
For Right Hereditary tax'd and fin'd,
He stuck to poverty with peace of mind;   65

---

[1] *I think Sir Godfrey*] An eminent Justice of Peace, who decided much in the manner of Sancho Pancha. P. Sir Godfrey Kneller. *Warburton.*

[2] See *Introductory Memoir*, p. ix. f.

[3] He had a partiality for this College in Oxford, in which he had spent many agreeable days with his friend Mr. Digby. *Warton.*

[The spelling is in deference to academical orthoëpy.]

[4] [The penal laws against the Roman Catholics, temporarily abolished by James II.'s illegal Declaration of Indulgence, came into force again, with new additions, after the Revolution which seated William III. on the throne.]

And me, the Muses help'd to undergo it;
Convict a Papist he, and I a Poet.
But (thanks to Homer)[1] since I live and thrive,
Indebted to no Prince or Peer alive,
Sure I should want the care of ten Monroes,[2] 70
If I would scribble, rather than repose.
Years follow'ng years, steal something ev'ry day,
At last they steal us from ourselves away;
In one our Frolics, one Amusements end,
In one a Mistress drops, in one a Friend: 75
This subtle Thief of life, this paltry Time,
What will it leave me, if it snatch my rhyme?
If ev'ry wheel of that unweary'd Mill,
That turn'd ten thousand verses, now stands still?

 But after all, what would you have me do? 80
When out of twenty I can please not two;
When this Heroics only deigns to praise,
Sharp Satire that, and that Pindaric lays?
One likes the Pheasant's wing, and one the leg
The vulgar boil, the learned roast an egg; 85
Hard task! to hit the palate of such guests,
When Oldfield loves, what Dartineuf[3] detests.

 But grant I may relapse, for want of grace,
Again to rhyme, can London be the place?
Who there his Muse, or self, or soul attends, 90
In crowds, and courts, law, business, feasts, and friends?
My counsel sends to execute a deed;
A Poet begs me, I will hear him read;
'In Palace-yard at nine you 'll find me there —'
'At ten for certain, Sir, in Bloomsb'ry square —' 95
'Before the Lords at twelve my Cause comes on —
'There 's a Rehearsal, Sir, exact at one.—'
"Oh but a Wit can study in the streets,
"And raise his mind above the mob he meets."
Not quite so well however as one ought; 100
A hackney coach may chance to spoil a thought;
And then a nodding beam, or pig of lead,
God knows, may hurt the very ablest head.
Have you not seen, at Guild-hall's narrow pass,
Two Aldermen dispute it with an Ass? 105
And Peers give way, exalted as they are,
Ev'n to their own S-r-v—nce in a Car?

 Go, lofty Poet! and in such a crowd,
Sing thy sonorous verse — but not aloud.
Alas! to Grottos and to Groves we run, 110
To ease and silence, ev'ry Muse's son:
Blackmore himself, for any grand effort,

---

[1] [See *Introductory Memoir*, p. xxvii.]
[2] *Monroes.*] Dr. Monroe, Physician to Bedlam Hospital. P.
[3] *Oldfield — Dartineuf*] Two celebrated Gluttons. *Warburton.* [Cf. as to the latter, *ante*, Bk. II. *Sat.* I. v. 46.]

Would drink and doze at Tooting or Earl's-Court [1]
How shall I rhyme in this eternal roar?
How match the bards whom none e'er match'd before?   115
The Man, who, stretch'd in Isis' calm retreat,
To books and study gives sev'n years complete,[2]
See! strew'd with learned dust, his night-cap on,
He walks, an object new beneath the sun!
The boys flock round him, and the people stare :   120
So stiff, so mute! some statue you would swear,
Stept from its pedestal to take the air!
And here, while town, and court, and city roars,
With mobs, and duns, and soldiers, at their doors ;
Shall I, in London, act this idle part?   125
Composing songs, for Fools to get by heart?
   The Temple late two brother Sergeants saw,
Who deem'd each other Oracles of Law ;
With equal talents, these congenial souls,
One lull'd th' Exchequer, and one stunn'd the Rolls ;   130
Each had a gravity would make you split,
And shook his head at Murray,[3] as a Wit.
"'T was, Sir, your law " — and " Sir, your eloquence — "
"Yours, Cowper's [4] manner" — and "yours, Talbot's [5] sense."
Thus we dispose of all poetic merit,   135
Yours Milton's genius, and mine Homer's spirit.
Call Tibbald Shakespear, and he 'll swear the Nine,
Dear Cibber! never match'd one Ode of thine.
Lord! how we strut thro' Merlin's Cave,[6] to see
No Poets there, but Stephen,[7] you, and me.   140
Walk with respect behind, while we at ease
Weave laurel Crowns, and take what names we please.
" My dear Tibullus!" if that will not do,
" Let me be Horace, and be Ovid you :
" Or, I 'm content, allow me Dryden's strains,   145
" And you shall rise up Otway for your pains."
Much do I suffer, much, to keep in peace
This jealous, waspish, wrong-head, rhyming race ;
And much must flatter, if the whim should bite
To court applause by printing what I write :   150
But let the Fit pass o'er, I 'm wise enough,
To stop my ears to their confounded stuff.
   In vain bad Rhymers all mankind reject,

[1] *Tooting — Earl's-Court.*] Two villages within a few miles of London. P.

[2] [The term for completing the M. A. Degree.]

[3] [Alluding to the common cant of that time, as if this eminent and accomplished person was more of a polite scholar than a profound lawyer. *Warton.* Cf. Bk. I. *Ep.* VI. *ante.*]

[4] [William first Earl Cowper, lord keeper in 1705, and one of the lords justices on the death of Queen Anne. Died 1723.]

[5] [Charles, Lord Talbot, Lord Chancellor.]

[6] [Cf. Pope's note to Bk. II. *Ep.* I. v. 355.]

[7] *but Stephen*] Mr. *Stephen Duck*, a modest and worthy man, who had the honour (which many, who thought themselves his betters in poetry, had not) of being esteemed by Mr. Pope. Queen Caroline chose this man for her favourite poet. *Warburton.*

They treat themselves with most profound respect;
'T is to small purpose that you hold your tongue: 155
Each prais'd within, is happy all day long;
But how severely with themselves proceed
The men, who write such Verse as we can read?
Their own strict Judges, not a word they spare
That wants or force, or light, or weight, or care,   160
Howe'er unwillingly it quits its place,
Nay tho' at Court (perhaps) it may find grace:
Such they 'll degrade; and sometimes, in its stead,
In downright charity revive the dead;
Mark where a bold expressive phrase appears,   165
Bright thro' the rubbish of some hundred years;
Command old words that long have slept, to wake,
Words, that wise Bacon, or brave Raleigh spake;[1]
Or bid the new be English, ages hence,
(For Use will farther what 's begot by Sense)   170
Pour the full tide of eloquence along,
Serenely pure, and yet divinely strong,   }
Rich with the treasures of each foreign tongue;   }
Prune the luxuriant, the uncouth refine,
But show no mercy to an empty line: 175
Then polish all, with so much life and ease,
You think 't is Nature, and a knack to please:
" But ease in writing flows from Art, not chance;
" As those move easiest who have learn'd to dance."[2]
    If such the plague and pains to write by rule,   180
Better (say I) be pleas'd, and play the fool;
Call, if you will, bad rhyming a disease,
It gives men happiness, or leaves them ease.
There liv'd *in Primo Georgii* (they record)
A worthy member, no small fool, a Lord;   185
Who, tho' the House was up, delighted sate,
Heard, noted, answer'd, as in full debate:
In all but this, a man of sober life,
Fond of his Friend, and civil to his Wife;
Not quite a mad-man, tho' a pasty fell,[3]   190
And much too wise to walk into a well.
Him, the damn'd Doctors and his Friends immur'd,
They bled, they cupp'd, they purg'd; in short, they cur'd.
Whereat the gentleman began to stare —

---

[1] ['In Bacon's *Essays* . . . though many Latinized words are introduced, even the solecisms are English, and the style is, in all probability, a fair picture of the language used at that time by men of the highest culture, in the conversational discussion of questions of practical philosophy, or what the Germans call *world-wisdom*.' Marsh, *Origin and History of the Eng. Language.* — Raleigh is said by Aubrey (cited by Warton) to have been accustomed to speak in a broad Devonshire dialect.]

[2] [Slightly altered from *Essay on Criticism*, vv. 362, 3.]

[3] [Cf. *Moral Essays*, Ep. II. v. 268. The original story of this sort of madness is traced by Warton to Aristotle and Ælian; and he compares Boileau's version in his Fourth Satire.]

"My Friends?" he cry'd, "p—x take you for your care!   195
That from a Patriot of distinguish'd note,
Have bled and purg'd me to a simple Vote."
Well, on the whole, plain Prose must be my fate :
Wisdom (curse on it) will come soon or late.
There is a time when Poets will grow dull :   200
I 'll e'en leave verses to the boys at school :
To rules of Poetry no more confin'd,
I learn to smooth and harmonize my Mind,
Teach ev'ry thought within its bounds to roll,
And keep the equal measure of the Soul.   205
   Soon as I enter at my country door,
My mind resumes the thread it dropt before ;
Thoughts which at Hyde-park-corner I forgot,
Meet and rejoin me, in the pensive Grot.
There all alone, and compliments apart,   210
I ask these sober questions of my heart.
   If, when the more you drink, the more you crave,
You tell the Doctor ; when the more you have,
The more you want ; why not with equal ease
Confess as well your Folly, as Disease?   215
The heart resolves this matter in a trice,
"Men only feel the Smart, but not the Vice."
   When golden Angels[1] cease to cure the Evil,
You give all royal Witchcraft to the Devil ;
When servile Chaplains cry,[2] that birth and place   220
Endue a Peer with honour, truth, and grace,
Look in that breast, most dirty D—! be fair,
Say, can you find out one such lodger there?
Yet still, not heeding what your heart can teach,
You go to church to hear these Flatt'rers preach.   225
   Indeed, could wealth bestow or wit or merit,
A grain of courage, or a spark of spirit,
The wisest man might blush, I must agree,
If D*** lov'd sixpence more than he.
   If there be truth in Law, and Use can give   230
A Property, that 's yours on which you live.
Delightful Abs-court,[3] if its fields afford
Their fruits to you, confesses you its lord :
All Worldly's hens, nay partridge,[4] sold to town :
His Ven'son too, a guinea makes your own :   235
He bought at thousands, what with better wit

---

[1] A golden coin, given as a fee by those who came to be touched by the royal hand for the Evil. *Warton.* [The scrofula. The office for the healing of the evil was originally included in the Book of Common Prayer ; the practice was kept up by Charles I. and Charles II., and was renewed by the Pretender.]

[2] The whole of this passage alludes to a dedi-cation of Mr., afterwards Bishop, Kennet to the Duke of Devonshire, to whom he was chaplain. *Bennet.* [This explains the blanks in vv. 222 and 229.]

[3] *delightful Abs-court,*] A farm over-against Hampton-Court. *Warburton.*

[4] [A plural ; as grouse, teal, &c.]

You purchase as you want, and bit by bit;
Now, or long since, what diff'rence will be found?
You pay a penny, and he paid a pound.
    Heathcote [1] himself, and such large-acred men,   240
Lords of fat E'sham, or of Lincoln fen,
Buy every stick of wood that lends them heat,
Buy every Pullet they afford to eat.
Yet these are Wights, who fondly call their own
Half that the Dev'l o'erlooks from Lincoln town.   245
The Laws of God, as well as of the land,
Abhor, a Perpetuity should stand:
Estates have wings, and hang in Fortune's pow'r
Loose on the point of ev'ry wav'ring hour,
Ready, by force or of your own accord,   250
By sale, at least by death, to change their lord.
Man? and *for ever?* wretch! what wouldst thou have?
Heir urges heir, like wave impelling wave.
All vast possessions (just the same the case
Whether you call them Villa, Park, or Chase)   255
Alas, my BATHURST! what will they avail?
Join Cotswood hills to Saperton's fair dale,[2]
Let rising Granaries and Temples here,
There mingled farms and pyramids appear,
Link towns to towns with avenues of oak,   260
Enclose whole downs in walls, 't is all a joke!
Inexorable Death shall level all,
And trees, and stones, and farms, and farmer fall.
    Gold, Silver, Iv'ry, Vases sculptur'd high,
Paint, Marble, Gems, and robes of Persian dye,   265
There are who have not — and thank heav'n there are,
Who, if they have not, think not worth their care.
    Talk what you will of Taste, my friend, you 'll find,
Two of a face, as soon as of a mind.
Why, of two brothers, rich and restless one   270
Ploughs, burns, manures, and toils from sun to sun;
The other slights, for women, sports, and wines,
All Townshend's Turnips,[3] and all Grosvenor's [4] mines:
Why one like Bu—[5] with pay and scorn content,
Bows and votes on, in Court and Parliament;   275
One, driv'n by strong Benevolence of soul,

---

[1] [Sir Gilbert Heathcote; cf. *Moral Essays*, Ep. III. v. 101.]

[2] [Alluding to the improvements made by Lord Bathurst on one of his Gloucestershire estates, at Daylingworth near Saperton in the Cotswold country.]

[3] *All Townshend's Turnips*] Lord Townshend, Secretary of State to George the First and Second, resigned office in 1730, and patriotically refrained from returning to public life, where he might have helped his political opponents the Tories to annoy his former rival Walpole. It was owing to him, says Lord Stanhope, that England, and more especially Norfolk, owes the introduction of the turnip from Germany.]

[4] [Sir Thomas Grosvenor succeeded to his brother Richard in 1733. They were the ancestors of the present Marquess of Westminster.]

[5] [Bubb Doddington, the *Bubo* of the IVth Ep. of the *Moral Essays*.]

Shall fly, like Oglethorpe,[1] from pole to pole :
Is known alone to that Directing Pow'r,
Who forms the Genius in the natal hour ;
That God of Nature, who, within us still,   280
Inclines our action, not constrains our will ;
Various of temper, as of face or frame,
Each individual : His great End the same.
    Yes, Sir, how small soever be my heap,
A part I will enjoy, as well as keep.   285
My heir may sigh, and think it want of grace
A man so poor would live without a place ;
But sure no statute in his favour says,[2]
How free, or frugal, I shall pass my days :
I, who at some times spend, at others spare,   290
Divided between carelessness and care.
'T is one thing madly to disperse my store ;
Another, not to heed to treasure more ;
Glad, like a Boy, to snatch the first good day,
And pleas'd, if sordid want be far away.   295
    What is 't to me (a passenger, God wot !)
Whether my vessel be first-rate or not ?
The Ship itself may make a better figure,
But I that sail, am neither less nor bigger.
I neither strut with ev'ry fav'ring breath,   300
Nor strive with all the tempest in my teeth.
In pow'r, wit, figure, virtue, fortune, plac'd
Behind the foremost, and before the last.
    "But why all this of Av'rice ? I have none."
I wish you joy, Sir, of a Tyrant gone ;   305
But does no other lord it at this hour,
As wild and mad : the Avarice of pow'r ?
Does neither Rage inflame, nor Fear appal ?
Not the black fear of death, that saddens all ?
With terrors round, can Reason hold her throne,   310
Despise the known, nor tremble at th' unknown ?
Survey both worlds, intrepid and entire,
In spite of witches, devils. dreams, and fire ?
Pleas'd to look forward, pleas'd to look behind,
And count each birth-day with a grateful mind ?   315
Has life no sourness, drawn so near its end ?
Canst thou endure a foe, forgive a friend ?

---

[1] *fly, like Oglethorpe,*] Employed in settling the Colony of Georgia. P.

[James Edward Oglethorpe, born in 1698, served under Prince Eugene against the Turks, settled the colony of Georgia, held a command during the year 1745, and in consequence of a difficulty which then occurred with the Duke of Cumberland (though Oglethorpe was acquitted by a court-martial) remained unemployed ever afterwards. Mr. Croker observes that to his supposed Jacobite leanings may be attributed much of the animosity displayed by the Whigs towards him, as well as of the friendliness subsisting between him and Pope and Johnson.]

[2] *But sure no statute*] Alluding to the statutes made in England and Ireland, to regulate the Succession of Papists, etc. *Warburton.* [A statute of William III. which was happily so interpreted by the Judges, as to produce much less effect than its authors had intended.]

DR. JOHN DONNE.

Has age but melted the rough parts away,
As winter-fruits grow mild ere they decay?
Or will you think, my friend, your business done,   320
When, of a hundred thorns, you pull out one?
  Learn to live well, or fairly make your will;
You 've play'd, and lov'd, and eat, and drank your fill:
Walk sober off; before a sprightlier age
Comes titt'ring on, and shoves you from the stage: 325
Leave such to trifle with more grace and ease,
Whom Folly pleases, and whose Follies please.

-----oo°o°oo-----

THE SATIRES

OF

DR. JOHN DONNE,

DEAN OF ST. PAUL'S,

VERSIFIED.

'Quid vetat et nosmet *Lucili* scripta legentes
Quærere, num illius, num rerum dura negarit
Versiculos natura magis factos, et euntes
Mollius?'   HOR. [*Sat.* LX. 56-9].

[These Satires, as Pope informs us in the Advertisement prefixed to the *Satires and Epistles of Horace Imitated* (ante, p. 289), were 'versified' by him at the request of Lords Oxford and Shrewsbury, and therefore in the main belong to an earlier period of his career than the *Satires* among which they were afterwards inserted. He called his labour 'versifying,' says Warburton, because indeed Donne's lines 'have nothing more of numbers than their being composed of a certain quantity of syllables' — a description exaggerated, but not untrue.

John Donne was born in 1573, and died in 1631; but though he wrote most of his poetry before the end of the 16th century, none of it was published till late in the reign of James I. The story of his life may be summed up as that of a popular preacher under pecuniary difficulties, which only towards its close terminated in the assurance of a competency (he died as Dean of St. Paul's). Donne has been, in deference to Pope's classification of poets, regarded as the father of the metaphysical, or fantastic school of English poets, which reached its height in the reign of Charles I. His poetry divides itself into two distinctly marked divisions — profane and religious. The former must be in the main regarded as consisting of purely intellectual exercitations; nor should the man be rashly confounded with the writer, or the Ovidian looseness of morals which he affects be supposed to have characterised his life. His *Songs* are full of the conceits criticised by Dr. Johnson; some of his *Epigrams* are very good; his *Elegies* are most offensively indecent; and the *Progress of the Soul* is a disgusting burlesque on the Pythagorean doctrine of metempsychosis. The *Funeral Elegies* already show the transition to sacred poetry; and it is on these and the *Holy Sonnets* that rests Donne's claim to be called a metaphysical poet.

Yet he states that he affected the metaphysics in his *Satires* and amorous verses as well. The former were first published, with the rest of his works, in 1633. In Dryden's opinion, quoted by Chalmers, the *Satires* of Donne, even if translated into numbers, would yet be found wanting in dignity of expression. It has however been doubted whether the irregularity of Donne's versification in the *Satires* was wholly undesigned. His lyrical poetry is fluent and easy; and the *Satires* of Hall, which preceded those of Donne by several years, show a comparative mastery over the heroic couplet which could surely have been compassed by the later Satirist. Pope has treated Donne's text with absolute freedom. Donne's *Third Satire*, in Warburton's opinion 'the noblest work not only of this but perhaps of any satiric poet,' was 'versified' by Parnell.]

SATIRE II.

YES; thank my stars! as early as I knew
This Town, I had the sense to hate it too;
Yet here; as ev'n in Hell, there must be still
One Giant-Vice, so excellently ill,
That all beside, one pities, not abhors;   5
As who knows Sappho, smiles at other whores.
 I grant that Poetry 's a crying sin;
It brought (no doubt) th' *Excise* and *Army* [1] in:
Catch'd like the Plague, or Love, the Lord knows how,
But that the cure is starving. all allow.   10
Yet like the Papist's, is the Poet's state,[2]
Poor and disarm'd, and hardly worth your hate !
 Here a lean Bard, whose wit could never give
Himself a dinner, makes an Actor live:
The Thief condemn'd, in law already dead,   15
So prompts, and saves a rogue who cannot read.
Thus, as the pipes of some carv'd Organ move,
The gilded puppets dance and mount above.
Heav'd by the breath th' inspiring bellows blow:
Th' inspiring bellows lie and pant below.   20
 One sings the Fair; but songs no longer move;
No rat is rhym'd to death, nor maid to love:
In love's, in nature's spite, the siege they hold,
And scorn the flesh, the dev'l, and all but gold.
 These write to Lords, some mean reward to get,   25
As needy beggars sing at doors for meat.
Those write because all write, and so have still
Excuse for writing, and for writing ill.
 Wretched indeed! but far more wretched yet
Is he who makes his meal on others' wit: 30
'T is chang'd, no doubt, from what it was before;
His rank digestion makes it wit no more:
Sense, past thro' him, no longer is the same;
For food digested takes another name.
 I pass o'er all those Confessors and Martyrs,   35
Who live like S—tt—n,[3] or who die like Chartres,
Out-cant old Esdras, or out-drink his heir,

---

[1] [i.e. the increased excise duties (which it was apprehended would become a general excise), and an army which must prove a standing one. Cf. *Moral Essays*, Ep. III. v. 119, and *Im. of Hor.* Bk. II. Sat. II. v. 160. The expressions are substituted for 'dearth and Spaniards' in Donne.]

[2] [Cf. *Im. of Hor.* Bk. II. Ep. II. v. 68.]

[3] Sir Robert Sutton, who was expelled the House of Commons on account of his share in the frauds of the company called the Charitable Corporation. *Carruthers.*

Out-usure Jews, or Irishmen out-swear ; [1]
Wicked as Pages, who in early years
Act sins which Prisca's Confessor [2] scarce hears.   40
Ev'n those I pardon, for whose sinful sake
Schoolmen new tenements in hell must make ;
Of whose strange crimes no Canonist can tell
In what Commandment's large contents they dwell.
  One, one man only breeds my just offence ;   45
Whom crimes gave wealth, and wealth gave Impudence :
Time, that at last matures a clap to pox,
Whose gentle progress makes a calf an ox,
And brings all natural events to pass,
Hath made him an Attorney of an Ass.   50
No young divine, new-benefic'd, can be
More pert, more proud, more positive than he
What further could I wish the fop to do,
But turn a wit, and scribble verses too ;
Pierce the soft lab'rinth of a Lady's ear   55
With rhymes of this *per cent.* and that *per year ?*
Or court a Wife, spread out his wily parts,
Like nets or lime-twigs, for rich Widows' hearts ;
Call himself Barrister to ev'ry wench,
And woo in language of the Pleas and Bench?   60
Language, which Boreas might to Auster hold
More rough than forty Germans when they scold.[3]
  Curs'd be the wretch, so venal and so vain :
Paltry and proud, as drabs in Drury Lane.
'T is such a bounty as was never known,   65
If PETER deigns to help you to your *own :*
What thanks, what praise, if *Peter* but supplies,
And what a solemn face if he denies!
Grave, as when pris'ners shake the head and swear
'T was only Suretyship that brought 'em there.   70
His *Office* keeps your Parchment fates entire,
He starves with cold to save them from the fire ;
For you he walks the streets thro' rain or dust,
For not in Chariots *Peter* puts his trust ;
For you he sweats and labours at the laws,   75
Takes God to witness he affects your cause,
And lies to ev'ry Lord in ev'ry thing,
Like a King's Favourite — or like a King.
These are the talents that adorn them all,
From wicked Waters ev'n to godly * * [4]   80

[1] Out-swear the Letanie. *Donne*.

[2] [Accentuated as in Donne.]

[3] [Donne's fine touch of satire against a historic wrong —

' Than when winds in our ruin'd abbeys roar,'
is exchanged by Pope for a cheap sneer against a then unpopular nationality.]

[4] Carruthers suggests the name of Paul Benfield, a financing M.P., for this hiatus.] [Lord Orrery says Paul Foley, son of Thomas who made a vast fortune out of iron. Paul studied law. Macaulay says " his morals were without stain." *Am. Ed.*]

Not more of Simony beneath black gowns,
Not more of bastardy in heirs to Crowns, [1]
In shillings and in pence at first they deal;
And steal so little, few perceive they steal;
Till, like the Sea, they compass all the land,   85
From *Scots* to *Wight*, from *Mount* to *Dover* strand:
And when rank Widows purchase luscious nights,
Or when a Duke to *Jansen* punts at White's,
Or City-heir in mortgage melts away;
·*Satan* himself feels far less joy than they.   90
Piecemeal they win this acre first, then that,
Glean on, and gather up the whole estate.
Then strongly fencing ill-got wealth by law,
Indentures, Cov'nants, Articles they draw,
Large as the fields themselves, and larger far   95
Than Civil Codes, with all their Glosses, are;
So vast, our new Divines, we must confess,
Are Fathers of the Church for writing less.
But let them write for you, each rogue impairs
The deeds, and dext'rously omits, *ses heirs*:   100
No Commentator can more slily pass
O'er a learn'd, unintelligible place;
Or, in quotation, shrewd Divines leave out
Those words, that would against them clear the doubt.
So Luther thought the Pater-noster long,[2]   105
When doom'd [3] to say his beads and Even-song;
But having cast his cowl, and left those laws,
Adds to Christ's pray'r, the *Pow'r and Glory* clause.
    The lands are bought; but where are to be found
Those ancient woods, that shaded all the ground?   110
We see no new-built palaces aspire,
No kitchens emulate the vestal fire.
Where are those troops of Poor, that throng'd of yore
The good old landlord's hospitable door?
Well, I could wish, that still in lordly domes   115
Some beasts were kill'd, tho' not whole hecatombs;
That both extremes were banish'd from their walls,
Carthusian fasts, and fulsome Bacchanals;
And all mankind might that just Mean observe,
In which none e'er could surfeit, none could starve.   120
These as good works, 't is true, we all allow;
But oh! these works are not in fashion now:
Like rich old wardrobes, things extremely rare,
Extremely fine, but what no man will wear.

---

[1] [Pointless here; but not so in Donne.]

[2] About this time of his life Dr. Donne had a strong propensity to Popery, which appears from several strokes in these satires. We find amongst his works, a short satirical thing called a *Catalogue of rare books*, one article of which is intitled, *M. Lutherus de abbreviatione Orationis Dominicæ*, alluding to Luther's omission of the [spurious] concluding Doxology in his two Catechisms; which shews the poet was fond of a joke. *Warburton.*

[3] [i.e. as an Augustine monk.]

Thus much I 've said, I trust, without offence;   125
Let no Court Sycophant pervert my sense,
Nor sly informer watch these words to draw
Within the reach of Treason, or the Law.

SATIRE IV.

WELL, if it be my time to quit the stage,
      Adieu to all the follies of the age!
I die in charity with fool and knave,
Secure of peace at least beyond the grave.
I 've had my Purgatory here betimes,   5
And paid for all my satires, all my rhymes.
The Poet's hell, its tortures, fiends, and flames,
To this were trifles, toys and empty names.
   With foolish pride my heart was never fir'd,
Nor the vain itch t' admire, or be admir'd;   10
I hop'd for no commission from his Grace;
I bought no benefice, I begg'd no place;
Had no new verses, nor new suit to show;
Yet went to Court! — the Dev'l would have it so.
But, as the Fool that in reforming days   15
Would go to Mass in jest (as story says)
Could not but think, to pay his fine was odd,
Since 't was no form'd design of serving God;
So was I punish'd, as if full as proud
As prone to ill, as negligent of good,   20
As deep in debt, without a thought to pay, ⎫
As vain, as idle, and as false, as they   ⎬
Who live at Court, for going once that way! ⎭
Scarce was I enter'd, when, behold! there came
A thing which Adam had been pos'd to name;   25
Noah had refus d it lodging in his Ark,
Where all the Race of Reptiles might embark:
A verier monster, that on Afric's shore
The sun e'er got, or slimy Nilus bore,
Or Sloane [1] or Woodward's [2] wondrous shelves contain,   30
Nay, all that lying Travellers can feign.
The watch would hardly let him pass at noon,
At night, would swear him dropt out of the Moon.
One whom the mob, when next we find or make
A popish plot, shall for a Jesuit take,   35
And the wise Justice starting from his chair
Cry: "By your Priesthood tell me what you are?"
   Such was the wight; th' apparel on his back
Tho' coarse, was rev'rend, and tho' bare, was black:

[1] [Cf. *Moral Essays*, Ep. IV. c. 10.]
[2] [John Woodward (1665-1728) the founder of the professorship of Geology in the University of Cambridge, to which he bequeathed his collections]

The suit, if by the fashion one might guess,   40
Was velvet in the youth of good Queen *Bess*,
But mere tuff-taffety what now remain'd ;
So Time, that changes all things, had ordain'd!
Our sons shall see it leisurely decay,
First turn plain rash, then vanish quite away.   45
   This thing has travell'd, speaks each language too,
And knows what 's fit for every state to do ;
Of whose best phrase and courtly accent join'd,
He forms one tongue, exotic and refin'd,
Talkers I 've learn'd to bear ; Motteux [1] I knew,   50
Henley [2] himself I 've heard, and Budgel [3] too.
The Doctor's Wormwood style, the Hash of tongues
A Pedant makes, the storm of Gonson's [4] lungs,
The whole Artill'ry of the terms of War,
And (all those plagues in one) the bawling Bar :   55
These I could bear ; but not a rogue so civil,
Whose tongue will compliment you to the Devil.
A tongue, that can cheat widows, cancel scores,
Make Scots speak treason, cozen subtlest whores,
With royal Favourites in flatt'ry vie,   60
And Oldmixon and Burnet both out-lie.[5]
   He spies me out, I whisper : 'Gracious God!
What sin of mine could merit such a rod?
That all the shot of dulness now must be
From this thy blunderbuss discharg'd on me!'   65
  " Permit," (he cries) " no stranger to your fame
" To crave your sentiment, if — 's your name.
" What *Speech* esteem you most?" ' The *King's*,'[6] said I.
" But the best *words* ? " — ' O Sir, the *Dictionary*.'
" You miss my aim ; I mean the most acute   70
" And perfect *Speaker* ?" — ' Onslow,[7] past dispute.'
" But, Sir, of writers?" ' Swift, for closer style,
' But Ho**y[8] for a period of a mile.'
" Why yes, 't is granted, these indeed may pass :
" Good common linguists, and so Panurge[9] was ;   75
" Nay troth th' Apostles (tho' perhaps too rough)
" Had once a pretty gift of Tongues enough :
" Yet these were all poor Gentlemen! I dare
" Affirm, 't was Travel made them what they were." [10]

---

[1] [*Motteux.* V. *Dunciad*, II. v. 412.]

[2] [*Henley.* V. *Dunciad*, III. v. 189 ff.]

[3] [*Budgel.* V. *Dunciad*, II. v. 397.]

[4] [Sir John Gonson, whose portrait, according to Bowles, is introduced into Hogarth's Harlot's Progress. v. *infra*, v. 256.]

[5] [Cf. *Ep. to Arbuthnot*, v. 146.]

[6] This sneer, said the ingenious Mr. Wilkes, is really indecent. *Warton.* [The phrase ' the King's English ' is not founded on the speech of either of the first two Georges.]

[7] [Arthur Onslow, sprung from a family,

members of which had already in two instances filled the chair, was elected Speaker in 1728, and occupied the post for 33 years, to the satisfaction of both parties in the House.]

[8] [Bishop Hoadley, here alluded to sarcastically on account of his loyalty to the House of Hanover.]

[9] [Vide *Rabelais*.]

[10] [The readers of recent satirical poetry can hardly fail to remember Mr. John P. Robinson's opinion of the shortcomings of the Apostles.]

Thus others' talents having nicely shown,   80
He came by sure transition to his own:
Till I cry'd out: 'You prove yourself so able,
'Pity! you was not Druggerman [1] at Babel;
'For had they found a linguist half so good,
'I make no question but the Tow'r had stood.'   85
    "Obliging Sir! for Courts you sure were made:
"Why then for ever bury'd in the shade?
"Spirits like you, should see and should be seen,
"The King would smile on you — at least the Queen."
'Ah gentle Sir! your Courtiers so cajole us —   90
'But Tully has it, *Nunquam minus solus:* [2]
'And as for Courts, forgive me, if I say
'No lessons now are taught the Spartan way:
'Tho' in his pictures Lust be full display'd,
'Few are the Converts Aretine [3] has made;   95
'And tho' the Court show Vice exceeding clear,
'None should, by my advice, learn Virtue there.'
    At this entranc'd, he lifts his hands and eyes,
Squeaks like a high-stretch'd lutestring, and replies:
"Oh 't is the sweetest of all earthly things   100
"To gaze on Princes, and to talk of Kings!"
'Then, happy Man who shows the Tombs!' said I,
'He dwells amidst the royal Family;
'He ev'ry day, from King to King can walk,
'Of all our Harries, all our Edwards talk, [4]   105
'And get by speaking truth of monarchs dead,
'What few can of the living, Ease and Bread.'
"Lord, Sir, a mere Mechanic! strangely low,
"And coarse of phrase, — your English all are so.
"How elegant your Frenchmen?" 'Mine, d'ye mean?   110
'I have but one, I hope the fellow's clean.'
"Oh! Sir, politely so! nay, let me die,
"Your only wearing is your Padua-soy." [5]
'Not, Sir, my only, I have better still,
'And this you see is but my dishabille —'   115
Wild to get loose, his Patience I provoke,
Mistake, confound, object at all he spoke.
But as coarse iron, sharpen'd, mangles more,
And itch most hurts when anger'd to a sore;
So when you plague a fool, 't is still the curse,   120
You only make the matter worse and worse.
    He past it o'er; affects an easy smile
At all my peevishness, and turns his style.

---

[1] [Dragoman, i.e. interpreter.]

[2] [Cicero (*de Officiis*, l. iii. c. 1) quotes from Cato major the saying of Scipio Africanus m.: 'that he was never less at leisure, than when at leisure; *and never less alone, than when alone.*']

[3] Alluding to the infamous sonnets which this [Florentine author of the age of Leo X.] composed to accompany some designs of Giulio Romano. *Warton.*

[4] ['The way to it is King Street.' *Donne.*]

[5] [Silk of Padua. *Am. Ed.*]

z

He asks, " What News?"   I tell him of new Plays,
New Eunuchs, Harlequins, and Operas.   125
He hears, and as a Still with simples in it
Between each drop it gives, stays half a minute,
Loth to enrich me with too quick replies,
By little and by little, drops his lies.
Mere household trash! of birth-nights, balls, and shows,   130
More than ten Holinsheds, or Halls, or Stowes.[1]
When the *Queen* frown'd, or smil'd, he knows; and what
A subtle Minister may make of that;
Who sins with whom: who got his Pension rug,[2]
Or quicken'd a Reversion by a drug;   135
Whose place is quarter'd out, three parts in four,
And whether to a Bishop, or a Whore;
Who having lost his credit, pawn'd his rent,
Is therefore fit to have a Government;
Who in the secret, deals in Stocks secure,   140
And cheats th' unknowing Widow and the Poor;
Who makes a Trust or Charity a Job,
And gets an Act of Parliament to rob;
Why Turnpikes rise, and now no Cit nor clown
Can gratis see the country, or the town;   145
Shortly no lad shall chuck, or lady vole,[3]
But some excising Courtier will have toll.
He tells what strumpet places sells for life,
What 'Squire his lands, what citizen his Wife:
And last (which proves him wiser still than all)   150
What Lady's face is not a whited wall.
     As one of Woodward's patients,[4] sick, and sore,
I puke, I nauseate, — yet he thrusts in more:
Trims Europe's balance, tops the statesman's part,[5]
And talks Gazettes and Post-boys [6] o'er by heart.   155
Like a big wife at sight of loathsome meat
Ready to cast, I yawn, I sigh, and sweat.
Then as a licens'd spy, whom nothing can
Silence or hurt, he libels the great Man;
Swears ev'ry place entail'd for years to come,   160
In sure succession to the day of doom;
He names the price for ev'ry office paid,
And says our wars thrive ill, because delay'd;
Nay hints, 't is by connivance of the Court,
That Spain robs on, and Dunkirk 's[7] still a Port.   165

---

[1] [Tudor chroniclers.]

[2] [Quære: *Snug* ?]

[3] [i.e. no boy shall play at chuck-farthing;
no lady win the vole (all the tricks) at cards.]

[4] *As one of Woodward's patients,*] Allud-
ing to the effects of his use of oils in bilious
disorders. *Warburton.*

[5] This originally stood thus:

'Shows Poland's int'rest, takes the Primate's
part.' *Warton.*

[6] [a newspaper.] [The *London Gazette*, the
first English newspaper, was started in 1665.
The Post-boy, Foreign and Domestic, first
appeared May 17, 1695. *Am. Ed.*]

[7] [Pope could apply to the difficulties with
Spain which brought about war in 1739 the

Not more amazement seiz'd on Circe's guests
To see themselves fall endlong into beasts,
Than mine, to find a subject staid and wise
Already half turn'd traitor by surprise.
I felt th' infection slide from him to me,   170
As in the pox, some give it to get free ;
And quick to swallow me, methought I saw
One of our Giant Statutes ope its jaw.
  In that nice moment, as another Lie
Stood just a-tilt the Minister came by.   175
To him he flies, and bows, and bows again,
Then, close as Umbra,[1] joins the dirty train,
Not Fannius'[2] self more impudently near,
When half his nose is in his Prince's ear.
I quak'd at heart; and still afraid, to see   180
All the Court fill'd with stranger things than he,
Ran out as fast, as one that pays his bail
And dreads more actions, hurries from a jail.
  Bear me, some God! oh quickly bear me hence
To wholesome Solitude, the nurse of sense :   185
Where Contemplation prunes her ruffled wings,[3]
And the free soul looks down to pity Kings!
There sober thought pursu'd th' amusing theme,
Till Fancy colour'd it, and form'd a Dream.
A Vision hermits can to Hell transport,   190
And forc'd ev'n me to see the damn'd at Court.
Not Dante dreaming all th' infernal state,
Beheld such scenes of envy, sin, and hate.
Base Fear becomes the guilty, not the free ;
Suits Tyrants, Plunderers, but suits not me :   195
Shall I, the Terror of this sinful town,
Care, if a liv'ry'd Lord or smile or frown?
Who cannot flatter, and detest who can,
Tremble before a noble Serving-man?
O my fair mistress, Truth! shall I quit thee   200
For huffing, braggart, puff'd Nobility?
Thou, who since yesterday hast roll'd o'er all
The busy, idle blockheads of the ball,
Hast thou, ol Sun! beheld an emptier fort,
Than such as swell this bladder of a court?   205
Now pox on those who show a *Court in wax!*[4]
It ought to bring all courtiers on their backs :
Such painted puppets! such a varnish'd race

---

reference in Donne to ' Spaniards and Dun-
kirkers.']

[1] [Bubb Doddington.] [Courthope says:
"One Walter Carey," Warden of the Mint and
later Clerk of the Privy Council. *Am. Ed.*]

[2] [Lord Hervey.]

[3] [From Milton's *Comus;* but possibly taken
by Pope from Hughes's *Thought in a Garden,*
or Mrs. Chandler's lines *on Solitude,* quoted by
Wakefield.]

[4] *Court in wax!*] A famous show of the
Court of France, in Wax-work. P. [Donne
alludes to] a show of the Italian Gardens in
Wax-work, in the time of King James I. P.

Of hollow gew-gaws, only dress and face!
Such waxen noses, stately staring things —   210
No wonder some folks bow, and think them Kings.
   See! where the British youth, engag'd no more
At Fig's, at White's, with felons,[1] or a whore,
Pay their last duty to the Court, and come
All fresh and fragrant, to the drawing-room;   .   215
In hues as gay, and odours as divine,
As the fair fields they sold to look so fine.
"That's velvet for a King!" the flatt'rer swears;
'T is true, for ten days hence 't will be King Lear's.
Our Court may justly to our stage give rules,[2]   220
That helps it both to fools-coats and to fools.
And why not players strut in courtiers' clothes?
For these are actors too, as well as those:
Wants reach all states; they beg but better drest,
And all is splended poverty at best.   225
   Painted for sight, and essenc'd for the smell,
Like frigates fraught with spice and cochinel,
Sail in the Ladies: how each pirate eyes
So weak a vessel, and so rich a prize!
Top-gallant he, and she in all her trim,   230
He boarding her, she striking sail to him:
"Dear Countess! you have charms all hearts to hit!"
And "Sweet Sir Fopling! you have so much wit!"
Such wits and beauties are not prais'd for nought,
For both the beauty and the wit are bought.   .   235
'T wou'd burst ev'n Heraclitus[3] with the spleen,
To see those antics, Fopling and Courtine:
The Presence seems, with things so richly odd,
The mosque of Mahound, or some queer Pagod.
See them survey their limbs by Durer's[4] rules,   240
Of all beau-kind the best-proportion'd fools!
Adjust their clothes, and to confession draw
Those venial sins, an atom, or a straw;
But oh! what terrors must distract the soul
Convicted of that mortal crime, a hole;   245
Or should one pound of powder less bespread
Those monkey tails that wag behind their head.
Thus finish'd, and corrected to a hair,
They march, to prate their hour before the Fair.
So first to preach a white-glov'd Chaplain goes,   250
With band of Lily, and with cheek of Rose,

---

[1] *At Fig's, at White's, with felons,*] White's was a noted gaming-house: Fig's, a Prize-fighter's Academy, where the young Nobility receiv'd instruction in those days. It was also customary for the nobility and gentry to visit the condemned criminals in Newgate. P.

[2] *our stage give rules,*] Alluding to the Chamberlain's Authority [as licenser of plays].
Warburton.

[3] ['The weeping philosopher.']

[4] [Albrecht Dürer, among other works on the theory of his art, published a work on the *Proportions* of the human figure.]

Sweeter than Sharon, in immac'late trim,
Neatness itself impertinent in him.
Let but the Ladies smile, and they are blest:
Prodigious! how the things *protest, protest:*　　　255
Peace, fools, or Gonson will for Papists seize you,
If once he catch you at your *Jesu! Jesu!*
　Nature made ev'ry Fop to plague his brother,
Just as one Beauty mortifies another.
But here 's the Captain that will plague them both,　　260
Whose air cries Arm! whose very look 's an oath:
The Captain 's honest,[1] Sirs, and that 's enough,
Tho' his soul 's bullet, and his body buff.
He spits fore-right; his haughty chest before,
Like batt'ring-rams, beats open ev'ry door:　　　265
And with a face as red, and as awry,
As Herod's hang-dogs in old Tapestry,[2]
Scarecrow to boys, the breeding woman's curse,
Has yet a strange ambition to look worse;
Confounds the civil, keeps the rude in awe,　　　270
Jests like a licens'd fool, commands like law.
　Frighted, I quit the room, but leave it so
As men from Jails to execution go;
For hung with deadly sins [3] I see the wall,
And lin'd with Giants deadlier than 'em all:　　　275
Each man an *Askapart*,[4] of strength to toss
For Quoits, both Temple-bar and Charing-cross.
Scar'd at the grizly forms, I sweat, I fly,
And shake all o'er, like a discover'd spy.
　Courts are too much for wits so weak as mine:　280
Charge them with Heav'n's Artill'ry, bold Divine!
From such alone the Great rebukes endure,
Whose Satire 's sacred, and whose rage secure:
　'T is mine to wash a few light stains, but theirs
To deluge sin, and drown a Court in tears.　　　285
Howe'er what 's now *Apocrypha*, my Wit,
In time to come, may pass for holy writ.[5]

---

[1] Much resembling Noll Bluff in Congreve's *Old Bachelor*, who was copied from *Thraso*, and also from Ben Jonson. *Warton.*

[2] [Cf. *Essay on Criticism*, v. 588.]

[3] *For hung with deadly sins*] The Room hung with old Tapestry, representing the seven deadly sins. P.

[4] A giant famous in Romances. P.

[5] 'Although I yet (With Maccabees modesty) the known merit Of my work lessen, yet some wise men shall, I hope, esteem my wits canonical.' *Donne.*

EPILOGUE TO THE SATIRES.

IN TWO DIALOGUES.

WRITTEN IN MDCCXXXVIII.

[The first part of these Satires was published under the title of *One Thousand Seven Hundred and Thirty-eight, a Dialogue something like Horace ;* and the second part followed in the same year. It is remarkable, says Boswell (in his *Life of Johnson*), that Johnson's *London* came out on the same morning in May as Pope's ' 1738 ' ; ' so that England had at once its Juvenal and Horace as poetical monitors.' Johnson's satire, though published anonymously and having nothing, like Pope's, to betray its author, appears to have created the stronger sensation.]

DIALOGUE I.

FR. NOT twice a twelve-month [1] you appear in Print,
        And when it comes, the Court see nothing in't
You grow correct, that once with Rapture writ,
And are, besides, too *moral* for a Writ.
Decay of Parts, alas! we all must feel —   5
Why now, this moment, don't I see you steal?
'T is all from Horace ; Horace long before ye
Said, "Tories call'd him Whig, and Whigs a Tory ; "
And taught his Romans, in much better metre,
"To laugh at Fools who put their trust in Peter."   10
    But Horace, Sir, was delicate, was nice ;
Bubo observes,[2] he lash'd no sort of *Vice :*
Horace would say, Sir Billy *serv'd the Crown*,[3]
Blunt could *do Bus'ness*, H—ggins [4] *knew the Town ;*
In Sappho touch the *Failings of the Sex*,   15
In rev'rend Bishops note some *small Neglects*,
And own, the Spaniard did a *waggish thing*,
Who cropt our Ears,[5] and sent them to the King.
His sly, polite, insinuating style
Could please at Court, and make AUGUSTUS smile :   20
An artful Manager, that crept between
His Friend and Shame, and was a kind of *Screen*.[6]

---

[1] *Not twice a twelve-month, &c.*] These two lines are from Horace; and the only lines that are so in the whole Poem; being meant to be a handle to that which follows in the character of an impertinent Censurer,

    '*T is all from Horace; &c.* P.
[The passage is at the commencement of Hor. *Sat.* II. III.]

[2] *Bubo observes,*] Some guilty person very fond of making such an observation. P. [Mr. Doddington, Lord Melcombe. *Am. Ed.*]

[3] [V. *Epistle to Arbuthnot*, v. 280.]

[4] *H—ggins*] Formerly Jailor of the Fleet prison, enriched himself by many exactions, for which he was tried and expelled. P. [This

Huggins] was the father of the author of the absurd and prosaic Translation of Ariosto.
                                            Warton.

[5] *Who cropt our Ears,*] Said to be executed by the Captain of a Spanish ship on one Jenkins, a Captain of an English one. He cut off his ears, and bid him carry them to the King his master. P. [Vide Mr. Carlyle's History of *Frederick the Great, passim.*]

[6] *Omne vafer vitium ridenti Flaccus amico Tangit, et admissus circum præcordia ludit.*
                                    PERS. [*Sat.* I. 116.] P.

    Screen] A metaphor peculiarly appropriated to a certain person in power. P.

But 'faith your very Friends will soon be sore ;
Patriots there are,[1] who wish you 'd jest no more —
And where 's the Glory? 't will be only thought   25
The Great man [2] never offer'd you a groat.
Go see Sir ROBERT —
      P. See Sir ROBERT! — hum —
And never laugh — for all my life to come?
Seen him I have, but in his happier hour [3]
Of Social Pleasure, ill-exchang'd for Pow'r ;   30
Seen him, uncumber'd [4] with the Venal tribe,
Smile without Art, and win without a Bribe.
Would he oblige me? let me only find,
He does not think me what he thinks mankind.[5]
Come, come, at all I laugh he laughs, no doubt ;   35
The only diff'rence is I dare laugh out.
  F. Why yes : with *Scripture* still you may be free ;
A Horse-laugh, if you please, at *Honesty* ;
A Joke on JEKYL,[6] or some odd *Old Whig*
Who never chang'd his Principle, or Wig :   40
A Patriot is a Fool in ev'ry age,
Whom all Lord Chamberlains allow the Stage :
These nothing hurts ; [7] they keep their Fashion still,
And wear their strange old Virtue, as they will.
If any ask you, "Who 's the Man, so near   45
"His Prince, that writes in Verse, and has his ear?"
Why, answer, LYTTELTON,[8] and I 'll engage
The worthy Youth shall ne'er be in a rage ;
But were his Verses vile, his Whisper base,
You 'd quickly find him in Lord *Fanny's* case.   50
Sejanus, Wolsey,[9] hurt not honest FLEURY,[10]
But well may put some Statesmen in a fury.

---

[1] *Patriots there are, &c.*] This appellation was generally given to those in opposition to the Court. Though some of them (which our author hints at) had views too mean and interested to deserve that Name. P.

[2] *The Great man*] A phrase by common use appropriated to the first minister. P.

[3] [Explained by Warburton to refer to the favour conferred by Walpole at Pope's request upon the Catholic priest Southcote. See *Introductory Memoir*, p. xi.]

[4] *Seen him, uncumber'd*] These two verses were originally in the poem, though omitted in all the first editions. P.

[5] [Bowles quotes Coxe's correction of the cynical saying commonly attributed to Sir R. Walpole. 'The political axiom was perverted by leaving out the word *those* ' referring to certain pretended patriots).]

[6] *A Joke on Jekyl,*] Sir Joseph Jekyl, Master of the Rolls, a true Whig in his principles,

and a man of the utmost probity. He sometimes voted against the Court, which drew upon him the laugh here described of ONE who bestowed it equally upon Religion and Honesty. He died a few months after the publication of this poem. P.   [*burton.*

[7] *These nothing hurts;*] i.e. offends. *War*-

[8] *Why, answer, Lyttelton,*] George Lyttelton, Secretary to the Prince of Wales, distinguished both for his writings and speeches in the spirit of Liberty. P. [V. *Im. of Hor.* Bk. I. Ep. i. v. 29.]

[9] *Sejanus, Wolsey,*] The one the wicked minister of Tiberius; the other, of Henry VIII. The writers against the Court usually bestowed these and other odious names on the Minister, without distinction, and in the most injurious manner. See Dial. II. v. 137. P.

[10] *Fleury,*] Cardinal : and Minister to Louis XV. It was a Patriot-fashion, at that time, to cry up his wisdom and honesty. P.

Laugh then at any, but at Fools or Foes ;
These you but anger, and you mend not those.
Laugh at your friends, and, if your Friends are sore,   55
So much the better, you may laugh the more.
To Vice and Folly to confine the jest,
Sets half the world, God knows, against the rest ;
Did not the Sneer of more impartial men
At Sense and Virtue, balance all again.   60
Judicious Wits spread wide the Ridicule,
And charitably comfort Knave and Fool.
    P. Dear Sir, forgive the Prejudice of Youth :
Adieu Distinction, Satire, Warmth, and Truth !
Come, harmless Characters, that no one hit ;   65
Come, Henley's Oratory, Osborne's[1] Wit !
The Honey dropping from Favonio's tongue,
The Flow'rs of Bubo, and the Flow of Y—ng ![2]
The gracious Dew[3] of Pulpit Eloquence,
And all the well-whipt Cream of Courtly Sense,   70
That First was H—vy's, F—'s next, and then
The S—te's, and then H—vy's once again.
O come, that easy Ciceronian style,[4]
So Latin, yet so English all the while,
As, tho' the Pride of Middleton[5] and Bland,[6]   75
All Boys may read, and Girls may understand !
Then might I sing, without the least offence,
And all I sung should be the *Nation's Sense* ;[7]
Or teach the melancholy Muse to mourn,
Hang the sad Verse on CAROLINA's[8] Urn,   80
And hail her passage to the Realms of Rest,
All Parts perform'd, and *all* her Children blest !
So — Satire is no more — I feel it die —
No *Gazetteer* more innocent than I — [9]

---

[1] *Henley — Osborne*] See them in their places in the Dunciad. P.

[2] [Sir William Yonge, not, as Bowles conjectures to be possible, Dr. Edward Young, author of *The Night Thoughts*, although to the latter Doddington (Bubo) was a constant friend.]

[3] *The gracious Dew*] Alludes to some court sermons, and florid panegyrical speeches ; particularly one very full of puerilities and flatteries ; which afterwards got into an address in the same pretty style ; and was lastly served up in an Epitaph, between Latin and English, published, by its author. P. An 'Epitaph' on Queen Caroline was written by Lord *Hervey*, and an address moved in the *House of Commons* (the Senate) on the occasion by *H. Fox*.
    Carruthers.

[4] *that easy Ciceronian style*,] A joke upon absurd Imitators ; who in light and familiar compositions, which require *ease*, affect a *Ciceronian style*, which is highly laboured, solemn, and pompous. *Warburton.*

[5] [Lord Hervey's friend, Dr. Conyers Middleton, author of the *Life of Cicero*.]

[6] Dr. Bland, of Eton, a very bad writer. *Bennet.*

[7] [According to Warburton, a cant term of politics at the time.]

[8] *Carolina*] Queen Consort to King George II. She died in 1737. Her death gave occasion, as is observed above, to many indiscreet and mean performances unworthy of her memory, whose last moments manifested the utmost courage and resolution. P.

[9] *No Gazetteer more innocent than I.*] The Gazetteer is one of the low appendices to the Secretary of State's office, to write the government's newspaper, published by authority. Sir Richard Steele had once this post. *Warburton.*

And let, a' God's name, ev'ry Fool and Knave   85
Be grac'd thro' Life, and flatter'd in his Grave.
  F. Why so? if Satire knows its Time and Place,
You still may lash the greatest — in Disgrace :
For Merit will by turns forsake them all :
Would you know when? exactly when they fall.   90
But let all Satire in all Changes spare
Immortal S—k, and grave De—re.[1]
Silent and soft, as Saints remove to Heav'n,
All Ties dissolv'd and ev'ry Sin forgiv'n,
These may some gentle ministerial Wing   95
Receive, and place for ever near a King!
There, where no Passion, Pride, or Shame transport,
Lull'd with the sweet Nepenthe of a Court ;
There, where no Father's, Brother's, Friend's disgrace
Once break their rest, or stir them from their Place : 100
But past the Sense of human Miseries,
All Tears are wip'd for ever from all eyes ;[2]
No cheek is known to blush, no heart to throb,
Save when they lose a Question, or a Job.
  P. Good Heav'n forbid, that I should blast their glory, 105
Who know how like Whig Ministers to Tory,
And, when three Sov'reigns died, could scarce be vext,
Consid'ring what a *gracious Prince* was next.
Have I, in silent wonder, seen such things
As Pride in Slaves, and Avarice in Kings ;   110
And at a Peer, or Peeress, shall I fret,
Who starves a Sister, or forswears a debt?[3]
Virtue, I grant you, is an empty boast ;[4]
But shall the Dignity of *Vice* be lost?
Ye Gods! shall Cibber's Son, without rebuke,   115
Swear like a Lord, or Rich[5] out-whore a Duke?[5]

---

[1] *Immortal S—k, and grave De—re!*] A title given *that* Lord by King James II. He was of the Bedchamber to King William; he was so to King George I.; he was so to King George II. *This* Lord was very skilful in all the forms of the House, in which he discharged himself with great gravity. P. Pope alludes to Charles Hamilton, third son of the Duke of Hamilton, who was created Earl of Selkirk in 1667. *Bowles*. [Is Lord Delaware the other?]

[2] [Cf. *Messiah*, v. 46 — a line altered at Steele's request.]

[3] In some editions,

Who starves a Mother, — *Warburton*.

I have been informed that these verses related to Lady M. W. Montagu and her sister the Countess of Mar. *Bowles*. [This charge against Lady M. W. M. rests on the scandal of Horace Walpole, in one of his letters to Sir H. Mann. She is there accused of having treated her sister hardly, while the latter was out of her senses, and of having frightened a Frenchman of the name of Ruzemonde (who had entrusted her with a large sum of money to buy stock for him) out of England by threats of betraying her intrigue with him, first to her husband, then to her brother-in-law. Lord Wharncliffe, in the Appendix to Vol. III. of his *Letters and Works of Lady M. W. M.*, states that the former accusation is utterly unfounded, and shews that the latter rests on a perversion of facts.]

[4] *Virtue, I grant you, is an empty boast;*] A satirical ambiguity — either that those *starve who have it*, or that those who *boast of it, have it not :* and both together (he insinuates) make up the present state of *modern virtue*. *Warburton*.

[5] *Cibber's Son, — Rich*] Two Players: look for them in the Dunciad. P. [Rich, IV. 261. He was the lessee of Covent-Garden theatre.]

A Fav'rite's Porter with his Master vie,
Be brib'd as often, and as often lie?
Shall Ward[1] draw Contracts with a Statesman's skill?
Or Japhet[2] pocket, like his Grace, a Will?	120
Is it for Bond,[3] or Peter, (paltry things)
To pay their Debts, or keep their Faith, like Kings?
If Blount[4] despatch'd himself, he play'd the man,
And so may'st thou, illustrious Passeran![5]
But shall a Printer, weary of his life,	125
Learn, from their Books, to hang himself and Wife?
This, this, my friend, I cannot, must not bear;
Vice thus abus'd, demands a Nation's care;
This calls the Church to deprecate our Sin,[7]
And hurls the Thunder of the Laws on *Gin.*[8]	130
    Let modest FOSTER, if he will, excel
Ten Metropolitans in preaching well:[9]
A simple Quaker, or a Quaker's Wife,[10]
Out-do Llandaff[11] in Doctrine, — yea in Life:
Let humble ALLEN,[12] with an awkward Shame,	135
Do good by stealth, and blush to find it Fame.
Virtue may choose the high or low Degree,
'T is just alike to Virtue, and to me;
Dwell in a Monk, or light upon a King,
She 's still the same, belov'd, contented thing.	140
Vice is undone, if she forgets her Birth,
And stoops from Angels to the Dregs of Earth:
But 't is the *Fall* degrades her to a Whore;

Swear like a Lord — or out-whore a Duke?] Elegance demands that these should be two proverbial expressions. *To swear like a Lord* is so. But to *out-whore a Duke* certainly is not. However this shews that the continence and conjugal virtues of the higher nobility must needs be very exemplary. SCRIBL.

[1] [Cf. *Moral Essays*, Ep. III. v. 20.]

[2] [Cf. 16, v. 86.]

[3] [Cf. *Dunciad*, III. v. 126.]

[4] *If Blount*] Author of an impious and foolish book called *the Oracles of Reason*, who being in love with a near kinswoman of his, and rejected, gave himself a stab in the arm, as pretending to kill himself, of the consequence of which he really died. P.

[5] *Passeran!*] Author of another book of the same stamp, called *A philosophical discourse on death*, being a defence of suicide. He was a nobleman of Piedmont, banished from his country for his impieties, and lived in the utmost misery, yet feared to practise his own precepts; and at last died a penitent. *Warburton.*

[6] *But shall a Printer, &c.*] A Fact that happened in London a few years past. The un-

happy man left behind him a paper justifying his action by the reasonings of some of these authors. P.

[7] *This calls the Church to deprecate our Sin,*] Alluding to the *forms of prayer,* composed in the times of public calamity; where the fault is generally laid upon the *People. Warburton.*

[8] *Gin.*] A spirituous liquor, the exorbitant use of which had almost destroyed the lowest rank of the People till it was restrained by an act of Parliament in 1736. P.

[9] An eloquent and persuasive preacher, who wrote an excellent Defence of Christianity against Tindal. *Warton.*

[10] Mrs. Drummond, celebrated in her time. *Warton.*

[11] *Llandaff*] A poor Bishoprick in Wales, as poorly supplied. P. By Dr. John Harris. *Carruthers.*

[12] [Ralph Allen, of Prior Park, an intimate friend and constant correspondent of Pope's, to whom he performed many kind services. He was afterwards a munificent patron to Fielding. Of his charitable habits there is evidence in Pope's Will.]

Let *Greatness* own her, and she 's mean no more; [1]
Her Birth, her Beauty, Crowds and Courts confess;   145
Chaste Matrons praise her, and grave Bishops bless;
In golden Chains the willing World she draws,
And hers the Gospel is, and hers the Laws,
Mounts the Tribunal, lifts her scarlet head,
And sees pale Virtue carted in her stead.   150
Lo! at the wheels of her Triumphal Car,
Old England's Genius, rough with many a Scar,
Dragg'd in the dust! his arms hang idly round,
His Flag inverted trails along the ground!
Our Youth, all livery'd o'er with foreign Gold,   155
Before her dance: behind her crawl the Old!
See thronging Millions to the Pagod run,
And offer Country, Parent, Wife, or Son!
Hear her black Trumpet thro' the Land proclaim,
That NOT TO BE CORRUPTED IS THE SHAME.   160
In Soldier, Churchman, Patriot, Man in Pow'r,
'T is Av'rice all. Ambition is no more!
See, all our Nobles begging to be Slaves!
See, all our Fools aspiring to be Knaves!
The Wit of Cheats, the Courage of a Whore,   165
Are what ten thousand envy and adore;
All, all look up with reverential Awe,
At Crimes that 'scape, or triumph o'er the Law;
While Truth, Worth, Wisdom, daily they decry —
"Nothing is Sacred now but Villainy."   170
   Yet may this Verse (if such a Verse remain)
Shew, there was one who held it in disdain.

DIALOGUE II.

FR. 'TIS all a Libel — Paxton [2] (Sir) will say.
      P. Not yet, my Friend! to-morrow 'faith it may; }
And for that very cause I print to-day.
How should I fret to mangle ev'ry line,
In rev'rence to the Sins of *Thirty nine!* [3]   5
Vice with such Giant strides comes on amain,
Invention strives to be before in vain;
Feign what I will, and paint it e'er so strong, [4]

---

[1] [Said by Warburton to refer to the Empress Theodora, the wife of Justinian, though Gibbon is sceptical as to the intended allusion.]

[2] *Paxton*] Late solicitor to the Treasury. *Warburton.* [Cf. infra, v. 141. He was, according to Carruthers, deeply involved in the charges against Sir R. Walpole; and temporarily imprisoned.]

[3] [i.e. of next year.]

[4] *Feign what I will, etc.*] The Poet has here introduced an oblique apology for himself with great art. You attack personal characters, say his enemies. No, replies he, so far from that, I paint from my invention; and to prevent a likeness I exaggerate every feature. But alas! the growth of vice is so monstrous quick, that it rises up to a resemblance before I can get from the press.

Some rising Genius sins up to my Song.
 F. Yet none but you by Name the guilty lash;   10
Ev'n Guthry [1] saves half Newgate by a Dash.
Spare then the Person, and expose the Vice.
 P. How, Sir? not damn the Sharper, but the Dice?
Come on then, Satire! gen'ral, unconfin'd,
Spread thy broad wing, and souse on all the kind.   15
Ye Statesmen, Priests, of one religion all!
Ye Tradesmen vile, in Army, Court, or Hall,
Ye Rev'rend Atheists — F. Scandal! name them! Who?
 P. Why, that's the thing you bid me not to do.
Who starv'd a Sister, who forswore a Debt,[2]   20
I never nam'd; the Town's enquiring yet.
The pois'ning Dame — F. You mean — P. I don't. — F. You do!
 P. See, now I keep the Secret, and not you!
The bribing Statesman — F. Hold, too high you go.
 P. The brib'd Elector — F. There you stoop too low. 25
 P. I fain would please you, if I knew with what;
Tell me, which Knave is lawful Game, which not?
Must great Offenders, once escap'd the Crown,[3]
Like royal Harts, be never more run down? [4]
Admit your Law to spare the Knight requires,   30
As Beasts of Nature may we hunt the Squires?
Suppose I censure — you know what I mean —
To save a Bishop, may I name a Dean?
 F. A Dean, Sir? no: his Fortune is not made;
You hurt a man that's rising in the Trade.   35
 P. If not the Tradesman who set up to-day,
Much less the 'Prentice who to-morrow may.
Down, down, proud Satire! tho' a Realm be spoil'd,
Arraign no mightier Thief than wretched *Wild*; [5]
Or, if a Court or Country's made a job,   40
Go drench a Pick-pocket, and join the Mob.
 But, Sir, I beg you (for the Love of Vice!)
The matter's weighty, pray consider twice;
Have you less pity for the needy Cheat,
The poor and friendless Villain, than the Great?   45
Alas! the small Discredit of a Bribe
Scarce hurts the Lawyer, but undoes the Scribe.
Then better sure it Charity becomes
To tax Directors, who (thank God) have Plums;

---

[1] *Ev'n Guthry*] The Ordinary of Newgate, who publishes the memoirs of the Malefactors, and is óften prevailed upon to be so tender of their reputation, as to set down no more than the initials of their name. P.

[2] Cf. ante, *Dial.* I. v. 112.]

[3] *Must great Offenders, etc.*] The case is archly put. Those who escape public justice being the particular property of the Satirist.

[4] *Like royal Harts, etc.*] Alluding to the old Game Laws. *Warburton.*

[5] *wretched Wild,*] Jonathan Wild, a famous Thief, and Thief-Impeacher, who was at last caught in his own train and hanged. P. [Fielding's *Jonathan Wild* appeared in 1743, nearly a quarter of a century after the death of its hero. But highwaymen flourished till a considerably later date.]

Still better, Ministers; or, if the thing   50
May pinch ev'n there — why lay it on a King.
   F. Stop! stop.
          P. Must Satire, then, nor rise nor fall?
Speak out, and bid me blame no Rogues at all.
   F. Yes, strike that *Wild*, I 'll justify the blow.
   P. Strike? why the man was hang'd ten years ago: 55
Who now that obsolete Example fears?
Ev'n Peter trembles only for his Ears.[1]
   F. What? always Peter? Peter thinks you mad;
You make men desp'rate if they once are bad:
Else might he take to Virtue some years hence —   60
   P. As S—k, if he lives, will love the PRINCE.
   F. Strange spleen to S—k!
          P. Do I wrong the Man?
God knows, I praise a Courtier where I can.
When I confess, there is who feels for Fame,
And melts to Goodness, need I SCARB'ROW[3] name?   65
Pleas'd let me own, in *Esher's* peaceful Grove[4]
(Where *Kent*[5] and Nature vie for PELHAM'S[6] Love)
The Scene, the Master, opening to my view,
I sit and dream I see my CRAGGS anew!
   Ev'n in a Bishop I can spy Desert;   70
Secker[7] is decent, *Rundel*[8] has a Heart,
Manners with Candour are to *Benson*[9] giv'n,
To *Berkeley*,[10] ev'ry Virtue under Heav'n.
   But does the Court a worthy Man remove?
That instant, I declare, he has my Love: 75
I shun his Zenith, court his mild Decline;

---

[1] *Ev'n Peter trembles only for his ears,*] Peter had, the year before this, narrowly escaped the Pillory for forgery: and got off with a severe rebuke only from the bench. P.

[2] [V. ante, *Dial.* I. v. 92.]

[3] *Scarb'row*] Earl of, and Knight of the Garter, whose personal attachments to the king appeared from his steady adherence to the royal interest, after his resignation of his great employment of Master of the Horse; and whose known honour and virtue made him esteemed by all parties. P. [He committed suicide in a fit of melancholy in 1740; and was mourned by Lord Chesterfield as 'the best man he ever knew, and the dearest friend he ever had.']

[4] *Esher's peaceful Grove,*] The house and gardens of Esher in Surrey, belonging to the Honourable Mr. Pelham, Brother of the Duke of Newcastle. The author could not have given a more amiable idea of his Character than in comparing him to Mr. Craggs. P.

[5] [The architect and friend of Lord Burlington.]

[6] [Henry Pelham became First Lord of the treasury in 1743, through Walpole's influence; and died in 1754, the King exclaiming on his death: 'Now I shall have no more peace.']

[7] [Thos. Secker (1693-1768), successively bishop of Bristol and of Oxford, and archbishop of Canterbury. His career is accounted for by his personal reputation for liberality and moderation.]

[8] [Dr. Rundel, bishop of Derry, esteemed equally by Pope and Swift. See their letters of Sept. 3, 1735 and foll.]

[9] [Bishop of Gloucester. He ordained Whitfield.]

[10] [Dr. Berkeley, bishop of Cloyne (born 1684, died 1707), the illustrious author of *Alciphron*. A very different bishop (Atterbury) said of him that 'so much understanding, so much knowledge, so much innocence, and such humility, I did not think had been the portion of any but angels, till I saw this gentleman.']

Thus SOMERS[1] once and HALIFAX,[2] were mine.
Oft, in the clear, still Mirror of Retreat,
I study'd SHREWSBURY,[3] the wise and great:
CARLETON'S[4] calm Sense, and STANHOPE'S[5] noble Flame,   80
Compar'd, and knew their gen'rous End the same;
How pleasing ATTERBURY'S[6] softer hour!
How shin'd the Soul, unconquer'd in the Tow'r!
How can I PULT'NEY,[7] CHESTERFIELD[8] forget,
While Roman Spirit charms, and Attic Wit: 85
ARGYLL, the State's whole Thunder born to wield,
And shake alike the Senate and the Field:[9]
Or WYNDHAM,[10] just to Freedom and the Throne,
The Master of our Passions, and his own?
Names, which I long have lov'd, nor lov'd in vain,   90
Rank'd with their Friends, not number'd with their Train;
And if yet higher the proud List should end,[11]
Still let me say: No Follower, but a Friend.
   Yet think not, Friendship only prompts my lays;
I follow *Virtue;* where she shines, I praise: 95

[1] *Somers*] John Lord Somers died in 1716. He had been Lord Keeper in the reign of William III. who took from him the seals in 1700. The author had the honour of knowing him in 1706. A faithful, able, and incorrupt minister; who, to the qualities of a consummate statesman, added those of a man of Learning and Politeness. P.

[2] *Halifax*] A peer, no less distinguished by his love of letters than his abilities in Parliament. He was disgraced in 1710, on the Change of Q. Anne's ministry. P.

[3] *Shrewsbury*,] Charles Talbot, Duke of Shrewsbury, had been Secretary of state, Embassador in France, Lord Lieutenant of Ireland, Lord Chamberlain, and Lord Treasurer. He several times quitted his employments, and was often recalled. He died in 1718. P.

[4] *Carleton*] Henry Boyle, Lord Carleton (nephew of the famous Robert Boyle), who was Secretary of state under William III. and President of the Council under Q. Anne. P.

[5] *Stanhope*] James Earl Stanhope. A Nobleman of equal courage, spirit, and learning. General in Spain, and Secretary of state. P. [The first Earl Stanhope, and the uncle of Chatham.]

[6] [Francis Atterbury, bishop of Rochester, the friend of Pope and Swift and a consistent Jacobite, was arrested in 1722 on a charge of treasonable complicity in a plot for bringing back the Pretender, and sentenced to banishment. He joined the Pretender's Court, and for some time directed his affairs. He died in 1731.]

[7] [William Pulteney (Earl of Bath in 1742), the great opponent of Sir Robert Walpole; eloquent as an orator and witty as a pamphleteer.]

[8] *Chesterfield*] Philip Earl of Chesterfield, commonly given by Writers of all Parties for an EXAMPLE to the Age he lives in, of *superior talents*, and *public Virtue. Warburton.* [Philip Dormer, Earl of Chesterfield, lord lieutenant of Ireland in 1744 and Secretary of State in 1747. His Irish administration is the highest point in his political career. As a writer he is famous for the sceptical *Letters to his Son;* of his wit some instances are given in Hayward's *Essay on Lord C.*]

[9] [This Duke of Argyll, after defending Scotland against the Pretender's invasion of 1715, played a very changeful part in political life; and at his death in 1744 was one of the chiefs of the opposition against the Whigs. The two lines in the text are said to have been added in consequence of a threat of the Duke's that he would run any man through the body who should dare to use his name in an invective.]

[10] *Wyndham*] Sir William Wyndham, Chancellor of the Exchequer under Queen Anne, made early a considerable figure; but since a much greater both by his ability and eloquence, joined with the utmost judgment and temper. P. [Bolingbroke's friend.]

[11] *And if yet higher, etc.*] He was at this time honoured with the esteem and favour of his Royal Highness the Prince of Wales. *Warburton.*

Point she to Priest or Elder, Whig or Tory,
Or round a Quaker's Beaver cast a Glory.
I never (to my scrrow I declare)
Din'd with the MAN of Ross,[1] or my LORD MAY'R.[2]
Some, in their choice of Friends (nay, look not grave)   100
Have still a secret Bias to a Knave:
To find an honest man I beat about,
And love him, court him, praise him, in or out.
   F. Then why so few commended?
                       P. Not so fierce!
Find you the Virtue, and I 'll find the Verse.   105
But random Praise — the task can ne'er be done;
Each Mother asks it for her booby Son,
Each Widow asks it for *the Best of Men*,
For him she weeps, and him she weds again.
Praise cannot stoop, like Satire, to the ground;   110
The Number may be hang'd, but not be crown'd.
Enough for half the Greatest of these days,
To 'scape my Censure, not expect my Praise.
And they riot Rich? what more can they pretend?
Dare they to hope a Poet for their Friend?   115
What RICH'LIEU wanted, LOUIS scarce could gain,[3]
And what young AMMON wish'd, but wish'd in vain.
No Pow'r the Muse's Friendship can command;
No Pow'r, when Virtue claims it, can withstand:
To *Cato, Virgil* pay'd one honest line;[4]   120
O let my Country's Friends illumine mine!
—What are you thinking? F. 'Faith the thought 's no sin:
I think your Friends are out, and would be in.
   P. If merely to come in, Sir, they go out,
The way they take is strangely round about.   125
   F. They too may be corrupted, you 'll allow?
   P. I only call those Knaves who are so now.
   Is that too little? Come then, I 'll comply —
Spirit of *Arnall!*[5] aid me while I lie.
COBHAM 's a Coward, POLWARTH[6] is a Slave,   130
And LYTTELTON a dark, designing Knave,
ST. JOHN has ever been a wealthy Fool —
But let me add, Sir ROBERT 's mighty dull,
Has never made a Friend in private life,
And was, besides, a Tyrant to his Wife.[7]   135

---

[1] [Cf. *Moral Essays*, Ep. III.]

[2] [Sir John Barnard. Cf. ante, Bk. I. Ep. ii. v. 85.]

[3] *Louis scarce could gain,*] By this expression finely insinuating, that the great *Boileau* always falls below himself in those passages where he flatters his Master. *Warburton.*

[4] *To Cato, Virgil pay'd one honest line;*] It is in the *Æn.* [VIII. 670] His *dantem jura Catonem. Warburton.*

[5] *Spirit of Arnall!*] Look for him in his place. *Dunc.* B. II. v. 315. P.

[6] *Polwarth*] The Hon. Hugh Hume, Son of Alexander Earl of Marchmont, Grandson of Patrick Earl of Marchmont, and distinguished, like them, in the cause of Liberty. P. [Afterwards one of Pope's Executors.]

[7] Walpole's maxim was ' to go his own way, and let madam go hers.' *Carruthers.*

But pray, when others praise him, do I blame?
Call Verres, Wolsey, any odious name?
Why rail they then, if but a Wreath of mine,
Oh All-accomplish'd St. John! deck thy shrine?
   What? shall each spur-gall'd Hackney of the day,   · 140
When Paxton gives him double Pots and Pay,
Or each new-pension'd Sycophant, pretend
To break my Windows, if I treat a Friend?
Then wisely plead, to me they meant no hurt,
But 't was my Guest at whom they threw the dirt?   145
Sure, if I spare the Minister, no rules
Of Honour bind me, not to maul his Tools;
Sure, if they cannot cut, it may be said
His Saws are toothless, and his Hatchet 's Lead.
   It anger'd TURENNE, once upon a day,   150
To see a Footman kick'd that took his pay:
But when he heard th' Affront the Fellow gave,
Knew one a Man of Honour, one a Knave;
The prudent Gen'ral turn'd it to a jest,
And begg'd, he 'd take the pains to kick the rest: 155
Which not at present having time to do—
F. Hold, Sir! for God's sake where 's th' Affront to you?
Against your worship when had S—k writ?[1]
Or P—ge pour'd forth the Torrent of his Wit?[2]
Or grant the Bard whose distich all commend[3]   160
[*In Pow'r a Servant, out of Pow'r a friend*][4]
To W—le guilty of some venial sin;
What 's that to you who ne'er was out nor in?
   The Priest whose Flattery be-dropt the Crown,[5]
How hurt he you? he only stain'd the Gown.   165
And how did, pray, the florid Youth[6] offend,[7]
Whose Speech you took, and gave it to a Friend?
P. 'Faith, it imports not much from whom it came; ⎫
Whoever borrow'd, could not be to blame,   ⎬
Since the whole House did afterwards the same.   ⎭ 170
Let Courtly Wits to Wits afford supply,
As Hog to Hog in huts of Westphaly;
If one, thro' Nature's Bounty or his Lord's,
Has what the frugal, dirty soil affords,

---

[1] Dr. Wm. Sherlock, Dean of St. Paul's, and the *bête noire* of the Nonjurors in the reign of William III.]

[2] [Judge Page. *Warton.*] [Sir Francis Page, who seems to have deserved his sobriquet of ' the hanging judge.' He died, according to Carruthers, in 1741.]

[3] *the Bard*] A verse taken out of a poem to Sir R. W. P. By Lord Melcombe [Bubb Doddington]. *Warton.* Some years afterwards Lord M. addressed *the same epistle* to Lord Bute. *Bowles.*

[4] [From a poem addressed by Doddington to Walpole. *Am. Ed.*]

[5] *The Priest, etc.*] Spoken not of any particular priest, but of many priests. P. [Meaning Dr. Alured Clarke, who wrote a panegyric on Queen Caroline.] *Warton.*

[6] Lord Hervey. Alluding to his painting himself. *Bowles.* [Croker says " Young Henry Fox." *Am. Ed.*]

[7] *And how did, etc.*] This seems to allude to a complaint made v. 71 of the preceding Dialogue. P.

From him the next receives it, thick or thin,   175
As pure a mess almost as it came in;
The blessed benefit, not there confin'd,
Drops to the third, who nuzzles close behind;
From tail to mouth, they feed and they carouse:
The last full fairly gives it to the *House*.   180
  F. This filthy simile, this beastly line
Quite turns my stomach —
                        P. So does Flatt'ry mine;
And all your courtly Civet-cats can vent,
Perfume to you, to me is Excrement.
But hear me further — Japhet, 't is agreed,   185
Writ not, and Chartres [1] scarce could write or read,
In all the Courts of Pindus guiltless quite;
But Pens can forge, my Friend, that cannot write;
And must no Egg in Japhet's face be thrown,
Because the Deed he forg'd was not my own?   190
Must never Patriot then declaim at Gin,[2]
Unless, good man! he has been fairly in?
No zealous Pastor blame a failing Spouse,
Without a staring Reason on his brows?
And each Blasphemer quite escape the rod,   195
Because the insult 's not on Man, but God?
  Ask you what Provocation I have had?
The strong Antipathy of Good to Bad.
When Truth or Virtue an Affront endures,
Th' Affront is mine, my friend, and should be yours.   200
Mine as a Foe profess'd to false Pretence,
Who think a Coxcomb's Honour like his Sense;
Mine, as a Friend to ev'ry worthy mind;
And mine as Man, who feel for all mankind.[3]
  F. You 're strangely proud.
                        P. So proud, I am no Slave: 205
So impudent, I own myself no Knave:
So odd, my Country's Ruin makes me grave.
Yes, I am proud; I must be proud to see
Men not afraid of God, afraid of me:[4]
Safe from the Bar, the Pulpit, and the Throne,   210
Yet touch'd and sham'd by Ridicule alone.
  O sacred weapon! left for Truth's defence,
Sole Dread of Folly, Vice, and Insolence!
To all but Heav'n-directed hands deny'd,
The Muse may give thee, but the Gods must guide: 215
Rev'rent I touch thee! but with honest zeal,

---

[1] *Japhet — Chartres*] See the Epistle to Lord Bathurst. P.

[2] [The Gin Act, passed in 1731, was repealed in 1743.]

[3] *And mine as Man, who feel for all man-* *kind.*] From Terence: "Homo sum: humani nihil a me alienum puto." P.

[4] [Then let him boast that honourable crime Of making *those who fear not God, fear* HIM. Lord Hervey's *Difference between Verbal and Practical Virtue, &c.*]

2 A

To rouse the Watchmen of the public Weal;
To Virtue's work provoke the tardy Hall,
And goad the Prelate slumb'ring in his Stall.
Ye tinsel Insects! whom a Court maintains,   220
That counts your Beauties only by your Stains,
Spin all your Cobwebs[1] o'er the Eye of Day!
The Muse's wing shall brush you all away:
All his Grace preaches, all his Lordship sings,
All that makes Saints of Queens, and Gods of Kings.   225
All, all but Truth, drops dead-born from the Press,
Like the last Gazette, or the last Address.[2]
    When black Ambition stains a public Cause,[3]
A Monarch's sword when mad Vain-glory draws,
Not Waller's Wreath can hide the Nation's Scar,   230
Nor Boileau turn the Feather to a Star.[4]
    Not so, when diadem'd with rays divine,
Touch'd with the Flame that breaks from *Virtue's* Shrine,
Her Priestless Muse forbids the Good to die,
And opes the Temple of *Eternity.*   235
There, other Trophies deck the truly brave,
Than such as Anstis[5] casts into the Grave;
Far other Stars than * and * * wear,
And may descend to Mordington from STAIR:[6]
(Such as on HOUGH'S[7] unsully'd Mitre shine,   240
Or beam, good DIGBY,[7] from a heart like thine)
Let *Envy* howl, while Heav'n's whole Chorus sings,
And bark at Honour not conferr'd by Kings;
Let *Flatt'ry* sickening see the Incense rise,
Sweet to the World, and grateful to the Skies: 245

---

[1] *Cobwebs*] Weak and slight sophistry against virtue and honour. Thin colours over vice, as unable to hide the light of Truth, as cobwebs to shade the sun. P.

[2] After v. 227 in the MS.

'Where's now the Star that lighted Charles to rise?

— With that which follow'd Julius to the skies.
Angels, that watch'd the Royal Oak so well,
How chanc'd ye nod, when luckless Sorel fell?
Hence, lying miracles! reduc'd so low
As to the regal-touch, and papal-toe;
Hence haughty Edgar's title to the Main,
Britain's to France, and thine to India, Spain!'
                  Warburton.

[3] *When black Ambition, etc.*] The cause of Cromwell in the civil war of England; (v. 229) of Louis XIV. in his conquest of the Low Countries. P. [Waller's *Panegyric to my Lord Protector* was written about 1654.]

[4] *Nor Boileau turn the Feather to a Star.*] See his Ode on Namur; where (to use his own words) "il a fait un Astre de la Plume blanche que le Roy porte ordinairement à son Chapeau, et qui est en effet une espèce de Comète, fatale à nos ennemis." P.

[5] *Anstis*] The chief Herald at Arms. It is the custom, at the funeral of great peers, to cast into the grave the broken staves and ensigns of honour. P.

[6] *Stair*] John Dalrymple, Earl of Stair, Knight of the Thistle; served in all the wars under the Duke of Marlborough; and afterwards as Ambassador in France. P. [Behnet, who supplies the blanks in v. 239 by the names of Kent and Grafton, has 'some notion that Lord Mordington kept a gaming-house.'] [Crocker insists that the asterisks stand for "George" and "Frederick." *Am. Ed.*]

[7] *Hough and Digby*] Dr. John Hough, Bishop of Worcester, and the Lord Digby. The one an assertor of the Church of England in opposition to the false measures of King James II. The other as firmly attached to the cause of that King. Both acting out of principle, and equally men of honour and virtue. P.

Truth guards the Poet, sanctifies the line,
And makes immortal, Verse as mean as mine.
   Yes, the last Pen for Freedom let me draw,
When Truth stands trembling on the edge of Law ;
Here, Last of Britons! let your Names be read ;   250
Are none, none living? let me praise the Dead,
And for that Cause which made your Fathers shine,
Fall by the Votes of their degen'rate Line.
   FR. Alas! alas! pray end what you began,
And write next winter more *Essays on Man.*[1]   255

[1] Ver. 255 in the MS.

Quit, quit these themes, and write Essays on
    Man.

   This was the last poem of the kind printed by our author, with a resolution to publish no more; but to enter thus, in the most plain and solemn manner he could, a sort of PROTEST against that insuperable corruption and depravity of manners, which he had been so unhappy as to live to see. Could he have hoped to have amended any, he had continued those attacks; but bad men were grown so shameless and so powerful, that Ridicule was become as unsafe as it was ineffectual. The Poem raised him, as he knew it would, some enemies; but he had reason to be satisfied with the approbation of good men, and the testimony of his own conscience. P.

THE DUNCIAD.

[IT may fairly be doubted whether the mystification in which every step connected with the publication of the various editions of the *Dunciad* was intentionally involved by Pope, has not answered an end beyond that proposed to himself by the poet, and provided a tangle of literary difficulties, which no learned ingenuity will ever suffice entirely to unravel. In the second volume of *Notes and Queries* for 1854 will be found an animated and sustained controversy on the subject, which even the editorial summing-up leaves to a certain degree *in suspenso*. It is therefore necessary in the following Remarks to confine ourselves to such an enumeration of editions as will suffice to indicate the main history of the work.

The earliest known edition of the *Dunciad* (in three Books), and in all probability the earliest actual edition, was published in May 1728. It bore the frontispiece of an Owl. The Edition with the notes Variorum and the Prolegomena of Martinus Scriblerus (accompanied by the *Letter to the Publisher*, infra, p. 363, signed William Cleland) appeared in 1729. It bore the vignette of an ass laden with a pile of books,[1] with an owl perched on the top of these. It contained nearly all the pieces with which the poem is surrounded in subsequent editions,[2] though these were afterwards varied as to both length and arrangement. The New Dunciad, 'as it was found in the year 1741,' appeared in 1742; and this is the first edition of the Fourth Book. The edition forming the third volume of Dodsley's edition of Pope's Works, in which Colley Cibber was by mere 'proclamation' (see p. lv.) substituted as hero for Theobald, appeared in 1743; and in the same year was published an edition 'according to the complete copy found in the year 1742,' which contained Warburton's *Dissertation* under the name of Ricardus Aristarchus, on the Hero of the Poem, and an *Advertisement* by the same hand (for which see p. 368).

It is uncertain what amount of influence should be ascribed to Swift upon the gradual growth of the original idea of the *Dunciad*. 'Without you,' Pope wrote to Swift, Nov. 12th, 1728, 'the poem had never been.' It cannot however be doubted that the original idea itself was Pope's own, except in so far as it was founded upon the supposed contents of the *Margites* ascribed to Homer (see note to p. 368), and upon Dryden's satire of MacFlecknoe. But MacFlecknoe (like Margites as it would seem) is only a Satire upon one dull poet; Pope from the first appears to have a wider scheme; for in his correspondence with Bolingbroke and Swift the embryo poem is mentioned under the titles of 'Dulness,'

---

[1] [The works of Welsted, Ward, Dennis, Theobald, Oldmixon and others, and the *Mist's Journal* being labelled with their authors' names.]

[2] [The 'Testimonies of Authors,' arguments and indices.]

FRONTISPIECE TO THE DUNCIAD.
(Quarto edition of 1729.)

or the 'Progress of Dulness.' Mr. Carruthers points out that the date of the action of the poem is 1720, when Sir George Thorold was Lord Mayor; and that this circumstance and the introduction of several dunces long dead 'seem to point to a period anterior to 1727' as the time when Pope commenced to work out his conception. In 1727, however, when Swift was in England, the main labour of the execution was accomplished; and to Swift, who had watched over its birth and influenced its character, the first complete edition (that of April 1729) was duly dedicated. The prolegomena of Scriblerus and the notes Variorum were the work of several hands, and Swift (see Pope's letter to him of June 28th, 1728) was specially invited to exercise his wit in a favourite direction. The deception practised upon the public in this matter was an innocent fraud. But such will hardly be the judgment which must be passed on the pretence as to the authorship of the letter signed 'William Cleland.' This Cleland was a real personage, a Major in the Army and a friend of the poet's; but it is impossible to doubt the correctness of Mr. Carruthers's conjecture, that at the most he re-cast 'in a somewhat freer and less author-like style' what the author had himself substantially dictated.

The original hero of the *Dunciad* was Lewis Theobald. He had earned this eminence by a quarrel originating in Pope's edition of Shakspere, which had made its appearance in 1725. In the following year Theobald had published a pamphlet under the title of *Shakspere Restored, or a Specimen of the many Errors committed as well as unamended by Mr. Pope in his late edition of this Poet.* Theobald (whose own edition of Shakspere was not published till 1733) was in the habit of contributing notes on passages of Shakspere to a weekly paper called *Mist's Journal* — 'crucifying Shakspere once a week,' according to a line omitted from the later editions of the *Dunciad.* He translated several Greek plays, and adapted Shakspere's *Richard II.* for the stage, besides producing several original pantomimes and palming off his tragedy of the *Double Falsehood* upon the world as a Shaksperian original. Upon the whole he constituted a very suitable hero for a Dunce-epic; and less injustice was done to him by the selection of his well-worn name for that office, than by Dryden to the worthy Flecknoe.

Theobald accepted his castigation very goodhumouredly; but such was not the spirit in which the other petty writers sacrificed by Pope met their fate. An endless series of retaliations, or attempts at retaliation ensued, in which Dennis was not behind-hand, and which were published in a collective form by Smedley. Pope and his friends retorted by an ironical series of criticisms in the *Grub-street Journal*, which lasted from 1730 to 1737; and concerning which see *Introductory Memoir.* Lady M. W. Montagu, who retorted upon the insult offered to her by a lampoon entitled a *Pop upon Pope*, appears to have remained unanswered.

The fourth book of the *Dunciad* was not published till March 1742, when Pope was in the constant society and under the constant influence of Warburton. 'The encouragement,' writes Pope to Warburton on Dec. 28, 1742, 'you gave me to add the fourth book first determined me to do so; and the approbation you seemed to give to it was what singly determined me to print it.' Colley Cibber, against whom Pope had borne a grudge ever since the mishaps which had attended his sole dramatic attempt, and who had recently succeeded to the Laureateship, was sarcastically alluded to in v. 20. He retorted by publishing a Letter which goaded Pope into sufficient resentment to induce him, in a new edition of the entire poem, to dethrone Theobald and place Cibber in his stead. To help the scheme, Warburton contributed the prefatory dissertation *Ricardus Aristarchus of the Hero of the Poem* and notes, to the new edition. Cibber replied by another epistle; but the change was made, and Cibber, not Theobald, remains the hero of the *Dunciad.*

The above is the barest outline of the history of this immortal satire. Elsewhere must be read, by those interested in such matters, the whole narrative of the mystifications which preceded, accompanied, and followed, its publication — of the proclamation of the Ass-Dunciad as the only true edition, of the prefaces and introductions and excerpts and keys (Curll's Key will be found occasionally quoted in the notes) and commentaries, issued by Pope to increase the notoriety of his work. On no occasion was he so thoroughly in his glory, and his glory was a wasp's nest which he had himself agitated into uncontrollable fury.

. As the *Dunciad* stands, it has a unity, notwithstanding the fact that its fourth book was added at a later date. This book represents the fulfilment of the prophecy of its predecessor; fulfilment and prophecy being of course equally imaginary. It cannot be disputed that the whole poem was marred by the author to gratify his spleen against the Laureate. Cibber's *Apology for his Life* is too well known a book to make it necessary to point out why he is an inappropriate hero for a Satire on Dulness. It is indeed full of vanity and egotism; but at the same time distinguished by vivacity throughout, and in many passages by really skilful pleading. He is a play-writer not only of uncommon skill, but of genuine though not very deep humour; and the tastes to which he occasionally pandered as manager of Drury Lane were those of the times, which he could hardly be expected to control. He adapted Shakspere so successfully that his ' improvements ' were retained by Garrick, and still in one tragedy at least are universally followed on the stage; and at all events in this respect he sinned no worse than Sheffield, Duke of Buckinghamshire, and a hundred others. (Cibber was born in 1671 and died in 1757; and his career as an author extends over not less than half a century.) But neither Cibber nor Theobald could more than represent extreme specimens of the genus to which in some degree they both belonged; they were merely brought into prominence as *primi inter pares.* Not an individual Dunce, but Dunces in general, are the theme of the poet. Herein lies the justification of Pope's Satire. It has frequently been argued that in the *Dunciad* he employs his satirical powers, intensified to their utmost degree, against objects undeserving of so serious an attack. He goes back, says a brilliant critic,[1] to the times of the deluge, he indulges in far-fetched historical tirades, he describes at length the reign of Dulness past, present and future, the burning of the Alexandria library by the Caliph Omar, the extinction of letters by the invasion of the barbarians and the superstitions of the Middle Ages, and the gradual spread and continuing encroachments of the reign of Insipidity in his own land — and for what end? To crush a petty insect like Dennis, whose day, like that of all *ephemeræ*, would have come to an end soon enough in any case, or a plodding antiquary like Theobald, or a

[1] Taine.

trumpery fribble like Cibber, or many others less noteworthy, and therefore less worthy of public exposure, than even these. The answer to such reproaches seems clear. Where Pope mixed up personal spleen, personal resentment for affronts real or imagined, with the execution of his self-imposed duty of general literary censor, he erred, and his error has avenged itself upon him severely enough. But Dulness was an enemy worthy of his steel. She is the natural foe of the true literary mind, and the true literary mind was typified in Pope more strongly than perhaps in any other English author. His hatred and contempt of Dulness is the most prominent characteristic of his entire career as an author. She is a monster with many heads, or apologies for heads, and many hands, with a pen in each. It was of little avail to cut off a single head, after the fashion of Dryden. *Uno avulso non deficit alter.* A crusade against the whole tribe was necessary to satisfy Pope's heroic indignation against the irrepressible enemy of all that he honoured in the microcosm which to him was his world — in the world of literature. The storm which Pope's effort created was of course unable to put an end to the tribe; and the Philistines of literature survived in the ashes of their sires. But Pope's Satire cleared the atmosphere; and his victims and their successors have never entirely recovered from its effects.

In the fourth book Pope, instigated by the influence of Warburton, carried the war into another field. The Dunces of philosophy and theology were indeed, and are, as fair game for the satirist as poetasters, mad antiquaries, and party-paid historians. Moreover, the 'cant of liberalism' which prevailed in the age of Bolingbroke, deserved the lash no less than the cant of orthodoxy which prevailed in the age of Warburton. But while literary imbecility and pretension were patent to the keen glance of Pope's own intellect, in questions as to matters such as those upon which he touches in the fourth book, he was too apt to judge and sentence imperfect knowledge, or at best second-hand information; and the fourth book, though it contains passages of genuine nobility and true elevation of feeling, is unhappily not devoid of misrepresentations and perversions of which the root is to be found in ignorance rather than malice. 'I mean this new edition of the *Dunciad*' (containing the fourth book), writes Pope to Warburton, Nov. 27th, 1742, 'as a kind of prelude or advertisement to the public, of your Commentaries on the *Essays on Man*, and on *Criticism.* . . . I have a particular reason to make you interest yourself in me and my writings. It will cause both them and me to make the better figure to posterity.' Posterity has judged otherwise. Dennis, Theobald and Cibber were Pope's own adversaries; but the divines and philosophers whom in the fourth book he has held up to scorn will not permanently be judged according to the canons set up by the moral assessor of Pope's later years.]

PREFACE

Prefixed to the five first imperfect Editions of the DUNCIAD, in three books, printed at DUBLIN and LONDON, in octavo and duodecimo, 1727.

The PUBLISHER[1] to the READER.

IT will be found a true observation, tho' somewhat surprizing, that when any scandal is vented against a man of the highest distinction and character, either in the state or in literature, the public in general afford it a most quiet reception; and the larger part accept it as favourably as if it were some kindness done to themselves: whereas if a known scoundrel or blockhead but chance to be touched upon, a whole legion is up in arms, and it becomes the common cause of all scribblers, booksellers, and printers whatsoever.

Not to search too deeply into the reason hereof, I will only observe as a fact, that every week for these two months past, the town has been persecuted with pamphlets, advertisements, letters, and weekly essays, not only against the wit and writings, but against the character and person of Mr. Pope. And that of all those men who have received pleasure from his works, which by modest computation may be about a hundred thousand[2] in these kingdoms of England and Ire-

---

[1] *The Publisher*] Who he was is uncertain; but Edward Ward tells us, in his preface to Durgen, "that most judges are of opinion this "preface is not of English extraction, but Hi- "bernian," &c. He means it was written by Dr. Swift, who, whether publisher or not, may be said in a sort to be author of the poem. For when he, together with Mr. Pope (for reasons specified in the preface to their Miscellanies) determined to own the most trifling pieces in which they had any hand, and to destroy all that remained in their power; the first sketch of this poem was snatched from the fire by Dr. Swift, who persuaded his friend to proceed in it, and to him it was therefore inscribed. But the occasion of printing it was as follows:

There was published in those Miscellanies a treatise of the Bathos, or Art of Sinking in Poetry, in which was a chapter, where the species of bad writers were ranged in classes, and initial letters of names prefixed, for the most part at random. But such was the Number of Poets eminent in that art, that some one or other took every letter to himself. All fell into so violent a fury, that for half a year, or more, the common Newspapers (in most of which they had some property, as being hired writers) were filled with the most abusive falsehoods and scurrilities they could possibly devise; a liberty no ways to be wondered at in those people, and in those papers, that for many years, during the

uncontrolled Licence of the press, had aspersed almost all the great characters of the age; and this with impunity, their own persons and names being utterly secret and obscure. This gave Mr. Pope the thought, that he had now some opportunity of doing good, by detecting and dragging into light these common Enemies of mankind; since to invalidate this universal slander, it sufficed to shew what contemptible men were the authors of it. He was not without hopes, that by manifesting the dulness of those who had only malice to recommend them; either the booksellers would not find their account in employing them, or the men themselves, when discovered, want courage to proceed in so unlawful an occupation. This it was that gave birth to the *Dunciad;* and he thought it an happiness, that, by the late flood of slander on himself, he had acquired such a peculiar right over their Names as was necessary to his design. P.

[2] *about a hundred thousand*] It is surprising with what stupidity this preface, which is almost a continued irony, was taken by those authors. All such passages as these were understood by Curl, Cook, Cibber, and others, to be serious. Hear the Laureate (Letter to Mr. Pope, p. 9). "Though I grant the *Dunciad* a "better poem of its kind than ever was writ; "yet, when I read it with those *vain-glorious* "encumbrances of Notes and Remarks upon it, "&c., it is amazing, that you, who have writ

land; (not to mention Jersey Guernsey, the Orcades, those in the new world and foreigners, who have translated him into their languages) of all this number not a man hath stood up to say one word in his defence.

The only exception is the author of the following poem,[1] who doubtless had either a better insight into the grounds of this clamour, or a better opinion of Mr. Pope's integrity, joined with a greater personal love for him, than any other of his numerous friends and admirers.

Farther, that he was in his peculiar intimacy, appears from the knowledge he manifests of the most private authors of all the anonymous pieces against him, and from his having in this poem attacked no man living,[2] who had not before printed, or published, some scandal against this gentleman.

How I came possest of it, is no concern to the reader; but it would have been a wrong to him had I detained the publication; since those names which are its chief ornaments die off daily so fast, as must render it too soon unintelligible. If it provoke the author to give us a more perfect edition, I have my end.

Who he is I cannot say, and (which is a great pity) there is certainly nothing in his style[3] and manner of writing, which can distinguish or discover him: For if it bears any resemblance to that of Mr. Pope, 't is not improbable but it might be done on purpose, with a view to have it pass for his. But by the frequency of his allusions to Virgil, and a laboured (not to say affected) *shortness* in imitation of him, I should think him more an admirer of the Roman poet than of the Grecian, and in that not of the same taste with his friend.

I have been well informed, that this work was the labour of full six years[4] of his life, and that he wholly retired himself from all the avocations and pleasures of the world, to attend diligently to its correction and perfection; and six years more he intended to bestow upon it, as it should seem by this verse of Statius,[5] which was cited at the head of his manuscript,

> *Oh mihi bissenos multum vigilata per annos,*
> *Duncia!*

Hence also we learned the true title of the poem; which with the same certainty as we call that of Homer the Iliad, of Virgil the Æneid, of Camoens the Lusiad, we may pronounce, could have been, and can be no other than

The DUNCIAD.

It is styled *Heroic*, as being *doubly* so; not only with respect to its nature, which, according to the best rules of the ancients, and strictest ideas of the mod-

---

" with such masterly spirit upon the ruling " Passion, should be so blind a slave to your " own, as not to see how far *a low avarice of* " *Praise*," &c. (taking it for granted that the notes of Scriblerus and others, were the authors' own). P.

[1] *the author of the following poem, &c.*] A very plain irony, speaking of Mr. Pope himself. P.

[2] The publisher in these words went a little too far; but it is certain, whatever names the reader finds that are unknown to him, are of such; and the exception is only of two or three, whose dulness, impudent scurrility, or self-conceit, all mankind agreed to have justly entitled them to a place in the *Dunciad*. P.

[3] *there is certainly nothing in his style, &c.*] This irony had small effect in concealing the author. The Dunciad, imperfect as it was, had not been published two days, but the whole Town gave it to Mr. Pope. P.

[4] *the labour of full six years, &c.*] This was also honestly and seriously believed by divers gentlemen of the Dunciad. P.

[5] [*Theb.* lib. XII. v. 810.]

erns, is critically such; but also with regard to the heroical disposition and high courage of the writer, who dared to stir up such a formidable, irritable, and implacable race of mortals.

There may arise some obscurity in chronology from the *Names* in the poem, by the inevitable removal of some authors, and insertion of others, in their niches. For whoever will consider the unity of the whole design will be sensible, that the *poem was not made for these authors, but these authors for the poem.* I should judge that they were clapped in as they rose, fresh and fresh, and changed from day to day; in like manner as when the old boughs wither, we thrust new ones into a chimney.

I would not have the reader too much troubled or anxious, if he cannot decipher them; since when he shall have found them out, he will probably know no more of the persons than before.

Yet we judged it better to preserve them as they are, than to change them for fictitious names; by which the satire would only be multiplied, and applied to many instead of one. Had the hero, for instance, been called Codrus,[1] how many would have affirmed him to have been Mr. T., Mr. E., Sir R. B. &c. but now all that unjust scandal is saved by calling him by a name, which by good luck happens to be that of a real person.

ADVERTISEMENT

To the FIRST EDITION with Notes, in Quarto, 1729.

IT will be sufficient to say of this edition, that the reader has here a much more correct and complete copy of the DUNCIAD, than has hitherto appeared. I cannot answer but some mistakes may have slipt into it; but a vast number of others will be prevented by the names being now not only set at length, but justified by the authorities and reasons given. I make no doubt, the author's own motive to use real rather than feigned names, was his care to preserve the innocent from any false application; whereas in the former editions, which had no more than the initial letters, he was made, by keys printed here, to hurt the inoffensive; and (what was worse) to abuse his friends, by an impression at Dublin.

The commentary which attends this poem was sent me from several hands, and consequently must be unequally written; yet will have one advantage over most commentaries, that it is not made upon conjectures, or at a remote distance of time: And the reader cannot but derive one pleasure from the very *Obscurity* of the persons it treats of, that it partakes of the nature of a *Secret*, which most people love to be let into, though the men or the things be ever so inconsiderable or trivial.

Of the *Persons* it was judged proper to give some account: For since it is only in this monument that they must expect to survive (and here survive they will, as long as the English tongue shall remain such as it was in the reigns of Queen ANNE and King GEORGE) it seemed but humanity to bestow a word or two upon each, just to tell what he was, what he writ, when he lived, and when he died.

If a word or two more are added upon the chief offenders, 'tis only as a paper pinned upon the breast, to mark the enormities for which they suffered; lest the correction only should be remembered, and the crime forgotten.

In some articles it was thought sufficient, barely to transcribe from Jacob, Curl, and other writers of their own rank, who were much better acquainted with them than any of the authors of this comment can pretend to be. Most of them had drawn each other's

---

[1] [Codrus, a name taken from Juvenal, was the designation under which Pope at an early age satirised Settle. See *To the author of a* *Poem entitled Successio;* in *Miscellaneous Poems.*]

characters on certain occasions; but the few here inserted are all that could be saved from the general destruction of such works.

Of the part of Scriblerus I need say nothing; his manner is well enough known, and approved by all but those who are too much concerned to be judges.

The Imitations of the Ancients are added, to gratify those who either never read, or may have forgotten them; together with some of the parodies and allusions to the most excellent of the Moderns. If, from the frequency of the former, any man think the poem too much a Cento,[1] our Poet will but appear to have done the same thing in jest which Boileau did in earnest; and upon which Vida, Fracastorius, and many of the most eminent Latin poets, professedly valued themselves.

A LETTER TO THE PUBLISHER,

FIRST CORRECT EDITION OF THE DUNCIAD.

IT is with pleasure I hear, that you have procured a correct copy of the DUNCIAD, which the many surreptitious ones have rendered so necessary; and it is yet with more, that I am informed it will be attended with a COMMENTARY: a Work so requisite, that I cannot think the Author himself would have omitted it, had he approved of the first appearance of this Poem.

Such *Notes* as have occurred to me, I herewith send you: you will oblige me by inserting them amongst those which are, or will be, transmitted to you by others; since not only the Author's friends, but even strangers, appear engaged by humanity, to take some care of an Orphan of so much genius and spirit, which its parent seems to have abandoned from the very beginning, and suffered to step into the world naked, unguarded, and unattended.

It was upon reading some of the abusive papers lately published, that my great regard to a Person, whose Friendship I esteem as one of the chief honours of my life, and a much greater respect to Truth, than to him or any man living, engaged me in enquiries, of which the inclosed *Notes* are the fruit.

I perceived, that most of these authors had been (doubtless very wisely) the first aggressors. They had tried, 'till they were weary, what was to be got by railing at each other: Nobody was either concerned or surprised, if this or that scribbler was proved a dunce. But every one was curious to read what could be said to prove Mr. POPE one, and was ready to pay something for such a discovery: A stratagem, which would they fairly own, it might not only reconcile them to me, but screen them from the resentment of their lawful Superiors, whom they daily abuse, only (as I charitably hope) to get that *by* them, which they cannot get *from* them.

I found this was not all: Ill success in that had transported them to Personal abuse, either of himself, or (what I think he could less forgive) of his Friends. They had called Men of virtue and honour bad Men, long before he had either leisure or inclination to call them bad Writers: and some had been such old offenders, that he had quite forgotten their persons as well as their slanders, 'till they were pleased to revive them.

Now what had Mr. POPE done before, to incense them? He had published those works which are in the hands of everybody, in which not the least mention is made of any of them. And what has he done since? He has laughed, and written the DUNCIAD. What has that said of them? A very serious truth, which the public had said before, that they were dull: and what it had no sooner said, but they themselves were at great pains to procure or even purchase room in the prints, to testify under their hands to the truth of it.

I should still have been silent, if either I had seen any inclination in my friend to be serious with such accusers, or if they had only meddled with his Writings; since whoever publishes, puts himself on his trial by his Country. But when his Moral character was attacked, and in a manner from which neither truth nor virtue can secure the most innocent, — in a manner, which, though it annihilates the credit of the accusation with

---

[1] [A *cento* is defined by Johnson as 'a composition formed by joining scraps from other authors.']

the just and impartial, yet aggravates very much the guilt of the accusers; I mean by Authors *without names:* then I thought, since the danger was common to all, the concern ought to be so; and that it was an act of justice to detect the Authors, not only on this account, but as many of them are the same who for several years past have made free with the greatest names in Church and State, exposed to the world the private misfortunes of Families, abused all, even to Women, and whose prostituted papers (for one or other party, in the unhappy divisions of their Country) have insulted the Fallen, the Friendless, the Exiled, and the Dead.

Besides this, which I take to be a public concern, I have already confessed I had a private one. I am one of that number who have long loved and esteemed Mr. POPE; and had often declared it was not his capacity or writings (which we ever thought the least valuable part of his character), but the honest, open, and beneficent man, that we most esteemed, and loved in him. Now, if what these people say were believed, I must appear to all my friends either a fool, or a knave; either imposed on myself, or imposing on them; so that I am as much interested in the confutation of these calumnies, as he is himself.

I am no Author, and consequently not to be suspected either of jealousy or resentment against any of the Men, of whom scarce one is known to me by sight; and as for their Writings, I have sought them (on this one occasion) in vain, in the closets and libraries of all my acquaintance. I had still been in the dark, if a Gentleman had not procured me (I suppose from some of themselves, for they are generally much more dangerous friends than enemies) the passages I send you. I solemnly protest I have added nothing to the malice or absurdity of them; which it behoves me to declare, since the vouchers themselves will be so soon and so irrecoverably lost. You may in some measure prevent it, by preserving at least their Titles,[1] and discovering (as far as you can depend on the truth of your information) the Names of the concealed authors.

The first objection I have heard made to the Poem is, that the persons are too *obscure* for satire. The persons themselves, rather than allow the objection, would forgive the satire; and if one could be tempted to afford it a serious answer, were not all assassinates, popular insurrections, the insolence of the rabble without doors, and of domestics within, most wrongfully chastised, if the Meanness of offenders indemnified them from punishment? On the contrary, Obscurity renders them more dangerous, as less thought of; Law can pronounce judgment only on open facts; Morality alone can pass censure on intentions of mischief; so that for secret calumny, or the arrow flying in the dark, there is no public punishment left, but what a good Writer inflicts.

The next objection is, that these sort of authors are *poor.* That might be pleaded as an excuse at the Old Bailey, for lesser crimes than Defamation (for 't is the case of almost all who are tried there); but sure it can be none: for who will pretend that the robbing another of his Reputation supplies the want of it in himself? I question not but such authors are poor, and heartily wish the objection were removed by any honest livelihood. But Poverty is here the accident, not the subject: He who describes Malice and Villainy to be pale and meagre, expresses not the least anger against Paleness or Leanness, but against Malice and Villainy. The Apothecary in *Romeo and Juliet* is poor; but is he therefore justified in vending poison? Not but Poverty itself becomes a just subject of satire, when it is the consequence of vice, prodigality, or neglect of one's lawful calling; for then it increases the public burden, fills the streets and highways with Robbers, and the garrets with Clippers, Coiners, and Weekly Journalists.

But admitting that two or three of these offend less in their morals, than in their writings: must Poverty make nonsense sacred? If so, the fame of bad authors would be much better consulted than that of all the good ones in the world; and not one of an hundred had ever been called by his right name.

They mistake the whole matter: It is not charity to encourage them in the way they follow, but to get them out of it; for men are not bunglers because they are poor, but they are poor because they are bunglers.

Is it not pleasant enough to hear our authors crying out on the one hand, as if their persons and characters were too sacred for Satire; and the public objection on the other, that they are too mean even for Ridicule? But whether Bread or Fame be their end, it must be allowed, our Author, by and in this Poem, has mercifully given them a little of both.

---

[1] Which we have done in a List printed in the Appendix. P.

There are two or three, who by their rank and fortune have no benefit from the former objections, supposing them good, and these I was sorry to see in such company. But if, without any provocation, two or three Gentlemen will fall upon one, in an affair wherein his interest and reputation are equally embarked; they cannot certainly, after they have been content to print themselves his enemies, complain of being put into the number of them.

Others, I am told, pretend to have been once his Friends. Surely they are their enemies who say so, since nothing can be more odious than to treat a friend as they have done. But of this I cannot persuade myself, when I consider the constant and eternal aversion of all bad writers to a good one.

Such as claim a merit from being his Admirers I would gladly ask, if it lays him under a personal obligation? At that rate he would be the most obliged humble servant in the world. I dare swear for these in particular, he never desired them to be his admirers, nor promised in return to be theirs. That had truly been a sign he was of their acquaintance; but would not the malicious world have suspected such an approbation of some motive worse than ignorance, in the author of the *Essay on Criticism?* Be it as it will, the reasons of their Admiration and of his Contempt are equally subsisting; for his works and theirs are the very same that they were.

One, therefore, of their assertions, I believe may be true: "That he has a contempt for their writings." And there is another, which would probably be sooner allowed by himself than by any good judge beside: "That his own have found too much success with the public." But as it cannot consist with his modesty to claim this as a justice, it lies not on him, but entirely on the public, to defend its own judgment.

There remains what in my opinion might seem a better plea for these people, than any they have made use of. If Obscurity or Poverty were to exempt a man from satire, much more should Folly or Dulness, which are still more involuntary; nay, as much so as personal Deformity. But even this will not help them : Deformity becomes an object of Ridicule when a man sets up for being handsome; and so must Dulness when he sets up for a Wit. They are not ridiculed, because Ridicule in itself is, or ought to be, a pleasure; but because it is just to undeceive and vindicate the honest and unpretending part of mankind from imposition; because particular interest ought to yield to general, and a great number, who are not naturally Fools, ought never to be made so, in complaisance to a few who are. Accordingly we find that in all ages, all vain pretenders, were they ever so poor or ever so dull, have been constantly the topics of the most candid satirists, from the Codrus of JUVENAL to the Damon of BOILEAU.[1]

Having mentioned BOILEAU, the greatest Poet and most judicious Critic of his age and country, admirable for his Talents, and yet perhaps more admirable for his Judgment in the proper application of them ; I cannot help remarking the resemblance betwixt him and our Author, in Qualities, Fame, and Fortune ; in the distinctions shewn them by their Superiors, in the general esteem of their Equals, and in their extended reputation amongst Foreigners ; in the latter of which ours has met with the better fate, as he has had for his Translators persons of the most eminent rank and abilities in their respective nations.[2] But the resemblance holds in nothing more, than in their being equally abused by the ignorant pretenders to Poetry of their times ; of which not the least memory will remain but in their own Writings, and in the Notes made upon them. What BOILEAU has done in almost all his poems, our Author has only in this : I dare answer for him he will do it in no more ; and on this principle, of attacking few but who had slandered him, he could not have done it at all, had he been confined from censuring obscure and worthless persons, for scarce any other were his enemies. However, as the parity is so remarkable, I hope it will continue to the last ; and if ever he shall give us an edition of this Poem himself, I may see some of them

---

[1] [Juv. *Sat.* I. & III.; Boileau *Sat.* I.]

[2] Essay on Criticism, in French verse, by General Hamilton; the same, in verse also, by Monsieur Roboton, Counsellor and Privy Secretary to King George I. after by the Abbé Reynel, in verse, with notes. Rape of the Lock, in French, by the Princess of Conti, Paris, 1728, and in Italian verse, by the Abbé Conti a Noble Venetian; and by the Marquis Rangoni, Envoy Extraordinary from Modena to King George II. Others of his works by Salvini of Florence, &c. His Essays and Dissertations on Homer, several times translated in French. Essay on Man, by the Abbé Reynel, in verse, by Monsieur Silhouet, in prose, 1737, and since by others in French, Italian, and Latin. P.

treated as gently, on their repentance or better merit, as Perrault and Quinault [1] were at last by BOILEAU.

In one point I must be allowed to think the character of our English Poet the more amiable. He has not been a follower of Fortune or Success; he has lived with the Great without flattery; been a friend to Men in power without pensions; from whom, as he asked, so he received no favour, but what was done Him in his Friends. As his Satires were the more just for being delayed, so were his Panegyrics; bestowed only on such persons as he had familiarly known, only for such virtues as he had long observed in them, and only at such times as others cease to praise, if not begin to calumniate them, — I mean when out of power or out of fashion.[2] A satire, therefore, on writers so notorious for the contrary practice, became no man so well as himself; as none, it is plain, was so little in their friendships, or so much in that of those whom they had most abused, namely the Greatest and Best of all Parties. Let me add a further reason, that, tho' engaged in their Friendships, he never espoused their Animosities; and can almost singly challenge this honour, not to have written a line of any man, which, through Guilt, through Shame, or through Fear, through variety of Fortune, or change of Interests, he was ever unwilling to own.

I shall conclude with remarking what a pleasure it must be to every reader of Humanity, to see all along, that our Author in his very laughter is not indulging his own ill-nature; but only punishing that of others. As to his Poem, those alone are capable of doing it justice, who, to use the words of a great writer,[3] know how hard it is (with regard both to his subject and his manner) VETUSTIS DARE NOVITATEM, OBSOLETIS NITOREM, OBSCURIS LUCEM, FASTIDITIS GRATIAM. I am

Your most humble servant,

St. James's,
Dec. 22, 1728. WILLIAM CLELAND.[4]

ADVERTISEMENT

To the First Edition of the Fourth Book of the DUNCIAD, when printed separately in the Year 1742.

WE apprehend it can be deemed no injury to the author of the three first books of the *Dunciad*, that we publish this Fourth. It was found merely by accident, in taking a survey of the *Library* of a late eminent nobleman; but in so blotted a condition, and in so many detached pieces, as plainly shewed it not only to be *incorrect*, but *unfinished*. That the author of the three first books had a design to extend and complete his poem in this manner, appears from the dissertation prefixed to it, where it is said, that *the design is more extensive, and that we may expect other episodes to complete it:*

[1] [Perrault, an academician and author of erotic poetry and of *Parallèles des Anciens et Modernes,* was attacked by Boileau in his ixth and xth Satires, and in several epigrams; Quinault, a more famous (dramatic) poet, in the earlier Satires. To the former Boileau became reconciled in 1700 (see his *Lettre à M. Perrault*); his reconciliation with the latter was very incomplete. See the allusion in the *Art Poétique,* ch. 1. v. 222 f.]

[2] As Mr. Wycherley, at the time the Town declaimed against his book of Poems; Mr. Walsh, after his death; Sir William Trumbull, when he had resigned the office of Secretary of State; Lord Bolingbroke, at his leaving England after the Queen's death; Lord Oxford, in his last decline of life; Mr. Secretary Craggs, at the end of the South Sea year, and after his death: others only in Epitaphs. P.

[3] Pliny, in *Hist. Nat., ad in.* § 15.

[4] This Gentleman was of Scotland, and bred at the University of Utrecht, with the Earl of Mar. He served in Spain under Earl Rivers. After the Peace, he was made one of the Commissioners of the Customs in Scotland, and then of Taxes in England, in which having shewn himself for twenty years diligent, punctual, and incorruptible, though without any other assistance of Fortune, he was suddenly displaced by the Minister in the sixty eighth year of his age; and died two months after, in 1741. He was a person of Universal Learning, and an enlarged Conversation; no man had a warmer heart for his Friend, or a sincerer attachment to the Constitution of his Country. P. — And yet for all this, the Public will not allow him to be the author of this Letter. *Warburton.*

and from the declaration in the argument to the third book, that *the accomplishment of the prophesies therein, would be the theme hereafter of a greater Dunciad.* But whether or no he be the author of this, we declare ourselves ignorant. If he be, we are no more to be blamed for the publication of it, than Tucca and Varius for that of the last six books of the *Æneid,* tho' perhaps inferior to the former.[1]

If any person be possessed of a more perfect copy of this work, or of any other fragments of it, and will communicate them to the publisher, we shall make the next edition more complete: In which we also promise to insert any *Criticisms* that shall be published (if at all to the purpose) with the *Names* of the *Authors;* or any letters sent us (though not to the purpose) shall yet be printed under the title of *Epistolæ Obscurorum Virorum;*[2] which, together with some others of the same kind formerly laid by for that end, may make no unpleasant addition to the future impressions of this poem.

ADVERTISEMENT

To the complete EDITION of 1743.

I HAVE long had a design of giving some sort of Notes on the works of this poet. Before I had the happiness of his acquaintance, I had written a commentary on his *Essay on Man,* and have since finished another on the *Essay on Criticism.* There was one already on the *Dunciad,* which had met with general approbation; but I still thought some additions were wanting (of a more serious kind) to the humourous notes of *Scriblerus,* and even to those written by Mr. *Cleland,* Dr. *Arbuthnot,* and others. I had lately the pleasure to pass some months with the author in the country, where I prevailed upon him to do what I had long desired, and favour me with his explanation of several passages in his works. It happened, that just at that juncture was published a ridiculous book against him, full of Personal Reflections, which furnished him with a lucky opportunity of improving *This Poem,* by giving it the only thing it wanted, a *more considerable Hero.* He was always sensible of its defect in that particular, and owned he had let it pass with the Hero it had, purely for want of a better; not entertaining the least expectation that such an one was reserved for this Post, as has since obtained the *Laurel:* But since that had happened, he could no longer deny this justice either to *him* or the *Dunciad.*

And yet I will venture to say, there was another motive which had still more weight with our Author: This person was one, who from every Folly (not to say Vice) of which another would be ashamed, has constantly derived a *Vanity;* and therefore was the *man in the world who would least be hurt by it. Warburton.*

ADVERTISEMENT.[3]

Printed in the JOURNALS, 1730.

WHEREAS, upon occasion of certain Pieces relating to the Gentlemen of the *Dunciad,* some have been willing to suggest, as if they looked upon them as an *abuse:* we can do no less than own, it is our opinion, that to call these Gentlemen *bad authors* is no sort of *abuse,* but a great *truth.* We cannot alter this opinion without some reason; but we promise to do it in respect to every person who thinks it an injury to be represented as no *Wit,* or *Poet,* provided he procures a Certificate of his being really such, from any *three of his companions* in the *Dunciad,* or from Mr. *Dennis singly,* who is esteemed equal to any three of the number.

---

[1] [According to Donatus, Vergil left to his friends Varius and Tucca (who had prevented him from burning the *Æneid*), his works, on condition that they should not introduce any emendations of their own. Augustus bade them interpret the proviso thus; that they might emend their author by omissions, but not by additions.]

[2] [This title is of course borrowed from that of the famous attacks on the schoolmen, in which Ulrich von Hutten took the most prominent part.]

[3] Taken from the *Grub-street Journal,* but printed with such variations as evidently shew a wish to conceal its origin. *Carruthers.*

MARTINUS SCRIBLERUS.

Of the POEM.

THIS poem, as it celebrateth the most grave and ancient of things, Chaos, Night, and Dulness; so is it of the most grave and ancient kind. Homer (saith Aristotle) was the first who gave the *Form*, and (saith Horace) who adapted the *Measure*, to heroic poesy. But, even before this, may be rationally presumed from what the Ancients have left written, was a piece by Homer composed, of like nature and matter with this of our poet. For of Epic sort it appeareth to have been, yet of matter surely not unpleasant, witness what is reported of it by the learned archbishop Eustathius, in *Odyss.* x. And accordingly Aristotle, in his *Poetic*, chap. iv., doth further set forth, that as the *Iliad* and *Odyssey* gave example to Tragedy, so did this poem to Comedy its first idea.

From these authors also it should seem, that the Hero, or chief personage of it was no less *obscure*, and his understanding and sentiments no less quaint and strange (if indeed not more so) than any of the actors of our poem. MARGITES was the name of this personage, whom Antiquity recordeth to have been *Dunce the first;* and surely, from what we hear of him, not unworthy to be the root of so spreading a tree, and so numerous a posterity. The poem, therefore, celebrating him was properly and absolutely a *Dunciad;* which though now unhappily lost, yet is its nature sufficiently known by the infallible tokens aforesaid. And thus it doth appear, that the first *Dunciad* was the first Epic poem, written by Homer himself, and anterior even to the *Iliad* or *Odyssey*.[1]

Now, forasmuch as our poet had translated those two famous works of Homer which are yet left, he did conceive it in some sort his duty to imitate that also which was lost: and was therefore induced to bestow on it the same form which Homer's is reported to have had, namely that of Epic poem: with a title also framed after the ancient Greek manner, to wit, that of *Dunciad*.

Wonderful it is, that so few of the moderns have been stimulated to attempt some *Dunciad!* since, in the opinion of the multitude, it might cost less pain and oil than an imitation of the greater Epic. But possible it is also, that, on due reflection, the maker might find it easier to paint a Charlemagne, a Brute,[2] or a Godfrey,[3] with just pomp and dignity heroic, than a Margites, a Codrus,[4] or a Flecknoe.

We shall next declare the occasion and the cause which moved our poet to this particular work. He lived in those days, when (after providence had permitted the invention of Printing as a scourge for the sins of the learned) Paper also became so cheap, and Printers so numerous, that a deluge of Authors covered the land: Whereby, not only the peace of the honest unwriting subject was daily molested, but unmerciful demands were made of his applause, yea of his money, by such as would neither earn the one, nor deserve the other. At the same time, the licence of the Press was such, that it grew dangerous to refuse them either; for they would forthwith publish slanders unpunished, the authors being anonymous, and skulking under the wings of Publishers, a set of men who never scrupled to vend either Calumny or Blasphemy, as long as the Town would call for it.

[5] Now our author, living in those times, did conceive it an endeavour well worthy an honest Satirist, to dissuade the dull, and punish the wicked, *the only way that was left.*

---

[1] [The *Margites* is ascribed to Homer by Aristotle (*Poet.* c. iv.), and stated to hold the same relation to comedy, that the *Iliad* and *Odyssey* hold to tragedy. K. O. Müller thinks that the iambic verses introduced into it were interpolated in a later version; and states that 'from the few fragments and notices relative to the poem which have come down to us, we can gather that it was a representation of a stupid man, who had a high opinion of his own cleverness, for he was said, 'to know many works, but know all badly.' The following is an attempt at rendering the beginning of the *M.:*

'Once to Colophon came an ancient and heavenly singer,

Votary he of the Muses and of far-darting Apollo,

And in his hands he held a well-tuned lyre.']

[2] [The fabulous King of Britain, the hero of Wace's and Layamon's poems.]

[3] [Godfrey of Bouillon, the hero of Tasso's *Jerusalem Delivered.*]

[4] [See *Ep. to Arbuthnot*, v. 85.]

[5] Vide Bossu, *Du Poëme Epique*, ch. VIII.

In that public-spirited view he la d the plan of his Poem, as the greatest service he was capable (without much hurt, or being slain) to render his dear country. First, taking things from their original, he co=sidereth the Causes creative of such Authors, namely *Dulness* and *Poverty;* the one born with them, the other contracted by neglect of their proper talents, through self-conzeit of greater abilities. This truth he wrappeth in an *Allegory*[1] (as the construction of Epic poesy requireth) and feigns that one of these Goddesses had taken up her abode with the other, and that they jointly inspired all such writers and such works. He proceedeth[2] to shew the *qualities* they bestow on these authors, and the *effects* they produce:[3] then the *materials*, or *stock* with which they furnish them;[4] and (above all) that *self-opinion*[5] which causeth it to seem to themselves vastly greater than it is, and is the prime motive of their setting up in this sad and sorry merchandise. The great power of these Goddesses acting in alliance (whereof as the one is the mother of Industry, so is the other of Plodding), was to be exemplified in some *one, great* and *remarkable Action :*[6] and none could be more so than that which our poet hath chosen, *viz.* the restoration of the reign of Chaos and Night, by the ministry of Dulness their Daughter, in the removal of her imperial seat from the City to the polite World; as the Action of the Æneid is the restoration of the empire of Troy, by the removal of the race from thence to Latium. But as Homer singing only the *Wrath* of Achilles, yet includes in his poem the whole history of the Trojan war; in like manner our author hath drawn into this *single Action* the whole history of Dulness and her children.

A *Person* must next be fixed upon to support this Action. This *Phantom* in the poet's mind must have a *Name :*[7] He finds it to be ——; and he becomes of course the Hero of the Poem.

The *Fable* being thus, according to the best Example, one and entire, as contained in the Proposition; the *Machinery* is a continued chain of Allegories, setting forth the whole Power, Ministry, and Empire of Dulness, extended through her subordinate instruments, in all her various operations.

This is branched into *Episodes*, each of which hath its Moral apart, though all conducive to the main end. The Crowd assembled in the second book demonstrates the design to be more extensive than to bad poets only, and that we may expect other Episodes of the Patrons, Encouragers, or Paymasters of such authors, as occasion shall bring them forth. And the third book, if well considered, seemeth to embrace the whole World. Each of the Games relateth to some or other vile class of writers: The first concerneth the Plagiary, to whom he giveth the name of Moore; the second, the libellous Novelist, whom he stylet Eliza; the third, the flattering Dedicator; the fourth, the bawling Critic, or noisy Poet; the fifth, the dark and dirty Party-writer; and so of the rest; assigning to each some *proper name* or other, such as he could find.

As for the *Characters*, the public hath already acknowledged how justly they are drawn: the manners are so depicted, and the sentiments so peculiar to those to whom applied, that surely to transfer them to any other or wiser personages would be exceeding difficult: and certain it is that every person concerned, being consulted apart, hath readily owned the resemblance of every portrait, his own excepted. So Mr. Cibber calls them, "a parcel of *poor wretches*, so many *silly flies :*[8] but adds, our Author's Wit is remarkably more bare and barren, whenever it would fall foul on *Cibber*, than upon any other Person whatever."

The *Descriptions* are singular, the *Comparisons* very quaint, the *Narration* various, yet of one colour: The purity and chastity of *Diction* is so preserved, that in the places most suspicious not the *words* but only the *images* have been censured, and yet are those images no other than have been sanctified by ancient and classical Authority (though, as was the manner of those good times, not so curiously wrapped up), yea, and commented upon by the most grave Doctors, and approved Critics.

As it beareth the name of *Epic*, it is thereby subjected to such severe indispensable rules as are laid on all Neoterics, a strict imitation of the Ancients; insomuch that any deviation, accompanied with whatever poetic beauties, hath always been censured

[1] Bossu, chap. VII.
[2] Book I. v. 32, &c.
[3] Ver. 45 to 54.
[4] Ver. 57 to 77.
[5] Ver. 80.

[6] Bossu, chap. VII, VIII.
[7] Ibid. chap. VIII. Vide Aristot. *Poetic,* cap. IX.
[8] Cibber's *Letter to Mr. P.* pp. 7, 9, &c.

by the sound Critic. How exact that Imitation hath been in this piece, appeareth not only by its general structure, but by particular allusions infinite, many whereof have escaped both the commentator and poet himself; yea divers by his exceeding diligence are so altered and interwoven with the rest, that several have already been, and more will be, by the ignorant abused, as altogether and originally his own.

In a word, the whole poem proveth itself to be the work of our Author, when his faculties were in full vigour and perfection; at that exact time when years have ripened the Judgment, without diminishing the Imagination: which, by good Critics, is held to be punctually at *forty.* For, at that season it was that Virgil finished his *Georgics;* and Sir Richard Blackmore, at the like age composing his *Arthurs,* declared the same to be the very *Acme* and pitch of life for Epic poesy: Though since he hath altered it to *sixty,* the year in which he published his *Alfred.*[1] True it is, that the talents for *Criticism,* namely, smartness, quick censure, vivacity of remark, certainty of asseveration, indeed all but acerbity, seem rather the gifts of Youth than of riper Age. But it is far otherwise in *Poetry;* witness the works of Mr. Rymer[2] and Mr. Dennis, who, beginning with Criticism, became afterwards such Poets as no age hath paralleled. With good reason therefore did our author choose to write his Essay on that subject at twenty, and reserve for his maturer years this great and wonderful work of the *Dunciad.* P.

BY AUTHORITY.

𝕭𝖞 𝖇𝖎𝖗𝖙𝖚𝖊 𝖔𝖋 𝖙𝖍𝖊 𝕬𝖚𝖙𝖍𝖔𝖗𝖎𝖙𝖞 𝖎𝖓 𝕌𝖘 𝖇𝖊𝖘𝖙𝖊𝖉 𝖇𝖞 𝖙𝖍𝖊 Act for subjecting Poets to the power of a Licenser, 𝖜𝖊 𝖍𝖆𝖛𝖊 𝖗𝖊𝖛𝖎𝖘𝖊𝖉 𝖙𝖍𝖎𝖘 𝕻𝖎𝖊𝖈𝖊; 𝖜𝖍𝖊𝖗𝖊 𝖋𝖎𝖓𝖉𝖎𝖓𝖌 𝖙𝖍𝖊 𝖘𝖙𝖞𝖑𝖊 𝖆𝖓𝖉 𝖆𝖕𝖕𝖊𝖑𝖑𝖆𝖙𝖎𝖔𝖓 𝖔𝖋 KING 𝖙𝖔 𝖍𝖆𝖛𝖊 𝖇𝖊𝖊𝖓 𝖌𝖎𝖛𝖊𝖓 𝖙𝖔 𝖆 𝖈𝖊𝖗𝖙𝖆𝖎𝖓 Pretender, Pseudo-Poet, 𝖔𝖗 Phantom, 𝖔𝖋 𝖙𝖍𝖊 𝖓𝖆𝖒𝖊 𝖔𝖋 TIBBALD; 𝖆𝖓𝖉 𝖆𝖕𝖕𝖗𝖊𝖍𝖊𝖓𝖉𝖎𝖓𝖌 𝖙𝖍𝖊 𝖘𝖆𝖒𝖊 𝖒𝖆𝖞 𝖇𝖊 𝖉𝖊𝖊𝖒𝖊𝖉 𝖎𝖓 𝖘𝖔𝖒𝖊 𝖘𝖔𝖗𝖙 𝖆 𝖗𝖊𝖋𝖑𝖊𝖈𝖙𝖎𝖔𝖓 𝖔𝖓 Majesty, 𝖔𝖗 𝖆𝖙 𝖑𝖊𝖆𝖘𝖙 𝖆𝖓 𝖎𝖓𝖘𝖚𝖑𝖙 𝖔𝖓 𝖙𝖍𝖆𝖙 𝕷𝖊𝖌𝖆𝖑 𝕬𝖚𝖙𝖍𝖔𝖗𝖎𝖙𝖞 𝖜𝖍𝖎𝖈𝖍 𝖍𝖆𝖘 𝖇𝖊𝖘𝖙𝖔𝖜𝖊𝖉 𝖔𝖓 𝖆𝖓𝖔𝖙𝖍𝖊𝖗 𝕻𝖊𝖗𝖘𝖔𝖓 𝖙𝖍𝖊 Crown of Poesy: 𝖂𝖊 𝖍𝖆𝖛𝖊 𝖔𝖗𝖉𝖊𝖗𝖊𝖉 𝖙𝖍𝖊 𝖘𝖆𝖎𝖉 Pretender, Pseudo-Poet, 𝖔𝖗 Phantom, 𝖚𝖙𝖙𝖊𝖗𝖑𝖞 𝖙𝖔 𝖛𝖆𝖓𝖎𝖘𝖍 𝖆𝖓𝖉 evaporate 𝖔𝖚𝖙 𝖔𝖋 𝖙𝖍𝖎𝖘 𝖜𝖔𝖗𝖐: 𝕬𝖓𝖉 𝖉𝖔 𝖉𝖊𝖈𝖑𝖆𝖗𝖊 𝖙𝖍𝖊 𝖘𝖆𝖎𝖉 𝕿𝖍𝖗𝖔𝖓𝖊 𝖔𝖋 𝕻𝖔𝖊𝖘𝖞 𝖋𝖗𝖔𝖒 𝖍𝖊𝖓𝖈𝖊𝖋𝖔𝖗𝖙𝖍 𝖙𝖔 𝖇𝖊 𝖆𝖇𝖉𝖎𝖈𝖆𝖙𝖊𝖉 𝖆𝖓𝖉 𝖛𝖆𝖈𝖆𝖓𝖙, 𝖚𝖓𝖑𝖊𝖘𝖘 𝖉𝖚𝖑𝖞 𝖆𝖓𝖉 𝖑𝖆𝖜𝖋𝖚𝖑𝖑𝖞 𝖘𝖚𝖕𝖕𝖑𝖎𝖊𝖉 𝖇𝖞 𝖙𝖍𝖊 LAUREATE himself. 𝕬𝖓𝖉 𝖎𝖙 𝖎𝖘 𝖍𝖊𝖗𝖊𝖇𝖞 𝖊𝖓𝖆𝖈𝖙𝖊𝖉, 𝖙𝖍𝖆𝖙 𝖓𝖔 𝖔𝖙𝖍𝖊𝖗 𝕻𝖊𝖗𝖘𝖔𝖓 𝖉𝖔 presume 𝖙𝖔 𝖋𝖎𝖑𝖑 𝖙𝖍𝖊 𝖘𝖆𝖒𝖊.

ↃC. Ch.

THE DUNCIAD:

To Dr. Jonathan Swift.[3]

BOOK THE FIRST.

ARGUMENT.

THE Proposition, the Invocation, and the Inscription. Then the Original of the great Empire of Dulness, *and cause of the continuance thereof. The College of the Goddess in the City, with her private Academy for Poets in particular; the Governors*

[1] See his *Essays.* P.

[2] [The author of a *Short View of Tragedy* (1693), which contains some absurd cavils against Shakspere as well as against later authors.]

[3] [In considering the relations between Pope

and Swift, concerning which see *Introductory Memoir,* it should never be left out of sight that their acquaintance commenced at a time (1713) when Swift was at the height of his influence as a political adviser as well as literary champion of the Tory party, while Pope had hardly se-

THE
DUNCI
AD

P. & K. Arthur
Tutchin's Rehard

DU
L E

Dennis's Works

Cibber's Plays

DUBLIN; Printed; LONDON: Reprinted for A. Dodd

FRONTISPIECE OF OWL.

(Edition of 1728.)

of it, and the four Cardinal Virtues. Then the Poem hastes into the midst of things, *presenting her, on the evening of a Lord Mayor's day, revolving the long succession of her Sons, and the glories past and to come. She fixes her eye on* Bays *to be the Instrument of that great Event which is the Subject of the Poem. He is described pensive among his Books, giving up the Cause, and apprehending the Period of her Empire : After debating whether to betake himself to the Church, or to Gaming, or to Party-writing, he raises an Altar of proper books, and (making first his solemn prayer and declaration) purposes thereon to sacrifice all his unsuccessful writings. As the pile is kindled, the Goddess, beholding the flame from her seat, flies and puts it out, by casting upon it the poem of* Thule. *She forthwith reveals herself to him, transports him to her Temple, unfolds her Arts, and initiates him into her Mysteries ; then denouncing the death of* Eusden *the Poet Laureate, anoints him, carries him to Court, and proclaims him Successor.*

BOOK I.

THE Mighty Mother,[1] and her Son, who brings
  The Smithfield Muses[2] to the ear of Kings,
I sing. Say you, her instruments the Great!
Call'd to this work by Dulness, Jove, and Fate:[3]
You by whose care, in vain decry'd and curst,   5
Still Dunce the second reigns like Dunce the first;
Say, how the Goddess bade Britannia sleep,
And pour'd her Spirit o'er the land and deep.
  In eldest time, ere mortals writ or read,
Ere Pallas issu'd from the Thund'rer's head,   10
Dulness o'er all possess'd her ancient right,
Daughter of Chaos and eternal Night:[4]
Fate in their dotage this fair Idiot gave,
Gross as her sire, and as her mother grave,
Laborious, heavy, busy, bold, and blind,   15
She rul'd, in native Anarchy, the mind.
  Still her old Empire to restore[5] she tries,
For, born a Goddess, Dulness never dies.
      O Thou whatever title please thine ear,

cured the first step on the ladder of fame. The composition of the *Dunciad* was as it were cradled by the friendship of Swift; and the dedication by which it was accompanied when first published in a complete form in April 1729, was therefore a tribute in every sense merited by the person to whom it was addressed. It must have reached him at the most miserable period of his life, after his return from his last visit to England and after the death of Stella.]

[1] *The Mighty Mother, &c.*] in the first Edd. it was thus,
'Books and the Man I sing, the first who brings
The Smithfield Muses to the ear of Kings,' &c.
                                        P.

[2] *The Smithfield Muses*] *Smithfield* is the place where Bartholomew Fair was kept, whose shows, machines, and dramatical entertainments, formerly agreeable only to the taste of the Rabble, were, by the Hero of this poem and others of equal genius, brought to the Theatres of Covent-garden, Lincolns-inn-fields, and the Haymarket, to be the reigning pleasures of the Court and Town. This happened in the reigns of King George I. and II. See Book III. P.

[3] *By Dulness, Jove, and Fate :*] i.e. by their *Judgments*, their *Interests*, and their *Inclinations.* P.

[4] Conformably to Milton's doctrine, *Par. Lost*, II. 894 and 960. *Wakefield.*

[5] *Still her old Empire to restore*] This Restoration makes the Completion of the Poem. *Vide* Book IV. P.

Dean, Drapier, Bickerstaff,[1] or Gulliver![2]   20
Whether thou choose Cervantes' serious air,[3]
Or laugh and shake in Rab'lais' easy chair,[4]
Or praise the Court, or magnify Mankind,[5]
Or thy griev'd Country's copper chains unbind;
From thy Bœotia tho' her Pow'r retires,[6]   25
Mourn not, my SWIFT, at aught our Realm acquires.[7]
Here pleas'd behold her mighty wings outspread
To hatch a new Saturnian age of Lead.[8]
   Close to those walls where Folly holds her throne,
And laughs to think Monroe[9] would take her down,   30
Where o'er the gates, by his fam'd father's hand,[10]
Great Cibber's brazen, brainless brothers stand;
One Cell there is, conceal'd from vulgar eye,
The Cave of Poverty and Poetry.[11]
Keen, hollow winds howl thro' the bleak recess,   35
Emblem of Music caus'd by Emptiness.
Hence Bards, like Proteus long in vain tied down,[12]
Escape in Monsters, and amaze the town.

[1] [In the Satire on John Partridge the Almanac-maker and subsequent publications. Steele borrowed the pseudonym of Isaac Bickerstaff from Swift, who was a contributor to a few of the earlier papers of the *Tatler*.]

[2] — *Drapier, Bickerstaff, or Gulliver!*] The several names and characters he assumed in his ludicrous, his splenetic, or his party-writings; which take in all his works. P.

[3] [In the *Travels of Gulliver*, as Warburton interprets the passage. But Mr. Booth, in Fielding's *Amelia*, is beyond a doubt right in his observation that 'he does not remember to have ever seen in Swift's works the least attempt in the manner of Cervantes,' and that the name of Lucian might have been appropriately introduced among those of the authors whom Swift studied above all others.]

[4] After Ver. 22 in the MS.

'Or in the graver Gown instruct mankind,
  Or silent let thy mortals tell thy mind.'

But this was to be understood, as the Poet says, *Ironicè*, like the 23rd Verse. P.

[5] *Or praise the Court, or magnify Mankind,*] *Ironicè*, alluding to *Gulliver's* representations of both. — The next line relates to the papers of the *Drapier* against the currency of *Wood's* copper coin in *Ireland*, which, upon the great discontent of the people, his Majesty was graciously pleased to recal. P.

[6] Bœotia of old lay under the raillery of the neighbouring wits, as Ireland does now; though each of those nations produced one of the greatest wits and greatest generals of their age. P.

[7] *Mourn not, my Swift, at aught our Realm*

acquires.] *Ironicè iterum.* The Politics of *England* and *Ireland* were at this time by some thought to be opposite, or interfering with each other: Dr. *Swift* of course was in the interest of the latter, our Author of the former. P.

[8] *To hatch a new Saturnian age of Lead.*] The ancient Golden Age is by Poets styled *Saturnian*, as being under the reign of Saturn; but in the Chemical language *Saturn* is Lead. She is said here only to be spreading her wings to hatch this age; which is not produced completely till the fourth book. P.

[9] [Physician to Bedlam Hospital.]

[10] Mr. Caius Gabriel Cibber, father of the Poet Laureate. The two Statues of the Lunatics over the gates of Bedlam Hospital were done by him, and (as the son justly says of them) are no ill monuments of his fame as an artist.

[11] *Poverty and Poetry*] I cannot here omit a remark that will greatly endear our Author to every one, who shall attentively observe that Humanity and Candour, which every where appear in him towards those unhappy objects of the ridicule of all mankind, the bad Poets. He here imputes all scandalous rhymes, scurrilous weekly papers, base flatteries, wretched elegies, songs, and verses (even from those sung at Court to ballads in the streets), not so much to malice or servility as to Dulness; and not so much to Dulness as to Necessity. And thus, at the very commencement of his Satire, makes an apology for all that are to be satirized. P.

· [12] Ov. *Metam.* XIII. [v. 918]. *Warburton.* A very close resemblance to the lines of Young

Hence Miscellanies spring, the weekly boast
Of Curl's chaste press, and Lintot's rubric post: 40
Hence hymning Tyburn's elegiac lines,[2]
Hence Journals, Medleys, Merc'ries, MAGAZINES; [3]
Sepulchral Lies [4] our holy walls to grace,
And New-year Odes,[5] and all the Grub-street race.
    In clouded Majesty here Dulness shone;   45
Four guardian Virtues, round, support her throne:
Fierce champion Fortitude, that knows no fears
Of hisses, blows, or want, or loss of ears:
Calm Temperance, whose blessings those partake
Who hunger, and who thirst for scribbling sake: 50
Prudence, whose glass presents th' approaching jail:
Poetic Justice, with her lifted scale,
Where, in nice balance, truth with gold she weighs,
And solid pudding against empty praise.
    Here she beholds the Chaos dark and deep,[6]   55
Where nameless Somethings in their causes sleep,
'Till genial Jacob,[7] or a warm Third day,
Call forth each mass, a Poem, or a Play:
How hints, like spawn, scarce quick in embryo lie,
How new-born nonsense first is taught to cry,   60
Maggots half-form'd in rhyme exactly meet,
And learn to crawl upon poetic feet.
Here one poor word an hundred clenches makes,[8]

in his first epistle on the authors of the age, addressed to Mr. Pope. *Warton.*

[1] *Curl's chaste press, and Lintot's rubric post:*] Two Booksellers, of whom see Book II. The former was fined by the Court of King's Bench for publishing obscene books; the latter usually adorned his shop with titles in red letters. P.

[2] Ver. 41 in the former Editions,
    'Hence hymning Tyburn's elegiac lay,
    Hence the soft sing-song on Cecilia's Day.'
                                    Warburton.

Hence hymning Tyburn's elegiac lines,] It is an ancient English custom for the Malefactors to sing a Psalm at their execution at Tyburn; and no less customary to print Elegies on their deaths, at the same time, or before. P.

[3] MAGAZINES.] The common name of those upstart collections in prose and verse; in which, at some times,
    — new born nonsense first is taught to cry;
at others, dead-born Scandal has its monthly funeral, where Dulness assumes all the various shapes of Folly to draw in and cajole the Rabble. The eruption of every miserable Scribbler; the scum of every dirty News-paper; or Fragments of Fragments, picked up from every Dunghill, under the title of *Papers, Essays,*

Reflections, Confutations, Queries, Verses, Songs, Epigrams, Riddles, &c. equally the disgrace of human Wit, Morality, Decency, and Common Sense. *P. and Warburton.*

[4] *Sepulchral Lies,*] Is a just satire on the Flatteries and Falsehoods admitted to be inscribed on the walls of Churches, in Epitaphs. P.

[5] *New-year Odes,*] Made by the Poet Laureate for the time being, to be sung at Court on every New-year's day, the words of which are happily drowned in the voices and instruments. The *New-year Odes* of the Hero of this work were of a cast distinguished from all that preceded him, and made a conspicuous part of his character as a writer, which doubtless induced our Author to mention them here so particularly. P.

[6] Compare Milton, *Par. Lost,* Bk. III. v. 11. *Wakefield.*

[7] [Jacob Tonson the bookseller: 'left-legged Jacob,' as he was afterwards called, who published for both Dryden and Pope.]

[8] *Here one poor word an hundred clenches makes,*] It may not be amiss to give an instance or two of these operations of *Dulness* out of the works of her Sons, celebrated in the Poem. A great Critic formerly held these clenches in such

And ductile Dulness new mæanders takes ;
There motley images her fancy strike,   65
Figures ill pair'd, and Similes unlike.
She sees a Mob of Metaphors advance,
Pleas'd with the madness of the mazy dance ;
How Tragedy and Comedy embrace ;
How Farce and Epic get a jumbled race ;   70
How Time himself[1] stands still at her command,
Realms shift their place, and Ocean turns to land.
Here gay Description Egypt glads with show'rs,
Or gives to Zembla fruits, to Barca flow'rs :
Glitt'ring with ice here hoary hills are seen,   75
There painted valleys of eternal green ;
In cold December fragrant chaplets blow,
And heavy harvests nod beneath the snow.
    All these and more the cloud-compelling Queen
Beholds thro' fogs, that magnify the scene.   80
She, tinsell'd o'er in robes of varying hues,
With self-applause her wild creation views ;
Sees momentary monsters rise and fall,
And with her own fools-colours gilds them all.
    'T was on the day when * * rich and grave,[2]   85
Like Cimon, triumph'd both on land and wave :
(Pomps without guilt, of bloodless swords and maces,
Glad chains, warm furs, broad banners, and broad faces)
Now Night descending, the proud scene was o'er,
But liv'd in Settle's numbers one day more.[3]   90
Now May'rs and Shrieves all hush'd and satiate lay,
Yet ate, in dreams, the custard of the day ;
While pensive Poets painful vigils keep,
Sleepless themselves, to give their readers sleep.

abhorrence, that he declared, "he that would pun, would pick a pocket." Yet Mr. Dennis's works afford us notable examples in this kind ; "*Alexander Pope* hath sent abroad into the world as many *Bulls* as his namesake Pope *Alexander.* — Let us take the initial and final letters of his name. *viz. A. P — E,* and they give you the idea of an *Ape.—Pope* comes from the Latin word *Popa,* which signifies a little Wart; or from *poppysma,* because he was continually *popping* out squibs of wit, or rather *Popysmata,* or *Popisms.*" DENNIS on *Hom.* and *Daily Journal, June* 11, 1728. P. [A ' clench' or ' clinch' was a common expression for a pun.

[1] *How Farce and Epic — How Time himself, &c.*] Allude to the transgressions of the *Unities* in the Plays of such Poets. For the Miracles wrought upon *Time* and *Place,* and the mixture of Tragedy and Comedy, Farce and Epic, see Pluto and Proserpine, Penelope, &c. if yet extant. P.

[2] Ver. 85 in the former Editions,
' 'T was on the day when Thorold, rich and grave.'
    Sir George Thorold, Lord Mayor of London in the year 1720. The Procession of a Lord Mayor is made partly by land, and partly by water. — Cimon, the famous Athenian General, obtained a victory by sea, and another by land, on the same day, over the Persians and Barbarians. P. [The battle of the Eurymedon.]

[3] *But liv'd in Settle's numbers one day more.*] A beautiful manner of speaking, usual with poets in praise of poetry. Settle was poet to the City of London. His office was to compose yearly panegyrics upon the Lord Mayors, and verses to be spoken in the pageants : But that part of the shows being at length frugally abolished, the employment of City-poet ceased; so that upon Settle's demise there was no successor to that place. P. [Part *om.*] [As to Elkanah Settle, see *To the Author of a Poem entitled Successio;* in *Miscellaneous Poems.*]

Much to the mindful Queen the feast recalls　　　　95
What City Swans once sung within the walls;
Much she revolves their arts, their ancient praise,
And sure succession down from Heywood's[1] days.
She saw, with joy, the line immortal run,
Each sire imprest, and glaring in his son:　　　　100
So watchful Bruin forms, with plastic care,
Each growing lump, and brings it to a Bear.
She saw old Prynne in restless Daniel[2] shine,
And Eusden eke out[3] Blackmore's endless line;
She saw slow Philips creep like Tate's poor page,　　105
And all the mighty Mad[4] in Dennis rage.
　　In each she marks her Image full exprest,
But chief in Bays's[5] monster-breeding breast:

[1] *John Heywood*, whose Interludes were printed in the time of Henry VIII. P.

[2] *Old Prynne in restless Daniel*] The first edition had it,

　She saw in Norton all his father shine:
a great mistake! for Daniel De Foe had parts, but Norton De Foe was a wretched writer, and never attempted Poetry. Much more justly is Daniel himself made successor to W. Pryn, both of whom wrote Verses as well as Politics. And both these authors had a semblance in their fates as well as writings, having been alike sentenced to the Pillory. P. [Part *om.* William Prynne was in the year 1633 sentenced to a fine of £5000, placed in the pillory, and sentenced to imprisonment till he should recant, on account of his *Histriomastix*, written in condemnation of plays and supposed to reflect on Queen Henrietta Maria. De Foe underwent a similar punishment in 1703 for his book *the Shortest Way with the Dissenters*, but was not, like Prynne, subjected to the penalty of losing his ears, as Pope implies *infra*, Bk. II. v. 147.]

[3] *And Eusden eke out, &c.*] Laurence Eusden, Poet Laureate [before Cibber]. Mr. Jacob gives a catalogue of some few only of his works, which were very numerous. Of Blackmore, see Book II. Of Philips, Book I. 262 and Book III. *prope fin.*

　Nahum Tate was Poet Laureate, a cold writer, of no invention; but sometimes translated tolerably when befriended by Mr. Dryden. In his second part of Absalom and Achitophel are above two hundred admirable lines together of that great hand, which strongly shine thro' the insipidity of the rest. Something parallel may be observed of another author here mentioned. P. [Part *om.*]

[4] *And all the mighty Mad*] This is by no means to be understood literally, as if Mr. Dennis were really mad, according to the Narrative of Dr. Norris in Swift and Pope's Miscellanies. No—it is spoken of that *Excellent* and *Divine Madness*, so often mentioned by Plato: that poetical rage and enthusiasm, with which Mr. D. hath, in his time, been highly possessed; and of those *extraordinary hints and motions* whereof he himself so feelingly treats in his preface to the *Rem. on Pr. Arth.* Mr. John Dennis was the son of a Saddler in London born in 1657. He paid court to Mr. Dryden; and having obtained some correspondence with Mr. Wycherley and Mr. Congreve, he immediately obliged the public with their Letters. He made himself known to the Government by many admirable schemes and projects; which the Ministry, for reasons best known to themselves, constantly kept private. For his character as a writer, it is given us as follows: " Mr. Dennis is *excellent* at Pindaric writings, *perfectly regular* in all his performances, and a person of *sound Learning.* That he is master of a great deal of *Penetration* and *Judgment*, his criticisms (particularly on *Prince Arthur*) do sufficiently demonstrate." From the same account it also appears " that he writ Plays more to get *Reputation* than *Money*." DENNIS himself. See Giles Jacob's *Lives of Dram. Poets*, p. 68, 69, compared with p. 286. [For an account of the life-long combat between Pope and his arch-enemy Dennis, of which the former had by no means invariably the best, see *Introductory Memoir. The Narrative on the Frenzy of J. D.* was written by Pope in 1713.]

[5] [As to Colley Cibber and Theobald see *Introductory Remarks* to the *Dunciad*.]

　But chief in Bays's, &c.] In the former Edd. thus,

' But chief, in Tibbald's monster-breeding breast;
Sees Gods with Dæmons in strange league ingage,
And earth, and heav'n, and hell her battles wage.

Bays, form'd by nature Stage and Town to bless,[1]
And act, and be, a Coxcomb with success.   110
Dulness, with transport eyes the lively Dunce,
Remembring she herself was Pertness once.
Now (shame to Fortune![2]) an ill Run at Play
Blank'd his bold visage, and a thin Third day:[3]
Swearing and supperless the Hero sate,   115
Blasphem'd his Gods, the Dice, and damn'd his Fate;
Then gnaw'd his pen, then dash'd it on the ground,
Sinking from thought to thought,[4] a vast profound!
Plung'd for his sense, but found no bottom there;
Yet wrote and flounder'd on in mere despair.   120
Round him much Embryo, much Abortion lay,[5]
Much future Ode, and abdicated Play;
Nonsense precipitate, like running Lead,
That slipp'd thro' Cracks and Zig-zags of the Head;
All that on Folly Frenzy could beget,   125
Fruits of dull Heat, and Sooterkins[6] of Wit,
Next, o'er his Books his eyes began to roll,
In pleasing memory of all he stole,
How here he sipp'd, how there he plunder'd snug,
And suck'd all o'er, like an industrious Bug.   130

She ey'd the Bard, where supperless he sate,
And pin'd, unconscious of his rising fate;
Studious he sate, with all his Books around,
Sinking from thought to thought,' &c. ——

Var. *Tibbald*] Author of a pamphlet intitled, *Shakespear restor'd*. During two whole years while Mr. Pope was preparing his Edition of Shakespear, he published Advertisements, requesting assistance, and promising satisfaction to any who could contribute to its greater perfection. But this Restorer, who was at that time soliciting favours of him by letters, did wholly conceal his design, till after its publication; (which he was since not ashamed to own, in a *Daily Journal* of *Nov.* 26, 1728). And then an outcry was made in the Prints, that our Author had joined with the Bookseller to raise an *extravagant subscription;* in which he had no share, of which he had no knowledge, and against which he had publickly advertised in his own proposals for *Homer*. Probably that proceeding elevated *Tibbald* to the dignity he holds in this Poem, which he seems to deserve no other way better than his brethren; unless we impute it to the share he had in the Journals, cited among the *Testimonies of Authors* prefixed to this work. P.

[1] *Bays, form'd by nature, &c.*] It is hoped the poet here hath done full justice to his Hero's character, which it were a great mistake to imagine was wholly sunk in stupidity: he is allowed to have supported it with a wonderful mixture of Vivacity. This character is heightened according to his own desire, in a Letter he wrote to our author. "Pert and dull at least you might have allowed me. What! am I only to be dull, and dull still, and again, and for ever." He then solemnly appealed to his own conscience, "that he could not think himself so, nor believe that our Poet did; but that he spoke worse of him than he could possibly think; and concluded it must be merely to shew his *Wit*, or for some *Profit* or *Lucre* to himself." Life of C. C. chap. vii. and Letter to Mr. P. pag. 15, 40, 53. P.

[2] *Shame to Fortune!*] Because she usually shews favour to persons of this Character, who have a three-fold pretence to it. P.

[3] [*A thin Third day*, i.e. of the performance of one of his plays.]

[4] From Lord Rochester on Man:
        ' Stumbling from thought to thought.'
                                    Warton.

[5] *Round him much Embryo, &c.*] In the former Editions thus,
' He roll'd his eyes that witness'd huge dismay
Where yet unpawn'd much learned lumber lay
Volumes, whose size the space exactly fill'd,
Or which fond authors were so good to gild,
Or where, by sculpture made for ever known,
The page admires new beauties not its own.
Here swells the shelf,' &c. —— *Warburton.*

[6] [False births.]

MOLIÈRE. (Mignard.)

Here lay poor Fletcher's half-eat scenes,[1] and here
The Frippery [2] of crucify'd Moliere;'
There hapless Shakespear,[3] yet of Tibbald sore,
Wish'd he had blotted [4] for himself before.
The rest on Out-side merit but presume,[5]   135
Or serve (like other Fools) to fill a room;
Such with their shelves as due proportion hold,
Or their fond parents drest in red and gold;
Or where the pictures for the page atone,
And Quarles [6] is sav'd by Beauties not his own.   140
Here swells the shelf with Ogilby the great;[7]
There, stamp'd with arms, Newcastle shines complete:[8]
Here all his suff'ring brotherhood retire,
And 'scape the martyrdom of jakes and fire:
A Gothic Library! of Greece and Rome   145

[1] *Poor Fletcher's half-eat scenes,*] A great number of them taken out to patch up his Plays. P.

[2] *The Frippery*] "When I fitted up an old play, it was as a good housewife will mend old linen, when she has not better employment." Life, p. 217. octavo. P.

[3] *Hapless Shakespear, &c.*] It is not to be doubted but Bays was a subscriber to Tibbald's Shakespear. He was frequently liberal this way; and, as he tells us, "subscribed to Mr. Pope's Homer, out of pure Generosity and Civility; but when Mr. Pope did so to his Nonjuror, he concluded it could be nothing but a joke." Letter to Mr. P. p. 24.
This Tibbald, or Theobald, published an edition of Shakespear, of which he was so proud himself as to say, in one of Mist's Journals, June 8, "That to expose any Errors in it was impracticable." And in another, April 27, "That whatever care might for the future be taken by any other Editor, he would still give above five hundred emendations, that *shall* escape them all." P.

[4] *Wish'd he had blotted*] It was a ridiculous praise which the Players gave to Shakespear, "that he never blotted a line." Ben Jonson honestly wish'd he had blotted a thousand; and Shakespear would certainly have wished the same, if he had lived to see those alterations in his works, which, not the Actors only (and especially the daring Hero of this poem) have made on the *Stage*, but the presumptuous Critics of our days in their *Editions.* P.

[5] *The rest on Out-side merit, &c.*] This Library is divided into three parts; the first consists of those authors from whom he stole, and whose works he mangled; the second, of such as fitted the shelves, or were gilded for shew, or adorned with pictures; the third class our author calls solid learning, old Bodies of Divinity, old Commentaries, old English Printers, or old English Translations; all very voluminous, and fit to erect altars to Dulness. P.

[6] [The author of the *Emblems*, whom Pope sneers at in *Imitations of Horace*, Bk. II. Ep. I. v. 377.]

[7] *Ogilby the Great;*] "John Ogilby was one, who, from a late initiation into literature, made such a progress as might well style him the prodigy of his time! sending into the world so many large *Volumes!* His translations of Homer and Virgil done *to the life*, and *with such excellent sculptures:* And (what added great grace to his works) he printed them all on *special good paper*, and in a *very good letter.*" *Winstanly, Lives of Poets.* P. [Ogilby (born 1600, died 1676,) began life as a dancing-master, and after being educated by charity at Cambridge, came before the public both as poet and printer. It is in the latter capacity that he is chiefly remarkable; from his press at Whitefriars he issued a large variety of works, among which his Maps became specially famous.]

[8] *There, stamp'd with arms, Newcastle shines complete:*] "The *Duchess of Newcastle* was one who busied herself in the ravishing delights of Poetry; leaving to posterity in print three *ample Volumes* of her studious endeavours." *Winstanly*, ibid. Langbane reckons up *eight* Folios of her Grace's; which were usually adorned with gilded covers, and had her coat of arms upon them. P. [The Duchess of Newcastle, in the times of the Commonwealth and Charles II., published a large number of poetical and 'philosophical' works, and a kind of narrative cyclopædia called the *World's Olio.*]

Well purg'd, and worthy Settle, Banks, and Broome.[1]
But, high above, more solid Learning [2] shone,
The Classics of an Age that heard of none;
There Caxton [3] slept, with Wynkyn at his side,
One clasp'd in wood, and one in strong cow-hide; 150
There sav'd by spice, like mummies, many a year,
Dry Bodies of Divinity appear;
De Lyra [4] there a dreadful front extends,
And here the groaning shelves Philemon [5] bends.
Of these twelve volumes, twelve of amplest size, 155
Redeem'd from tapers and defrauded pies,
Inspir'd he seizes; these an altar raise;
An hecatomb of pure unsully'd lays
That altar crowns; A folio Common-place
Founds the whole pile, of all his works the base; 160
Quartos, octavos, shape the less'ning pyre;
A twisted Birth-day Ode completes the spire.[6]
Then he: "Great Tamer of all human art!
First in my care, and ever at my heart;
Dulness! whose good old cause I yet defend, 165
With whom my Muse began, with whom shall end.
E'er since Sir Fopling's Periwig [7] was Praise,

---

[1] *Worthy Settle, Banks, and Broome.*] The Poet has mentioned these three authors in particular, as they are parallel to our Hero in three capacities: 1. Settle was his brother Laureate; only indeed upon half-pay, for the City instead of the Court; but equally famous for unintelligible flights in his poems on public occasions, such as Shows, Birth-days, &c. 2. Banks was his Rival in *Tragedy* (tho' more successful) in one of his Tragedies, the *Earl of Essex*, which is yet alive: *Anna Boleyn*, the *Queen of Scots*, and *Cyrus the Great*, are dead and gone. These he drest in a sort of *Beggar's Velvet*, or a happy Mixture of the *thick Fustian* and *thin Prosaic;* exactly imitated in *Perolla and Isidora*, *Cæsar in Egypt*, and the *Heroic Daughter.* 3. Broome was a serving-man of Ben Jonson, who once picked up a *Comedy* from his Betters, or from some cast scenes of his Master, not entirely contemptible. P.

[2] *More solid Learning*] Some have objected, that books of this sort suit not so well the library of our Bays, which they imagine consisted of Novels, Plays, and obscene books; but they are to consider, that he furnished his shelves only for ornament, and read these books no more than the *Dry Bodies of Divinity*, which, no doubt, were purchased by his father, when he designed him for the Gown. See the note on v. 200. P.

[3] *Caxton*] A Printer in the time of Edward IV. Rich. III. and Hen. VII.; Wynkyn de

Word, his successor, in that of Hen. VII. and VIII. The former translated into prose Virgil's Æneis, as a history; of which he speaks, in his Proeme, in a very singular manner, as of a book hardly known. P. [Part *om.*]

[4] *Nich. de Lyra*, or Harpsfield, a very voluminous commentator, whose works, in five vast folios, were printed in 1472. P.

[5] *Philemon Holland*, Doctor in Physic. " He translated *so many books*, that a man would think he had done *nothing else;* insomuch that he might be called *Translator general of his age.* The books alone of his turning into English are sufficient to make a *Country Gentleman* a *complete Library. Winstanly.*
           P.

[6] *A twisted, &c.*] in the former Edd.
' And last, a little Ajax tips the spire.'
        Warburton.
A little Ajax] in *duodecimo*, translated from Sophocles by Tibbald. P. [The birthday Ode of course substituted in allusion to Cibber's laureateship. Cf. v. 168.]

[7] *E'er since Sir Fopling's Periwig*] The first visible cause of the passion of the Town for our Hero was a fair flaxen full-bottom'd periwig, which, he tells us, he wore in his first play of the *Fool in fashion.* This remarkable Periwig usually made its entrance upon the stage in a sedan, brought in by two chairmen, with infinite approbation of the audience. P. [Part *om.*]

To the last honours of the Butt and Bays :
O thou! of Bus'ness the directing soul!
To this our head like bias to the bowl,   170
Which, as more pond'rous, made its aim more true,
Obliquely waddling to the mark in view :
O! ever gracious to perplex'd mankind,
Still spread a healing mist before the mind ;
And, lest we err by Wit's wild dancing light,   175
Secure us kindly in our native night.
Or, if to Wit a coxcomb make pretence,[1]
Guard the sure barrier between that and Sense ;
Or quite unravel all the reas'ning thread,
And hang some curious cobweb in its stead!   180
As, forc'd from wind-guns, lead itself can fly,[2]
And pond'rous slugs cut swiftly thro' the sky ;
As clocks to weight their nimble motion owe,
The wheels above urg'd by the load below :
Me Emptiness, and Dulness could inspire,   185
And were my Elasticity and Fire.·
Some Dæmon stole my pen (forgive th' offence)
And once betray'd me into common sense :
Else all·my Prose and Verse were much the same ;
This prose on stilts, that poetry fall'n lame.   190
Did on the stage my Fops appear confin'd?
My life gave ampler lessons to mankind.
Did the dead letter unsuccessful prove?
The brisk Example never fail'd to move.
Yet sure had Heav'n decreed to save the State,   195
Heav'n had decreed these works a longer date.
Could Troy be sav'd by any single hand,
This grey-goose weapon must have made her stand.
What can I now? my Fletcher[3] cast aside,

---

[1] *Or, if to Wit, &c.*] in the former Edd.
'Ah! still o'er Britain stretch that peaceful
    wand,
Which lulls th' Helvetian and Batavian land;
Where rebel to thy throne if Science rise,
She does but shew her coward face, and dies:
There thy good Scholiasts with unweary'd pains
Make Horace flat, and humble Maro's strains:
Here studious I unlucky Moderns save,
Nor sleeps one Error in its father's grave,
Old puns restore, lost blunders nicely seek,
And crucify poor Shakespeare once a week.
For thee supplying, in the worst of days,
Notes to dull books, and prologues to dull plays;
Not that my quill to critics was confin'd,
My verse gave ampler lessons to mankind;
So gravest precepts may successless prove,
But sad examples never fail to move.
As forc'd from wind-guns,' &c.   *Warburton.*

[2] *As, forc'd from wind-guns, &c.*] The
thought of these four verses is found in a poem
of our Author's of a very early date (namely
written at fourteen years old, and soon after
printed) to the author of a poem called *Suc-
cessio.* [See *Miscellaneous Poems.*] *War-
burton.*

[3] *My Fletcher*] A familiar manner of speak-
ing, used by modern Critics, of a favourite au-
thor. Bays might as justly speak thus of
Fletcher, as a French Wit did of Tully, seeing
his works in his library, "Ah! mon cher Cice-
ron; je le connois bien; c'est le même que Marc
Tulle." But he had a better title to call Fletcher
his own, having made so free with him. P. [In
our day, Pope's spleen would have inevitably
been aroused by the corresponding practice on
the part of 'critics' who make free with the Chris-
tian names of ' Sam Johnson' and his equals.]

THE DUNCIAD.

Take up the Bible, once my better guide?[1]   200
Or tread the path by vent'rous Heroes trod,
This Box my Thunder, this right hand my God?
Or chair'd at White's amidst the Doctors sit,
Teach Oaths to Gamesters, and to Nobles Wit?
Or bidst thou rather Party to embrace?   205
(A friend to Party thou, and all her race;
'T is the same rope at diff'rent ends they twist;
To Dulness Ridpath is as dear as Mist.[2])
Shall I, like Curtius, desp'rate in my zeal,
O'er head and ears plunge for the Commonweal?   210
Or rob Rome's ancient geese of all their glories,
And cackling save the Monarchy of Tories?
Hold — to the Minister I more incline;
To serve his cause, O Queen! is serving thine.
And see! thy very Gazetteers[3] give o'er,   215
Ev'n Ralph[4] repents, and Henley writes no more.
What then remains? Ourself. Still, still remain
Cibberian forehead, and Cibberian brain.
This brazen Brightness, to the 'Squire so dear;
This polish'd Hardness, that reflects the Peer: 220
This arch Absurd, that wit and fool delights;
This Mess, toss'd up of Hockley-hole[5] and Whites;
Where Dukes and Butchers join to wreathe my crown,
At once the Bear and Fiddle of the town.
  " O born in sin, and forth in folly brought![6]   225
Works damn'd, or to be damn'd! (your father's fault)
Go, purify'd by flames ascend the sky,
My better and more christian progeny![7]
Unstain'd, untouch'd, and yet in maiden sheets;
While all your smutty sisters walk the streets.   230
Ye shall not beg, like gratis-given Bland,
Sent with a Pass,[8] and vagrant thro' the land;

---

[1] *Take up the Bible, once my better guide?*]
When, according to his Father's intention, he had
been a *Clergyman*, or (as he thinks himself) a
Bishop of the Church of England. P. [Part *om.*]

  This learned Critic is to be understood alle-
gorically: The DOCTORS in this place mean no
more than *false Dice*, a Cant phrase used
amongst Gamesters. So the meaning of these
four sonorous lines is only this, " Shall I play
fair or foul?" P.

[2] *Ridpath — Mist.*] George Ridpath author
of a Whig paper, called the Flying-post; Na-
thaniel Mist, of a famous Tory Journal. P.

[3] *Gazetteers*] A band of ministerial writers,
hired at the price mentioned in the note on
Book II. ver. 316, who, on the very day their
patron quitted his post, laid down their paper,
and declared they would never more meddle in
Politics. P.

[4] [*Ralph;* cf. Pope's note to Bk. III. v. 165.]
[5] [*Hockley-hole.* Cf. *Imit. of Hor.* Bk. II.
Sat. I. v. 49.]

[6] *O born in sin, &c.*] This is a tender and
passionate Apostrophe to his own works, which
he is going to sacrifice agreeable to the nature
of man in great affliction; and reflecting like a
parent on the many miserable fates to which
they would otherwise be subject. P.

[7] *My better and more christian progeny!*]
" It may be observable, that my muse and my
spouse were equally prolific; that the one was
seldom the mother of a Child, but in the same
year the other made me father of a Play. I
think we had a dozen of each sort between us;
of both which kinds some *died* in their *Infancy*,"
&c. Life of C. C. P.

[8] *Gratis-given Bland, Sent with a Pass,*]
It was a practice so to give the Daily Gazetteer

Not sail with Ward, to Ape-and-monkey climes,[1]
Where vile Mundungus trucks for viler rhymes:
Not sulphur-tipt emblaze an Ale-house fire;   235
Not wrap up Oranges, to pelt your sire!
O! pass more innocent, in infant state,
To the mild Limbo of our Father Tate:[2]
Or peaceably forgot, at once be blest
In Shadwell's[3] bosom with eternal Rest!   240
Soon to that mass of Nonsense to return,
Where things destroy'd are swept to things unborn."
    With that, a Tear (portentous sign of Grace!)
Stole from the Master of the sev'nfold Face;
And thrice he lifted high the Birth-day brand,   245
And thrice he dropt it from his quiv'ring hand;
Then lights the structure, with averted eyes:
The rolling smoke involves the sacrifice.
The op'ning clouds disclose each work by turns:
Now flames the Cid,[3] and now Perolla[4] burns;[5] 250
Great Cæsar roars, and hisses in the fires;
King John in silence modestly expires;[6]
No merit now the dear Nonjuror claims,
Moliere's old stubble[7] in a moment flames.
Tears gush'd again, as from pale Priam's eyes   255
When the last blaze sent Ilion to the skies.[8]

and ministerial pamphlets (in which this B. was a writer), and to send them *Post-free* to all the Towns in the kingdom. P. Bland was the Provost of Eton. *Warton.*

[1] — *With Ward, to Ape-and-monkey climes,*] "Edward Ward, a very voluminous Poet in Hudibrastic verse, but best known by the London Spy, in prose. He has of late years kept a public house in the City (but in a genteel way), and with his wit, humour, and good liquor (ale) afforded his guests a pleasurable entertainment, especially those of the high-church party." JACOB, Lives of Poets, vol. II. p. 225. Great number of his works were yearly sold into the Plantations. — Ward, in a book called Apollo's Maggot, declared this account to be a great falsity, protesting that his public house was not in the *City*, but in *Moorfields.* P. [According to Bowles, this Ward had given no special cause of offence to Pope.]

[2] *Tate — Shadwell*] Two of his predecessors in the Laurel. P.

[3] ['Ximenes,' founded on Corneille's Cid.]

[4] ['Perolla and Izadora.']

[5] *Now flames the Cid, &c.*] In the first notes on the Dunciad it was said, that this Author was particularly excellent at Tragedy. "This (says he) is as unjust as to say I could not dance on a Rope." But certain it is that he

had attempted to dance on this Rope, and fell most shamefully, having produced no less than four Tragedies (the names of which the Poet preserves in these few lines), the three first of them were fairly printed, acted, and damned; the fourth suppressed, in fear of the like treatment. P.

[6]   ['such was the Hiss
Welcom'd his *Cæsar* to th' Ægyptian shore,
Such was the Hiss, in which great *John* should
        have expired:
But wherefore do I strive in vain to number
Those glorious Hisses, which from age to age
Our family has borne triumphant from the
        stage?"
        Pistol (Theophilus Cibber) in *Fielding's
                Historical Register for* 1736.]

[7] *The dear Nonjuror — Moliere's old stubble*] A Comedy threshed out of Moliere's Tartuffe, and so much the Translator's favourite, that he assures us all our author's dislike to it could only arise from *disaffection to the Government.* P. [Part *om.* This play, however, is still occasionally performed.]

[8] *When the last blaze sent Ilion to the skies.*] See Virgil, Æn. II. where I would advise the reader to peruse the story of Troy's destruction, rather than in Wynkyn. SCRIBL. [Part *om.*]

Rous'd by the light, old Dulness heav'd the head,
Then snatch'd a sheet of Thule [1] from her bed;
Sudden she flies, and whelms it o'er the pyre;
Down sink the flames, and with a hiss expire.   260
    Her ample presence fills up all the place;
A veil of fogs dilates her awful face: [2]
Great in her charms! as when on Shrieves and May'rs
She looks, and breathes herself into their airs.
She bids him wait her to her sacred Dome: [3]   265
Well pleas'd he enter'd, and confess'd his home.
So Spirits ending their terrestrial race
Ascend, and recognize their Native Place.
This the Great Mother [4] dearer held than all
The clubs of Quidnuncs, or her own Guildhall: 270
Here stood her Opium, here she nurs'd her Owls,
And here she plann'd th' Imperial seat of Fools.
    Here to her Chosen all her works she shews;
Prose swell'd to verse, verse loit'ring into prose:
How random thoughts now meaning chance to find,   275
Now leave all memory of sense behind;
How Prologues into Prefaces decay,
And these to Notes are fritter'd quite away.
How Index-learning turns no student pale,
Yet holds the eel of science by the tail: 280
How, with less reading than makes felons scape,
Less human genius than God gives an ape,
Small thanks to France, and none to Rome or Greece,
A vast, vamp'd, future, old, reviv'd, new piece,
'Twixt Plautus, Fletcher, Shakespear, and Corneille,   285
Can make a Cibber, Tibbald,[5] or Ozell.[6]
    The Goddess then, o'er his anointed head,
With mystic words, the sacred Opium shed.

[1] *Thule*] An unfinished poem of that name, of which one sheet was printed many years ago, by Amb. Philips, a northern author. It is an usual method of putting out a fire, to cast wet sheets upon it. Some critics have been of opinion that this sheet was of the nature of the Asbestos, which cannot be consumed by fire: but I rather think it an allegorical allusion to the coldness and heaviness of the writing. P.

[2] [Wakefield traces the origin of this line to Dryden's *MacFlecknoe:*
' His brows thick fogs, instead of glories, grace,
And lambent dulness play'd around his face.']

[3] *Sacred Dome:*] Where he no sooner enters, but he reconnoitres the place of his original, as Plato says the spirits shall, at their entrance into the celestial regions. P.

[4] *Great Mother*] *Magna mater*, here applied to *Dulness.* The *Quidnuncs*, a name given to the ancient members of certain political clubs, who were constantly enquiring *quid nunc?* what news? P.

[5] *Tibbald,*] Lewis Tibbald (as pronounced) or Theobald (as written) was bred an Attorney, and son to an Attorney (says Mr. Jacob) of Sittenburn in Kent. He was author of some forgotten Plays, Translations, and other pieces. He was concerned in a paper called the Censor, and a Translation of Ovid. P. [Part *om.*]

[6] *Ozell.*] " Mr. John Ozell (if we credit Mr. Jacob) did go to school in Leicestershire, where *somebody* left him *something* to live on, when he shall retire from business. He was designed to be sent to Cambridge, in order for priesthood; but he chose rather to be placed in an *office of accounts*, in the City, being qualified for the same by his skill in *arithmetic*, and writing the necessary *hands.* He has obliged the world with many translations of French Plays." Jacob, Lives of *Dram. Poets*, p. 198. P. [Part *om.*]

And lo! her bird (a monster of a fowl,
Something betwixt a Heideggre [1] and Owl)
Perch'd on his crown. "All hail! and hail again,
My son: the promis'd land expects thy reign.
Know, Eusden thirsts no more for sack or praise; [2]
He sleeps among the dull of ancient days;
Safe, where no Critics damn, no duns molest,
Where wretched Withers,[3] Ward, and Gildon [4] rest,
And high-born Howard,[5] more majestic sire,
With Fool of Quality completes the quire.
Thou, Cibber! thou, his Laurel shalt support,
Folly, my son, has still a Friend at Court.
Lift up your Gates, ye Princes, see him come!
Sound, sound, ye Viols; be the Cat-call dumb!
Bring, bring the madding Bay, the drunken Vine;
The creeping, dirty, courtly Ivy join.
And thou! his Aid-de-camp, lead on my sons,
Light-arm'd with Points, Antitheses, and Puns.
Let Bawdry, Billingsgate, my daughters dear,
Support his front, and Oaths bring up the rear:
And under his, and under Archer's wing,
Gaming and Grub-street skulk behind the King.[6]
   "O! when shall rise a Monarch all our own,

290

295

300

305

310

---

[1] *A Heideggre*] A strange bird from Switzerland, and not (as some have supposed) the name of an eminent person who was a man of parts, and, as was said of Petronius, *Arbiter Elegantiarum*. P. [The German Heydegger, who held the Opera-house with Handel, and managed it, according to Dibdin, 'like another Cibber,' introduced masquerades into England. He brought them into such vogue, that in 1729 he was presented as a nuisance by the Grand Jury. He said of himself that ' he had come to England out of Switzerland without a farthing, and had then found means to get £500 a year, and spend it.' In a facetious fragment by Pope, published in Roscoe's *Supplement* [1825], he is apostrophised as " false Heidegger who wert so wicked To let in the Devil."]

[2] Ver. 293. *Know, Eusden, &c.*] In the former Editions.

'Know, Settle, cloy'd with custard and with praise,
Is gather'd to the dull of ancient days,
Safe where no critics damn, no duns molest,
Where Gildon, Banks, and high-born Howard rest.
I see a King! who leads my chosen sons
To lands that flow with clenches and with puns:
Till each fam'd theatre my empire own;
Till Albion, as Hibernia, bless my throne!
I see! I see! — then rapt she spoke no more,

God save King Tibbald! Grubstreet alleys roar.
So when Jove's block,' &c. *Warburton.*

[3] *Withers,*] ' George Withers was a great pretender to poetical zeal against the vices of the times, and abused the greatest personages in power, which brought upon him *frequent correction*. The Marshalsea and Newgate were no strangers to him.' *Winstanley.* P. [He went over from the Royalist to the Parliamentary side; yet his honesty is undoubted and his power as a satirist now generally acknowledged.]

[4] *Gildon*] Charles Gildon, a writer of criticisms and libels of the last age, bred at St. Omer's with the Jesuits; but renouncing popery, he published Blount's books against the divinity of Christ, the Oracles of Reason, &c. He signalized himself as a critic, having written some very bad Plays; abused Mr. P. very scandalously in an anonymous pamphlet of the Life of Mr. Wycherley, printed by Curl; in another called the New Rehearsal, printed in 1714: in a third, entitled, the Complete Art of English Poetry, in two volumes; and others. P. [See *note* to *Epistle to Arbuthnot*, v. 151.]

[5] *Howard,*] Hon. Edward Howard, author of the British Princes, and a great number of wonderful pieces, celebrated by the late Earls of Dorset and Rochester, Duke of Buckingham, Mr. Waller, &c. P.

[6] *Under Archer's wing, — Gaming, &c.*]

And I, a Nursing-mother, rock the throne;
'Twixt Prince and People close the Curtain draw,
Shade him from Light, and cover him from Law;
Fatten the Courtier, starve the learned band,　　　　　315
And suckle Armies, and dry-nurse the land:
Till Senates nod to Lullabies divine,
And all be sleep, as at an Ode of thine."
　　She ceas'd.　Then swells the Chapel-royal [1] throat:
" God save King Cibber! " mounts in ev'ry note.　　320
Familiar White's, " God save King Colley! " cries;
" God save King Colley! " Drury-lane replies:
To Needham's quick the voice triumphal rode,
But pious Needham [2] dropt the name of God;
Back to the Devil [3] the last echoes roll,　　　　325
And " Coll! " each Butcher roars at Hockley-hole.
　　So when Jove's block descended from on high
(As sings thy great forefather Ogilby [4])
Loud thunder to its bottom shook the bog,
And the hoarse nation croak'd, " God save King Log! "　330

THE DUNCIAD.

BOOK THE SECOND.

ARGUMENT.

The King being proclaimed, the solemnity is graced with public Games, and sports of various kinds; not instituted by the Hero, as by Æneas in Virgil, but for greater honour by the Goddess in person (in like manner as the games Pythia, Isthmia, &c. were

When the Statute against Gaming was drawn up, it was represented, that the King, by ancient custom, plays at Hazard one night in the year; and therefore a clause was inserted, with an exception as to that particular. Under this pretence, the Groom-porter had a room appropriated to Gaming all the summer the Court was at Kensington, which his Majesty accidentally being acquainted of with a just indignation prohibited. It is reported the same practice is yet continued wherever the Court resides, and the Hazard Table there open to all the professed Gamesters in town.

'Greatest *and* justest Sov'REIGN! *know you this?*
Alas! no more than Thames' *calm* head *can know*
Whose meads his arms *drown or whose corn o'erflow.'* Donne to Queen Eliz. P.

[Cf. *The Basset-Table*, v. 99. The Groom-porter was an officer in the royal household who had succeeded to most of the functions of the Master of the Revels. As to the practice referred to by Pope, see Evelyn's *Diary*, 8 Jan. 1667-8, *et al.*]

[1] *Chapel-royal*] The voices and instruments used in the service of the Chapel-royal being also employed in the performance of the Birth-day and New-year Odes. P.

[2] *But pious Needham*] A Matron of great fame, and very religious in her way; whose constant prayer it was, that she might " get enough by her profession to leave it off in time, and make her peace with God." But her fate was not so happy; for being convicted and set in the pillory, she was (to the lasting shame of all her great Friends and Votaries) so ill used by the populace, that it put an end to her days. P.

[3] *Back to the Devil*] The Devil Tavern in Fleet-street, where these Odes are usually rehearsed before they are performed at Court. P. [Cf. *Imit. of Hor.* Bk. II. Ep. I. v. 91.]

[4] *Ogilby) — God save King Log!*] See Ogilby's Æsop's Fables, where, in the story of the Frogs and their King, this excellent hemistic is to be found. P. [Part *om.*]

anciently said to be ordained by the Gods, and as Thetis herself appearing, according to Homer, Odyss. xxiv. *proposed the prizes in honour of her son Achilles). Hither flock the Poets and Critics, attended, as is but just, with their Patrons and Booksellers. The Goddess is first pleased, for her disport, to propose games to the Booksellers, and setteth up the Phantom of a Poet, which they contend to overtake. The Races described, with their divers accidents. Next, the game for a Poetess. Then follow the Exercises for the Poets, of tickling, vociferating, diving: The first holds forth the arts and practices of Dedicators, the second of Disputants and fustian Poets, the third of profound, dark, and dirty Party-writers. Lastly, for the Critics, the Goddess proposes (with great propriety) an Exercise, not of their parts, but their patience, in hearing the works of two voluminous Authors, one in verse, and the other in prose, deliberately read without sleeping: The various effects of which, with the several degrees and manners of their operation, are here set forth; till the whole number, not of Critics only, but of spectators, actors, and all present, fall asleep; which naturally and necessarily ends the games.*

BOOK II.

HIGH on a gorgeous seat, that far out-shone
    Henley's gilt tub,[1] or Fleckno's Irish throne,[2]
Or that where on her Curls the Public pours,[3]
All-bounteous, fragrant Grains and Golden show'rs,
Great Cibber sate: The proud Parnassian sneer,   5
The conscious simper, and the jealous leer,
Mix on his look: All eyes direct their rays
On him, and crowds turn Coxcombs as they gaze:
His Peers shine round him with reflected grace,
New edge their dulness, and new bronze their face,   10
So from the Sun's broad beam in shallow urns

[1] *Henley's gilt tub,*] The pulpit of a Dissenter is usually called a Tub; but that of Mr. Orator Henley was covered with velvet, and adorned with gold. He had also a fair altar, and over it this extraordinary inscription, *The Primitive Eucharist.* See the history of this person, Book III. [v. 199]. P.

[2] *Or Fleckno's Irish throne,*] Richard Fleckno was an Irish priest, but had laid aside (as himself expressed it) the mechanic part of priesthood. He printed some plays, poems, letters, and travels. I doubt not our Author took occasion to mention him in respect to the poem of Mr. Dryden, to which this bears some resemblance, though of a character more different from it than that of the Æneid from the Iliad, or the Lutrin of Boileau from the Défait de Bouts rimées of Sarazin. P. [It is not known whether Fleckno had actually died about the time (1682) when Dryden wrote his famous satire, or whether the latter with careless malice gave unenviable notoriety to a harmless living writer, who had to the best of his ability honoured Dryden himself. As to the relations between the *Dunciad* and Dryden's Satire see *Introduction to Dunciad*, p. 349.]

It may be just worth mentioning, that the Eminence, from whence the ancient Sophists entertained their auditors, was called by the pompous name of a throne; — ἐπὶ θρόνον τινὸς ὑψηλοῦ μάλα σοφιστικῶς καὶ σοβαρῶς. Themistius, Orat. I. P.

[3] *Or that where on her Curls the Public pours,*] Edmund Curl stood in the pillory at Charingcross, in March 1727-8. "This (saith Edmund Curl) is a false assertion —— I had indeed the corporal punishment of what the Gentlemen of the long robe are pleased jocosely to call *mounting the Rostrum* for one hour; but that scene of action was not in the month of *March*, but in *February.*" And of *the History of his being tost in a Blanket*, he saith, "Here, *Scriblerus!* thou leeseth in what thou assertest concerning the blanket; it was not a *blanket*, but a *rug.*" Much in the same manner Mr. *Cibber* remonstrated, that his Brothers, at Bedlam, mentioned Book I. were not *Brazen*, but *Blocks;* yet our Author let it pass unaltered, as a trifle that no way altered the relationship. *Scriblerus.*

2 C

Heav'n's twinkling Sparks draw light, and point their horns.
  Not with more glee, by hands pontific crown'd,
With scarlet hats wide-waving circled round,
Rome in her Capitol saw Querno sit,[1]   15
Thron'd on seven hills, the Antichrist of wit.
  And now the Queen, to glad her sons, proclaims,
By herald Hawkers, high heroic Games.
They summon all her Race: an endless band
Pours forth, and leaves unpeopled half the land.   20
A motley mixture! in long wigs, in bags,
In silks, in crapes,[2] in Garters, and in Rags,
From drawing-rooms, from colleges, from garrets,
  On horse, on foot, in hacks, and gilded chariots:
All who true Dunces in her cause appear'd,   25
And all who knew those Dunces to reward.
  Amid that area wide they took their stand,
Where the tall may-pole once o'er-look'd the Strand.
But now (so ANNE and Piety ordain)
A Church collects the saints of Drury-lane.[3]   30
  With Authors, Stationers[4] obey'd the call,
(The field of glory is a field for all).
Glory, and gain, th' industrious tribe provoke;
And gentle Dulness ever loves a joke.
A Poet's form she plac'd before their eyes,   35
And bade the nimblest racer seize the prize;
No meagre, muse-rid mope, adust and thin,
In a dun night-gown of his own loose skin;
But such a bulk as no twelve bards could raise,
Twelve starv'ling bards of these degen'rate days.   40
All as a partridge plump, full-fed, and fair,
She form'd this image of well-body'd air;
With pert flat eyes she window'd well its head:

---

[1] *Rome in her Capitol saw Querno sit,*] Camillo Querno was of Apulia, who, hearing the great Encouragement which Leo X. gave to poets, travelled to Rome with a harp in his hand, and sung to it twenty thousand verses of a poem called Alexias. He was introduced *as a Buffoon* to Leo, and promoted to the honour of the *Laurel;* a jest which the Court of Rome and the Pope himself entered into so far, as to cause him to ride on an elephant to the Capitol, and to hold a solemn festival on his coronation; at which it is recorded the Poet himself was so transported as to *weep for joy*. He was ever after a constant frequenter of the Pope's table, drank abundantly, and poured forth verses without number. PAULUS JOVIUS. Some idea of his poetry is given by Fam. Strada, in his Prolusions. P.

[2] [The material of an ordinary clergyman's gown. Cf. *Moral Essays*, Ep. I. v. 137.]

[3] ['In front of the spot now occupied by St. Mary-le-Strand, commonly called the New Church, anciently stood a cross, at which, says Stowe, "in the year 1294, and other times, the justices itinerant sat without London." In the place of this cross was set up a May-pole, which having been taken down in 1713, a new one was erected opposite Somerset House. This second May-pole had two gilt balls and a vane on the summit, and was decorated on holidays with flags and garlands. It was removed in 1718, probably being thought in the way of the new church which was then being erected. Sir Isaac Newton begged it of the parish, and afterwards sent it to the Rector of Wanstead, who set it up in Wanstead Park to support the then largest telescope in Europe.' Leigh Hunt's *Town*.]

[4] [*Stationers*, i.e. booksellers.]

A brain of feathers, and a heart of lead ;
And empty words she gave, and sounding strain, 45
But senseless, lifeless! idol void and vain!
Never was dash'd out, at one lucky hit,
A fool, so just a copy of a wit ;
So like, that critics said, and courtiers swore,
A Wit it was, and call'd the phantom Moore.[1] 50
    All gaze with ardour : some a poet's name,
Others a sword-knot and lac'd suit inflame.
But lofty Lintot [2] in the circle rose :
" This prize is mine ; who tempt it are my foes ;
" With me began this genius, and shall end." 55
He spoke : and who with Lintot shall contend?
    Fear held them mute. Alone, untaught to fear,
Stood dauntless Curl ; [3] " Behold that rival here!
" The race by vigour, not by vaunts is won ;
" So take the hindmost, Hell," (he said) " and run." 60
Swift as a bard the bailiff leaves behind,
He left huge Lintot, and out-stripp'd the wind.
As when a dab-chick [4] waddles thro' the copse
On feet and wings, and flies, and wades, and hops :
So lab'ring on, with shoulders, hands, and head, 65
Wide as a wind-mill all his figure spread,
With arms expanded Bernard rows his state,
And left-legg'd Jacob seems to emulate.
Full in the middle way there stood a lake,
Which Curl's Corinna [5] chanc'd that morn to make : 70

---

[1] [Pope has a note too long for insertion on the sins of this hated personage, James Moore Smythe, the son of Arthur Moore. James was an admirer of Teresa Blount, and intimate with her family, as well as an occasional associate of Pope's literary circle. He was the author of a comedy called the *Rival Modes*, in which he was accused by Pope of having plagiarised the lines addressed by the latter to Martha Blount on her birth-day. See note *ad loc.*]

[2] *But lofty Lintot*] We enter here upon the episode of the Booksellers: Persons, whose names being more known and intimate in the learned world than those of the Authors in this poem, do therefore need less explanation. The action of Mr. Bernard Lintot here imitates that of Dares in Virgil, rising just in this manner to lay hold on a *Bull*. This eminent Bookseller printed the *Rival Modes* before-mentioned. P. [Young, in Spence's *Anecdotes*, calls Lintot ' a great sputtering fellow.']

[3] *Stood dauntless Curl;* We come now to a character of much respect, that of Mr. Edmund Curl. As a plain repetition of great actions is the best praise of them, we shall only say of this eminent man, that he carried the Trade many

lengths beyond what it ever before had arrived at ; and that he was the envy and admiration of all his profession. He possessed himself of a command over all authors whatever ; he caused them to write what he pleased ; they could not call their very *Names* their own. He was not only famous among these ; he was taken notice of by the *State*, the *Church*, and the *Law*, and received particular marks of distinction from each. P. [Part *om.*]

[4] [A dab-chick is a small water-fowl which is constantly dabbling under the water.]

[5] *Curl's Corinna*] This name, it seems, was taken by one Mrs. T——, who procured some private letters of Mr. Pope, while almost a boy, to Mr. Cromwell, and sold them without the consent of either of those Gentlemen to Curl, who printed them in 12mo, 1727. We only take this opportunity of mentioning the manner in which those letters got abroad, which the author was ashamed of as very trivial things, full not only of levities, but of wrong judgments of men and books, and only excusable from the youth and inexperience of the writer. P. Mrs. Elizabeth Thomas was first styled Corinna by Dryden, to whom she sent a copy of verses. She

(Such was her wont, at early dawn to drop
Her evening cates before his neighbour's shop,)
Here fortun'd Curl to slide; loud shout the band,
And " Bernard! Bernard! " rings thro' all the Strand.
Obscene with filth the miscreant lies bewray'd,   75
Fall'n in the plash his wickedness had laid:
Then first (if Poets aught of truth declare)
The caitiff Vaticide conceiv'd a pray'r.
   " Hear, Jove! whose name my bards and I adore,
As much at least as any God's, or more;   80
And him and his if more devotion warms,
Down with the Bible, up with the Pope's Arms." [1]
   A place there is, betwixt earth, air, and seas, [2]
Where, from Ambrosia, Jove retires for ease.
There in his seat two spacious vents appear,   85
On this he sits, to that he leans his ear,
And hears the various vows of fond mankind;
Some beg an eastern, some a western wind:
All vain petitions, mounting to the sky,
With reams abundant this abode supply;   90
Amus'd he reads, and then returns the bills
Sign'd with that Ichor which from Gods distils. [3]
   In office here fair Cloacina [4] stands,
And ministers to Jove with purest hands.
Forth from the heap she pick'd her Vot'ry's pray'r,   95
And plac'd it next him, a distinction rare!
Oft had the Goddess heard her servants call,
From her black grottos near the Temple-wall,
List'ning delighted to the jest unclean
Of link-boys vile, and watermen obscene;   100
Where as he fish'd her nether realms for Wit, [5]
She oft had favour'd him, and favours yet.
Renew'd by ordure's sympathetic force,
As oil'd with magic juices [6] for the course,
Vig'rous he rises; from th' effluvia strong   105
Imbibes new life, and scours and stinks along;
Re-passes Lintot, vindicates the race,
Nor heeds the brown dishonours of his face.
   And now the victor stretch'd his eager hand,

---

died, in want, in 1730. *Carruthers.* [On the
subject of this ' unwarranted publication' see
Introductory Memoir, p. xxxiii.]

   [1] *Down with the Bible, up with the Pope's
Arms.*] The Bible, Curl's sign; the Cross-
key's, Lintot's. P.

   [2] See Lucian's Icaro-Menippus, where this
fiction is more extended. P.

   [3] Ver. 92. Alludes to Homer, Iliad v. [v. 339].
—— ῥέε δ' ἄμβροτον αἷμα Θεοιο,
'Ιχὼρ οἷος πέρ τε ῥέει μακάρεσσι Θεοῖσιν.

*A stream of nect'rous humour issuing flow'd,
Sanguine, such as celestial sp'rits may bleed.*
                    Milton [*Par. Lost*, Bk. vi. v. 332].

   [4] *Cloacina*] The Roman Goddess of the
common-sewers. P.

   [5] *Where as he fish'd, &c.*] See the preface
to Swift's and Pope's *Miscellanies.* P.

   [6] *As oil'd with magic juices*] Alluding to
the opinion that there are ointments used by
witches to enable them to fly in the air, &c. P.

Where the tall Nothing stood, or seem'd to **stand**;　　110
A shapeless shade, it melted from his sight,
Like forms in clouds, or visions of the night.
To seize his papers, Curl, was next thy care;
His papers light fly diverse, tost in air;
Songs, sonnets, epigrams the winds uplift,　　115
And whisk 'em back to Evans, Young, and Swift.[1]
Th' embroider'd suit at least he deem'd his prey;
That suit an unpaid tailor[2] snatch'd away.
No rag, no scrap, of all the beau, or wit,
That once so flutter'd, and that once so writ.　　120
　Heav'n rings with laughter. Of the laughter vain,
Dulness, good Queen, repeats the jest again.
Three wicked imps of her own Grubstreet choir,
She deck'd like Congreve, Addison, and Prior;[3]
Mears, Warner, Wilkins[4] run: delusive thought!　　125
Breval, Bond, Besaleel, the varlets caught.
Curl stretches after Gay, but Gay is gone:
He grasps an empty Joseph[5] for a John;
So Proteus, hunted in a nobler shape,
Became, when seiz'd, a puppy or an ape.　　130
　To him the Goddess: "Son! thy grief lay down,
And turn this whole illusion on the town:[6]
As the sage dame, experienc'd in her trade,
By names of Toasts retails each batter'd jade;
(Whence hapless Monsieur much complains at Paris　　135
Of wrongs from Duchesses and Lady Maries;[7])

---

[1] *Evans, Young, and Swift.*] Some of those persons, whose writings, epigrams, or jests he had owned. See Note on v. 50. Dr. Evans, of St. John's College, Oxford, author of the *Apparition*, a Satire on Tindal. *Warton.*

[2] *An unpaid tailor*] This line has been loudly complained of in Mist, June 8, Dedic. to Sawney, and others, as a most inhuman satire on the *poverty* of *Poets*: But it is thought our Author would be acquitted by a jury of *Tailors*. To me this instance seems unluckily chosen; if it be a satire on any body, it must be on a bad *paymaster*, since the person to whom they have here applied it was a man of fortune. Not but poets may well be jealous of so great a prerogative as *non-payment*; which Mr. Dennis so far asserts, as boldly to pronounce, that "if Homer himself was not in debt, it was because nobody would trust him."
　　　　　　　　　　　　　　　P.

[3] *Like Congreve, Addison, and Prior;*] These authors being such whose names will reach posterity, we shall not give any account of them, but proceed to those of whom it is necessary. — Besaleel Morris was author of some satires on the translators of Homer, with many other things printed in news-papers. — "Bond writ a satire against Mr. P. — Capt. "Breval was author of the Confederates, an in- "genious dramatic performance, to expose Mr. "P., Mr. Gay, Dr. Arb. and some ladies of "quality," says Curl. P.

[4] *Mears, Warner, Wilkins*] Booksellers, and Printers of much anonymous stuff. P. [As to Breval, see v. 237; Bond's and Besaleel Morris's works seem according to Carruthers to have disappeared.]

[5] *Joseph Gay,* a fictitious name put by Curl before several pamphlets, which made them pass with many for Mr. Gay's. P. The antiquity of the word *Joseph*, which likewise signifies a loose upper-coat, gives much pleasantry to the idea. *Warburton.* [Wakefield also points out the allusion to *Iliad* III. 376, and to the story of Ixion embracing a cloud instead of Juno.]

[6] *And turn this whole illusion on the town:*] It was a common practice of this bookseller to publish vile pieces of obscure hands under the names of eminent authors. P.

[7] [See note to *Epilogue to Satires*, Dial. I. v. 112.]

Be thine, my stationer! this magic gift;
Cook shall be Prior,[1] and Concanen,[2] Swift:
So shall each hostile name become our own,
And we too boast our Garth and Addison."[3]   140
   With that she gave him (piteous of his case,
Yet smiling at his rueful length of face)
A shaggy Tap'stry,[4] worthy to be spread
On Codrus' old, or Dunton's modern bed;[5]
Instructive work! whose wry-mouth'd portraiture   145
Display'd the fates her confessors endure.
Earless on high, stood unabash'd De Foe,[6]
And Tutchin[7] flagrant from the scourge below.
There Ridpath, Roper,[8] cudgell'd might ye view;
The very worsted still look black and blue.   150
Himself among the story'd chiefs he spies,[9]
As, from the blanket, high in air he flies;
And " Oh!" (he cry'd) " what street, what lane but knows

---

[1] *Cook shall be Prior,*] The man here specified writ a thing called The Battle of Poets, in which Philips and Welsted were the Heroes, and Swift and Pope utterly routed. He also published some malevolent things in the British, London, and Daily Journals; and at the same time wrote letters to Mr. Pope, protesting his innocence. His chief work was a translation of Hesiod, to which Theobald writ notes and half notes, which he carefully owned. P.

[2] [See Pope's note to v. 299.]

[3] *And we too boast our Garth and Addison.*] Nothing is more remarkable than our author's love of praising good writers. He has in this very poem celebrated Mr. Locke, Sir Isaac Newton, Dr. Barrow, Dr. Atterbury, Mr. Dryden, Mr. Congreve, Dr. Garth, Mr. Addison; in a word, almost every man of his time that deserved it; even Cibber himself (presuming him to be author of the Careless Husband). It was very difficult to have that pleasure in a poem on this subject, yet he has found means to insert their panegyric, and has made even Dulness out of her own mouth pronounce it. It must have been particularly agreeable to him to celebrate Dr. Garth; both as his constant friend, and as he was his predecessor in this kind of satire. P. [Part *om.*]

[4] *A shaggy Tap'stry*] A sorry kind of Tapestry frequent in old inns, made of worsted or some coarser stuff, like that which is spoken of by Donne — *Faces as frightful as theirs who whip Christ in old hangings.* The imagery woven in it alludes to the mantle of Cloanthus, in Æn. v. [v. 250, ff.] P.

[5] *On Codrus' old, or Dunton's modern bed;*] Of Codrus the poet's bed, see Juvenal,

describing his *poverty* very copiously, Sat. III. 103, &c. But Mr. Concanen, in his dedication of the letters, advertisements, &c. to the author of the Dunciad, assures us, " that Juvenal never satirized the Poverty of Codrus." P.

John Dunton was a broken bookseller, and abusive scribbler; he writ Neck or Nothing, a violent satire on some ministers of state; a libel on the Duke of Devonshire and the Bishop of Peterborough, &c. P.

[6] [Cf. ante, note to Bk. I. v. 103.]

[7] *And Tutchin flagrant from the scourge*] John Tutchin, author of some vile verses, and of a weekly paper called the Observator: He was sentenced to be whipped through several towns in the west of England, upon which he petitioned King James II. to be hanged. When that prince died in exile, he wrote an invective against his memory, occasioned by some humane elegies on his death. He lived to the time of Queen Anne. P. [He was the author of *The Foreigner*, the Satire on William III. which provoked De Foe's *True-born Englishman.* The sentence to which Pope refers was pronounced by Judge Jeffreys, but remitted in return for a bribe which reduced the prisoner to poverty. See Macaulay's *History of England*, chap. 5.]

[8] *There Ridpath, Roper,*] Author of the Flying-post and Post-boy, two scandalous papers on different sides, for which they equally and alternately deserved to be cudgelled, and were so. P.

[9] *Himself among the story'd chiefs he spies,*] The history of Curl's being tossed in a blanket, and whipped by the scholars of Westminster, is well known. P. [Part *om.*]

Our purgings, pumpings, blanketings, and blows?
In ev'ry loom our labours shall be seen,   155
And the fresh vomit run for ever green!"
  See in the circle next, Eliza [1] plac'd,
Two babes of love close clinging to her waist;
Fair as before her works she stands confess'd,
In flow'rs and pearls by bounteous Kirkall [2] dress'd.   160
The Goddess then: "Who best can send on high
"The salient spout, far-streaming to the sky;
"His be yon Juno of majestic size,
"With cow-like udders, and with ox-like eyes.
"This China Jordan let the chief o'ercome   165
"Replenish, not ingloriously, at home."
  Osborne [3] and Curl accept the glorious strife,
(Tho' this his Son dissuades, and that his Wife).
One on his manly confidence relies;
One on his vigour and superior size.   170
First Osborne lean'd against his letter'd post;
It rose, and labour'd to a curve at most.
So Jove's bright bow displays its wat'ry round,
(Sure sign that no spectator shall be drown'd).
A second effort brought but new disgrace: 175
The wild Mæander wash'd the Artist's face;
Thus the small jet, which hasty hands unlock,
Spirts in the gard'ner's eyes who turns the cock.
Not so from shameless Curl; impetuous spread
The stream, and smoking flourish'd o'er his head.   180
So (fam'd like thee for turbulence and horns)
Eridanus his humble fountain scorns;
.Thro' half the heav'ns he pours th' exalted urn;
His rapid waters in their passage burn.
  Swift as it mounts, all follow with their eyes: 185
Still happy Impudence obtains the prize.
Thou triumph'st, Victor of the high-wrought day,
And the pleas'd dame, soft smiling, lead'st away.
Osborne, thro' perfect modesty o'ercome,
Crown'd with the Jordan, walks contented home.   190
  But now for Authors nobler palms remain;

---

[1] *Eliza Haywood*] This woman was authoress of those most scandalous books called the Court of Carimania, and the new Utopia. P. [Part *om.*]

[2] *Kirkall*, the name of an Engraver. Some of this Lady's works were printed in four volumes in 12mo, with her picture thus dressed up before them. P.

[3] *Osborne, Thomas*] A bookseller in Gray's-inn, very well qualified by his impudence to act this part; and therefore placed here instead of a less deserving Predecessor. This man published advertisements for a year together, pretending to sell Mr. Pope's subscription books of Homer's Iliad at half the price: Of which books he had none, but cut to the size of them (which was Quarto) the common books in folio, without Copper-plates, on a worse paper, and never above half the value. P. [Part *om.*] Of Osborne Johnson used to say, that he had no sense of any shame, but that of being poor. *Bannister* [quoted by Bowles, who refers to the well-known episode in Boswell, concerning J.'s summary chastisement of O. See Boswell *ad ann.* 1742.]

"Room for my Lord!" three jockeys in his train;
Six huntsmen with a shout precede his chair:
He grins, and looks broad nonsense with a stare.
His Honour's meaning Dulness thus exprest,   195
"He wins this Patron, who can tickle best."
    He chinks his purse, and takes his seat of state:
With ready quills the Dedicators wait;
Now at his head the dext'rous task commence,
And, instant, fancy feels th' imputed sense;   200
Now gentle touches wanton o'er his face,
He struts Adonis, and affects grimace:
Rolli [1] the feather to his ear conveys,
Then his nice taste directs our Operas:
Bentley [2] his mouth with classic flatt'ry opes,   205
And the puff'd orator bursts out in tropes.
But Welsted [3] most the Poet's healing balm
Strives to extract from his soft, giving palm;
Unlucky Welsted! thy unfeeling master,
The more thou ticklest, gripes his fist the faster.   210
    While thus each hand promotes the pleasing pain,
And quick sensations skip from vein to vein;
A youth unknown to Phœbus, in despair,[4]
Puts his last refuge all in heav'n and pray'r.
What force have pious vows! The Queen of Love   215
His sister sends, her vot'ress, from above.
As, taught by Venus, Paris learnt the art
To touch Achilles' only tender part;
Secure, thro' her, the noble prize to carry,
He marches off his Grace's Secretary.   220
    "Now turn to diff'rent sports," (the Goddess cries)
" And learn, my sons, the wond'rous pow'r of Noise.
To move, to raise, to ravish ev'ry heart,
With Shakespear's nature, or with Jonson's art,

---

[1] *Paolo Antonio Rolli*, an Italian Poet, and writer of many Operas in that language, which, partly by the help of his genius, prevailed in England near twenty years. He taught Italian to some fine Gentlemen, who affected to direct the Operas. P.

[2] *Bentley his mouth, &c.*] Not spoken of the famous Dr. Richard Bentley, but of one Tho. Bentley, a small critic, who aped his uncle in a *little Horace*. The great one who was intended to be dedicated to the Lord Halifax, but (on a change of the Ministry) was given to the Earl of Oxford; for which reason the little one was dedicated to his son the Lord Harley. P. [Part *om.*]

[3] *Welsted*] Leonard Welsted, author of the Triumvirate, or a Letter in verse from Palæmon to Cælia at Bath, which was meant for a satire

on Mr. P. and some of his friends about the year 1718. He writ other things which we cannot remember. You have him again in Book III. 169. P. [Part *om.*] [He was a hanger-on of the Whigs, and a copious writer.]

[4] *A youth unknown to Phœbus, &c.*] The satire of this Episode, being levelled at the base flatteries of authors to worthless wealth or greatness, concludes here with an excellent lesson to such men: That altho' their pens and praises were as exquisite as they conceit of themselves, yet (even in their own mercenary views) a creature unlettered, who serveth the passions, or pimpeth to the pleasures of such vain, braggart, puft Nobility, shall with those patrons be much more inward, and of them much higher rewarded. SCRIBL.

Let others aim: 't is yours to shake the soul 225
With Thunder rumbling from the mustard-bowl,[1]
With horns and trumpets now to madness swell,
Now sink in sorrows with a tolling bell;[2]
Such happy arts attention can command,
When fancy flags, and sense is at a stand. 230
Improve we these. Three Cat-calls[3] be the bribe
Of him, whose chatt'ring shames the monkey-tribe;
And his this Drum, whose hoarse heroic bass
Drowns the loud clarion of the braying Ass."
　　Now thousand tongues are heard in one loud din; 235
The monkey-mimics rush discordant in;
'T was chatt'ring, grinning, mouthing, jabb'ring all,
And Noise and Norton,[4] Brangling and Breval,
Dennis and Dissonance, and captious Art,
And Snip-snap short, and Interruption smart, 240
And Demonstration thin, and Theses thick,
And Major, Minor, and Conclusion quick.
"Hold!" (cry'd the Queen), "a Cat-call each shall win
Equal your merits! equal is your din!
But that this well-disputed game may end, 245
Sound forth, my Brayers, and the welkin rend."
　　As, when the long-ear'd milky mothers wait
At some sick miser's triple bolted gate,
For their defrauded, absent foals they make
A moan so loud, that all the guild awake; 250
Some sighs sir Gilbert,[5] starting at the bray,
From dreams of millions, and three groats to pay.
So swells each wind-pipe; Ass intones to Ass;
Harmonic twang! of leather, horn, and brass;
Such as from lab'ring lungs th' Enthuiast blows, 255
High Sound, attemper'd to the vocal nose;
Or such as bellow from the deep Divine;
There, Webster! peal'd thy voice, and Whitfield![6] thine.

---

[1] *With Thunder rumbling from the mustard-bowl,*] The old way of making Thunder and Mustard were the same; but since, it is more advantageously performed by troughs of wood with stops in them. Whether Mr. Dennis was the inventor of that improvement, I know not; but it is certain, that being once at a Tragedy of a new author, he fell into a great passion at hearing some, and cried, "'Sdeath! that is *my* 'Thunder.'" P. [Dennis' tragedy was *Appius and Virginia;* and 'his thunder' was used in *Macbeth*. See note to *Essay on Criticism*, v. 586.]

[2] *— with a tolling bell;*] A mechanical help to the Pathetic, not unuseful to the modern writers of Tragedy. P.

[3] *Three Cat-calls*] Certain musical instruments used by one sort of Critics to confound the poets of the Theatre. P.

[4] *Norton,*] See ver. 417. — *J. Durant Breval,* author of a very extraordinary Book of Travels, and some Poems. See before, note on ver. 126. P. [The word 'brangle' (to oscillate; another form of brandle, Fr. branler) was confounded with 'wrangle.']

[5] *Sir Gilbert* [Heathcote, cf. *Moral Essays*, Ep. III. v. 101].

[6] *Webster — and Whitfield!*] The one the writer of a News-paper called the Weekly Miscellany, the other a Field-preacher. *Warburton.* [George Whitfield, the early associate of the Wesleys, was born in 1714 and first attracted general attention by his preaching at Bristol and London in 1736. John Wesley was induced by his example to commence field-preaching. He died in America in 1770.]

But far o'er all, sonorous Blackmore's strain;
Walls, steeples, skies, bray back to him again.   260
In Tot'nham fields, the brethren, with amaze,
Prick all their ears up, and forget to graze;
Long Chanc'ry-lane [1] retentive rolls the sound,
And courts to courts return it round and round;
Thames wafts it thence to Rufus' roaring hall,[2]   265
And Hungerford re-echoes bawl for bawl.
All hail him victor in both gifts of song,
Who sings so loudly, and who sings so long,[3]
    This labour past, by Bridewell all descend,[4]
(As morning pray'r and flagellation end) [5]   270
To where Fleet-ditch with disemboguing streams
Rolls the large tribute of dead dogs to Thames,
The king of dykes! than whom no sluice of mud
With deeper sable blots the silver flood.
" Here strip, my children! here at once leap in,   275
" Here prove who best can dash thro' thick and thin,
" And who the most in love of dirt excel,
" Or dark dexterity [6] of groping well.
" Who flings most filth, and wide pollutes around
" The stream, be his the Weekly Journals [7] bound;   280
" A pig of lead to him who dives the best;
" A peck of coals a-piece shall glad the rest."
    In naked majesty Oldmixon stands,[8]

---

[1] *Long Chanc'ry-lane*] The place where the offices of Chancery are kept. The long detention of Clients in that Court, and the difficulty of getting out, is humorously allegorized in these lines. P.

[2] [Westminster Hall; built by William II. A.D. 1097.]

[3] *Who sings so loudly, and who sings so long,*] A just character of Sir Richard Blackmore knight, who (as Mr. Dryden expresseth it)

Writ to the rumbling of the coach's wheels,

and whose indefatigable Muse produced no less than six Epic poems: Prince and King Arthur, twenty books; Eliza, ten; Alfred, twelve; the Redeemer, six; besides Job, in folio; the whole book of Psalms; the Creation, seven books; Nature of Man, three books; and many more. 'T is in this sense he is styled afterwards the *everlasting Blackmore.* P. [Part *om.*]

[4] [The scene is on the site of the modern Bridge Street.]

[5] (*As morning pray'r and flagellation end*)] It is between eleven and twelve in the morning, after church service, that the criminals are whipt in Bridewell. — This is to mark punctually the *time* of the day: Homer does it by the circumstance of the Judges rising from court, or of the Labourer's dinner; our author by one very

proper both to the *Persons* and the *Scene* of his poem, which we may remember commenced in the evening of the Lord-mayor's day: The first book passed in that *night;* the next *morning* the games begin in the Strand, thence along Fleet-street (places inhabited by Booksellers); then they proceed by Bridewell toward Fleet-ditch, and lastly thro' Ludgate to the City and the Temple of the Goddess. P.

[6] — *dash thro' thick and thin,* — *love of dirt* — *dark dexterity*] The three chief qualifications of Party-writers: to stick at nothing, to delight in flinging dirt, and to slander in the dark by guess. P.

[7] *The Weekly Journals*] Papers of news and scandal intermixed, on different sides and parties, and frequently shifting from one side to the other, called the London Journal, British Journal, Daily Journal, &c. the concealed writers of which for some time were Oldmixon, Roome, Arnall, Concanen, and others; persons never seen by our Author. P. .

[8] *In naked majesty Oldmixon stands,*] Mr. JOHN OLDMIXON, next to Mr. Dennis, the most ancient Critic of our nation; and unjust censurer of Mr. Addison. In his Essay on Criticism, and the Arts of Logic and Rhetoric, he frequently reflects on our Author. But the top of his char-

And Milo-like surveys his arms and hands;
Then, sighing thus, "And am I now three-score?   285
"Ah why, ye Gods, should two and two make four?"
He said, and climb'd a stranded lighter's height,
Shot to the black abyss, and plung'd downright.
The Senior's judgment all the crowd admire,
Who but to sink the deeper, rose the higher.   290
   Next Smedley div'd;[1] slow circles dimpled o'er
The quaking mud, that clos'd, and op'd no more,
All look, all sigh, and call on Smedley lost;
"Smedley" in vain resounds thro' all the coast.
   Then * essay'd;[2] scarce vanish'd out of sight,   295
He buoys up instant, and returns to light:
He bears no token of the sabler streams,
And mounts far off among the Swans of Thames.
   True to the bottom see Concanen[3] creep,
A cold, long-winded native of the deep;   300
If perseverance gain the Diver's prize,
Not everlasting Blackmore this denies;
No noise, no stir, no motion canst thou make,
Th' unconscious stream sleeps o'er thee like a lake.
   Next plung'd a feeble, but a desp'rate pack,   305
With each a sickly brother at his back:

acter was a Perverter of History, in that scandalous one of the Stuarts, in folio, and his Critical History of England, two volumes, octavo. Being employed by Bishop Kennet, in publishing the Historians in his Collection, he falsified Daniel's Chronicle in numberless places. He was all his life a virulent Party-writer for hire, and received his reward in a small place, which he enjoyed to his death. He is here likened to Milo, in allusion to Ovid [*Metam.* Bk. xv. v. 229]. P. [Part *om.*]

[1] *Next Smedley div'd;*] The person here mentioned, an Irishman, was author and publisher of many scurrilous pieces, a weekly Whitehall Journal, in the year 1722, in the name of Sir James Baker; and particularly whole volumes of Billingsgate against Dr. Swift and Mr. Pope, called Gulliveriana and Alexandriana, printed in octavo, 1728. P.

Jonathan Smedley, a staunch Whig, and Dean of Clogher. *Carruthers* [who quotes his lines 'The Devil's last game' against Swift].

[2] *Then * essay'd*] A gentleman of genius and spirit, who was secretly dip in some papers of this kind, on whom our Poet bestows a panegyric instead of a satire, as deserving to be better employed than in party quarrels, and personal invectives. P. Supposed to be *Aaron Hill;* but Pope denied it. *Warton.* [Hill, however,

called Pope to account by a poetical rejoinder; though, as Bowles remarks, the compliment in the above lines infinitely exceeds the abuse. Cf. *Intr. Memoir,* p. xxxvi. Hill wrote no less than seventeen dramatic pieces, and was, besides, according to Dibdin, 'the projector of nut oil, of masts of ships from Scotch firs, of cultivating Georgia, and of potash!']

[3] *Concanen*] MATTHEW CONCANEN, an Irishman, bred to the law. He was author of several dull and dead scurrilities in the British and London Journals, and in a paper called the Speculatist. In a pamphlet, called a Supplement to the Profund, he dealt very unfairly with our Poet, not only frequently imputing to him Mr. Broome's verses (for which he might indeed seem in some degree accountable, having corrected what that gentleman did) but those of the duke of Buckingham and others: To this rare piece somebody humorously caused him to take for his motto, *De profundis clamavi.* He was since a hired scribbler in the Daily Courant, where he poured forth much Billingsgate against the lord Bolingbroke, and others; after which this man was surprisingly promoted to administer Justice and Law in Jamaica. P. [Part *om.*] This is the scribbler to whom Warburton wrote his famous Letter, published by Dr. Akenside. *Warton.*

Sons of a Day![1] just buoyant on the flood,
Then number'd with the puppies in the mud.
Ask ye their names? I could as soon disclose
The names of these blind puppies as of those.   310
Fast by, like Niobe [2] (her children gone)
Sits Mother Osborne,[3] stupefy'd to stone!
And Monumental brass this record bears,
" These are, — ah no! these were, thè Gazetteers!"
   Not so bold Arnall; [4] with a weight of skull,   315
Fùrious he dives, precipitately dull.
Whirlpools and storms his circling arm invest,
With all the might of gravitation blest.
No crab more active in the dirty dance,
Downward to climb, and backward to advance.   320
He brings up half the bottom on his head,
And loudly claims the Journals and the Lead.
   The plunging Prelate,[5] and his pond'rous Grace,
With holy envy gave one Layman place.
When lo! a burst of thunder shook the flood;   325
Slow rose a form, in majesty of Mud;
Shaking the horrors of his sable brows,
And each ferocious feature grim with ooze.
Greater he looks, and more than mortal stares;
Then thus the wonders of the deep declares.   330
   First he relates, how sinking to the chin,
Smit with his mien the Mud-nymphs suck'd him in:
How young Lutetia,[6] softer than the down,
Nigrina black, and Merdamante brown,

---

[1] *With each a sickly brother at his back: Sons of a Day! &c.*] These were daily papers, a number of which, to lessen the expense, were printed one on the back of another. P.

[2] *Like Niobe*] See the story in Ovid, Met. VII. where the miserable petrefaction of this old Lady is pathetically described. P.

[3] *Osborne*] A name assumed by the eldest and gravest of these writers, who at last, being ashamed of his Pupils, gave his paper over, and in his age remained silent. P.

[4] *Arnall*] WILLIAM ARNALL, bred an Attorney, was a perfect Genius in this sort of work. He began under twenty with furious Party-papers; then succeeded Concanen in the British Journal. At the first publication of the Dunciad, he prevailed on the Author not to give him his due place in it, by a letter professing his detestation of such practices as his predecessor's. But since, by the most unexampled insolence, and personal abuse of several great men, the Poet's particular friends, he most amply deserved a nitch in the Temple of Infamy: He writ for hire, and valued himself upon it; not indeed without cause, it appearing by the aforesaid REPORT, that he received " for Free Britons, and other writings, in the space of *four years*, no less than *ten thousand nine hundred and ninety seven pounds, six shillings, and eight pence*, out of the Treasury." But frequently, thro' his fury or folly, he exceeded all the bounds of his commission, and obliged his honourable Patron to disavow his scurrilities. P. [Part *om.*]

[5] Sir Robert Walpole, who was Bishop Sherlock's contemporary at Eton College, used to relate, that when some of the scholars, going to bathe in the Thames, stood shivering on the bank, S. plunged in immediately over head and ears. *Warton.* [Hence this was understood to refer to S.; but Pope indignantly repudiated the insinuation. The next allusion could only refer to an Archbishop; possibly ' leaden Gilbert ' of IV. 608. These two lines are wanting in the earlier editions.]

[6] [A play on the fancied etymology of the Latin name of Paris (Lutetia Parisiorum.)]

Vied for his love in jetty bow'rs below, 335
As Hylas fair[1] was ravished long ago.
Then sung, how shown him by the Nut-brown maids
A branch of Styx[2] here rises from the Shades,
That tinctur'd as it runs with Lethe's streams,
And wafting Vapours from the Land of dreams, 340
(As under seas Alpheus' secret sluice
Bears Pisa's off'rings to his Arethuse)
Pours into Thames: and hence the mingled wave
Intoxicates the pert, and lulls the grave:
Here brisker vapours o'er the TEMPLE creep, 345
There, all from Paul's to Aldgate drink and sleep.
Thence to the banks where rev'rend Bards repose,
They led him soft; each rev'rend Bard arose;
And Milbourn[3] chief, deputed by the rest,
Gave him the cassock, surcingle, and vest. 350
" Receive " (he said) " these robes which once were mine,
" Dulness is sacred in a sound divine."
He ceas'd, and spread the robe; the crowd confess
The rev'rend Flamen in his lengthen'd dress.
Around him wide a sable Army stand, 355
A low-born, cell-bred, selfish, servile band,
Prompt or to guard or stab, to saint or damn,
Heav'n's Swiss, who fight for any God or Man.[4]
Thro' Lud's fam'd gates,[5] along the well-known Fleet,
Rolls the black troop, and overshades the street; 360
'Till show'rs of Sermons, Characters, Essays,
In circling fleeces whiten all the ways:
So clouds, replenish'd from some bog below,
Mount in dark volumes, and descend in snow.
Here stopt the Goddess; and in pomp proclaims 365
A gentler exercise to close the games.
" Ye Critics in whose heads, as equal scales,

---

[1] *As Hylas fair*] Who was ravished by the water-nymphs and drawn into the river. The story is told at large by Valerius Flaccus, lib. III. *Argon.* See VIRGIL, *Ecl.* VI. P.

[2] *A branch of Styx, &c.*] Cf. Homer, *Il.* II. [vv. 751–755]. Of the land of Dreams in the same region, he makes mention, *Odyss.* XXIV. See also Lucian's True History. *Lethe* and the *Land of Dreams* allegorically represent the *Stupefaction* and *visionary Madness* of Poets, equally dull and extravagant. Of Alpheus's waters gliding secretly under the sea of Pisa, to mix with those of Arethuse in Sicily, see Moschus, *Idyl.* VIII. Virg. *Ecl.* X. vv. 3, 4. And again, *Æn.* III. vv. 693-5. P.

[3] *And Milbourn*] Luke Milbourn, a Clergyman, the fairest of Critics; who, when he wrote against Mr. Dryden's Virgil, did him

justice in printing at the same time his own translations of him, which were intolerable. His manner of writing has a great resemblance with that of the Gentlemen of the Dunciad against our Author. P. [Part *om.*] [Cf. *Essay on Criticism*, v. 463.]

[4] The expression is taken from Dryden's *Hind and Panther:* ' Those Swisses fight for any side for pay.' *Warton.* [The well-known proverb ' Point d'argent, point de Suisse' contains a similar sarcasm. The French Kings had a Swiss guard from the time of Louis XI. to that of Louis XVI.]

[5] [Ludgate, according to popular tradition, built by King Lud, (see *Faerie Queene*, Bk. II. Canto x. st. 46), probably is the same as Flood (or Fleet) gate. The gate, after being rebuilt several times, was finally removed in 1760.]

"I weigh what author's heaviness prevails;
"Which most conduce to soothe the soul in slumbers,
"My H—ley's [1] periods, or my Blackmore's numbers;   370
"Attend the trial we propose to make:
"If there be man, who o'er such works can wake,
"Sleep's all-subduing charms who dares defy,
"And boasts Ulysses' ear with Argus' eye; [2]
"To him we grant our amplest pow'rs to sit   375
"Judge of all present, past, and future wit;
"To cavil, censure, dictate, right or wrong;
"Full and eternal privilege of tongue."
    Three College Sophs,[3] and three pert Templars came,
The same their talents, and their tastes the same;   380
Each prompt to query, answer, and debate,
And smit with love of Poesy and Prate,
The pond'rous books two gentle readers bring;
The heroes sit, the vulgar form a ring.
The clam'rous crowd is hush'd with mugs of Mum,[4]   385
'Till all, tun'd equal, send a gen'ral hum.
Then mount the Clerks, and in one lazy tone
Thro' the long, heavy, painful page drawl on;
Soft creeping, words on words, the sense compose;
At ev'ry line they stretch, they yawn, they doze.   390
As to soft gales top-heavy pines bow low
Their heads, and lift them as they cease to blow:
Thus oft they rear, and of the head decline,
As breathe, or pause, by fits, the airs divine;
And now to this side, now to that they nod,   395
As verse, or prose, infuse the drowsy God.
Thrice Budgel aim'd to speak,[5] but thrice supprest
By potent Arthur,[6] knock'd his chin and breast.
Toland and Tindal, prompt at priests to jeer,[7]

---

[1] [*Henley's* in the early editions; probably the blank was substituted to leave an opportunity for supplying it with the name of *Hoadley.*]

[2] See Hom. *Odyss.* XII. Ovid, *Met.* I. .P.

[3] [A Sophister is properly a disputant at an exercise of dialectics; the term from its use at the old examinations for the Degree at Cambridge has come to mean those who have been one year or two years in residence at the University (Junior and Senior Sophs.)]

[4] [*Mum* was a strong ale, said to derive its name from its inventor, Christian Mumme of Brunswick.]

[5] *Thrice Budgel aim'd to speak,*] Famous for his speeches on many occasions about the South Sea scheme, &c. "He is a very ingenious gentleman, and hath written some excellent Epilogues to Plays, and *one small* piece on Love, which is very pretty." Jacob, *Lives of Poets.* But this gentleman since made himself

much more eminent, and personally well known to the greatest Statesmen of all parties, as well as to all the Courts of Law in this nation. P. Budgell was a relation of Addison whom he accompanied as clerk to Ireland. He afterwards rose to be Under Secretary of State. After Addison's death he was involved in losses by the South Sea Bubble; a stain fell on his character in consequence of Tindal's bequest in his favour being set aside, and he committed suicide in 1737. *Carruthers.* [Cf. *Epistle to Arbuthnot*, vv. 378, 9; and *notes.*]

[6] [Blackmore.]

[7] Ver. 399; in the first Edition it was:

'Collins and Tindal, prompt at priests to jeer.'
                                        Warburton.

Toland and Tindal,] Two persons, not so happy as to be obscure, who writ against the Religion of their Country. *Toland*, the author of the Atheist's Liturgy, called *Pantheisticon,*

Yet silent bow'd to *Christ's No kingdom here.*[1]   400
Who sate the nearest, by the words o'ercome,
Slept first; the distant nodded to the hum.
Then down are roll'd the books; stretch'd o'er 'em lies
Each gentle clerk, and mutt'ring seals his eyes,
As what a Dutchman plumps into the lakes,   405
One circle first, and then a second makes;
What Dulness dropt among her sons imprest
Like motion, from one circle to the rest;
So from the mid-most the mutation spreads
Round and more round, o'er all the *sea of heads.*   410
At last Centlivre[2] felt her voice to fail;
Motteux[3] himself unfinish'd left his tale;
Boyer the State, and Law the Stage gave o'er;[4]
Morgan[5] and Mandevil[6] could prate no more;
Norton,[7] from Daniel and Ostrœa sprung,   415
Bless'd with his father's front, and mother's tongue,

was a spy, in pay to lord Oxford. *Tindal* was author of the *Rights of the Christian Church,* and *Christianity as old as the Creation.* P. [Part *om.*] [John Toland's most famous work *Christianity not mysterious* was published in 1696; Matthew Tindal's *Christianity as old as the Creation,* rather later. Anthony Collins, who probably lost his place in the text for the sake of the alliteration, brought out his *Discourse of free Thinking* in 1713.]

[1] *Christ's No kingdom, &c.*] This is said by Curl, Key to Dunc. to allude to a sermon of a reverend Bishop. P. It alludes to Bishop Hoadley's sermons preached before George I., in 1717, *on the Nature* of the Kingdom of Christ, which occasioned a long, vehement, and learned debate, known as the Bangorian Controversy, of which see Hoadley was at that time bishop. *Wakefield.*

[2] *Centlivre*] Mrs. Susanna Centlivre, wife to Mr. Centlivre, Yeoman of the Mouth to his Majesty. She writ many Plays, and a Song (says Mr. Jacob) before she was seven years old. She also writ a Ballad against Mr. Pope's Homer before he began it. P. [Some of her plays still keep the stage.]

[3] Peter Anthony Motteux, the excellent translator of Don Quixote, and author of a number of forgotten dramatic pieces. Dryden addressed a complimentary Epistle to him. He died in 1718. *Carruthers.*

[4] *Boyer the State, and Law the Stage gave o'er;*] A. Boyer, a voluminous compiler of Annals, Political Collections, &c. — William Law, A.M. wrote with great zeal against the Stage; Mr. Dennis answered with as great: Their books were printed in 1726. The same Mr.

Law is author of a book, intitled, *An Appeal to all that doubt of or disbelieve the truth of the gospel;* in which he has detailed a system of the rankest Spinozism, for the most exalted Theology; and amongst other things as rare, informed us of this, that Sir Isaac Newton stole the principles of his philosophy from one *Jacob Bœhmen,* a German cobbler. P.

[5] A man of some learning, and uncommon acuteness, with a strong disposition to Satire, which very often degenerated into scurrility. His most celebrated work is the *Moral Philosopher,* first published in the year 1737. *Bowles.*

[6] [Bernard de Mandeville was born in Holland, in 1670, and after residing in England during the latter half of his life, died in 1733. The *Fable of the Bees,* to which he owed his fame, first appeared in 1708 in the form of a short poem, and was afterwards republished with explanatory notes and essays, which drew upon the author the threat of a prosecution. In its enlarged form it bore the second title of *Private Vices Public Benefits,* which explains the moral or object of the Fable. Though Mandeville only meant to shew that under the system of Providence good is wrought out of evil, he would have done well to leave no doubt as to both the meaning and the limitations of his doctrine.]

[7] *Norton*] Norton De Foe, offspring of the famous Daniel. *Fortes creantur fortibus.* One of the authors of the Flying Post, in which well-bred work Mr. P. has sometime the honour to be abused with his betters; and of many hired scurrilities and daily papers, to which he never set his name. P. [Does *Ostrœa* here signify an oyster-wife?]

Hung silent down his never-blushing head;
And all was hush'd, as Folly's self lay dead.
   Thus the soft gifts of Sleep conclude the day,
And stretch'd on bulks, as usual, Poets lay.   420
Why should I sing, what bards the nightly Muse
Did slumb'ring visit, and convey to stews;
Who prouder march'd, with magistrates in state,
To some fam'd round-house, ever open gate!
How Henley lay inspir'd beside a sink,   425
And to mere mortals seem'd a Priest in drink:
While others, timely, to the neighb'ring Fleet [1]
(Haunt of the Muses) made their safe retreat.

THE DUNCIAD.

BOOK THE THIRD.

ARGUMENT.

After the other persons are disposed in their proper places of rest, the Goddess trans-
ports the King to her Temple, and there lays him to slumber with his head on her lap;
a position of marvellous virtue, which causes all the visions of wild enthusiasts, project-
ors, politicians, inamoratos, castle-builders, chemists, and poets. He is immediately car-
ried on the wings of Fancy, and led by a mad Poetical Sibyl to the Elysian shade; *where,*
on the banks of Lethe, *the souls of the dull are dipped by* Bavius, *before their entrance*
into this world. There he is met by the ghost of Settle, *and by him made acquainted*
with the wonders of the place, and with those which he himself is destined to perform.
He takes him to a Mount of Vision, *from whence he shews him the past triumphs of the*
Empire of Dulness, then the present, and lastly the future : how small a part of the
world was ever conquered by Science, how soon those conquests were stopped, and those
very nations again reduced to her dominion. Then distinguishing the Island of Great-
Britain, *shews by what aids, by what persons, and by what degrees it shall be brought to*
her Empire. Some of the persons he causes to pass in review before his eyes, describing
each by his proper figure, character, and qualifications. On a sudden the Scene shifts,
and a vast number of miracles and prodigies appear, utterly surprising and unknown to
the King himself, till they are explained to be the wonders of his own reign now com-
mencing. On this subject Settle *breaks into a congratulation, yet not unmixed with con-*
cern, that his own times were but types of these. He prophesies how first the nation shall
be over-run with Farces, Operas, *and* Shows; *how the throne of Dulness shall be*
advanced over the Theatres, *and set up even at* Court; *then how her Sons shall pre-*
side in the seats of Arts *and* Sciences: *giving a glimpse or Pisgah-sight of the future*
Fulness of her Glory, the accomplishment whereof is the subject of the fourth and last
book.

BOOK III.

BUT in her Temple's last recess enclos'd,
  On Dulness' lap th' Anointed head repos'd.
Him close she curtains round with Vapours blue,
And soft besprinkles with Cimmerian dew.
Then raptures high the seat of Sense o'erflow,   5

---

[1] *Fleet*] A prison for insolvent Debtors on the bank of the Ditch. P.

Which only heads refin'd from Reason know.
Hence, from the straw where Bedlam's Prophet nods,
He hears loud Oracles, and talks with Gods :
Hence the Fool's Paradise, the Statesman's Scheme,
The air-built Castle, and the golden Dream,   10
The Maid's romantic wish, the Chemist's flame,
And Poet's vision of eternal Fame.
    And now, on Fancy's easy wing convey'd,
The King descending views th' Elysian Shade.
A slip-shod Sibyl led his steps along,   15
In lofty madness meditating song ;
Her tresses staring from Poetic dreams,
And never wash'd, but in Castalia's streams.
Taylor,[1] their better Charon, lends an oar,
(Once swan of Thames, tho' now he sings no more.)   20
Benlowes,[2] propitious still to blockheads, bows ;
And Shadwell nods the Poppy [3] on his brows.
Here, in a dusky vale where Lethe rolls,
Old Bavius sits,[4] to dip poetic souls,
And blunt the sense, and fit it for a skull   25
Of solid proof, impenetrably dull :
Instant, when dipt, away they wing their flight,
Where Brown and Mears [5] unbar the gates of Light,
Demand new bodies, and in Calf's array
Rush to the world, impatient for the day.   30
Millions and millions on these banks he views,
Thick as the stars of night, or morning dews,

---

[1] *Taylor*] John Taylor the Water-poet, an honest man, who owns he learned not so much as the Accidence : A rare example of modesty in a Poet!

I must confess I do want eloquence,
And never scarce did learn my Accidence;
For having got from possum to posset,
I there was gravell'd, could no farther get.

He wrote fourscore books in the reign of James I. and Charles I. and afterwards (like Edward Ward) kept an Ale-house in Long-Acre. He died in 1654. P. [Carruthers corrects this date to 1653; and refers for an account of the poetic waterman to Southey's *Lives of Uneducated Poets*. A splendid edition of Taylor's poems has recently been published by the Spenser Society.]

[2] *Benlowes*,] A country gentleman, famous for his own bad poetry, and for patronizing bad poets, as may be seen from many Dedications of Quarles and others to him. Some of these anagram'd his name, *Benlowes into Benevolus:* to verify which he spent his whole estate upon them. P.

[3] *And Shadwell nods the Poppy &c.*] Shadwell took Opium for many years, and died

of too large a dose, in the year 1692. P. [The hero of *MacFlecknoe.*]

[4] *Old Bavius sits,*] Bavius was an ancient Poet, celebrated by Virgil for the like cause as Bays by our Author, though not in so christian-like a manner: For heathenishly it is declared by Virgil of Bavius, that he ought to be *hated* and *detested* for his evil works; *Qui Bavium non* odit; Whereas we have often had occasion to observe our Poet's great *Good Nature* and *Mercifulness* thro' the whole course of this Poem. SCRIBLERUS.

Mr. Dennis warmly contends, that Bavius was no inconsiderable author; nay, that " He and Mævius had (even in Augustus's days) a very formidable party at Rome, who thought them much superior to Virgil and Horace: For (saith he) I cannot believe they would have fixed that eternal brand upon them, if they had not been coxcombs in more than ordinary credit." Rem. on Pr. Arthur, part II. c. I. An argument which, if this poem should last, will conduce to the honour of the gentlemen of the Dunciad. P.

[5] *Brown and Mears*] Booksellers, Printers for any body. P. [Part *om.*]

2 D

As thick as bees o'er vernal blossoms fly,
As thick as eggs at Ward in pillory.[1]
   Wond'ring he gaz'd: When lo! a Sage[2] appears,   35
By his broad shoulders known, and length of ears,
Known by the band and suit which Settle[3] wore
(His only suit) for twice three years before:
All as the vest, appear'd the wearer's frame,
Old in new state; another, yet the same.   40
Bland and familiar as in life, begun
Thus the great Father to the greater Son.
   "Oh born to see what none can see awake!
Behold the wonders of th' oblivious Lake.
Thou, yet unborn, hast touch'd this sacred shore;   45
The hand of Bavius drench'd thee o'er and o'er.
But blind to former, as to future fate,
What mortal knows his pre-existent state?
Who knows how long thy transmigrating soul
Might from Bœotian to Bœotian roll?   50
How many Dutchmen she vouchsaf'd to thrid?
How many stages thro' old Monks she rid?
And all who since, in mild benighted days,
Mix'd the Owl's ivy with the Poet's bays?
As man's Mæanders to the vital spring   55
Roll all their tides; then back their circles bring;
Or whirligigs twirl'd round by skilful swain,
Suck the thread in, then yield it out again:
All nonsense thus, of old or modern date,
Shall in thee centre, from thee circulate.   60
For this our Queen unfolds to vision true
Thy mental eye, for thou hast much to view:
Old scenes of glory, times long cast behind
Shall, first recall'd, rush forward to thy mind:
Then stretch thy sight o'er all her rising reign,   65
And let the past and future fire thy brain.
   "Ascend this hill, whose cloudy point commands
Her boundless empire over seas and lands.
See, round the Poles[4] where keener spangles shine,
Where spices smoke beneath the burning Line,   70
(Earth's wide extremes) her sable flag display'd,
And all the nations cover'd in her shade.

[1] *Ward in pillory.*] John Ward of Hackney, Esq. Member of Parliament, being convicted of forgery, was first expelled the House, and then sentenced to the Pillory on the 17th of February 1727. P. [Part *om.*] [Cf. *Moral Essays*, Ep. III. 20, *note.*]

[2] [Dante.]

[3] *Settle*] Elkanah Settle was once a Writer in vogue as well as Cibber, both for Dramatic Poetry and Politics. He was author or publisher of many noted pamphlets in the time of King Charles II. He answered all Dryden's political poems; and, being carried up on *one side*, succeeded not a little in his Tragedy of the *Empress of Morocco*. P. [Part *om.*] [For an account of this extremely sensational play, against which strictures were indited by Dryden, Shadwell and Crown, see Geneste, *u. s.* Vol. I. p. 154.]

[4] *See, round the Poles &c.*] Almost the whole Southern and Northern Continent wrapt in ignorance. P.

" Far eastward cast thine eye, from whence the Sun [1]
And orient Science their bright course begun :
One god-like Monarch [2] all that pride confounds, 75
He, whose long wall the wand'ring Tartar bounds ;
Heav'ns! what a pile! whole ages perish there,
And one bright blaze turns Learning into air.
" Thence to the south extend thy gladden'd eyes ;
There rival flames with equal glory rise, 80
From shelves to shelves see greedy Vulcan roll, [3]
And lick up all the Physic of the Soul.
How little, mark! that portion of the ball,
Where, faint at best, the beams of Science fall :
Soon as they dawn, from Hyperborean skies 85
Embody'd dark, what clouds of Vandals rise!
Lo! where Mæotis sleeps, and hardly flows
The freezing Tanais thro' a waste of snows, [4]
The North by myriads pours her mighty sons,
Great nurse of Goths, of Alans, [5] and of Huns! 90
See Alaric's stern port! the martial frame
Of Genseric! and Attila's [6] dread name!
See the bold Ostrogoths on Latium fall ;
See the fierce Visigoths on Spain and Gaul!
See, where the morning gilds the palmy shore 95
(The soil that arts and infant letters bore [7])
His conqu'ring tribes th' Arabian prophet draws,
And saving Ignorance enthrones by Laws.
See Christians, Jews, one heavy sabbath keep,
And all the western world believe and sleep. 100
" Lo! Rome herself, proud mistress now no more
Of arts, but thund'ring against heathen lore ; [8]
Her grey-hair'd Synods damning books unread,

[1] Ver. 73; in the former Editions:
' Far eastward cast thine eye, from whence the
Sun
And orient Science *at a birth begun.'*
Warburton.
Our Author favours the opinion that all Sci-
ences came from the Eastern nations. • P.

[2] Chi Ho-am-ti Emperor of China, the same
who built the great wall between China and
Tartary, destroyed all the books and learned
men of that empire. P.

[3] The Caliph, Omar I., having conquered
Ægypt, caused his General to burn the Ptole-
mæan library, on the gates of which was this
inscription, ΨΥΧΗΣΙΑΤΡΕΙΟΝ, the Physic of
the Soul. P. [A.D. 641. Gibbon was strongly
inclined to dispute the fact, but fresh authorities
corroborating it have been adduced by Mil-
man.]

[4] I have been told that this was the couplet
by which Pope declared his own ear to be most

gratified; but the reason of this preference I
cannot discover. *Johnson.*

[5] [The Alemanni, who twice invaded Gaul.]

[6] [Kings of the Goths, Vandals and Huns
respectively.]

[7] (*The soil that arts and infant letters
bore*)] Phœnicia, Syria, &c. where Letters are
said to have been invented. In these countries
Mahomet began his conquests. P.

[8] [Pope has a long note attempting to bring
home this charge against Pope Gregory I. (the
Great). His hatred of classical learning is un-
doubted; his destruction of ancient buildings
rests only on later evidence. See Gibbon, chap·
XLV. Compare on this and the whole subject of
the prejudices of the Church against profane
learning the first chapter of Hallam's *Lit. of
Europe.* The establishment of the *Index Ex-
purgatorius* belongs to the century of the
Reformation.]

And Bacon trembling for his brazen head.[1]
Padua, with sighs, beholds her Livy burn,[2]   105
And ev'n th' Antipodes Virgilius mourn.
See the Cirque falls, th' unpillar'd Temple nods,
Streets pav'd with Heroes, Tiber chok'd with Gods:
'Till Peter's keys some christ'ned Jove adorn,[3]
And Pan to Moses lends his pagan horn;   110
See, graceless Venus to a Virgin turn'd,
Or Phidias broken, and Apelles burn'd.
   " Behold yon' Isle, by Palmers, Pilgrims trod,
Men bearded, bald, cowl'd, uncowl'd, shod, unshod,
Peel'd, patch'd, and pyebald, linsey-wolsey brothers,   115
Grave Mummers! sleeveless some, and shirtless others.
That once was Britain — Happy! had she seen
No fiercer sons, had Easter never been.[4]
In peace, great Goddess, ever be ador'd;
How keen the war, if Dulness draw the sword!   120
Thus visit not thy own! on this blest age
Oh spread thy Influence, but restrain thy Rage!
   " And see, my son! the hour is on its way,
That lifts our Goddess to imperial sway:
This fav'rite Isle, long sever'd from her reign,   125
Dove-like, she gathers [5] to her wings again.
Now look thro' Fate! behold the scene she draws!
What aids, what armies to assert her cause!
See all her progeny, illustrious sight!
Behold, and count them, as they rise to light.   130
As Berecynthia, while her offspring vie
In homage to the mother of the sky,
Surveys around her, in the blest abode,
An hundred sons, and ev'ry son a God:
Not with less glory mighty Dulness crown'd   135
Shall take thro' Grubstreet her triumphant round;
And her Parnassus glancing o'er at once,
Behold an hundred sons, and each a Dunce.

---

[1] [Roger Bacon lived in the 13th century; the earliest English cultivator of mathematical science. His ' brazen head' was a popular superstition connected with his experiments in magic; and is alluded to in Butler's *Hudibras*.]

[2] [Livy is said to have been burnt among other authors by Gregory I.]

[3] *'Till Peter's keys some christ'ned Jove adorn,*] After the government of Rome devolved to the Popes, their zeal was for some time exerted in demolishing the Heathen Temples and Statues, so that the Goths scarce destroyed more monuments of Antiquity out of rage, than these out of devotion. At length they spared some of the temples, by converting them into Churches; and some of the Statues, by modifying them into images of Saints. In much later times, it was thought necessary to change the statues of Apollo and Pallas, on the tomb of Sannazarius, into David and Judith; the Lyre easily became a Harp, and the Gorgon's head turned to that of Holofernes. P. [Abundant instances of this will be found in any description of Rome.]

[4] *Happy! — had Easter never been.*] Wars in England anciently, about the right time of celebrating Easter. P. [It was not till the visit of St. Augustine in 596 that the British Church conformed to the decision of the Council of Nice as to the day on which Easter should be kept.]

[5] *Dove-like she gathers*] This is fulfilled in the fourth book. P.

"Mark first that youth who takes the foremost place,
And thrust his person full into your face.   140
With all thy Father's virtues blest, be born![1]
And a new Cibber shall the stage adorn.
  "A second see, by meeker manners known,
And modest as the maid that sips alone ;
From the strong fate of drams if thou get free,   145
Another Durfey,[2] Ward! shall sing in thee.
Thee shall each ale-house, thee each gill-house mourn,
And answ'ring gin-shops sourer sights return.
  "Jacob, the scourge of Grammar, mark with awe,[3]
Nor less revere him, blunderbuss of Law.   150
Lo P—p—le's brow, tremendous to the town,
Horneck's fierce eye, and Roome's[4] funereal frown.
Lo sneering Goode,[5] half malice and half whim,
A friend in glee, ridiculously grim.
Each Cygnet sweet, of Bath and Tunbridge race,   155
Whose tuneful whistling makes the waters pass ;[6]
Each Songster, Riddler, ev'ry nameless name,
All crowd, who foremost shall be damn'd to Fame.[7]
Some strain in rhyme ; the Muses, on their racks,
Scream like the winding of ten thousand jacks ;   160
Some free from rhyme or reason, rule or check,

---

[1] [As to Cibber's father see Pope's note to Bk. I. v. 30.]

[2] [Durfey; v. *Essay on Criticism*, v. 618.]

[3] *Jacob, the scourge of Grammar, mark with awe*,] "This *Gentleman* is son of a *considerable Maltster* of Romsey in Southamptonshire, and bred to the Law under a *very eminent Attorney :* Who, between his *more laborious* studies, has *diverted* himself with Poetry. He is a great admirer of poets and their works, which has occasioned him to try his genius that way.— He has written in prose the *Lives* of the *Poets, Essays*, and a great many Law-books, *The Accomplished Conveyancer, Modern Justice, &c.* GILES JACOB of himself, *Lives of Poets*, vol. 1. He very grossly, and unprovok'd, abused, in that book the Author's Friend, Mr. *Gay*. P.

[4] *Horneck and Roome*] These two were virulent party-writers, worthily coupled together, and one would think prophetically, since, after the publishing of this piece, the former dying, the latter succeeded him in *Honour* and *Employment*. The first was Phil p Horneck, author of a Billingsgate paper called The High German Doctor. Edward Roome was son of an Undertaker for Funerals in Fleet-street, and writ some of the papers called Pasquin, where by malicious innuendos he endeavoured to rep-

resent our Author guilty of malevolent practices with a great man then under prosecution of Parliament. Of this man was made the following Epigram :
"You ask why Roome diverts you with his jokes,
Yet if he writes, is dull as other folks?
You wonder at it— This, sir, is the case,
The jest is lost unless he prints his face."
Popple was the author of some vile Plays and Pamphlets. He published abuses on our Author in a paper called the Prompter. P.

[5] *Goode*,] An ill-natur'd Critic, who writ a satire on our Author, called *The mock Æsop*, and many anonymous Libels in News-papers for hire. P.

[6] [Borrowed from two lines of *Young's Universal Passion*, Sat. 6.] *Warton.*

Whose tuneful whistling makes the waters pass :] There were several successions of these sort of minor poets, at Tunbridge, Bath, &c. singing the praise of the Annuals flourishing for that season ; whose names indeed would be nameless, and therefore the Poet slurs them over with others in general. P.

[7] After Ver. 158 in the former Editions followed :
' How proud, how pale, how earnest all appear!
How rhymes eternal jingle in their ear!'
                          Warburton.

Break Priscian's[1] head, and Pegasus's neck;
Down, down they larum, with impetuous whirl,
The Pindars, and the Miltons of a Curl.
    "Silence, ye Wolves! while Ralph[2] to Cynthia howls,[3]   165
And makes night hideous — Answer him, ye Owls!
    "Sense, speech, and measure, living tongues and dead,
Let all give way, and Morris[4] may be read.
Flow, Welsted, flow! like thine inspirer, Beer,
Tho' stale, not ripe; tho' thin, yet never clear;   170
So sweetly mawkish, and so smoothly dull;
Heady, not strong; o'erflowing, tho' not full.
    "Ah Dennis![5] Gildon ah! what ill-starr'd rage
Divides a friendship long confirm'd by age?
Blockheads with reason wicked wits abhor;   175
But fool with fool is barb'rous civil war.
Embrace, embrace, my sons! be foes no more!
Nor glad vile Poets with true Critics' gore.
    "Behold yon Pair,[6] in strict embraces join'd;
How like in manners, and how like in mind!   180
Equal in wit, and equally polite,
Shall this a *Pasquin*, that a *Grumbler* write;
Like are their merits, like rewards they share,
That shines a Consul, this Commissioner.[7]
    "But who is he, in closet close y-pent,   185
Of sober face, with learned dust besprent?

---

[1] [Priscian, the celebrated Roman grammarian, lived in the time of Justinian, who appointed him teacher of grammar at Constantinople.]

[2] *Ralph*] James Ralph, a name inserted after the first editions, not known to our Author till he writ a swearing-piece called *Sawney*, very abusive of Dr. Swift, Mr. Gay, and himself. These lines allude to a thing of his, intitled, *Night*, a Poem: This low writer attended his own works with panegyrics in the Journals, and once in particular praised himself highly above Mr. Addison. He was wholly illiterate, and knew no language, not even *French*. Being advised to read the rules of dramatic poetry before he began a play, he smiled and replied, "*Shakespear* writ without rules." He ended at last in the common sink of all such writers, a political News-paper, to which he was recommended by his friend Arnal, and received a small pittance for pay. P.

[3] [Shaksp. *Jul. Cæs.* Act iv. Sc. 3: 'I'd rather be a dog and bay the moon, &c.' But Wakefield has pointed out two lines by Ambrose Philips parodied in the above.]

[4] *Morris,*] Besaleel. See Book ii. [v. 126]. P.

[5] *Ah Dennis! &c.*] The reader, who has seen thro' the course of these notes, what a constant attendance Mr. Dennis paid to our Author and all his works, may perhaps wonder he should be mentioned but twice, and so slightly touched, in this poem. But in truth he looked upon him with some esteem, for having (more generously than all the rest) *set his Name* to such writings. He was also a very old man at this time. By his own account of himself in Mr. *Jacob's Lives*, he must have been above threescore, and happily lived many years after. So that he was senior to Mr. *Durfey*, who hitherto of all our poets enjoyed the longest bodily life. P.

[6] *Behold yon Pair, &c.*] One of these was author of a weekly paper called the *Grumbler*, as the other was concerned in another called *Pasquin*, in which Mr. *Pope* was abused with the duke of *Buckingham*, and Bishop of *Rochester*. They also joined in a piece against his first undertaking to translate the *Iliad*, intituled *Homerides*, by Sir *Iliad Doggrel*, printed 1715. P. [Part *om.*]

[7] *That shines a* Consul, *this* Commissioner.] Such places were given at this time to such sort of writers. P.

Right well mine eyes arede[1] the myster wight,
On parchment scraps y-fed, and Wormius hight.[2]
To future ages may thy dulness last,
As thou preserv'st the dulness of the past!   190
" There, dim in clouds, the poring Scholiasts mark,
Wits, who, like owls,[3] see only in the dark,
A Lumber-house of books in ev'ry head,
For ever reading, never to be read!
" But, where each Science lifts its modern type,   195
Hist'ry her Pot, Divinity her Pipe,
While proud Philosophy repines to show,
Dishonest sight! his breeches rent below;
Embrown'd with native bronze, lo! Henley stands,[4]
Turning his voice, and balancing his hands.   200
How fluent nonsense trickles from his tongue!
How sweet the periods, neither said, nor sung!
Still break the benches, Henley! with thy strain,
While Sherlock, Hare, and Gibson[5] preach in vain.
Oh great Restorer of the good old Stage,   205
Preacher at once, and Zany of thy age!
Oh worthy thou of Ægypt's wise abodes,
A decent priest, where monkeys were the gods!

[1] *arede*] *Read*, or *peruse;* though sometimes used for *counsel.* P. [*Myster*, like *arede* and *besprent*, is a word used by Spenser. But Pope explains it wrongly: it is equivalent to manner, craft or trade (French *métier*, probably from *magister*). ' *The* myster wight' is nonsense; 'such myster wight' would be sense.] *Myster wight*] Uncouth morta.. P.

[2] Wormius *hight.*] Let not this name, purely fictitious, be conceited to mean the learned *Olaus Wormius ;* much less (as it was unwarrantably foisted into the surreptitious editions) our own Antiquary Mr. *Thomas Hearne*, who had no way aggrieved our Poet, but on the contrary published many curious tracts which he hath to his great contentment perused. P. [Part *om.*]

hight] " In Cumberland they say to *hight*, for to *promise*, or *vow ;* but HIGHT, usually signifies *was called ;* and so it does in the North even to this day, notwithstanding what is done in Cumberland." *Hearne.* P. [The old hâtan means to call and to promise (German *heissen*, *verheissen*).]

[3] *Wits, who, like owls, &c.*] These few lines exactly describe the right verbal critic: The darker his author is, the better he is pleased; like the famous Quack Doctor, who put up in his bills, *he delighted in matters of difficulty.* Some body said well of these men, that their heads were *Libraries out of order.* P.

[4] *lo! Henley stands, &c.*] J. Henley the Orator; he preached on the Sundays upon Theological matters, and on the Wednesdays upon all other sciences. Each auditor paid one shilling. He declaimed some years against the greatest persons, and occasionally did our Author that honour. After having stood some Prosecutions, he turned his rhetoric to buffoonery upon all publick and private occurrences. This man nad an hundred pounds a year given him for the secret service of a weekly paper of unintelligible nonsense, called the Hyp-Doctor. P. [Part *om.*] [John Henley, a native of Leicestershire, had graduated at Cambridge; but set up a scheme of Universology on his own account, establishing his ' Oratory ' in a wooden booth in Newport market in 1726. Three years later he removed his pulpit to the corner of Lincoln's Inn Fields, and though subjected to a prosecution for profaning the clerical character, continued his exhibitions till the middle of the century. See Wright's *Caric. Hist. of the Georges*, and Jesse, *George Selwyn and his Contemporaries*, Vol. I., where Henley is said to have been a man of real learning and of poetical talent. He died in 1756.]

[5] *Sherlock, Hare, Gibson,*] Bishops of Salisbury, Chichester, and London; whose Sermons and Pastoral Letters did honour to their country as well as stations. P.

But fate with butchers placed thy priestly stall,
Meek modern faith to murder, hack, and maul;					210
And bade thee live, to crown Britannia's praise,
In Toland's, Tindal's, and in Woolston's days.[1]
    "Yet oh, my sons, a father's words attend:
(So may the fates preserve the ears you lend)
'Tis yours a Bacon or a Locke to blame,					215
A Newton's genius, or a Milton's flame:
But oh! with One, immortal One dispense;
The source of Newton's Light, of Bacon's Sense.
Content, each Emanation of his fires
That beams on earth, each Virtue he inspires,					220
Each Art he prompts, each Charm he can create,
Whate'er he gives, are giv'n for you to hate.
Persist, by all divine in Man unaw'd,
But 'Learn, ye DUNCES! not to scorn your God.'"[2]
    Thus he, for then a ray of Reason stole					225
Half thro' the solid darkness of his soul;
But soon the cloud return'd — and thus the Sire:
"See now, what Dulness and her sons admire!
See what the charms, that smite the simple heart
Not touch'd by Nature, and not reach'd by Art."					230
    His never-blushing head he turn'd aside,
(Not half so pleas'd when Goodman prophesy'd [3])
And look'd, and saw a sable Sorc'rer [4] rise,
Swift to whose hand a winged volume flies:
All sudden, Gorgons hiss, and Dragons glare,					235
And ten-horn'd fiends and Giants rush to war.
Hell rises, Heav'n descends, and dance on Earth:[5]
Gods, imps, and monsters, music, rage, and mirth,

---

[1] *Of Toland* and *Tindal*, see Book II. [v. 399]. *Tho. Woolston* was an impious madman, who wrote in a most insolent style against the Miracles of the Gospel, in the years 1726, &c. P.

[2] *But, 'Learn, ye Dunces! not to scorn your God.'*] Virg. *Æn.* VI. [v. 619]. The hardest lesson a *Dunce* can learn. For being bred to *scorn* what he does not understand, that which he understands least he will be apt to *scorn* most. Of which, to the disgrace of all Government, and (in the Poet's opinion) even of that of DULNESS herself, we have had a late example in a book intitled, *Philosophical Essays concerning human Understanding.* P.

'*not to scorn your God.*'] See this subject pursued in Book IV. P.

[3] (*Not half so pleas'd when Goodman prophesy'd*)] Mr. Cibber tells us, in his Life, p. 149, that Goodman being at the rehearsal of a play, in which he had a part, clapped him on

the shoulder and cried, "If he does not make a good actor, I'll be d——d." — And (says Mr. Cibber) I make it a question, whether Alexander himself, or Charles the Twelfth of Sweden, when at the head of their first victorious armies, could feel a greater transport in their bosoms than I did in mine. P.

[4] *a sable Sorc'rer*] Dr. Faustus, the subject of a set of Farces, which lasted in vogue two or three seasons, in which both Play-houses strove to outdo each other for some years. All the extravagances in the sixteen lines following were introduced on the Stage, and frequented by persons of the first quality in England, to the twentieth and thirtieth time. P. [Probably revivals of Mountfort's harlequinade founded on Marlowe's tragedy.]

[5] *Hell rises, Heav'n descends, and dance on Earth:*] This monstrous absurdity was actually represented in Tibbald's *Rape of Proserpine.* P.

A fire, a jig, a battle, and a ball,
'Till one wide conflagration swallows all.   240
    Thence a new world to Nature's laws unknown,
Breaks out refulgent, with a heav'n its own:
Another Cynthia her new journey runs,
And other planets circle other suns.
The forests dance, the rivers upward rise,   245
Whales sport in woods, and dolphins in the skies;
And last, to give the whole creation grace,
Lo! one vast Egg [1] produces human race.
    Joy fills his soul, joy innocent of thought;
'What pow'r,' he cries, 'what pow'r these wonders wrought?' 250
"Son, what thou seek'st is in thee! Look, and find
Each monster meets his likeness in thy mind.
Yet would'st thou more? in yonder cloud behold,
Whose sars'net skirts are edg'd with flamy gold,
A matchless youth! his nod these worlds controls,   255
Wings the red lightning, and the thunder rolls.
Angel of Dulness, sent to scatter round
Her magic charms o'er all unclassic ground:
Yon stars, yon suns, he rears at pleasure higher,
Illumes their light, and sets their flames on fire.   260
Immortal Rich! [2] how calm he sits at ease
'Mid snows of paper, and fierce hail of pease;
And proud his Mistress' orders to perform,
Rides in the whirlwind, and directs the storm.
    "But lo! to dark encounter in mid air [3]   265
New wizards rise; I see my Cibber there!
Booth [4] in his cloudy tabernacle shrin'd, [5]
On grinning dragons thou shalt mount the wind. [6]
Dire is the conflict, dismal is the din,
Here shouts all Drury, there all Lincoln's-inn; [7]   270
Contending Theatres our empire raise,
Alike their labours, and alike their praise.
    "And are these wonders, Son, to thee unknown?
Unknown to thee? these wonders are thy own. [8]

---

[1] *Lo! one vast Egg*] In another of these
Farces, Harlequin is hatched upon the stage
out of a large Egg. P.

[2] *Immortal Rich!*] Mr. John Rich, Mas-
ter of the Theatre Royal in Covent-garden, was
the first that excelled this way. P.

[3] [Join their dark encounter in mid-air. Mil-
ton, *Par. Lost*, II. v. 718.]

[4] *Booth* and *Cibber* were joint managers of
the Theatre in Drury-lane. P.

[5] [as Harlequin.]

[6] *On grinning dragons thou shalt mount
the wind.*] In his Letter to Mr. P. Mr. C.
solemnly declares this not to be *literally true.*

We hope therefore the reader will understand it
allegorically only. P.

[7] [The Theatre called the Duke's was built
in Portugal Street, Lincoln's Inn Fields, at the
time of the Restoration. It was here Rich first
brought out his harlequinades; but soon after
his removal it was closed (1737).]

[8] After ver. 274 in the former Edd. followed:
For works like these let deathless Journals tell
    "None but thyself can be thy parallel."
                                    Warburton.

    Var. *None but thyself can be thy parallel*]
A marvellous line of *Theobald;* unless the Play
called the *Double Falsehood* be (as he would
have it believed) *Shakespear's.* P.

These Fate reserv'd to grace thy reign divine,   275
Foreseen by me, but ah! withheld from mine.
In Lud's old walls tho' long I rul'd, renown'd
Far as loud Bow's stupendous bells resound;
Tho' my own Aldermen conferr'd the bays,
To me committing their eternal praise,   280
Their full-fed Heroes, their pacific May'rs
Their annual trophies,[1] and their monthly wars;
Tho' long my Party [2] built on me their hopes,
For writing Pamphlets, and for roasting Popes; [3]
Yet lo! in me what authors have to brag on!   285
Reduc'd at last to hiss in my own dragon.
Avert it, Heav'n! that thou, my Cibber, e'er
Should'st wag a serpent-tail in Smithfield fair!
Like the vile straw that's blown about the streets,
The needy Poet sticks to all he meets,   290
Coach'd, carted, trod upon, now loose, now fast,
And carry'd off in some Dog's tail at last.
Happier thy fortunes! like a rolling stone,
Thy giddy dulness still shall lumber on,
Safe in its heaviness, shall never stray,   295
But lick up ev'ry blockhead in the way.
Thee shall the Patriot, thee the Courtier taste,[4]
And ev'ry year be duller than the last.
Till rais'd from booths, to Theatre, to Court,
Her seat imperial Dulness shall transport.   300
Already Opera prepares the way,
The sure fore-runner of her gentle sway:
Let her thy heart, next Drabs and Dice, engage,
The third mad passion of thy doting age.
Teach thou the warbling Polypheme [5] to roar,   305
And scream thyself as none e'er scream'd before!
To aid our cause, if Heav'n thou can'st not bend,
Hell thou shalt move; for Faustus is our friend:

---

[1] *Annual trophies*, on the Lord-mayor's day; and *monthly wars* in the Artillery-ground. P.

[2] *Tho' long my Party*] Settle, like most Party-writers, was very uncertain in his political principles. He was employed to hold the pen in the *Character* of a *popish successor*, but afterwards printed his *Narrative* on the other side. He had managed the ceremony of a famous Pope-burning on Nov. 17, 1680; then became a trooper in King James's army, at Hounslow-heath. After the Revolution he kept a booth at Bartholomew-fair, where, in the droll called *St. George for England*, he acted in his old age in a Dragon of green leather of his own invention; he was at last taken into the Charter-house, and there died, aged sixty years. P. [Carruthers observes that Settle

was really seventy-six at the time of his death (1724).]

[3] After ver. 284 in the former Edd. followed:
' Diff'rent our parties, but with equal grace
The Goddess smiles on Whig and Tory race.'
Warburton.

[4] *Thee shall the Patriot, thee the Courtier taste,*] It stood in the first edition with blanks * * *and* * *. Concanen was sure "they must needs mean no body but *King GEORGE* and *Queen CAROLINE;* and said he would insist it was so, till the Poet cleared himself by filling up the blanks otherwise, agreeably to the context, and consistent with his *allegiance.*" P.

[5] *Polypheme*] He translated the Italian Opera of *Polifemo;* but unfortunately lost the whole jest of the story. P. [Part *om.*]

Pluto[1] with Cato thou for this shalt join,
And link the Mourning Bride[2] to Proserpine.   310
Grubstreet! thy fall should men and Gods conspire,
Thy stage shall stand, ensure it but from Fire.[3]
Another Æschylus appears![4] prepare
For new abortions, all ye pregnant fair!
In flames, like Semele's,[5] be brought to bed,   315
While op'ning Hell spouts wild-fire at your head.
  " Now, Bavius, take the poppy from thy brow,
And place it here! here all ye Heroes bow!
This, this is he, foretold by ancient rhymes:
Th' Augustus born to bring Saturnian times.   320
Signs following signs lead on the mighty year!
See! the dull stars roll round and re-appear.
See, see, our own true Phœbus wears the bays![6]
Our Midas sits Lord Chancellor of Plays!
On Poets' Tombs see Benson's titles writ![7]   325
Lo! Ambrose Philips[8] is preferr'd for Wit!
See under Ripley rise a new White-hall,
While Jones' and Boyle's united Labours fall;[9]

[1] *Faustus, Pluto, &c.*] Names of miserable Farces, which it was the custom to act at the end of the best Tragedies, to spoil the digestion of the audience. P.

[2] [Congreve's tragedy.]

[3] *ensure it but from Fire.*] In Tibbald's farce of Proserpine, a corn-field was set on fire: whereupon the other play-house had a barn burnt down for the recreation of the spectators. They also rival'd each other in showing the burnings of hell-fire, in Dr. Faustus. P.

[4] *Another Æschylus appears!*] It is reported of Æschylus, that when his Tragedy of the Furies was acted, the audience were so terrified that the children fell into fits. P.

[5] *like Semele's,*] See Ovid, Met. III. P.

[6] Ver. 323. *See, see, our own &c.*] In the former Edd.:

' Beneath his reign shall Eusden wear the bays,
Cibber preside Lord Chancellor of plays,
Benson sole Judge of Architecture sit,
And Namby Pamby be preferr'd for Wit!
I see th' unfinish'd Dormitory wall,
I see the Savoy totter to her fall;
Hibernian Politics, O Swift! thy doom,
And Pope's, translating three whole years with
  Broome:
Proceed great days, &c.' *Warburton.*

[7] *On Poets' Tombs see Benson's Titles writ!*] W—m Benson (Surveyor of the Buildings to his Majesty King George I.) gave in a report to the Lords, that their House and the Painted-chamber adjoining were in immediate danger of falling. Whereupon the Lords met

in a committee to appoint some other place to sit in, while the House should be taken down. But it being proposed to cause some other builders first to inspect it, they found it in very good condition. In favour of this man, the famous Sir Christopher Wren, who had been Architect to the Crown for above fifty years, who built most of the churches in London, laid the first stone of St. Paul's, and lived to finish it, had been displaced from his employment at the age of near ninety years. P. [Part *om.*]

[8] *Ambrose Philips*] " He was (saith Mr. JACOB) one of the wits at Button's and a justice of the peace; " But he hath since met with higher preferment in Ireland. He endeavoured to create some misunderstanding between our Author and Mr. Addison, whom also soon after he abused as much. His constant cry was, that Mr. P. was an *Enemy to the government;* and in particular he was the avowed author of a report very industriously spread, that he had a hand in a Party-paper called the *Examiner:* A falsehood well-known to those yet living, who had the direction and publication of it. P. [As to the reasons for Pope's aversion from A. P. see *Introductory Memoir,* pp. xv, xxviii.]

[9] *While Jones' and Boyle's united Labours fall;*] At the time when this poem was written, the banqueting-house at White-hall, the church and piazza of Covent-garden, and the palace and chapel of Somerset-house, the works of the famous Inigo Jones, had been for many years so neglected, as to be in danger of ruin. The portico of Covent-garden church had been

While Wren with sorrow to the grave descends;[1]
Gay dies unpension'd[2] with a hundred friends;   330
Hibernian Politics, O Swift! thy fate;[3]
And Pope's, ten years to comment and translate.[4]
  " Proceed, great days! till Learning fly the shore,
Till Birch shall blush with noble blood no more,
Till Thames see Eton's sons for ever play,   335
Till Westminster's whole year be holiday,

just then restored and beautified at the expense of the earl of Burlington and [Richard Boyle]; who, at the same time, by his publication of the designs of that great Master and Palladio, as well as by many noble buildings of his own, revived the true taste of Architecture in this kingdom. P. [As to Ripley, Sir Robert Walpole's architect who, according to Wakefield, was employed in repairing Whitehall, cf. *Moral Essays*, Ep. IV. v. 18 and *note*.]

[1] [Sir Christopher Wren died in 1723, at the age of 91. 'The length of his life enriched the reigns of several princes, and disgraced the last of them.' *Horace Walpole, Anecdotes of Printing*, quoted by *Warton*.]

[2] *Gay dies unpension'd &c.*] See Mr. Gay's fable of the *Hare and many Friends*. This gentleman was early in the friendship of our Author, which continued to his death. He wrote several works of humour with great success, the Shepherd's Week, Trivia, the What-d'ye-call-it, Fables; and, lastly, the celebrated Beggar's Opera; a piece of satire which hits all tastes and degrees of men, from those of the highest quality to the very rabble. That verse of Horace,

Primores populi arripuit, populumque tributim,

could never be so justly applied as to this. The vast success of it was unprecedented, and almost incredible: What is related of the wonderful effects of the ancient music or tragedy hardly came up to it: Sophocles and Euripides were less followed and famous. It was acted in London sixty-three days, uninterrupted; and renewed the next season with equal applauses. It spread into all the great towns of England, was played in many places to the thirtieth and fortieth time, at Bath and Bristol fifty, &c. It made its progress into Wales, Scotland, and Ireland, where it was performed twenty-four days together: It was last acted in Minorca. The fame of it was not confined to the Author only; the ladies carried about with them the favourite songs of it in fans; and houses were furnished with it in screens. The person who acted Polly, till then obscure, became all at once the favourite of the town; her pictures

were engraved, and sold in great numbers; her life written, books of letters and verses to her published; and pamphlets made even of her sayings and jests.

Furthermore, it drove out of England, for that season, the Italian Opera, which had carried all before it for ten years. That idol of the Nobility and people, which the great Critic Mr. Dennis by the labours and outcries of a whole life could not overthrow, was demolished by a single stroke of this gentleman's pen. This happened in the year 1728. Yet so great was his modesty, that he constantly prefixed to all the editions of it this motto, *Nos hæc novimus esse nihil*. P. [See Epitaph No. xii. and *Introductory Memoir*, p. xxvi.]

[3] Ver. 331, in the former Editions thus:

'—— O Swift! thy doom,
And Pope's, translating ten whole years with
Broome.'

On which was the following Note, " He concludes his irony with a stroke upon himself; for whoever imagines this a sarcasm on the other ingenious person is surely mistaken. The opinion our Author had of him was sufficiently shewn by his joining him in the undertaking of the *Odyssey*; in which Mr. Broome, having engaged without any previous agreement, discharged his part so much to Mr. Pope's satisfaction, that he gratified him with the full sum of *Five hundred pounds*, and a present of all those books for which his own interest could procure him subscribers, to the value of *One hundred more*. The Author only seems to lament, that he was employed in Translation at all." P.

Hibernian Politics, O Swift! thy fate;] See Book I. ver. 26. P.

[4] *And Pope's, ten years to comment and translate.*] The Author here plainly laments that he was so long employed in translating and commenting. He began the Iliad in 1713, and finished it in 1719. The edition of Shakespear (which he undertook merely because no body else would) took up near two years more in the drudgery of comparing impressions, rectifying the Scenery, &c., and the translation of half the Odyssey employed him from that time to 1725. P.

Till Isis' Elders reel, their pupils' sport,
Till Alma Mater lie dissolv'd in Port!"[1]
'Enough! enough!' the raptur'd Monarch cries;
And thro' the Iv'ry Gate the Vision flies.　　　　　340

THE DUNCIAD.

BOOK THE FOURTH.

ARGUMENT.

The Poet being, in this Book to declare the Completion *of the* Prophecies *mentioned at the end of the former, makes a new* Invocation; *as the greater Poets are wont, when some high and worthy matter is to be sung. He shews the Goddess coming in her Majesty, to destroy Order and Science, and to substitute the* Kingdom *of the Dull upon earth. How she leads captive the Sciences, and silenceth the Muses, and what they be who succeed in their stead. All her Children, by a wonderful attraction, are drawn about her; and bear along with them divers others, who promote her Empire by connivance, weak resistance, or discouragement of Arts; such as Half-wits, tasteless Admirers, vain Pretenders, the Flatterers of Dunces, or the Patrons of them. All these crowd round her; one of them offering to approach her is driven back by a Rival; but she commends and encourages both. The first who speak in form are the Geniuses of the Schools, who assure her of their care to advance her Cause, by confining Youth to Words, and keeping them out of the way of real Knowledge. Their Address, and her gracious Answer; with her Charge to them and the Universities. The Universities appear by their proper Deputies, and assure her that the same method is observed in the progress of Education. The speech of Aristarchus on this subject. They are drawn off by a band of young Gentlemen returned from* Travel *with their Tutors; one of whom delivers to the Goddess, in a polite oration, an account of the whole Conduct and Fruits of their Travels: presenting to her at the same time a young Nobleman perfectly accomplished. She receives him graciously, and endues him with the happy quality of Want of Shame. She sees loitering about her a number of Indolent Persons abandoning all business and duty, and dying with laziness : To these approaches the Antiquary Annius, intreating her to make them Virtuoso's, and assign them over to him. But Mummius, another Antiquary, complaining of his fraudulent proceeding, she finds a method to reconcile their difference. Then enter a troop of people fantastically adorned, offering her strange and exotic presents : Amongst them one stands forth and demands justice on another, who had deprived him of one of the greatest Curiosities in nature; but he justifies himself so well, that the Goddess gives them both her approbation. She recommends to them to find proper employment for the Indolents before-mentioned, in the study of Butterflies, Shells, Birds-nests, Moss, &c. but with particular caution, not to proceed beyond Trifles, to any useful or extensive views of Nature, or of the Author of Nature. Against the last of these apprehensions, she is secured by a hearty address from the Minute Philosophers and Freethinkers, one of whom speaks in the name of the rest. The Youth, thus instructed and principled, are delivered to her in a body, by the hands of Silenus and then admitted to taste the cup of the Magus her High Priest, which causes a total oblivion of all Obligations, divine, civil, moral, or rational. To these her Adepts she sends Priests, Attendants, and Comforters of various kinds; confers on them Orders and Degrees; and then dismissing them with a speech, confirming to each his Privileges, and telling what she expects from each, concludes with a Yawn of extraordinary virtue : The Progress and Effects whereof on all Orders of men, and the Consummation of all, in the restoration of Night and Chaos, conclude the Poem.*

---

[1] [Cf. Book IV. v. 202.]

BOOK IV.[1]

YET, yet a moment, one dim Ray of Light
  Indulge, dread Chaos, and eternal Night!
Of darkness visible so much be lent,
As half to shew, half veil, the deep Intent.
Ye Pow'rs! whose Mysteries restor'd I sing,   5
To whom Time bears me on his rapid wing,
Suspend awhile your Force inertly strong,[2]
Then take at once the Poet and the Song.
  Now flam'd the Dog-star's unpropitious ray,
Smote ev'ry Brain, and wither'd ev'ry Bay;   10
Sick was the Sun, the Owl forsook his bow'r,
The moon-struck Prophet felt the madding hour:
Then rose the Seed of Chaos, and of Night,
To blot out Order, and extinguish Light,
Of dull and venal a new World[3] to mould,   15
And bring Saturnian days of Lead and Gold.
  She mounts the Throne: her head a Cloud conceal'd,
In broad Effulgence all below reveal'd;
('T is thus aspiring Dulness ever shines)
Soft on her lap her Laureate son reclines.   20
  Beneath her footstool,[4] *Science* groans in Chains,
And *Wit* dreads Exile, Penalties, and Pains.
There foam'd rebellious *Logic*, gagg'd and bound,
There, stript, fair *Rhet'ric* languish'd on the ground;
His blunted Arms by *Sophistry* are borne,   25
And shameless *Billingsgate* her Robes adorn.
Morality, by her false guardians drawn,
Chicane in Furs, and *Casuistry* in Lawn,
Gasps, as they straiten at each end the cord,

---

[1] This Book may properly be distinguished from the former, by the Name of the GREATER DUNCIAD, not so indeed in Size, but in Subject; and so far contrary to the distinction anciently made of the *Greater* and *Lesser Iliad*. But much are they mistaken who imagine this Work in any wise inferior to the former, or of any other hand than of our Poet; of which I am much more certain than that the *Iliad* itself was the work of *Solomon*, or the *Batrachomuomachia* of *Homer*, as *Barnes* hath affirmed. ' BENTLEY.' P.

[2] *Force inertly strong,*] Alluding to the *Vis inertiæ of Matter*, which, tho' it really be no Power, is yet the Foundation of all the Qualities and Attributes of that sluggish Substance. P. *and Warburton.*

[3] *a new World*] In allusion to the Epicurean opinion, that from the Dissolution of the natural World into Night and Chaos a new one should arise; this the Poet alluding to, in the Production of a new moral World, makes it partake of its original Principles. P. *and Warburton.*

[4] *Beneath her footstool, &c.*] We are next presented with the pictures of those whom the Goddess leads in captivity. *Science* is only depressed and confined so as to be rendered useless; but *Wit* or *Genius*, as a more dangerous and active enemy, punished, or driven away: *Dulness* being often reconciled in some degree with Learning, but never upon any terms with Wit. And accordingly it will be seen that she admits something *like* each Science, as Casuistry, Sophistry, &c. but nothing like *Wit*, *Opera* alone supplying its place. P. *and Warburton.*

And dies, when Dulness gives her Page the word.[1]   30
Mad *Máthesis*[2] alone was unconfin'd,
Too mad for mere material chains to bind,
Now to pure Space lifts her ecstatic stare,
Now running round the Circle finds it square.[3]
But held in ten-fold bonds the *Muses* lie,   35
Watch'd both by Envy's and by Flatt'ry's eye:[4]
There to her heart sad Tragedy addrest
The dagger wont to pierce the Tyrant's breast;
But sober History restrain'd her rage,
And promis'd Vengeance on a barb'rous age.   40
There sunk Thalia, nerveless, cold, and dead,
Had not her Sister Satire held her head:
Nor could'st thou, CHESTERFIELD![5] a tear refuse,
Thou wept'st, and with thee wept each gentle Muse.
When lo! a Harlot form[6] soft sliding by,   45
With mincing step, small voice, and languid eye:
Foreign her air, her robe's discordant pride
In patch-work flutt'ring, and her head aside:
By singing Peers up-held on either hand,
She tripp'd and laugh'd, too pretty much to stand;   50
Cast on the prostrate Nine a scornful look,
Then thus in quaint Recitativo spoke.
"O *Cara! Cara!* silence all that train:
Joy to great Chaos! let Division reign:[7]

---

[1] *gives her* Page *the word.*] There was a Judge of this name, always ready to hang any Man that came before him, of which he was suffered to give a hundred miserable examples during a long life, even to his dotage. P. *and Warburton.* [Cf. *Epilogue to Satires,* Dial. II. v. 159.]

[2] *Mad* Máthesis] Alluding to the strange Conclusions some Mathematicians have deduced from their principles, concerning the *real Quantity of Matter,* the *Reality of Space, &c.* P. *and Warburton.*

[3] *running round the* Circle *finds it square.*] Regards the wild and fruitless attempts of *squaring the Circle.* P. *and Warburton.*

[4] *Watch'd both by* Envy's *and by* Flatt'ry's *eye.*] One of the misfortunes falling on Authors from the *Act* for subjecting *Plays* to the power of a *Licenser,* being the false representations to which they were exposed, from such as either gratify'd their Envy to Merit, or made their Court to Greatness, by perverting general Reflections against Vice into Libels on particular Persons. P. *and Warburton.* [A licensing Act had been introduced by Sir John Barnard in 1735, but immediately abandoned; the Act of 1737 was occasioned by the political strokes in Fielding's *Pasquin* and the scurrilities of

other plays. The bill was carried by Walpole, notwithstanding the vigorous opposition of Lord Chesterfield, who treated it as a first step towards a censorship of the press. Though the powers conferred by this Act are still retained by the Lord Chamberlain, they are used so sparingly and temperately (in 14 years, from 1852 to 1865, only 19 plays were rejected out of 2,816) that the restriction is practically little felt by managers, authors or public.]

[5] [*Chesterfield,* cf. *Epil. to Satires,* Dial. II. v. 84.]

[6] *When lo! a Harlot form*] The Attitude given to this Phantom represents the nature and genius of the *Italian* Opera; its affected airs, its effeminate sounds, and the practice of patching up these Operas with favourite Songs, incoherently put together. These things were supported by the subscriptions of the Nobility. This circumstance that OPERA should prepare for the opening of the grand Sessions was prophesied of in Book III. ver. 304. P. *and Warburton.*

[7] *let Division reign:*] Alluding to the false taste of playing tricks in Music with numberless divisions, to the neglect of that harmony which conforms to the Sense, and applies to the Passions. Mr. *Handel* had introduced a great

Chromatic tortures [1] soon shall drive them hence,   55
Break all their nerves, and fritter all their sense :
One Trill shall harmonize joy, grief, and rage,
Wake the dull Church, and lull the ranting Stage ;
To the same notes thy sons shall hum, or snore,
And all thy yawning daughters cry, *encore.*   60
Another Phœbus, thy own Phœbus, reigns, [2]
Joys in my jigs, and dances in my chains.
But soon, ah soon, Rebellion will commence,
If Music meanly borrows aid from Sense.
Strong in new Arms, lo! Giant HANDEL [3] stands,   65
Like bold Briareus, with a hundred hands ;
To stir, to rouse, to shake the soul he comes,
And Jove's own Thunders follow Mars's Drums.
Arrest him, Empress ; or you sleep no more — "
She heard, and drove him to th' Hibernian shore.   70
    And now had Fame's posterior Trumpet [4] blown,
And all the Nations summon'd to the Throne.
The young, the old, who feel her inward sway,
One instinct seizes, and transports away.
None need a guide, by sure attraction led,   75
And strong impulsive gravity of Head ;
None want a place, for all their Centre found,
Hung to the Goddess, and coher'd around.
Not closer, orb in orb, conglob'd are seen
The buzzing Bees about their dusky Queen.   80
    The gath'ring number, as it moves along,
Involves a vast involuntary throng,
Who gently drawn, and struggling less and less,
Roll in her Vortex, and her pow'r confess.
Not those alone who passive own her laws,   85
But who, weak rebels, more advance her cause.

number of Hands, and more variety of Instruments into the Orchestra, and employed even Drums and Cannon to make a fuller Chorus; which proved so much too manly for the fine Gentlemen of his age, that he was obliged to remove his music into *Ireland.* After which they were reduced, for want of Composers, to practise the patch-work above-mentioned. P. *and Warburton.*

[1] *Chromatic tortures*] That species of the ancient music called the *Chromatic* was a variation and embellishment, in odd irregularities, of the *Diatonic* kind. They say it was invented about the time of *Alexander,* and that the *Spartans* forbad the use of it, as languid and effeminate. *Warburton.*

[2] *thy own* Phœbus *reigns,*
    ' Tuus jam regnat Apollo.'
        Virg. [*Ecl.* v. 10]. P.

[3] [Handel, who came to England in 1710, was an inmate of Lord Burlington's house from 1715 to 1718, during which time Pope must have frequently met him. His *Messiah* was produced in 1741.] It is remarkable, that in the earlier part of his life, Pope was so very insensible to the charms of music, that he once asked his friend, Dr. Arbuthnot, who had a fine ear, ' whether, at Lord Burlington's concerts, the rapture which the company expressed upon hearing the compositions and performance of Handel did not proceed wholly from affectation.' *Warton.*

[4] *Fame's posterior Trumpet*] According to Hudibras:
    ' She blows not both with the same Wind,
    But one before and one behind;
    And therefore modern Authors name
    One good, and t'other evil Fame.'
        P. *and Warburton.* [Part *om.*]

Whate'er of dunce in College or in Town
Sneers at another, in toupee [1] or gown;
Whate'er of mongrel no one class admits,
A wit with dunces, and a dunce with wits.   90
    Nor absent they, no members of her state,
Who pay her homage in her sons, the Great;
Who, false to Phœbus, bow the knee to Baal;
Or, impious, preach his word without a call.
Patrons, who sneak from living worth to dead,   95
Withhold the pension, and set up the head;
Or vest dull Flatt'ry in the sacred Gown;
Or give from fool to fool the Laurel crown.
And (last and worst) with all the cant of wit,
Without the soul, the Muse's Hypocrite.   100
    There march'd the bard and blockhead, side by side,
Who rhym'd for hire, and patroniz'd for pride.
Narcissus, prais'd with all a Parson's pow'r,
Look'd a white lily sunk beneath a show'r.[2]
There mov'd Montalto with superior air;   105
His stretch'd-out arm display'd a volume fair;
Courtiers and Patriots in two ranks divide,
Thro' both he pass'd, and bow'd from side to side:[3]
But as in graceful act, with awful eye
Compos'd he stood, bold Benson [4] thrust him by: 110
On two unequal crutches propt he came,
Milton's on this, on that one Johnston's name.
The decent Knight [5] retir'd with sober rage,
Withdrew his hand, and clos'd the pompous page.[6]
But (happy for him as the times went then)   115
Appear'd Apollo's May'r and Aldermen,
On whom three hundred gold-capt youths await,
To lug the pond'rous volume off in state.
    When Dulness, smiling — "Thus revive [7] the Wits!

---

[1] [The curl of the wig at the top of the head.]

[2] Means Dr. Middleton's laboured encomium on Lord Hervey, in his dedication of the *Life of Cicero. Warton.*

[3] *bow'd from side to side:*] As being of no one party. *Warburton.*

[4] *bold* Benson] This man endeavoured to raise himself to Fame by erecting monuments, striking coins, setting up heads, and procuring translations, of *Milton ;* and afterwards by as great passion for *Arthur Johnston,* a *Scotch* physician's version of the *Psalms,* of which he printed many fine editions. See more of him, Book III. ver. 325. P. *and Warburton.*

[5] *The decent* Knight] An eminent person, who was about to publish a very pompous edition of a great Author, *at his own expense.* P. *and Warburton.* Sir Thomas Hanmer. *Wakefield.* [His edition of Shakspere was

published at Oxford in 1744, 'with a kind of sanction from the University, as it was printed at the theatre with the imprimatur of the Vice-Chancellor, and had no publisher's name on the title-page.' It was beautifully printed and obtained much favour, but its text is characterised by the editors of the *Cambridge Shakspere* (Preface, p. xxxiv.) as better indeed than Pope's, inasmuch as many of Theobald's restorations and some probable emendations were introduced, but showing no trace of collation of the earlier Folios or any of the Quartos.]

[6] Ver. 114. "What! no respect, he cry'd, for SHAKESPEAR's page?"

[7] *Thus revive, &c.*] The Goddess applauds the practice of tacking the obscure names of Persons not eminent in any branch of learning, to those of the most distinguished Writers; either by printing *Editions* of their works with

2 E

But murder first, and mince them all to bits ;　　　　120
As erst Medea (cruel, so to save!)
A new Edition of old Æson ¹ gave ;
Let standard-authors, thus, like trophies borne,
Appear more glorious as more hack'd and torn
And you, my Critics! in the chequer'd shade,　　　　125
Admire new light thro' holes yourselves have made.
　Leave not a foot of verse, a foot of stone,
A Page,² a Grave, that they can call their own ;
But spread, my sons, your glory thin or thick,
On passive paper, or on solid brick.　　　　　　　　130
So by each Bard an Alderman ³ shall sit,⁴
A heavy Lord shall hang at ev'ry Wit,
And while on Fame's triumphal Car they ride,
Some Slave of mine be pinion'd to their side."
　Now crowds on crowds around the Goddess press,　135
Each eager to present their first Address.
Dunce scorning Dunce beholds the next advance,
But Fop shews Fop superior complaisance.
When lo! a Spectre rose, whose index-hand
Held forth the virtue of the dreadful wand ;　　　　140
His beaver'd brow a birchen garland wears,
Dropping with Infant's blood, and Mother's tears.
O'er ev'ry vein a shudd'ring horror runs ;
Eton and Winton ⁵ shake thro' all their Sons.
All Flesh is humbled, Westminster's bold race　　　145
Shrink, and confess the genius of the place : ⁶
The pale Boy-Senator yet tingling stands,
And holds his breeches close with both his hands.
Then thus. 'Since Man from beast by Words is known,
Words are Man's province, Words we teach alone.　150
When Reason doubtful, like the Samian letter,⁷
Points him two ways, the narrower is the better.
Plac'd at the door ⁸ of Learning, youth to guide,

---

impertinent alterations of their Text, as in the former instances; or by setting up *Monuments* disgraced with their own vile names and inscriptions, as in the latter. P. *and Warburton.*

¹ *old Æson*] Of whom Ovid (very applicable to these restored authors),

　　' Æson *miratur,*
　　Dissimilemque animum *subiit'* —
P. *and Warburton.* [*Met.* VII. 292 ? where the story of Medea making Æson, the father of Iason, young again is narrated concluded. The quotation is garbled.]

² *A Page,*] *Pagina,* not *Pedissequus.* A Page of a Book; not a Servant, Follower, or Attendant; no Poet having had a *Page* since the death of Mr. Thomas Durfey. *Scriblerus.* P. *and Warburton.*

³ *So by each Bard an Alderman, &c.*]

Vide the *Tombs of the Poets,* Editio Westmonasteriensis. P. *and Warburton.*

⁴ *an Alderman shall sit,*] Alluding to the monument erected for Butler by Alderman Barber. P.

⁵ [Winchester.]

⁶ [Personified in Dr. Busby, who wielded his ferule at Westminster School from 1640 to 1695.]

⁷ *like the Samian letter,*] The letter Y, used by Pythagoras as an emblem of the different roads of Virtue and Vice.

　' Et tibi quæ Samios diduxit litera ramos.'
　Pers. [*Sat.* III. v. 56]. P. *and Warburton.*

⁸ *Plac'd at the door, &c.*] This circumstance of the *Genius Loci* (with that of the Index-hand before) seems to be an allusion to the *Table of Cebes,* where the Genius of human

We never suffer it to stand too wide.[1]
To ask, to guess, to know, as they commence,   155
As Fancy opens the quick springs of Sense,
We ply the Memory, we load the brain,
Bind rebel Wit and double chain on chain ;
Confine the thought, to exercise the breath ;
And keep them in the pale of Words till death.   160
Whate'er the talents, or howe'er design'd,
We hang one jingling padlock on the mind :
A Poet the first day he dips his quill ;
And what the last? A very Poet still.
Pity! the charm works only in our wall,   165
Lost, lost too soon in yonder House or Hall.[2]
There truant WYNDHAM [3] ev'ry Muse gave o'er,
There TALBOT [4] sunk, and was a Wit no more!
How sweet an Ovid, MURRAY [5] was our boast!
How many Martials were in PULT'NEY [6] lost!   170
Else sure some Bard, to our eternal praise,
In twice ten thousand rhyming nights and days,
Had reach'd the Work, the all that mortal can ;
And South beheld that Master-piece of Man.'[7]
     " Oh " (cry'd the Goddess) "for some pedant Reign!   175
Some gentle JAMES,[8] to bless the land again ;
To stick the Doctor's Chair into the Throne,
Give law to Words, or war with Words alone,
Senates and Courts with Greek and Latin rule,
And turn the Council to a Grammar School!   180
For sure, if Dulness sees a grateful Day,
'T is in the shade of Arbitrary Sway.
O! if my sons may learn one earthly thing,
Teach but that one, sufficient for a king ;
That which my Priests, and mine alone, maintain,   185
Which as it dies, or lives, we fall, or reign :
May you, may Cam and Isis, preach it long!
'The RIGHT DIVINE of Kings to govern wrong.' "[9]

Nature points out the road to be pursued by those entering into life. P. *and Warburton.*

[1] *to stand too wide.*] A pleasant allusion to the description of the door of Wisdom in the *Table of Cebes. Warburton.*

[2] *in yonder* House *or* Hall.] Westminster-hall and the House of Commons. P.

[3] [Sir William Wyndham, a leading member of the opposition against Walpole, died in 1740.]

[4] [Cf. *Imit. of Hor.* Bk. II. Ep. ii. v. 154.]

[5] [Cf. *Imit. of Hor.* Bk. I. Ep. vi.]

[6] [Cf. *Epil. to Satires,* Dial. II. v. 84.]

[7] *that Master-piece of Man.*] Viz. an *Epigram.* The famous Dr. South declared a perfect Epigram to be as difficult a performance as an Epic Poem. And the Critics say, " an Epic Poem is the greatest work human nature is capable of." P. *and Warburton.*

[8] *Some gentle* JAMES, *&c.*] Wilson tells us that this King, *James* the First, took upon himself to teach the Latin tongue to Car, earl of Somerset; and that Gondomar the Spanish ambassador would speak false Latin to him, on purpose to give him the pleasure of correcting it, whereby he wrought himself into his good graces.

This great Prince was the first who assumed the title of *Sacred Majesty. Warburton.* [Part *om.*]

[9] [The theory of the divine right of the sovereign and its absolute independence of the law, was first fully developed in Cowell's *Interpre-*

Prompt at the call,[1] around the Goddess roll
Broad hats, and hoods, and caps, a sable shoal :   190
Thick and more thick the black blockade extends,
A hundred head of Aristotle's friends.[2]
Nor wert thou, Isis! wanting to the day,
[Tho' Christ-church long kept prudishly away.[3]]
Each staunch Polemic, stubborn as a rock,   195
Each fierce Logician, still expelling Locke,[4]
Came whip and spur, and dash'd thro' thin and thick
On German Crouzaz,[5] and Dutch Burgersdyck.
As many quit the streams[6] that murm'ring fall
To lull the sons of Marg'ret and Clare-hall,   200
Where Bentley late tempestuous wont to sport
In troubled waters, but now sleeps in Port.[7]
Before them march'd that awful Aristarch ;
Plough'd was his front with many a deep Remark :
His Hat, which never vail'd to human pride,   · 205

ter (1607); and carried out to its logical conse-
quences in Filmer's *Patriarca*, which has been
termed by Gneist the standard of this theory of
government under Charles I.]

[1] [*Prompt at the call, — Aristotle's friends*]
The Author, with great propriety, hath made
these, who were so *prompt at the call* of Dul-
ness, to become preachers of the Divine Right
of Kings, to be the *friends* of *Aristotle ;* for
this philosopher, in his *politics*, hath laid it
down as a principle, that some men were, by
nature, made to serve, and others to command.
Warburton.

[2] *A hundred head of Aristotle's friends.*]
The Philosophy of *Aristotle* hath suffered a long
disgrace in this learned University: being first
expelled by the *Cartesian*, which, in its turn,
gave place to the *Newtonian*. But it had all
this while some faithful followers in secret,
who never bowed the knee to *Baal*, nor ac-
knowledged any strange God in Philosophy.
These, on this new appearance of the Goddess,
came out like Confessors, and made an open
profession of the ancient faith, in the *ipse
dixit* of their Master. SCRIBLERUS.

[Dr. Law speaks of the old scholastic method
which clung to ' the dull, crabbed system of
Aristotle's logic ' as still prevailing in our pub-
lic forms of education a short time before this
satire was written (1723). See Mullinger's
Essay on *Cambridge in the Seventeenth Cen-
tury*.]

[3] [*Tho' Christ-church*]   This line is doubt-
less spurious, and foisted in by the impertinence
of the Editor; and accordingly we have put it be-
tween Hooks.   For I affirm this Cóllege came as
early as any other, by its *proper Deputies ;* nor
did any College pay homage to Dulness in its

whole body. ' BENTLEY.'   P. *and Warbur-
ton.*

[4] *still expelling* Locke,]   In the year 1703
there was a meeting of the heads of the Uni-
versity of Oxford to censure Mr. Locke's Essay
on Human Understanding, and to forbid the
reading it. See his Letters in the last Edit.
P.   [But he was never expelled, only deprived
of his studentship at Christ-Church; and this
on the ground of political suspicions, *before* he
had written his great *Essay*.]

[5] [The hostility of Pope to Crouzaz is readily
accounted for by the attack made by the latter
on the *Essay on Man*. But Pope committed
a gross mistake in introducing his adversary
among Locke's Aristotelian opponents, as C.
had formed his philosophy in the school of
Locke. *Dugald Stewart*, quoted by *Roscoe*.]

[6] *the streams*]   The river Cam, running by
the walls of these Colleges, which are particu-
larly famous for their skill in Disputation. P.
and Warburton.

[7] *sleeps in Port.*]   Viz. "now retired into
harbour, after the tempests that had long agi-
tated his society." So SCRIBLERUS.   But the
learned *Scipio Maffei* understands it of a cer-
tain wine called *Port*, from *Oporto* a city of
Portugal, of which this Professor invited him to
drink abundantly. SCIP. MAFF. *De Compota-
tionibus Academicis*.   P. *and Warburton.*
[Bentley's quarrel with his College virtually
came to an end with the death of the Visitor,
bp. Greene, whose right to decide the dispute
between the Master and Society he had origi-
nally challenged.   This event happened in
1738; the quarrel with the University had ended
in 1725 by the restoration of all Bentley's rights
and degrees by royal mandamus.]

Walker [1] with rev'rence took, and laid aside.
Low bow'd the rest: He, kingly, did but nod;
So upright Quakers please both Man and God.
" Mistress! dismiss that rabble from your throne:
Avaunt —— is Aristarchus [2] yet unknown?   210
Thy mighty Scholiast, whose unweary'd pains
Made Horace dull, and humbled Milton's strains. [3]
Turn what they will to Verse, their toil is vain,
Critics like me [4] shall make it Prose again.
Roman and Greek Grammarians! know your Better: 215
Author of something yet more great than Letter; [5]
While tow'ring o'er your Alphabet, like Saul,
Stands our Digamma, [6] and o'er-tops them all.
'T is true, on Words is still our whole debate,
Disputes of *Me* or *Te*, [7] of *aut* or *at*,   220
To sound or sink in *cano*, O or A,
Or give up Cicero to C or K. [8]
Let Freind [9] affect to speak as Terence spoke,
And Alsop [9] never but like Horace joke:
For me, what Virgil, Pliny may deny,   225
Manilius [10] or Solinus [11] shall supply:
For Attic Phrase in Plato let them seek,
I poach in Suidas [12] for unlicens'd Greek.
In ancient Sense if any needs will deal,
Be sure I give them Fragments, not a Meal;   230

[1] John Walker, Vice-Master of Trin. Coll. Cambridge, while Bentley was Master. *Carruthers.*

[He laboured faithfully for Bentley, both in literary and personal matters. Thuillier (*Corr. of Bentley* II. p. 549) calls him ' dignum tanto Magistro discipulum.']

[2] *Aristarchus*] A famous Commentator, and Corrector of Homer, whose name has been frequently used to signify a complete Critic. The compliment paid by our Author to this eminent Professor, in applying to him so great a Name, was the reason that he hath omitted to comment on this part which contains his own praises. We shall therefore supply that loss to our best ability. SCRIBL. P. *and Warburton.*

[3] [Bentley's editions of Horace and of *Paradise Lost*, published in 1711 and 1731 respectively.]

[4] *Critics like me*] Alluding to two famous Editions of Horace and Milton; whose richest veins of Poetry he hath prodigally reduced to the poorest and most beggarly prose. SCRIBL.

[5] *Author of something yet more great than Letter;*] Alluding to those Grammarians, such as Palmedes and Simonides, who invented *single letters*. But Aristarchus, who had found out a *double* one, was therefore worthy of double honour. SCRIBL.

[6] *While tow'ring o'er your Alphabet, like Saul, Stands our* Digamma,] Alludes to the boasted restoration of the Æolic Digamma, in his long projected Edition of Homer. P. [Bentley never lived to finish this crowning work of his life.]

[7] *of* Me *or* Te,] It was a serious dispute, about which the learned were much divided, and some treatises written: Had it been about *Meum* or *Tuum*, it could not be more contested, than whether at the end of the first Ode of Horace, to read, Me *doctarum hederæ præmia frontium*, or, Te *doctarum hederæ —.* SCRIBL.

[8] *Or give up* Cicero *to* C *or* K.] Grammatical disputes about the manner of pronouncing Cicero's name in Greek. *Warburton.* [Rather, of course, in Latin.]

[9] *Freind, Alsop*] Dr. Robert Freind, master of Westminster-school, and canon of Christ-church — Dr. Anthony Alsop, a happy imitator of the Horatian style. P. *and Warburton.*

[10] [Author of the *Astronomicon* — a writer of the Augustan age.]

[11] [Author of the *Polyhistor*, a compilation from Pliny's Natural History.]

[12] [The famous lexicographer, of whose work Küster (infra, v. 237) brought out the Cambridge editions.]

What Gellius or Stobæus[1] hash'd before,
Or chew'd by blind old Scholiasts o'er and o'er.
The critic Eye, that microscope of Wit,
Sees hairs and pores, examines bit by bit:
How parts relate to parts, or they to whole,   235
The body's harmony, the beaming soul,
Are things which Kuster, Burman, Wasse[2] shall see,
When Man's whole frame is obvious to a *Flea*.
 "Ah, think not, Mistress! more true Dulness lies
In Folly's Cap, than Wisdom's grave disguise.   240
Like buoys that never sink into the flood,
On Learning's surface we but lie and nod.
Thine is the genuine head of many a house,
And much Divinity, without a Noῦς.
Nor could a BARROW[3] work on ev'ry block,   245
Nor has one ATTERBURY[4] spoil'd the flock.
See! still thy own, the heavy Canon[5] roll,
And Metaphysic smokes involve the Pole.
For thee we dim the eyes, and stuff the head
With all such reading as was never read: 250
For thee explain a thing till all men doubt it,
And write about it, Goddess, and about it:
So spins the silk-worm small its slender store,
And labours till it clouds itself all o'er.
 "What tho' we let some better sort of fool   255
Thrid ev'ry science, run thro' ev'ry school?
Never by tumbler thro' the hoops was shown

---

[1] *Suidas, Gellius, Stobæus*] The first a Dictionary-writer, a collector of impertinent facts and barbarous words; the second a minute Critic; the third an author, who gave his Common-place book to the public, where we happen to find much Mince-meat of old books. P. *and Warburton.*

[A. Gellius' *Noctes Atticæ* is little but a scrap-book from other authors, and Stobæus' famous work was *Eclogæ*, or selections from about 500 authors.]

[2] Burmann, Küster and Wasse were men of real and useful erudition. *Warton.* [Burmann is Peter Burmann, who died at Utrecht in 1741, the most illustrious of a family of scholars.] Ludolf Küster, of Amsterdam, the editor of Aristophanes and a correspondent of Bentley's, died in 1716. — Joseph Wasse, fellow of Queen's College Cambridge, was co-editor with Jebb, of the *Bibliotheca Litteraria* (1722); and also edited Sallust.

[3] *Barrow, Atterbury*] Isaac Barrow, Master of Trinity, Francis Atterbury, Dean of Christ-church, both great Geniuses and eloquent Preachers; one more conversant in the sublime Geometry; the other in classical Learning; but who equally made it their care to advance the polite Arts in their several Societies. P. *and Warburton.*

[Dr. Isaac Barrow, the illustrious author of the treatise *On the Supremacy of the Pope*, master of Trinity, Cambridge, with which college his name is indelibly associated, and successively Professor of Greek and Lucasian Professor of Mathematics. To him more than any other man is owing the direction taken by Cambridge towards mathematical studies. He died in 1677.]

[4] [Cf. *Epitaph* No. xiii.]

[5] *Canon* here, if spoken of Artillery, is in the plural number; if of the *Canons of the House*, in the singular, and meant only of *one;* in which case I suspect the *Pole* to be a false reading, and that it should be the *Poll*, or *Head* of that Canon. It may be objected, that this is a mere *Paronomasia* or *Pun*. But what of that? Is any figure of speech more apposite to our gentle Goddess, or more frequently used by her and her Children, especially of the University? *Scriblerus. Pope and Warburton.* [Part *om.*] [Some Canon of Christ-Church is evidently alluded to.]

Such skill in passing all, and touching none;[1]
He may indeed (if sober all this time)
Plague with Dispute, or persecute with Rhyme.   260
We only furnish what he cannot use,
Or wed to what he must divorce, a Muse:
Full in the midst of Euclid dip at once,
And petrify a Genius to a Dunce:
Or set on Metaphysic ground to prance,   265
Show all his paces, not a step advance.
With the same CEMENT, ever sure to bind,
We bring to one dead level ev'ry mind.
Then take him to develop, if you can,
And hew the Block off,[2] and get out the Man.   270
But wherefore waste I words? I see advance
Whore, Pupil, and lac'd Governor from France.
Walker! our hat "—— nor more he deign'd to say,
But, stern as Ajax' spectre, strode away.[3]
        In flow'd at once a gay embroider'd race,   275
And titt'ring push'd the Pedants off the place:
Some would have spoken, but the voice was drown'd
By the French horn, or by the op'ning hound.
The first came forwards, with as easy mien,
As if he saw St. James's and the Queen.   280
When thus th' attendant Orator begun,
"Receive, great Empress! thy accomplish'd Son:
Thine from the birth, and sacred from the rod,
A dauntless infant! never scar'd with God.
The Sire saw one by one, his Virtues wake: 285
The mother begg'd the blessing of a Rake.
Thou gav'st that Ripeness, which so soon began,
And ceas'd so soon, he ne'er was Boy, nor Man,
Thro' School and College, thy kind cloud o'ercast,
Safe and unseen the young Æneas past: 290
Thence bursting glorious,[4] all at once let down,
Stunn'd with his giddy Larum half the town.
Intrepid then, o'er seas and lands he flew:

---

[1] These two verses are verbatim from an epigram of Dr. Evans, of St. John's College, Oxford; given to my father twenty years before the *Dunciad* was written. *Warton.*

[2] *And hew the Block off,*] A notion of Aristotle, that there was originally in every block of marble a Statue, which would appear on the removal of the superfluous parts. P. *and Warburton.*

[3] *stern as Ajax' spectre strode away.*] See Homer, Odyss. xi., where the Ghost of Ajax turns sullenly from Ulysses the *Traveller*, who had succeeded against him in the dispute for the arms of Achilles. There had been the same contention between the *Travelling*

and the *University* tutor, for the spoils of our young heroes, and fashion adjudged it to the former; so that this might well occasion the sullen dignity in departure, which Longinus so much admired. SCRIBL. *Warburton and Warton.*

[4] *unseen the young Æneas past: Thence bursting glorious,*] See Virg. Æn. 1. [vv. 411-417], where he enumerates the causes why his mother took this care of him: to wit, 1. that nobody might touch or correct him: 2. might stop or detain him: 3. examine him about the progress he had made, or so much as guess why he came there. P. *and Warburton.*

Europe he saw, and Europe saw him too.
There all thy gifts and graces we display,   295
Thou, only thou, directing all our way!
To where the Seine, obsequious as she runs,
Pours at great Bourbon's feet her silken sons;
Or Tiber, now no longer Roman, rolls,
Vain of Italian Arts, Italian Souls: 300
To happy Convents, bosom'd deep in vines,
Where slumber Abbots, purple as their wines:[1]
To Isles of fragrance, lily-silver'd vales,[2]
Diffusing languor in the panting gales:
To lands of singing, or of dancing slaves,   305
Love-whisp'ring woods, and lute-resounding waves.
But chief her shrine where naked Venus keeps,
And Cupids ride the Lion of the Deeps;[3]
Where, eas'd of Fleets, the Adriatic main
Wafts the smooth Eunuch and enamour'd swain.   310
Led by my hand, he saunter'd Europe round,
And gather'd ev'ry Vice on Christian ground;
Saw ev'ry Court, heard ev'ry King declare
His royal Sense of Op'ras or the Fair;
The Stews and Palace equally explor'd,   315
Intrigu'd with glory, and with spirit whor'd;
Try'd all *hors-d'œuvres*, all *liqueurs* defin'd,
Judicious drank, and greatly-daring din'd;
Dropt the dull lumber of the Latin store,
Spoil'd his own language, and acquir'd no more;   320
All Classic learning lost on Classic ground;
And last turn'd *Air*, the Echo of a Sound![4]
See now, half-cur'd, and perfectly well-bred,
With nothing but a Solo in his head;[5]
As much Estate, and Principle, and Wit,   325
As Jansen, Fleetwood, Cibber[6] shall think fit;
Stol'n from a Duel, follow'd by a Nun,

[1] [This phrase, which Warton traces to J. B. Rousseau, alludes to the purple stockings worn by Abbés.]

[2] *lily-silver'd vales,*] Tuberoses. P.

[3] *And Cupids ride the Lion of the Deeps;*] The winged Lion, the Arms of Venice. This Republic heretofore the most considerable in Europe, for her Naval Force and the extent of her Commerce; now illustrious for her *Carnivals.* P. *and Warburton.*

[4] *And last turn'd* Air, *the Echo of a Sound!*] Yet less a Body than Echo itself; for Echo reflects *Sense* or *Words* at least, this Gentleman only *Airs* and *Tunes:*

'Sonus *est, qui vivit in* illo.'

Ovid, Met. [III. v. 401]. SCRIBLERUS.

[5] *With nothing but a* Solo *in his head;*] With nothing but a *Solo?* Why, if it be a *Solo,*

how should there be any thing else? Palpable Tautology! Read boldly an *Opera*, which is enough of conscience for such a head as has lost all its Latin. 'BENT.'

[6] *Jansen, Fleetwood, Cibber*] Three very eminent persons, all Managers of *Plays;* who, tho' not Governors by profession, had, each in his way, concerned themselves in the Education of Youth: and regulated their Wits, their Morals, or their Finances, at that period of their age which is the most important, their entrance into the polite world. Of the last of these, and his Talents for this end, see Book I. ver. 199, &c. P. *and Warburton.* [Fleetwood was patentee of Drury-Lane Theatre from 1734 to 1745; it was the attempted secession of his actors in 1743 which gave rise to the famous quarrel of Macklin with Garrick.]

And, if a Borough choose him not, undone; [1]
See, to my country happy I restore
This glorious Youth, and add one Venus more.   330
Her too receive (for her my soul adores)
So may the sons of sons of sons of whores,
Prop thine, O Empress! like each neighbour Throne,
And make a long Posterity thy own."
Pleas'd, she accepts the Hero, and the Dame   335
Wraps in her Veil, and frees from sense of Shame.
    Then look'd, and saw a lazy, lolling sort,
Unseen at Church, at Senate, or at Court,
Of ever-listless Loit'rers, that attend
No Cause, no Trust, no Duty, and no Friend.   340
Thee too, my Paridel! [2] she mark'd thee there,
Stretch'd on the rack of a too easy chair,
And heard thy everlasting yawn confess
The Pains and Penalties of Idleness.
She pity'd! but her Pity only shed   345
Benigner influence on thy nodding head.
    But Annius, [3] crafty Seer, with ebon wand,
And well dissembled em'rald on his hand,
False as his Gems, and canker'd as his Coins,
Came, cramm'd with capon, from where Pollio dines. [4]   350
Soft, as the wily Fox is seen to creep,
Where bask on sunny banks the simple sheep,
Walk round and round, now prying here, now there,
So he; but pious, whisper'd first his pray'r.
    "Grant, gracious Goddess! grant me still to cheat,   355
O may thy cloud still cover the deceit!
Thy choicer mists on this assembly shed,
But pour them thickest on the noble head.
So shall each youth, assisted by our eyes,
See other Cæsars, other Homers rise;   360
Thro' twilight ages hunt th' Athenian fowl, [5]
Which Chalcis Gods, and mortals call an Owl,
Now see an Attys, now a Cecrops [6] clear,

---

[1] [This seems to allude to the protection of a member of Parliament against arrest for debt.]

[2] *Thee too, my* Paridel!] The Poet seems to speak of this young gentleman with great affection. The name is taken from Spenser, who gives it to a *wandering Courtly 'Squire*, that travelled about for the same reason, for which many young Squires are now fond of travelling, and especially to *Paris*. P. *and Warburton*. [Paridell narrates his lineage in Canto x. of Book III. of the *Faerie Queene*; and acts in accordance with it in the following Canto.]

[3] *Annius*,] The name taken from Annius the Monk of Viterbo, famous for many Impositions and Forgeries of ancient manuscripts and inscrip-

tions, which he was prompted to by mere vanity, but our Annius had a more substantial motive. P. *and Warburton*. Sir Andrew Fountaine. *Warton*. [But this is doubted by *Roscoe*, since Sir A. F. was a friend of Swift's.]

[4] This seems more obscure than almost any other passage in the whole. Perhaps he meant the Prince of Wales's dinners. *Bowles*.

[5] *hunt th' Athenian fowl*,] The Owl stamp'd on the reverse on the ancient money of Athens. 'Which *Chalcis* Gods, and mortals call an Owl,' is the verse by which Hobbes renders that of Homer [*Il.* XIV. 291]. P. *and Warburton*. [Κύμινδις is a kind of hawk.]

[6] *Attys, Cecrops*] The first Kings of Athens,

Nay, Mahomet! the Pigeon at thine ear;
Be rich in ancient brass, tho' not in gold,   365
And keep his Lares, tho' his house be sold;
To headless Phœbe his fair bride postpone,
Honour a Syrian Prince above his own;
Lord of an Otho, if I vouch it true;
Blest in one Niger, till he knows of two." [1] 370
 Mummius [2] o'erheard him; Mummius, Fool-renown'd,[3]
Who like his Cheops [4] stinks above the ground,
Fierce as a startled Adder, swell'd, and said,
Rattling an ancient Sistrum [5] at his head:
'Speak'st thou of Syrian Princes? [6] Traitor base! 375
Mine, Goddess! mine is all the horned race.
True, he had wit, to make their value rise;
From foolish Greeks to steal them, was as wise;
More glorious yet, from barb'rous hands to keep,
When Sallee Rovers chas'd him on the deep. 380
Then taught by Hermes, and divinely bold,
Down his own throat he risk'd the Grecian gold,
Receiv'd each Demi-God,[7] with pious care,
Deep in his Entrails — I rever'd them there,
I bought them, shrouded in that living shrine, 385
And, at their second birth, they issue mine.'
 "Witness, great Ammon! [8] by whose horns I swore,"
(Reply'd soft Annius) " this our paunch before

of whom it is hard to suppose any Coins are extant; but not so improbable as what follows, that there should be any of Mahomet, who forbad all Images; and the story of whose Pigeon was a monkish fable. Nevertheless one of these Annius's made a counterfeit medal of that Impostor, now in the collection of a learned Nobleman. P. *and Warburton.*

[1] [Compare with this passage *Moral Essays*, Ep. v.]

[Said by Warton to refer to Dr. Mead, which is highly improbable.]

[2] *Mummius*] This name is not merely an allusion to the Mummies he was so fond of, but probably referred to the Roman General of that name, who burned Corinth, and committed the curious Statues to the Captain of a ship, assuring him, " that if any were lost or broken, he should procure others to be made in their stead: " by which it should seem (whatever may be pretended) that Mummius was no Virtuoso. P. *and Warburton.*

[3] *Fool-renown'd,*] A compound epithet in the Greek manner, *renown'd by Fools,* or *renown'd for making Fools.* P.

[4] *Cheops*] A King of Egypt, whose body was certainly to be known, as being buried alone in his Pyramid, and is therefore more genuine than

any of the Cleopatras. This Royal Mummy, being stolen by a wild Arab, was purchased by the Consul of Alexandria, and transmitted to the Museum of Mummius; for proof of which he brings a passage in Sandys's Travels, where that accurate and learned Voyager assures us that he saw the Sepulchre empty; which agrees exactly (saith he) with the time of the theft above-mentioned. But he omits to observe that Herodotus tells the same thing of it in his time. P. *and Warburton.*

[5] [The rattle used in the worship of Isis.]

[6] *Speak'st thou of Syrian Princes? &c.*] The strange story following, which may be taken for a fiction of the Poet, is justified by a true relation in Spon's Voyages [of Vaillant, the French historian of the Syrian kings, swallowing twenty gold medals when the ship in which he was returning to France was attacked by Sallee pirates]. P. *and Warburton.*

[7] *Each* Demi-God,] They are called Θεοὶ on their Coins. P. *and Warburton.*

[8] *Witness, great* Ammon!] Jupiter Ammon is called to witness, as the father of Alexander, to whom those Kings succeeded in the division of the Macedonian Empire, and whose *Horns* they wore on their Medals. P. *and Warburton.*

Still bears them, faithful; and that thus I eat,
Is to refund the Medals with the meat.   390
To prove me, Goddess! clear of all design,
Bid me with Pollio sup, as well as dine:
There all the Learn'd shall at the labour stand,
And Douglas [1] lend his soft, obstetric hand."
    The Goddess smiling seem'd to give consent;   395
So back to Pollio, hand in hand, they went.
    Then thick as Locusts black'ning all the ground,
A tribe, with weeds and shells fantastic crown'd.
Each with some wond'rous gift approach'd the Pow'r,
A Nest, a Toad, a Fungus, or a Flow'r.   400
But far the foremost, two, with earnest zeal,
And aspect ardent to the Throne appeal.
    The first thus open'd: "Hear thy suppliant's call,
Great Queen, and common Mother of us all!
Fair from its humble bed I rear'd this Flow'r,   405
Suckled, and cheer'd, with air, and sun, and show'r,
Soft on the paper ruff its leaves I spread,
Bright with the gilded button tipt its head;
Then thron'd in glass, and named it CAROLINE; [2]
Each maid cry'd, Charming! and each youth, Divine!   410
Did Nature's pencil ever blend such rays,
Such vary'd light in one promiscuous blaze?
Now prostrate! dead! behold that Caroline:
No maid cries, Charming! and no youth, Divine!
And lo the wretch! whose vile, whose insect lust   415
Laid this gay daughter of the Spring in dust.
Oh punish him, or to the Elysian shades
Dismiss my soul, where no Carnation fades!"
He ceas'd, and wept. With innocence of mien,
Th' Accus'd stood forth, and thus address'd the Queen.   420
    "Of all th' enamell'd race, whose silv'ry wing
Waves to the tepid Zephyrs of the spring,
Or swims along the fluid atmosphere,
Once brightest shin'd this child of Heat and Air.
I saw, and started from its vernal bow'r,   425
The rising game, and chas'd from flow'r to flow'r.
It fled, I follow'd; now in hope, now pain;
It stopt, I stopt; it mov'd, I mov'd again.
At last it fix'd, 't was on what plant it pleas'd,
And where it fix'd, the beauteous bird I seiz'd: 430

---

[1] *Douglas*] A Physician of great Learning and no less Taste; above all curious in what related to *Horace*, of whom he collected every Edition, Translation, and comment, to the number of several hundred volumes. P. *and Warburton.*

[2] *and named it* Caroline:] It is a compliment which the Florists usually pay to Princes and great persons, to give their names to the most curious Flowers of their raising: Some have been very jealous of vindicating this honour, but none more than that ambitious Gardener at Hammersmith, who caused his Favourite to be painted on his sign, with this inscription, *This is My Queen Caroline.* P. *and Warburton.*

Rose or Carnation was below my care;
I meddle, Goddess! only in my sphere.
I tell the naked fact without disguise,
And, to excuse it, need but shew the prize;
Whose spoils this paper offers to your eye,　　　　435
Fair ev'n in death! this peerless *Butterfly*."
　"My sons!" (she answer'd) "both have done your parts:
Live happy both, and long promote our arts!
But hear a Mother, when she recommends
To your fraternal care our sleeping friends.[1]　　　　440
The common Soul, of Heav'n's more frugal make,
Serves but to keep fools pert, and knaves awake:
A drowsy Watchman, that just gives a knock,
And breaks our rest, to tell us what's a-clock.
Yet by some object ev'ry brain is stirr'd;　　　　445
The dull may waken to a humming-bird;
The most recluse, discreetly open'd, find
Congenial matter in the Cockle-kind;
The mind, in Metaphysics at a loss,
May wander in a wilderness of Moss;[2]　　　　450
The head that turns at super-lunar things,
Pois'd with a tail, may steer on Wilkins' wings.[3]
　"O! would the Sons of Men once think their Eyes
And Reason giv'n them but to study *Flies*!
See Nature in some partial narrow shape,　　　　455
And let the Author of the Whole escape:
Learn but to trifle; or, who most observe,
To wonder at their Maker, not to serve!"
　"Be that my task" (replies a gloomy Clerk,
Sworn foe to Myst'ry, yet divinely dark;　　　　460
Whose pious hope aspires to see the day
When Moral Evidence shall quite decay,[4]

[1] *our sleeping friends.*] Of whom see ver. 345 above. P.

[2] *a wilderness of Moss;*] Of which the Naturalists count I can't tell how many hundred species. P. *and Warburton.*

[3] Wilkins' *wings*] One of the first Projectors of the Royal Society, who, among many enlarged and useful notions, entertained the extravagant hope of a possibility to fly to the Moon; which has put some volatile Geniuses upon making wings for that purpose. P. *and Warburton.*

[Dr. John Wilkins was successively Warden of Wadham College, Oxford, and master of Trinity, Cambridge. He married a sister of Oliver Cromwell. His first publication (written in 1638, many years before the foundation of the Royal Society) was the famous *Discovery of a New World, or a Discourse to prove that it is probable there may be another habitable world in the moon; with a Discourse concerning the possibility of a passage thither.*

The Royal Society, in those early transactions which Butler so copiously ridiculed, never seems to have taken up this subject in its original fulness.]

[4] *When Moral Evidence shall quite decay,*] Alluding to a ridiculous and absurd way of some Mathematicians, in calculating the gradual decay of Moral Evidence by mathematical proportions: according to which calculation, in about fifty years it will be no longer probable that Julius Cæsar was in Gaul, or died in the Senate-house. See Craig's *Theologiæ Christianæ Principia Mathematica.* But as it seems evident, that facts of a thousand years old, for instance, are now as probable as they were five hundred years ago; it is plain that if in fifty more they quite disappear, it must be owing, not to their Arguments, but to the extraordinary Power of our Goddess; for whose help therefore they have reason to pray. P. *and Warburton.*

And damns implicit faith, and holy lies,
Prompt to impose, and fond to dogmatize :)
" Let others creep by timid steps, and slow,   465
On plain Experience lay foundations low,
By common sense to common knowledge bred,
And last, to Nature's Cause thro' Nature led.
All-seeing in thy mists, we want no guide,
Mother of Arrogance, and Source of Pride!   470
We nobly take the high Priori Road,[1]
And reason downward, till we doubt of God ;
Make Nature still[2] encroach upon his plan ;
And shove him off as far as e'er we can :
Thrust some Mechanic Cause into his place ;[3]   475
Or bind in Matter, or diffuse in Space.
Or, at one bound o'er-leaping all his laws,
Make God Man's Image, Man the final Cause,
Find Virtue local, all Relation scorn,
See all in *Self,* and but for self be born :   480
Of naught so certain as our *Reason* still,
Of naught so doubtful as of *Soul* and *Will,*
Oh hide the God still more! and make us see
Such as Lucretius drew,[4] a God like Thee :
Wrapt up in Self, a God without a Thought,   485
Regardless of our merit or default.
Or that bright Image [5] to our fancy draw,
Which Theocles in raptur'd vision saw,[6]
While thro' Poetic scenes the GENIUS roves,

---

[1] *the high Priori Road,*] Those who, from the effects in this Visible world, deduce the Eternal Power and Godhead of the First Cause, tho' they cannot attain to an adequate idea of the Deity, yet discover so much of him, as enables them to see the End of their Creation, and the Means of their Happiness : whereas they who take this high Priori Road (such as Hobbes, Spinoza, Des Cartes, and some better Reasoners) for one that goes right, ten lose themselves in Mists, or ramble after Visions, which deprive them of all sight of their End, and mislead them in the choice of wrong means. P. *and Warburton.*

An oblique censure of Dr. S Clarke's celebrated demonstration of the Being and Attributes of God à priori. *Wakefield.*

[2] *Make Nature still*] This relates to such as, being ashamed to assert a mere Mechanic Cause, and yet unwilling to forsake it entirely, have had recourse to a certain *Plastic Nature, Elastic Fluid, Subtile Matter, &c.* P. *and Warburton.*

[3] *Thrust some* Mechanic Cause *into his place,*
Or bind in Matter, *or diffuse in* Space.]

The first of these Follies is that of Des Cartes ; the second of Hobbes ; the third of some succeeding Philosophers. P. *and Warburton.* I am afraid that Pope suffered himself so far to be misled by the malignity of Warburton, as to aim a secret stab at Newton and Clarke, by associating their figurative, and not altogether unexceptionable, language concerning space (which they called the sensorium of the Deity) with the opinion of Spinoza. *Dugald Stewart,* cited by *Roscoe.*

[4] *Such as Lucretius drew,*] Lib. I. vv. i. 57–60. SCRIBL. P. *and Warburton* [*part om.*].

[5] *Or that* bright Image] *Bright Image* was the title given by the later Platonists to that Vision of *Nature,* which they had formed out of their own fancy, so bright, that they called it Αὐτοπτον ᾿Αγαλμα, or the *Self-seen Image,* i.e. seen by its own light. SCRIBL.

[6] [Explained in P. and Warburton's note by quotations from *The Moralists,* a dialogue in Shaftesbury's *Characteristics,* in which Theocles is an interlocutor. Warton truly observes that an injustice is done by the insinuation to Shaftesbury, who was a consistent Deist.]

Or wanders wild in Academic Groves;   490
That NATURE our Society adores,[1]
Where Tindal dictates, and Silenus [2] snores."
  Rous'd at his name, up rose the bousy Sire,
And shook from out his Pipe the seeds of fire; [3]
Then snapt his box, and strok'd his belly down: 495
Rosy and rev'rend, tho' without a Gown.
Bland and familiar to the throne he came,
Led up the Youth, and call'd the Goddess *Dame:*
Then thus: "From Priest-craft happily set free,
Lo! ev'ry finish'd Son returns to thee: 500
First slave to Words, then vassal to a Name,
Then dupe to Party; child and man the same;
Bounded by Nature, narrow'd still by Art,
A trifling head, and a contracted heart.
Thus bred, thus taught, how many have I seen,   505
Smiling on all, and smil'd on by a Queen? [4]
Mark'd out for Honours, honour'd for their Birth,
To thee the most rebellious things on earth:
Now to thy gentle shadow all are shrunk,
All melted down, in Pension, or in Punk!   510
So K * so B * * sneak'd into the grave,[5]
A Monarch's half, and half a Harlot's slave.
Poor W * * [6] nipt in Folly's broadest bloom,
Who praises now? his Chaplain on his Tomb.
Then take them all, oh take them to thy breast!   515
Thy *Magus,* Goddess! shall perform the rest."
  With that, a WIZARD OLD his *Cup* extends;
Which whoso tastes, forgets his former friends,
Sire, Ancestors, Himself. One casts his eyes
Up to a *Star,* and like Endymion dies: [7]   520
A *Feather,* shooting from another's head,
Extracts his brain; and Principle is fled;
Lost is his God, his Country, ev'ry thing;
And nothing left but Homage to a King! [8]

---

[1] *That Nature our Society adores,*] See the *Pantheisticon,* with its liturgy and rubrics, composed by *Toland. Warburton.*

[2] *Silenus*] Silenus was an Epicurean Philosopher, as appears from Virgil, Eclog. vi. where he sings the principles of that Philosophy in his drink. P. *and Warburton.* By Silenus he means Thos. Gordon, the translator of Tacitus, who published the *Independent Whig,* and obtained a place under government. *Warton.*

[3] *seeds of fire;*] The Epicurean language, *Semina rerum,* or Atoms, Virg. Eclog. vi.
  ' Semina ignis — semina flammæ —' P.

[4] *smil'd on by a Queen?*] i.e. This Queen or Goddess of Dulness. P. [Of course with an allusion to Queen Caroline.]

[5] [Carruthers conjectures that K* may be the Duke of Kent, who died in 1740. B** it is impossible, from the abundant choice offering itself, even conjecturally to identify.]

[6] Philip Duke of Wharton. *Bowles.* [v. *Moral Essays,* Ep. i. vv. 179 ff.]

[7] [i.e. is immersed in perpetual slumber.]

[8] *Lost is his God, his Country — And nothing left but Homage to a king.*] So strange as this must seem to a mere English reader, the famous Mons. de la Bruyère declares it to be the character of every good Subject in a Monarchy: "Where (says he) *there is no such thing as Love of our Country,* the Interest, the Glory, and Service of the *Prince* supply its place." *De la République,* chap. x. P.

The vulgar herd turn off to roll with Hogs,   525
To run with Horses, or to hunt with Dogs;
But, sad example! never to escape
Their Infamy, still keep the human shape.
But she, good Goddess, sent to ev'ry child
Firm Impudence, or Stupefaction mild;   530
And straight succeeded, leaving shame no room,
Cibberian forehead, or Cimmerian gloom.
  Kind Self-conceit to some her glass applies,
Which no one looks in with another's eyes:
But as the Flatt'rer or Dependant paint,   535
Beholds himself a Patriot, Chief, or Saint.
  On others' Int'rest her gay liv'ry flings,
Int'rest that waves on Party-colour'd wings:
Turn'd to the Sun, she casts a thousand dyes,
And, as she turns, the colours fall or rise.   540
  Others the Syren Sisters warble round,
And empty heads console with empty sound.
No more, alas! the voice of Fame they hear,
The balm of Dulness trickling in their ear.[1]
Great C**, H**, P**, R**, K*,   545
Why all your Toils? your Sons have learn'd to sing.
How quick Ambition hastes to ridicule!
The Sire is made a Peer, the Son a Fool.
  On some, a Priest succinct in amice white [2]
Attends; all flesh is nothing in his sight!   550
Beeves, at his touch, at once to jelly turn,
And the huge Boar is shrunk into an Urn:
The board with specious miracles he loads,[3]
Turns Hares to Larks, and Pigeons into Toads.
Another (for in all what one can shine?)   555
Explains the *Sève* and *Verdeur* [4] of the Vine.
What cannot copious Sacrifice atone?
Thy Truffles, Perigord! thy Hams, Bayonne!
With French Libation, and Italian Strain,
Wash Bladen white, and expiate Hays's stain.[5]   560

---

[1] *The balm of Dulness*] The true *Balm of Dulness*, called by the Greek Physicians Κολακεία, is a *Sovereign* remedy against Inanity, and has its poetic name from the Goddess herself. Its ancient Dispensators were *her Poets ;* and for that reason our Author, Book II. ver. 207, calls it, *the Poet's healing balm :* but now it is got into as many hands as Goddard's Drops or Daffy's Elixir. It is prepared by the *Clergy,* as appears from several places of this poem: And by ver. 534, 535, it seems as if the *Nobility* had it made up in their own houses. This, which *Opera* is here said to administer, is but a spurious sort. See my Dissertation on the *Silphium* of the *Antients.* 'BENTL.' *Warburton.*

[2] [*amice* (amictus), a coat, is a word used by Spenser and Milton.]

[3] This good Scholiast (Scriblerus), not being acquainted with modern Luxury, was ignorant that these were only the miracles of *French Cookery,* and that particularly *Pigeons en crapeau* were a common dish. P. *and Warburton.*

[4] Sève *and* Verdeur] French Terms relating to Wines, which signify their flavour and poignancy. P.

[5] *Bladen — Hays*] Names of Gamesters. Bladen is a black man. ROBERT KNIGHT, Cashier of the South-sea Company, who fled from England in 1720 (afterwards pardoned in 1742) ⸺

KNIGHT lifts the head, for what are crowds undone,
To three essential Partridges in one?
Gone ev'ry blush, and silent all reproach,
Contending Princes mount them in their Coach.
   Next, bidding all draw near on bended knees,   565
The Queen confers her *Titles* and *Degrees.*
Her children first of more distinguish'd sort,
Who study Shakespeare at the Inns of Court,[1]
Impale a Glow-worm, or Vertú profess,
Shine in the dignity of F.R.S.[2]   570
Some, deep Free-Masons, join the silent race
Worthy to fill Pythagoras's place:
Some Botanists, or Florists at the least,
Or issue Members of an Annual feast.
Nor past the meanest unregarded, one   575
Rose a Gregorian, one a Gormogon.[3]
The last, not least in honour or applause,
Isis and Cam made DOCTORS of her LAWS.[4]
   Then, blessing all, "Go, Children of my care!
To Practice now from Theory repair.   580
All my commands are easy, short, and full:
My Sons! be proud, be selfish, and be dull.
Guard my Prerogative, assert my Throne:
This Nod confirms each Privilege your own.[5]
The Cap and Switch be sacred to his Grace;   585
With Staff and Pumps the Marquis lead the Race;
From Stage to Stage the licens'd Earl may run,
Pair'd with his Fellow-Charioteer the Sun;
The learned Baron Butterflies design,

These lived with the utmost magnificence at Paris, and kept open Tables frequented by persons of the first Quality of England, and even by Princes of the Blood of France. *P. and Warburton.* Colonel Martin Bladen was a man of some literature and translated Cæsar's *Commentaries.* I never could learn that he had offended Pope. He was uncle to Wm. Collins, the poet, whom he left an estate. *Warton.*

[1] *Her Children first of more distinguish'd sort, Who study* Shakespeare *at the Inns of Court.*] Mr. THOMAS EDWARDS, a *Gentleman,* as he is pleased to call himself, of *Lincoln's Inn;* but, in reality, a Gentleman only of the Dunciad; or, to speak him better, in the plain language of our honest Ancestors to such Mushrooms, *A Gentleman of the last Edition:* who, nobly eluding the solicitude of his careful Father, very early retained himself in the cause of *Dulness* against *Shakespear,* and with the wit and learning of his Ancestor *Tom Thimble* in the *Rehearsal,* and with the air of good nature and politeness of *Caliban* in the *Tempest,* hath now happily finished the *Dunce's progress* in perso-

nal abuse. SCRIBL. [Part *om.*] P. This attack on Mr. Edwards is not of weight sufficient to weaken the effects of his excellent Canons of Criticism. *Warton.*

[2] A line taken from Bramston's *Men of Taste. Warton.*

[3] *a Gregorian, one a Gormogon.*] A sort of Lay-brothers, *Slips* from the Root of the Free-Masons. P. *and Warburton.* ['*Gregorians*' are mentioned as 'a convivial sect,' and 'a kind of Masons, but without their sign,' in Crabbe's *Borough,* Letter x.]

[4] Pope refused this degree when offered to him on a visit undertaken to Oxford with Warburton, because the University would not confer the degree of D.D. upon Warburton, to whom some of its members had proposed it. *Roscoe.*

[5] *each* Privilege *your own, &c.*] This speech of Dulness to her Sons at parting may possibly fall short of the Reader's expectation; who may imagine the Goddess might give them a charge of more consequence, and, from such a Theory as is before delivered, incite them to the practice of something more extraordinary, than to personate

Or draw to silk Arachne's subtile line ; [1] 590
The Judge to dance his brother Sergeant call ; [2]
The Senator at Cricket urge the Ball ;
The Bishop stow (Pontific Luxury!)
An hundred Souls of Turkeys in a pie ;
The sturdy Squire to Gallic masters stoop, 595
And drown his Lands and Manors in a Soupe.
Others import yet nobler arts from France,
Teach Kings to fiddle,[3] and make Senates dance.
Perhaps more high some daring son may soar,
Proud to my list to add one Monarch more! 600
And nobly conscious, Princes are but things
Born for First Ministers, as Slaves for Kings,
Tyrant supreme! shall three Estates command,
And MAKE ONE MIGHTY DUNCIAD OF THE LAND!"
 More she had spoke, but yawn'd — All Nature nods : 605
What Mortal can resist the Yawn of Gods ? [4]
Churches and Chapels instantly it reach'd ;
(St. James's first, for leaden G—— preach'd) [5]
Then catch'd the Schools ; the Hall scarce kept awake ;
The Convocation gap'd, but could not speak : 610
Lost was the Nation's Sense, nor could be found,
While the long solemn Unison went round :
Wide, and more wide, it spread o'er all the realm ;
Ev'n Palinurus nodded at the Helm : [6]
The Vapour mild o'er each Committee crept ; 615
Unfinish'd Treaties in each Office slept ;
And Chiefless Armies doz'd out the Campaign ;

Running-Footmen, Jockeys, Stage Coachmen, &c.

But if it be well considered, that whatever inclination they might have to do mischief, her sons are generally rendered harmless by their Inability ; and that it is the common effect of Dulness (even in her greatest efforts) to defeat her own design ; the Poet, I am persuaded, will be justified, and it will be allowed that these worthy persons, in their several ranks, do as much as can be expected from them. *P. and Warburton.*

[1] *Arachne's subtile line ;* This is one of the most ingenious employments assigned, and therefore recommended only to Peers of Learning. Of weaving Stockings of the Webs of Spiders, see the *Philosophical Transactions. P. and Warburton.*

[2] *The Judge to dance his brother Sergeant call ;*] Alluding perhaps to that ancient and solemn *Dance,* intituled, *A Call of Sergeants. P. and Warburton.*

[3] *Teach Kings to fiddle*] An ancient amusement of Sovereign Princes, (viz.) Achilles, Alex-

ander, Nero ; tho' despised by Themistocles, who was a Republican — *Make Senates dance,* either after their Prince, or to Pontoise, or Siberia. P. *and Warburton.* [The Parliament of Paris was in 1720 relegated *en masse* to Pontoise, for having resisted the last desperate financial measures of Law, the author of the Mississippi scheme, and then director of the Bank of France.]

[4] *What Mortal can resist the Yawn of Gods ?*] This verse is truly Homerical ; as is the conclusion of the Action, where the great Mother composes all, in the same manner as Minerva at the period of the Odyssey. P. [*Part om.*]

[5] Dr. Gilbert Archbishop of York, who had attacked Dr. King of Oxford whom Pope much respected. *Warton.* [*Bowles* was informed that this prelate was a most eloquent preacher.]

[6] Young's *Sat.* VII. v. 215 :

'What felt thy Walpole, pilot of the realm?
Our Palinurus slept not at the helm. — '
         Wakefield.

2 F

And Navies yawn'd for Orders on the Main.[1]
O Muse! relate (for you can tell alone,
Wits have short Memories,[2] and Dunces none),   620
Relate, who first, who last resign'd to rest;
Whose Heads she partly, whose completely, blest;
What Charms could Faction, what Ambition lull,
The Venal quiet, and entrance the Dull;
'Till drown'd was Sense, and Shame, and Right, and Wrong—
O sing, and hush the Nations with thy Song!   626

　　　*　　　*　　　*　　　*　　　*　　　*

In vain, in vain—the all-composing Hour
Resistless falls: the Muse obeys the Pow'r.
She comes! she comes! the sable Throne behold [3]
Of *Night* primæval and of *Chaos* old!   630
Before her, *Fancy's* gilded clouds decay,
And all its varying Rain-bows die away.
Wit shoots in vain its momentary fires,
The meteor drops, and in a flash expires.
As one by one, at dread Medea's strain,[4]   635
The sick'ning stars fade off th' ethereal plain;
As Argus' eyes by Hermes' wand opprest,
Clos'd one by one to everlasting rest;
Thus at her felt approach, and secret might,
Art after *Art* goes out, and all is Night.   640
See skulking *Truth* to her old cavern fled,[5]
Mountains of Casuistry heap'd o'er her head!
Philosophy, that lean'd on Heav'n before,[6]
Shrinks to her second cause, and is no more.
Physic of *Metaphysic* begs defence,   645
And *Metaphysic* calls for aid on *Sense*!
See *Mystery* to *Mathematics* fly!
In vain! they gaze, turn giddy, rave, and die.
Religion blushing veils her sacred fires,
And unawares *Morality* expires.   650

---

[1] These verses were written many years ago, and may be found in the State Poems of that time. P. *and Warburton.* V. 616 is from a poem by Halifax. *Wakefield.*

[2] *Wits have short Memories,*] This seems to be the reason why the Poets, whenever they give us a Catalogue, constantly call for help on the Muses, who, as the Daughters of *Memory*, are obliged not to forget any thing. So Homer, *Iliad* II. vv. 788 ff. And Virgil, *Æn.* VII. [vv. 645-6]. SCRIBL. P.

[3] *She comes! she comes! &c.*] Here the Muse, like Jove's Eagle, after a sudden stoop at ignoble game, soareth again to the skies. As Prophecy hath ever been one of the chief provinces of Poesy, our Poet here foretells from what we feel, what we are to fear; and, in the style of other prophets, hath used the future tense for the preterite: since what he says shall be, is already to be seen, in the writings of some even of our most adored authors, in Divinity, Philosophy, Physics, Metaphysics, &c. who are too good indeed to be named in such company. P.

[4] [Cf. Ov. *Met.* VII. v. 209.]

[5] *Truth to her old Cavern fled,*] Alluding to the saying of Democritus, That Truth lay at the bottom of a deep well, from whence he had drawn her: Though Butler says, *He first put her in, before he drew her out. Warburton.*

[6] Ver. 643, in the former Edd. stood thus,
Philosophy, that reach'd the Heav'ns before,
Shrinks to her hidden cause, and is no more.
And this was intended as a censure of the Newtonian philosophy. *Warburton.*

For *public* Flame, nor *private*, dares to shine;
Nor *human* Spark is left, nor Glimpse *divine!*
Lo! thy dread Empire, CHAOS! is restor'd;
Light dies before thy uncreating word;
Thy hand, great Anarch! lets the curtain fall,   655
And universal Darkness buries All.

IMITATIONS.

BOOK I

Ver. 1. *Say, great Patricians! since your-
selves inspire These wondrous works*]
' Dii cœptis (nam vos mutastis et illas).'
                        Ovid, *Met.* I. [v. 2.]

Ver. 6. Alluding to a verse of Mr. Dryden,
not in MacFleckno (as is said ignorantly in the
Key to the Dunciad, p. 1), but in his verses to
Mr. Congreve,
' And Tom the second reigns like Tom the first.'
                        [*Epistle* XII. v. 48.]

Ver. 41, 42. *Hence hymning Tyburn's —
Hence, &c.*]
        ' Genus unde Latinum,
Albanique patres, atque altæ mœnia Romæ.'
                        Virg. *Æn.* I. [vv. 6, 7.]

Ver. 45. *In clouded Majesty*]
                ' the Moon
        Rising in clouded Majesty.'
Milton [*Par. Lost*], Book IV. [vv. 606, 7.]

Ver. 48. *— that knows no fears Of hisses,
blows, or want, or loss of ears :*]
' Quem neque pauperies, neque mors, neque vin-
        cula terrent.'
        Hor. [*Lib.* I. *Sat.* VII. v. 84.]

Ver. 55. *Here she beholds the Chaos dark
and deep, Where nameless Somethings, &c.*]
That is to say, unformed things, which are either
made into Poems or Plays, as the Booksellers or
the Players bid most. These lines allude to the
following in Garth's *Dispensary*, Cant. VI.
' Within the chambers of the globe they spy
The beds where sleeping vegetables lie,
'Till the glad summons of a genial ray
Unbinds the glebe, and calls them out to day.'

Ver. 64. *And ductile Dulness, &c.*] A
parody on a verse in Garth, Cant. I.
' How ductile matter new meanders takes.'

Ver. 79. *The cloud-compelling Queen*] From
Homer's Epithet of Jupiter, νεφεληγερέτα Ζεύς.

Var. *He rolled his eyes that witness'd huge
dismay.*
        ' round he throws his [baleful] eyes,
That witness'd huge affliction and dismay.'
        Milt. [*Par. Lost*], Bk. I. [vv. 56, 7.]
The progress of a bad poet in his thoughts,
being (like the progress of the Devil in Milton)
through a *Chaos*, might probably suggest this
imitation.

Ver. 140 in the former Edd. *The page ad-
mires new beauties not its own.*]
' Miraturque novas frondes et non sua poma.'
                Virg. *Geor.* II. [v. 82.]

Ver. 166. *With whom my Muse began,
with whom shall end.*]
        ' A te principium, tibi desinet.' —
                Virg. *Ecl.* VIII. [v. 11.]
'Εκ Διὸς ἀρχώμεσθα, καὶ εἰς Δία λήγετε,
        Μοῦσαι.
                Theoc. [*Id.* XVII. v. 1.]
' Prima dicte mihi, summa dicende Camœna.'
        Hor. [*Lib.* I. *Epist.* I. v. 1.]

Ver. 195. *Had Heav'n decreed, &c.*]
' Me si cœlicolæ voluissent ducere vitam,
Has mihi servassent sedes.'
                Virg. *Æn.* II. [vv. 641, 2.]

Ver. 197, 198. *Could Troy be sav'd — This
grey-goose weapon*]
                ' Si Pergama dextra
Defendi possent, etiam hac defensa fuissent.'
                Virg. ibid. [vv. 291, 2.]

Ver. 202. *This Box my Thunder, this right
hand my God.*]
' Dextra mihi *Deus*, et telum *quod missile
libro.*'
        Virgil, of the Gods of Mezentius.
                [*Æn.* x. v. 773.]
Var. *And visit Alehouse,*] Waller [*to the
King*] *on his Navy*]
' Those tow'rs of Oak o'er fertile plains might go,
And visit mountains where they once did grow.'

Ver. 229. *Unstain'd, untouch'd, &c.*]
'Felix Priamëia virgo!
Jussa mori: quæ sortitus non pertulit ullos,
Nec victoris heri tetigit captiva cubile!
Nos, patria incensa, diversa per æquora vectæ,
&c.'
Virg. *Æn.* III. [v. 320 ff.]

Ver. 245. *And thrice he lifted high the
Birthday brand,*] Ovid, of Althæa on a like
occasion, burning her offspring:
'Tum conata quater flammis imponere torrem,
Cœpta quater tenuit.'
[*Metam.* VIII. vv. 462, 3.]

Ver. 250. *Now flames the Cid, &c.*]
'Jam Deïphobi dedit ampla ruinam,
Vulcano superante domus; jam proximus ardet
Ucalegon.' —   *Æn.* II. [vv. 310–2.]

Ver. 263. *Great in her charms! as when
on Shrieves and May'rs She looks and
breathes herself into their airs.*]
'Alma parens confessa Deam; qualisque videri
Cœlicolis, et quanta solet.'
Virg. *Æn.* II. [vv. 591, 2.]
'Et lætos oculis afflavit honores.'
Id. *Æn.* I. [v. 591.]

Ver. 269. *This the Great Mother, &c.*]
'Urbs antiqua fuit
Quam Juno fertur terris magis omnibus unam
Posthabita coluisse Samo: hic illius arma,
Hic currus fuit: hic regnum Dea gentibus esse
(Si qua fata sinant) jam tum tenditque fovetque.'
Virg. *Æn.* I. [vv. 12 ff.]

Ver. 304. *The creeping, dirty, courtly Ivy
join.*]
'Quorum Imagines lambunt,
Hederæ sequaces.'
Pers. [*Prol.* vv. 5, 6.]

Ver. 311. *O! when shall rise a Monarch,
&c.*] Boileau, *Lutrin*, Chant. II. [vv. 123, 4.]
'Hélas! qu'est devenu ce temps, cet heureux
temps,
Où les Rois s'honoraient du nom de Fainéans:
&c.'

BOOK II.

Ver. 1. *High on a gorgeous seat*] Parody
of Milton [*Par. Lost*], Book II. [vv. 1. ff.]
'High on a throne of royal state, that far
Outshone the wealth of Ormus and of Ind,
Or where the gorgeous East with richest hand
Show'rs on her Kings Barbaric pearl and gold,
Satan exalted sate.'

Ver. 35. *A Poet's form she plac'd before
their eyes,*] This is what Juno does to deceive
Turnus, *Æn.* X. [vv. 636–40.]

'Tum Dea nube cava, tenuem *sine viribus
umbram*
In faciem Æneæ (visu mirabile monstrum!)
Dardaniis ornat telis, clypeumque jubasque
Divini assimilat capitis —
Dat *inania verba,*
Dat *sine mente sonum.*'
The reader will observe how exactly some of
these verses suit with their allegorical applica-
tion here to a Plagiary: There seems to me a
great propriety in this Episode, where such an
one is imagined by a phantom that deludes the
grasp of the expecting Bookseller.

Ver. 39. *But such a bulk as no twelve bards
could raise,*]
'Vix illud lecti bis sex [cervice subirent,]
Qualia nunc hominum producit corpora tellus.'
Virg. *Æn.* XII. [vv. 899, 900.]

Ver. 60. *So take the hindmost, Hell.*]
'Occupet extremum scabies; mihi turpe relin-
qui est.'
Hor. *de Arte* [v. 417].

Ver. 61, &c. Something like this is in Homer,
Il. X. v. 220, of Diomed. Two different man-
ners of the same author in his similes are also
imitated in the two following; the first, of the
Bailiff, is short, unadorned, and (as the Critics
well know) from *familiar life;* the second,
of the Water-fowl, more extended, picturesque,
and from *rural life.* The 59th verse is likewise
a literal translation of one in Homer.[1]

Ver. 64, 65. *On feet and wings, and flies,
and wades, and hops; So lab'ring on, with
shoulders, hands, and head,*]
'So eagerly the Fiend
O'er bog, o'er steep, thro' streight, rough, dense,
or rare,
With head, hands, wings, or feet pursues his
way,
And swims, or sinks, or wades, or creeps, or
flies.'
Milton [*Par. Lost*], Book II. [v. 947 ff.]

Ver. 67, 68. *With arms expanded, Bernard
rows his state, And left-legg'd Jacob seems to
emulate.*]   Milton, of the motion of the Swan,
'rows
His state with oary feet.'
Par. Lost [Book VII.] v. 440.
And Dryden, of another's, —*With two left legs.*

Ver. 73. *Here fortun'd Curl to slide;*]
'Labitur infelix, cæsis ut forte juvencis
Fusus humum viridesque super madefecerat
herbas
Concidit, immundoque fimo, sacroque cruore.'
Virg. *Æn.* v. of Nisus [v. 329 ff.]

[1] [After a diligent search I am disposed to doubt this. Perhaps the allusion is to *Iliad* XXIII. v. 479.]

Ver. 74. *And Bernard! Bernard!*]
' Ut littus, Hyla, Hyla, omne sonaret.'
Virg. *Ecl.* VI. [v. 44.]

Ver. 83. *A place there is, betwixt earth, air, and seas,*]
' Orbe locus medio est, inter terrasque, fretumque,
Cœlestesque plagas.'
Ovid. *Met.* XII. [xv. 39, 40.]

Ver. 108. *Nor heeds the brown dishonours of his face.*]
' faciem ostentabat, et udo
Turpia membra fimo.'
Virg. *Æn.* V. [vv. 357, 8.]

Ver. 111. *A shapeless shade, &c.*]
' Effugit imago
Par levibus ventis, volucrique similima somno.'
Virg. *Æn.* VI. [vv. 701, 2.]

Ver. 114. *His papers light, fly diverse, tost in air;*] Virg. *Æn.* VI. of the Sibyl's leaves,
' Carmina
turbata volent rapidis ludibria ventis.'
[vv. 74, 5.]

Ver. 141, 142. *—piteous of his case, Yet smiling at his rueful length of face.*]
' Risit pater optimus illi.'
' Me liceat casum misereri insontis amici —
Sic fatus, tergum Gætuli immane leonis, &c.
Virg. *Æn.* [v. 353; vv. 350, 1.]

Ver. 151. *Himself among the story'd chiefs he spies,*]
' Se quoque principibus permixtum agnovit Achivis —
Constitit, et lacrymans: Quis jam locus, inquit, Achate!
Quæ regio in terris nostri non plena laboris?'
Virg. *Æn.* I. [v. 488; vv. 459, 60.]

Ver. 156. *And the fresh vomit run for ever green!*] A parody on these lines of a late noble author:
' His bleeding arm had furnish'd all their rooms,
And run for ever purple in the looms.'

Ver. 158. *Two babes of love close clinging to her waist;*]
' Cressa genus, Pholoë, geminique sub ubere nati.' Virg. *Æn.* V. [v. 285.]

Ver. 163. *yon Juno—With cow-like udders, and with ox-like eyes.*] In allusion to Homer's
Βοῶπις πότνια Ἥρη.

Ver. 165. *This China Jordan*]
' Tertius Argolica hac galea contentus abito.'
Virg. *Æn.* V. [v. 314.]
In the games of Homer, *Il.* XXIII. there are set together, as prizes, a Lady and a Kettle, as in this place Mrs. Haywood and a Jordan. But there the preference in value is given to the Kettle, at which Mad. Dacier is justly displeased. Mrs. H. is here treated with distinction, and acknowledged to be the more valuable of the two.

Ver. 169, 170. *One on his manly confidence relies, One on his vigour*]
' Ille — melior motu, fretusque juventa;
Hic membris et mole valens.'
Virg. *Æn.* V. [vv. 430, 1.]

Ver. 173, 174. *So Jove's bright bow . . . (Sure sign)* The words of Homer, of the Rainbow, in *Iliad* XI. [vv. 27, 8.]
' ἅς τε Κρονίων
Ἐν νέφεϊ στήριξε, τέρας μερόπων ἀνθρώπων.'
' Que le fils de Saturn a fondés dans les nües, pour être dans tous les âges une signe à tous les mortels.'
Dacier.

Ver. 181, 182. *So (fam'd like thee for turbulence and horns) Eridanus*] Virgil mentions these two qualifications of Eridanus,
Georg. IV. [vv. 371-3.]
' Et gemina auratus taurino *cornua* vultu,
Eridanus, quo non alius per pinguia culta
In mare purpureum *violentior* influit amnis.'
The Poets fabled of this river Eridanus, that it flowed through the skies. Denham, *Cooper's Hill:*
' Heav'n her Eridanus no more shall boast,
Whose fame in thine, like lesser currents lost;
Thy nobler stream shall visit Jove's abodes,
To shine among the stars, and bathe the Gods.'

Ver. 223, 225. *To move, to raise, &c. Let others aim: 'T is yours to shake, &c.*]
' Excudent alii spirantia mollius æra,
Credo equidem, vivos ducent de marmore vultus, &c.'
' Tu regere imperio populos, Romane, memento,
Hæ tibi erunt artes ' —
[*Æn.* VI. vv. 847 ff.; vv. 851, 2.]

Ver. 243. *A Cat-call each shall win, &c.*]
' Non nostrum inter vos tantas componere lites,
Et vitula tu dignus, et hic.'
Virg. *Ecl.* III. [vv. 108, 9.]

Ver. 247. *As when the &c.*] A Simile with a long tail, in the manner of Homer.

Ver. 260. *bray back to him again.*] A figure of speech taken from Virgil:
' Et vox assensu nemorum ingeminata remugit.'
Georg. III. [v. 45.]
' He hears his numerous herds low o'er the plain,
While neighb'ring hills *low* back to them again.'
Cowley.
The poet here celebrated, Sir R. B. delighted

much in the word *bray*, which he endeavoured to ennoble by applying it to the sound of *Armour*, *War*, &c. In imitation of him, and strengthened by his authority, our author has here admitted it into Heroic poetry.

Ver. 262. *Prick all their ears up, and forget to graze;*]
' Immemor herbarum quos est mirata juvenca.'
　　　　　　　　　　　　Virg. *Ecl.* VIII. [v. 2.]

The progress of the sound from place to place, and the scenery here of the bordering regions, Tottenham-fields, Chancery-lane, the Thames, Westminster-hall, and Hungerford-stairs, are imitated from Virgil, *Æn.* VII. on the sounding the horn of Alecto:

' Audiit et Triviæ longe lacus, audiit amnis
Sulphurea Nar albus aqua, fontesque Velini,
　　&c.'　　　　　　　　　　　[v. 516 ff.]

Ver. 273. *The king of dykes, &c.*]
' Fluviorum rex Eridanus,
— quo non alius, per pinguia culta,
In mare purpureum violentior influit amnis.'
　　　　　Virg. [*Georg.* I. v. 482; IV. vv. 372, 3.]

Ver. 285. *Then sighing thus, And am I now threescore ? &c.*]
' — Fletque Milon senior, cum spectat inanes
Herculeis similes, fluidos pendere lacertos.'
　　　　　　　　　　Ovid [*Met.* XV. 229, 30].

Ver. 293. *and call on Smedley lost; &c.*]
' Alcides wept in vain for Hylas lost,
Hylas, in vain, resounds thro' all the coast.'
　　　　　　　Lord Roscommon's Translat. of
　　　　　　　　　　　　Virgil's *Ecl.* VI.

Ver. 302. *Not everlasting Blackmore*]
' Nec bonus Eurytion prælato invidit honori,
　　&c.'　　　　　　Virg. *Æn.* [VI. v. 44.]

Ver. 329. *Greater he looks, and more than mortal stares :*]　Virg. *Æn.* VI. of the Sibyl:
　　　　　' majorque videri,
　　Nec mortale sonans.'　　　[vv. 49, 50.]

Ver. 346. *Thence to the banks, &c.*]
' Tum canit errantem Permessi ad flumina Gallum,
Utque viro Phœbi chorus assurrexerit omnis;
Ut Linus hæc illi divino carmine pastor,
Floribus atque apio crines ornatus amaro,
Dixerit, Hos tibi dant calamos, en accipe, Musæ,
Ascræo quos ante seni &c.'
　　　　　　　　　[Virg. *Ecl.* VI. vv. 64 ff.]

Ver. 380, 381. *The same their talents . . . Each prompt &c.*]
　　' Ambo florentes ætatibus, Arcades ambo,
　　Et certare pares, et respondere parati.'
　　　　　　　　　Virg. *Ecl.* VII. [vv. 4, 5.]

Ver. 382. *And smit with love of Poetry and Prate.*]
　　' Smit with the love of sacred song.'
　　　　　Milton [*Par. Lost*, Bk. III. v. 29.]

Ver. 384. *The heroes sit, the vulgar form a ring;*]
　　' Consedere duces, et vulgi stante corona.'
　　　　　　　　　　Ovid, *Met.* XIII. [v. I.]

Ver. 410. *o'er all the sea of heads.*]
' A waving sea of heads was round me spread,
And still fresh streams the gazing deluge fed.'
　　　　　　　　　　　　Blackm. *Job.*

Ver. 418. *And all was hush'd, as Folly's self lay dead.*] Alludes to Dryden's verse in the *Indian Emperor* [Act III. Sc. 2. v. I];
' All things are hush'd, as Nature's self lay dead.'

Book III.

Ver. 7, 8. *Hence from the straw where Bedlam's Prophet nods, He hears loud Oracles, and talks with Gods :*]
' Et varias audit voces, fruiturque deorum
　Colloquio.'　　　Virg. *Æn.* VII. [vv. 91, 2.]

Ver. 15. *A slipshod Sibyl &c.*]
' Conclamat Vates
　　　furens antro se immisit aperto.'
　　　　　Virg. [*Æn.* VI. vv. 259, 262.]

Ver. 23. *Here, in a dusky vale &c.*]
' Videt Æneas in valle reducta
Seclusum nemus . . .　　　　　•
Lethæumque domos placidas qui prænatat
amnem,' &c.
Hunc circum innumeræ gentes, &c.'
　　　　　　Virg. *Æn.* VI. [vv. 703 ff.]

Ver. 24. *Old Bavius sits, to dip poetic souls,*] Alluding to the story of Thetis dipping Achilles to render him impenetrable:
' At pater Anchises penitus convalle virenti
Inclusas animas, superumque ad lumen ituras,
Lustrabat.'　　Virg. *Æn.* VI. [vv. 679–81.]

Ver. 28. *unbar the gates of Light,*] An Hemistic of Milton.

Ver. 31, 32. *Millions and millions — Thick as the stars, &c.*]
' Quam multa in silvis autumni frigore primo
Lapsa cadunt folia, aut ad terram gurgite ab alto
Quam multæ glomerantur aves, &c.'
　　　　　　Virg. *Æn.* VI. [vv. 309 ff.]

Ver. 54. *Mix'd the Owl's ivy with the Poet's bays,*]
　　　　　' sine tempora circum
Inter victrices hederam tibi serpere lauros.'
　　　　　　Virg. *Ecl.* VIII. [vv. 12, 13.]

Ver. 61, 62. *For this our Queen unfolds to vision true Thy mental eye, for thou hast much to view:*] This has a resemblance to that passage in Milton [*Par. Lost*], Book XI. [vv. 411 ff.] where the Angel

'To nobler sights from Adam's eye remov'd
The film;
          Then purg'd with Euphrasie and Rue
The visual nerve—*for he had much to see.*'

There is a general allusion in what follows to that whole Episode.

Ver. 117, 118. *Happy !—had Easter never been !*]

'Et fortunatam, si nunquam armenta fuissent.'
Virg. *Ecl.* VI. [v. 45.]

Ver. 127, 129. *Now look thro' Fate !—See all her Progeny, &c.*]

'Nunc age, Dardaniam prolem quæ deinde sequatur
Gloria, qui maneant Itala de gente nepotes,
Illustres animas, nostrumque in nomen ituras,
Expediam.' Virg. *Æn.* VI. [vv. 756 ff.]

Ver. 131. *As Berecynthia &c.*]

'Felix prole virûm, qualis Berecynthia mater
Invehitur curru Phrygias turrita per urbes,
Læta deûm partu, centum complexa nepotes,
Omnes cœlicolas, omnes supera alta tenentes.'
Virg. *Æn.* VI. [vv. 784 ff.]

Ver. 139. *Mark first that Youth, &c.*]

'Ille vides, pura juvenis qui nititur hasta,
Proxima forte tenet lucis loca.'
Virg. *Æn.* VI [vv. 760, 1.]

Ver. 141. *With all thy Father's virtues blest, be born !*] A manner of expression used by Virgil, *Ecl.* VIII. [v. 17.]

'Nascere! præque diem veniens, age, Lucifer.'
As also that of *patriis virtutibus*, Ecl. IV. [v. 17.]

It was very natural to shew to the Hero, before all others, his own Son, who had already begun to emulate him in his theatrical, poetical, and even political capacities. By the attitude in which he here presents himself, the reader may be cautioned against ascribing wholly to the Father the merit of the epithet *Cibberian*, which is equally to be understood with an eye to the Son.

Ver. 145. *From the strong fate of drams if thou get free,*]

'si qua fata aspera rumpas,
Tu Marcellus eris!'
Virg. *Æn.* VI. [vv. 882, 3.]

Ver. 147. *Thee shall each ale-house &c.*]

'Te nemus Anguitiæ, vitrea te Fucinus unda,
Te liquidi flevere lacus.'
Virg. *Æn.* VII. [vv. 759, 60.]

Virgil again, *Ecl.* X. [v. 13.]

'Illum etiam lauri, illum flevere myricæ, &c.'

Ver. 150. 'duo fulmina belli
Scipiadas, cladem Libyæ!'
Virg. *Æn.* VI. [vv. 842, 3.]

Ver. 166. *And makes Night hideous*]

'Visit thus the glimpses of the moon,
Making Night hideous.'
Shakesp. [*Hamlet*, Act I. Sc. 4.]

Ver. 169. *Flow, Welsted, flow ! &c.*] Parody on Denham, *Cooper's Hill.*

'O could I flow like thee, and make thy stream
My great example, as it is my theme:
Tho' deep, yet clear; tho' gentle, yet not dull;
Strong without rage; without o'erflowing, full!'

Ver. 177. *Embrace, embrace, my sons ! be foes no more !*]

'Ne tanta animis assuescite bella,
Neu patriæ validas in viscera vertite vires:
Tuque prior, tu parce—sanguis meus!'
Virg. *Æn.* VI. [v. 832 ff.]

Ver. 179. *Behold yon Pair, in strict embraces join'd ;*]

'Illæ autem paribus quas fulgere cernis in armis,
Concordes animæ.' Virg. *Æn.* VI. [vv. 826, 7.]

'Euryalus, forma insignis viridique juventa,
Nisus amore pio pueri.'
Virg. *Æn.* V. [vv. 295, 6.]

Ver. 185. *But who is he, &c.*] Virgil. *Æn.* VI. [vv. 808 ff.] questions and answers in this manner, of *Numa:*

'Quis procul ille autem ramis insignis olivæ,
Sacra ferens?—nosco crines, incanaque menta,
&c.'

Ver. 224. *Learn ye Dunces ! not to scorn your God.*]

'Discite justitiam moniti, et non temnere divos.'
Virg. [*Æn.* VI. v. 620.]

Ver. 244. *And other planets*]

'solemque *suum, sua* sidera norunt.'
Virg. *Æn.* VI. [v. 641.]

Ver. 246. *Whales sport in woods, and dolphins in the skies ;*]

'Delphinum sylvis appingit, fluctibus aprum.'
Hor. [*de Arte Poet.* v. 30.]

Ver. 251. *Son ? what thou seek'st is in thee :*]

'(Quod petis in te est)
Ne te quæsiveris extra.'
Pers. [*Sat.* I. v. 7. The first part of this seems to be loosely quoted from Hor. *Lib.* I. *Epist.* XI. v. 29.]

Ver. 256. *Wings the red light'ning, &c.*] Like Salmoneus in *Æn.* VI. [vv. 586, 590, 1.]

'Dum flammas Jovis, et sonitus imitatur
Olympi.'
        'Nimbos, et non imitabile fulmen,
Ære et cornipedum cursu simularat equorum.'

Ver. 258. *o'er all unclassic ground :*] Al-
ludes to Mr. Addison's verse, in the praises of
Italy:
'Poetic fields encompass me around,
And still I seem to tread on classic ground.'
                [*Letter from Italy to Lord Halifax.*]
As v. 264 is a parody on a noble one of the
same author in *The Campaign ;* and v. 259,
260, on two sublime verses of Dr. Y[oung].

Ver. 319, 320. *This, this is he, foretold by
ancient rhymes, Th' Augustus, &c.*]
'Hic vir, hic est! tibi quem promitti sæpius
audis,
Augustus Cæsar, divum genus; aurea condet
Secula qui rursus Latio, regnata per arva
Saturno quondam.'
                Virg. *Æn.* VI. [vv. 791 ff.]
Saturnian here relates to the age of *Lead,*
mentioned book I. v. 26.

Ver. 340. *And thro' the Iv'ry Gate, &c.*]
'Sunt geminæ Somni portæ; quarum altera
fertur
Cornea, qua veris facilis datur exitus umbris
Altera candenti perfecta nitens elephanto,
Sed falsa ad cœlum mittunt insomnia manes.'
                Virg. *Æn.* VI. [vv. 893 ff.]

BOOK IV.

Ver. 54. *Joy to great Chaos !*]
        'Joy to great Cæsar.'
The beginning of a famous old Song.

Ver. 126. *Admire new light &c.*]
'The Soul's dark cottage, batter'd and decay'd,
Lets in new light, through chinks that time has
made.'
Waller. [Lines *On his Divine Poems.*]

Ver. 142. *Dropping with infant's blood,
&c.*]
'First Moloch, horrid King, besmear'd with
blood
Of human Sacrifice, and parents' tears.'
                Milton [*Par. Lost,* I. vv. 392, 3].

Ver. 207. *He, kingly, did but nod ;*]
        'He, kingly, from his State
Declin'd not.'
                Milton [*Par. Lost,* XI. vv. 249, 50].

Ver. 210. *is* Aristarchus *yet unknown ?*]
        'Sic notus *Ulysses ?*'
                Virg. [*Æn.* II. v. 44.]
'Dost thou not feel me, *Rome ?*'
Ben. Jonson [first verse of *Catiline*].

Ver. 215. *Roman and Greek* Grammarians,
&c.] Imitated from Propertius speaking of the
Æneid. [*Lib.* II. *Eleg.* XXV. vv. 65, 6.]
'Cedite, *Romani* scriptores, cedite *Graii !*
Nescio quid majus nascitur Iliade.'

Ver. 284. *A dauntless infant never scar'd
with God.*]
        'sine Dis animosus Infans.'
                Hor. [*Lib.* III. *Od.* IV. v. 20.]

Ver. 332. *So may the sons of sons &c.*]
'Et nati natorum, et qui nascentur ab illis.'
                Virg. [*Æn.* III. v. 98.]

Ver. 342. *Stretch'd on the rack And heard
&c.*]
                'Sedet, *æternumque sedebit,*
Infelix Theseus, Phlegyasque *miserrimus*
omnes
Admonet.'   Virg. [*Æn.* VI. v. 617 ff.]

Ver. 355. *grant me still to cheat ! O may
thy cloud still cover the deceit !*]
        'Pulchra Laverna,
Da mihi fallere . . .
Noctem peccatis et fraudibus objice nubem.'
                Hor. [Lib. I. Epist. XVI. vv. 60-2.]

Ver. 383. *Receiv'd each Demi-God,*]
'Emissumque ima de sede Typhoëa terræ
Cœlitibus fecisse metum ; cunctosque dedisse,
Terga fugæ : donec fessos Ægyptia tellus
Ceperit.'   Ovid [*Metam.* V. vv. 321 ff.].

Ver. 405. *Fair from its humble bed, &c.
nam'd it* Caroline!
'Each Maid cry'd, *charming !* and each Youth,
        divine !
Now prostrate! dead! behold that *Caroline :*
No Maid cries, *charming !* and no Youth,
        divine !'
These Verses are translated from Catullus,
Epith. [vv. 39 ff.]
'Ut flos in septis secretus nascitur hortis,
Quam mulcent auræ, firmat Sol, educat imber,
Multi illum pueri, multæ optavere puellæ :
Idem quum tenui carptus defloruit ungui,
Nulli illum pueri, nullæ optavere puellæ, &c.'

Ver. 421. *Of all th' enamel'd race,*] The
poet seems to have an eye to Spenser, *Muiopot-
mos.* [vv. 17, 18.]
'Of all the race of silver-winged Flies
Which do possess the Empire of the Air.'

Ver. 427, 428. *It fled, I follow'd, &c.*]
        'I started back,
It started back ; but pleas'd I soon return'd,
Pleas'd it return'd as soon.'
                Milton [*Par. Lost,* IV. vv. 402, 3.]

Ver. 518. *Which whoso tastes, forgets his former friends, Sire, &c.*]

‘ Αὐτίκ’ ἄρ’ εἰς οἶνον βάλε φάρμακον, ἔνθεν
    ἔπινον

Νηπενθές τ’ ἀχολόν τε, κακῶν ἐπίληθον
    ἁπάντων.’

Homer of the Nepenthe, *Odyss.* IV. [vv. 220, 1.]

Ver. 622. Virg. *Æn.* XI. 664, 5. *Warburton.*

Ver. 637. *As Argus' eyes, &c.*]

‘ Et quamvis sopor est oculorum parte receptus,

Parte tamen vigilat.’

    ‘ Vidit Cyllenius omnes

Succubuisse oculos, &c.’

        Ovid. *Met.* I. [vv. 685, 6; 713, 4.]

BY THE AUTHOR

A DECLARATION.

𝖂𝖍𝖊𝖗𝖊𝖆𝖘 certain Haberdashers of Points and Particles, being instigated by the spirit of Pride, and assuming to themselves the name of Critics and Restorers, have taken upon them to adulterate the common and current sense of our Glorious Ancestors, Poets of this Realm, by clipping, coining, defacing the images, mixing their own base allay, or otherwise falsifying the same; which they publish, utter, and send as genuine: The said haberdashers having no right thereto, as neither heirs, executors, administrators, assigns, or in any sort related to such Poets, to all or any of them: Now, We, having carefully revised this our Dunciad, beginning with the words The Mighty Mother, and ending with the words buries All, containing the entire sum of One thousand seven hundred and fifty four verses, declare every word, figure, point, and comma of this impression to be authentic: And do therefore strictly enjoin and forbid any person or persons whatsoever to erase, reverse, put between hooks, or by any other means, directly or indirectly, change or mangle any of them. And we do hereby earnestly exhort all our brethren to follow this our example, which we heartily wish our great Predecessors had heretofore set, as a remedy and prevention of all such abuses. Provided always, that nothing in this Declaration shall be construed to limit the lawful and undoubted right of every subject of this Realm, to judge, censure, or condemn, in the whole or in part, any Poem or Poet whatsoever.

Given under our hand at London, this third day of January, in the year of our
    Lord One thousand, seven hundred, thirty and two.

Declarat' cor' me,

JOHN BARBER, Mayor.   P.

A LIST OF BOOKS, PAPERS, AND VERSES,

In which our Author was abused, before the Publication of the DUNCIAD; with the true Names of the Authors.

REFLECTIONS critical and satyrical on a late Rhapsody, called an Essay on Criticism. By Mr. Dennis, printed by B. Lintot, price 6d.

A New Rehearsal, or Bays the younger; containing an Examen of Mr. Rowe's plays, and a word or two on Mr. Pope's Rape of the Lock. Anon. (by Charles Gildon) printed for J. Roberts, 1714, price 1s.

Homerides, or a Letter to Mr. Pope, occasioned by his intended translation of Homer. By Sir Iliad Dogrel. (Tho. Burnet and G. Ducket, Esquires), printed for W. Wilkins, 1715, price 9d.

Æsop at the Bear-garden; a vision, in imitation of the Temple of Fame. By Mr. Preston. Sold by John Morphew, 1715, price 6d.

The Catholic Poet, or Protestant Barnaby's Sorrowful Lamentation; a Ballad about Homer's Iliad. By Mrs. Centlivre, and others, 1715, price 1d.

An Epilogue to a Puppet-shew at Bath, concerning the said Iliad. By George Ducket, Esq. printed by E. Curl.

A complete Key to the What d'ye call it. Anon. (by Griffin, a player, supervised by Mr. Th——) printed by J. Roberts, 1715.

A true Character of Mr. P. and his writings, in a letter to a friend. Anon. (Dennis) printed for S. Popping, 1716, price 3d.

The Confederates, a Farce. By Joseph Gay (J. D. Breval) printed for R. Burleigh, 1717, price 1s.

Remarks upon Mr. Pope's translation of Homer; with two letters concerning the Windsor Forest, and the Temple of Fame. By Mr. Dennis, printed for E. Curl, 1717, price 1s. 6d.

Satyrs on the translators of Homer, Mr. P. and Mr. T. Anon. (Bez. Morris) 1717, price 6d.

The Triumvirate: or, a Letter from Palæmon to Celia at Bath. Anon. (Leonard Welsted), 1711, folio, price 1s.

The Battle of Poets, an heroic poem. By Tho. Cooke, printed for J. Roberts, folio, 1725.

Memoirs of Lilliput. Anon. (Eliza Haywood), octavo, printed in 1727.

An Essay on Criticism, in prose. By the Author of the Critical History of England (J. Oldmixon), octavo, printed 1728.

Gulliveriana and Alexandriana; with an ample preface and critique on Swift and Pope's Miscellanies. By Jonathan Smedley, printed by J. Roberts, octavo, 1728.

Characters of the Times; or, an account of the writings, characters, &c. of several gentlemen libelled by S—— and P——, in a late Miscellany. Octavo, 1728.

Remarks on Mr. Pope's Rape of the Lock, in letters to a friend. By Mr. Dennis; written in 1724, though not printed till 1728, octavo. P.

VERSES, LETTERS, ESSAYS, OR ADVERTISEMENTS, IN THE PUBLIC PRINTS.

British Journal, Nov. 25, 1727. A Letter on Swift and Pope's Miscellanies. (Writ by M. Concanen.)

Daily Journal, March 18, 1728. A Letter by Philo-mauri. James-Moore Smith.

Id. March 29. A letter about Thersites; accusing the author of disaffection to the Government. By James-Moore Smith.

Mist's Weekly Journal, March 30. An Essay on the Arts of a Poet's sinking in reputation; or, a Supplement to the Art of Sinking in Poetry. (Supposed by Mr. Theobald.)

Daily Journal, April 3. A Letter under the name of Philo-ditto. By James-Moore Smith.

Flying Post, April 4. A Letter against Gulliver and Mr. P. (By Mr. Oldmixon.)

Daily Journal, April 5. An Auction of Goods at Twickenham. By James-Moore Smith.

The Flying Post, April 6. A Fragment of a Treatise upon Swift and Pope. By Mr. Oldmixon.

The Senator, April 9. On the same. By Edward Roome.

Daily Journal, April 8. Advertisement by James-Moore Smith.

Flying Post, April 13. Verses against Dr. Swift, and against Mr. P—'s Homer. By J. Oldmixon.

Daily Journal, April 23. Letter about the translation of the character of Thersites in Homer. By Thomas Cooke, &c.

Mist's Weekly Journal, April 27. A Letter of Lewis Theobald.

Daily Journal, May 11. A Letter against Mr. P. at large. Anon. (John Dennis.)

All these were afterwards reprinted in a pamphlet, entituled A Collection of all the Verses, Essays, Letters, and Advertisements occasion'd by Mr. Pope and Swift's Miscellanies, prefaced by Concanen, Anonymous, octavo, and printed for A. Moore, 1728, price 1s. Others of an elder date, having lain as waste Paper many years, were, upon the publication of the Dunciad, brought out, and their Authors betrayed by the mercenary Booksellers (in hope of some possibility of vending a few) by advertising them in this manner — " The Confeder- " ates, a farce. By Capt. Breval (for which he " was put into the Dunciad). An Epilogue to " Powel's Puppet-show. By Col. Ducket (for " which he is put into the Dunciad). Essays, &c. " By Sir Richard Blackmore. (N.B. It was for " a passage of this book that Sir Richard was put " into the Dunciad.) " And so of others.

AFTER THE DUNCIAD, 1728.

An Essay on the Dunciad. Octavo, printed for J. Roberts. (In this book, p. 9. it was formally declared, " That the complaint of the " aforesaid Libels and Advertisements was forged " and untrue; that all mouths had been silent, " except in Mr. Pope's praise; and nothing " against him published, but by Mr. Theobald.")

Sawney, in blank verse, occasioned by the Dunciad; with a Critique on that poem. By J. Ralph (a person never mentioned in it at first, but inserted after), printed for J. Roberts, octavo.

A complete Key to the Dunciad. By E. Curl, 12mo. price 6d.

A second and third edition of the same, with additions, 12mo.

The Popiad. By E. Curl, extracted from J. Dennis, Sir Richard Blackmore, &c. 12mo. price 6d.

The Curliad. By the same E. Curl.

The Female Dunciad. Collected by the same Mr. Curl, 12mo. price 6d. With the Metamorphosis of P. into a stinging Nettle. By Mr. Foxton, 12mo.

The Metamorphosis of Scriblerus into Snarlerus. By J. Smedley, printed for A. Moore, folio, price 6d.

The Dunciad dissected. By Curl and Mrs. Thomas, 12mo.

An Essay on the Taste and Writings of the present times. Said to be writ by a gentleman of C. C. C. Oxon, printed for J. Roberts, octavo.

The Arts of Logic and Rhetoric, partly taken from Bouhours with new Reflections, &c. By John Oldmixon, octavo.

Remarks on the Dunciad. By Mr. Dennis, dedicated to Theobald, octavo.

A Supplement to the Profund. Anon. by Matthew Concanen, octavo.

Mist's Weekly Journal, June 8. A long letter, signed W. A. Writ by some or other of the Club of Theobald, Dennis, Moore, Concanen, Cooke, who for some time held constant weekly meetings for these kind of performances.

Daily Journal, June 11. A Letter signed Philoscriblerus, on the name of Pope — Letter to Mr. Theobald, in verse, signed B. M. (Bezaleel Morris) against Mr. P—. Many other little epigrams about this time in the same papers, by James Moore, and others.

Mist's Journal, June 22. A Letter by Lewis Theobald.

Flying Post, August 8. Letter on Pope and Swift.

Daily Journal, August 8. Letter charging the Author of the Dunciad with Treason.

Durgen: a plain satire on a pompous satirist. By Edward Ward, with a little of James Moore.

Apollo's Maggot in his Cups. By E. Ward.

Gulliveriana secunda. Being a Collection of many of the Libels in the News-papers, like the former Volume, under the same title, by Smedley. Advertised in the Craftsman, Nov. 9, 1728, with this remarkable promise, that " *any thing* " which *any body* should send as Mr. Pope's or " Dr. Swift's, should be inserted and published " as theirs."

Pope Alexander's supremacy and infallibility examined, &c. By George Ducket, and John Dennis, quarto.

Dean Jonathan's Paraphrase on the fourth chapter of Genesis. Writ by E. Roome, folio, 1729.

Labeo. A paper of verses by Leonard Welsted, which after came into *One Epistle*, and was published by James Moore, quarto, 1730. Another part of it came out in Welsted's own name, under the just title of Dulness and Scandal, folio, 1731.

There have been since published:

Verses on the Imitator of Horace. By a Lady (or between a Lady, a Lord, and a Court-'squire). Printed for J. Roberts, folio.

An Epistle from a Nobleman to a Doctor of Divinity, from Hampton-court (Lord H——y). Printed for J. Roberts also, folio.

A Letter from Mr. Cibber to Mr. Pope. Printed for W. Lewis in Covent-garden, octavo.

P.

INDEX

OF PERSONS CELEBRATED IN THIS POEM.

(The first Number shews the BOOK, the second the VERSE.)

INDEX

OF MATTERS CONTAINED IN THIS POEM AND NOTES.

(The first Number denotes the BOOK, the second the VERSE and NOTE on it. *Test.* Testimonies.[1])

[1] [*The Testimonies of Authors concerning our Poet and his Works*, published by P. under the name of Martinus Scriblerus, but omitted here.]

MISCELLANEOUS PIECES IN VERSE.

———o○○○○○———

IMITATIONS OF HORACE.

[Of the following *Imitations of Horace* the first two are rather imitations of Swift, Horace merely supplying the text for the travesty. For (as previous editors have not failed to point out), no styles could be found less alike one another than the bland and polite style of Horace and the downright, and often cynically plain, manner of Swift. With Pope the attempt to write in Swift's style was a mere *tour de force*, which he could indeed carry out with success through a few lines, but not further, without relapsing into his own more elaborate manner. Swift's marvellous precision and *netteté* of expression are something very different from Pope's pointed and rhetorical elegance. The latter was as ill suited by the Hudibrastic metre patronised by Swift, as was the comic genius of Butler himself by the wider, but nowise easier, garment of the heroic couplet. As it was Swift, and not Horace, whom Pope imitated in the first two of the following pieces, it is needless to follow Warton into a comparison between them and previous attempts at a real version of Horace. The *Ode to Venus*, which was first published in 1737, more nearly approaches the character of a translation.]

BOOK I. EPISTLE VII.[1]

Imitated in the Manner of Dr. SWIFT.

'TIS true, my Lord, I gave my word,
  I would be with you, June the third;
Chang'd it to August, and (in short)
Have kept it — as you do at Court.
You humour me when I am sick,   5
Why not when I am splenetic?
In town, what Objects could I meet?
The shops shut up in ev'ry street,
And Fun'rals black'ning all the Doors,
And yet more melancholy Whores: 10
And what a dust in every place!
And a thin Court that wants your Face,
And Fevers raging up and down,
And W * and H * * both in town![2]

---

[1] [Horace's Epistle, which serves as the groundwork of the above, is addressed to Mæcenas, and intended as an excuse and a justification for his protracted absence from Rome. Only about half of Horace's Epistle is followed by Pope.]

[2] [Possibly Ward and Henley, as two representative quacks for bodily and mental ailments.]

451

"The Dog-days are no more the case."   15
'T is true; but Winter comes apace:
Then southward let your Bard retire,
Hold out some months 'twixt Sun and Fire,
And you shall see the first warm Weather,
Me and the Butterflies together.   20
    My Lord, your Favours well I know;
'T is with Distinction you bestow;
And not to ev'ry one that comes,
Just as a Scotsman does his Plums.
"Pray take them, Sir, — Enough 's a Feast: 25
"Eat some, and pocket up the rest "—
What? rob your Boys? those pretty rogues!
"No, Sir, you 'll leave them to the Hogs."
Thus Fools with Compliments besiege ye,
Contriving never to oblige ye.   30
Scatter your Favours on a Fop,
Ingratitude 's the certain crop;
And 't is but just, I 'll tell ye wherefore,
You give the things you never care for.
A wise man always is or should   35
Be mighty ready to do good;
But makes a diff'rence in his thought
Betwixt a Guinea and a Groat.
    Now this I 'll say: you 'll find in me
A safe Companion, and a free;   40
But if you 'd have me always near —
A word, pray, in your Honour's ear.
I hope it is your Resolution
To give me back my Constitution!
The sprightly Wit, the lively Eye,[1]   45
Th' engaging Smile, the Gaiety,
That laugh'd down many a Summer Sun,
And kept you up so oft till one:
And all that voluntary Vein,
As when Belinda[2] rais'd my Strain.   50
    A Weasel once made shift to slink
In at a Corn-loft thro' a Chink;
But having amply stuff'd his skin,
Could not get out as he got in:
Which one belonging to the House   55
('T was not a Man, it was a Mouse)
Observing, cry'd, "You 'scape not so,
"Lean as you came, Sir, you must go."
    Sir, you may spare your Application,
I 'm no such Beast, nor his Relation;   60
Nor one that Temperance advance,
Cramm'd to the throat with Ortolans:

---

[1] [Cf. *Epistle to Arbuthnot*, v. 118.]   himself and the public on his *Rape of the Lock.*
[2] *As when Belinda*] A compliment he pays   *Warburton.*

Extremely ready to resign
All that may make me none of mine.
South-sea Subscriptions take who please,   65
Leave me but Liberty and Ease.
'T was what I said to Craggs and Child,[1]
Who prais'd my Modesty, and smil'd.
Give me, I cry'd, (enough for me)
My Bread, and Independency!   70
So bought an Annual Rent or two,
And liv'd — just as you see I do;
Near fifty, and without a Wife,
I trust that sinking Fund, my Life.
Can I retrench? Yes, mighty well,   75
Shrink back to my Paternal Cell,[2]
A little House, with Trees a-row,
And, like its Master, very low.
There died my Father, no man's Debtor,
And there I 'll die, nor worse nor better.   80
   To set this matter full before ye,
Our old Friend Swift will tell his Story.
   " Harley,[3] the Nation's great Support," —
But you may read it; I stop short.

BOOK II. SATIRE VI.[4]

The first Part imitated in the Year 1714, by Dr. SWIFT; the latter Part
added afterwards.

I 'VE often wish'd that I had clear
   For life, six hundred pounds a year,
A handsome House to lodge a Friend,
A River at my garden's end,
A Terrace-walk, and half a Rood   5
Of Land, set out to plant a Wood,
   Well, now I have all this and more,
I ask not to increase my store;
But here a Grievance seems to lie,
All this is mine but till I die;   10
I can't but think 't would sound more clever,
To me and to my Heirs for ever.
   If I ne'er got or lost a groat,
By any Trick, or any Fault;

[1] *Craggs and Child,*] Mr. Craggs gave him some South-sea subscriptions. He was so indifferent about them as to neglect making any benefit of them. He used to say it was a satisfaction to him that he did not grow rich (as he might have done) by the public calamity. *Warburton.* [Cf. *Introductory Memoir,* p. xxxv.] Sir Francis Child, the banker. *Bowles.*

[2] [Pope's father died at Chiswick in 1717.]
[3] [Harley, Earl of Oxford, the friend of Swift. See the following *Imitation.*]
[4] [In this Satire an opportunity is afforded for judging how far Pope succeeds in imitating the style of his friend. Pope's performance begins at v. 125.]

And if I pray by Reason's rules,   15
And not like forty other Fools:
As thus, "Vouchsafe, oh gracious Maker!
" To grant me this and t' other Acre:
" Or, if it be thy Will and Pleasure,
" Direct my Plough to find a Treasure: "   20
But only what my Station fits,
And to be kept in my right wits.[1]
Preserve, Almighty Providence,
Just what you gave me, Competence:
And let me in these shades compose   25
Something in Verse as true as Prose;
Remov'd from all th' Ambitious Scene,
Nor puff'd by Pride, nor sunk by Spleen.
    In short, I 'm perfectly content,
Let me but live on this side Trent;   30
Nor cross the Channel twice a year,
To spend six months with Statesmen here.[2]
    I must by all means come to town,
'T is for the service of the Crown.
" Lewis, the Dean will be of use,   35
" Send for him up, take no excuse."
The toil, the danger of the Seas;
Great Ministers ne'er think of these;
Or let it cost five hundred pound,
No matter where the money 's found,   40
It is but so much more in debt,
And that they ne'er consider'd yet.
    " Good Mr. Dean, go change your gown,
" Let my Lord know you 're come to town."
I hurry me in haste away,   45
Not thinking it is Levee-day;
And find his Honour in a Pound,
Hemm'd by a triple Circle round,
Chequer'd with Ribbons blue and green:[3]
How should I thrust myself between?   50
Some Wag observes me thus perplext,
And, smiling, whispers to the next,
" I thought the Dean had been too proud,
" To jostle here among a crowd."
Another in a surly fit,   55
Tells me I have more Zeal than Wit,
" So eager to express your love,

---

[1] [Swift's apprehension of idiotcy, to be so terribly justified at the close of his life, haunted him from an early period. Its most terrible expression is the description of the Struldbrugs in Gulliver's voyage to the Houyhnhms.]

[2] [Swift appears never to have absolutely relinquished the hope of English preferment till his last visit to England in 1727. But he never condescended to ask it either of friend or foe.]

[3] [The orders of the Garter and Shamrock. The Bath was not revived till 1725 (by Sir R. Walpole). At Lilliput, Gulliver observed the nobles leaping over a stick, in order to be decorated with blue, red and green threads.]

"You ne'er consider whom you shove,
"But rudely press before a Duke."
I own I 'm pleas'd with this rebuke,   60
And take it kindly meant to show
What I desire the World should know.
    I get a whisper, and withdraw;
When twenty Fools I never saw
Come with Petitions fairly penn'd,   65
Desiring I would stand their friend.
    This, humbly offers me his Case —
That, begs my int'rest for a Place —
A hundred other Men's affairs,
Like bees, are humming in my ears.   70
"To-morrow my Appeal comes on,
"Without your help the Cause is gone" —
"The Duke expects my Lord and you,
"About some great Affair, at Two — "
"Put my Lord Bolingbroke in mind,   75
"To get my Warrant quickly sign'd:
"Consider, 't is my first request." —
'Be satisfied, I 'll do my best : ' —
Then presently he falls to tease,
"You may for certain, if you please;   80
"I doubt not, if his Lordship knew —
"And, Mr. Dean, one word from you" —
    'T is (let me see) three years and more,
(October next it will be four)[1]
Since HARLEY bid me first attend,   85
And chose me for an humble friend;
Would take me in his Coach to chat,
And question me of this and that;
As, "What 's o'clock ?" And, "How 's the Wind?"
"Whose Chariot 's that we left behind?"   90
Or gravely try to read the lines
Writ underneath the Country Signs;
Or, "Have you nothing new to-day
"From Pope, from Parnell,[2] or from Gay?"
Such tattle often entertains   95
My Lord and me as far as Staines,
As once a week we travel down
To Windsor, and again to Town,
Where all that passes, *inter nos*,
Might be proclaim'd at Charing-Cross.   100
    Yet some I know with envy swell,

---

[1] [Swift commenced his literary labours for the Tories in 1710.]

[2] [Thomas Parnell (born in 1679), author of the *Hermit*, and a lyrical poet of real merit, went over, like Swift, from the Whigs to the Tories, and was one of the members of the Scriblerus Club. He died in 1717; and Pope published his poems in 1722, with a dedication to the Earl of Oxford (v. infra, p. 460). Parnell wrote the Life of Homer for Pope's *Iliad*, and translated the *Batrachomyomachia*. His biography was afterwards written by Goldsmith.]

Because they see me us'd so well:
"How think you of our Friend the Dean?
"I wonder what some people mean;
"My Lord and he are grown so great,   105
"Always together, *tête à tête;*
"What, they admire him for his jokes—
"See but the fortune of some Folks!"
There flies about a strange report
Of some Express arriv'd at Court;   110
I'm stopp'd by all the Fools I meet,
And catechis'd in ev'ry street.
"You, Mr. Dean, frequent the Great;
"Inform us, will the Emp'ror treat?
"Or do the Prints and Papers lie?"   115
'Faith, Sir, you know as much as I.'
"Ah Doctor, how you love to jest?
"'T is now no secret"—'I protest
''T is one to me'—"Then tell us, pray,
"When are the Troops to have their pay?"   120
And, tho' I solemnly declare
I know no more than my Lord Mayor,
They stand amaz'd, and think me grown
The closest mortal ever known.

Thus in a sea of folly toss'd,   125
My choicest Hours of life are lost;
Yet always wishing to retreat,
Oh, could I see my Country Seat!
There, leaning near a gentle Brook,
Sleep, or peruse some ancient Book,[1]   130
And there in sweet oblivion drown
Those Cares that haunt the Court and Town.
O charming Noons! and Nights divine!
Or when I sup, or when I dine.
My Friends above, my Folks below,   135
Chatting and laughing all-a-row,
The Beans and Bacon set before 'em,[2]
The Grace-cup serv'd with all decorum:
Each willing to be pleas'd, and please,
And ev'n the very Dogs at ease!   140
Here no man prates of idle things,
How this or that Italian sings,
A Neighbour's Madness, or his Spouse's,
Or what's in either of the Houses:
But something much more our concern,   145

---

[1] [Charles Fox, on a summer's day at St. Ann's, declared it the right time for lying in the shade with a book. 'Why with a book?' asked Sheridan.]

[2] ['(For one whole day) we have had nothing for dinner but mutton-broth, beans and bacon, and a barn-door fowl.' *Pope to Swift* (from Dawley), June 28, 1728.]

And quite a scandal not to learn :
Which is the happier, or the wiser,
A man of Merit, or a Miser?
Whether we ought to choose our Friends,
For their own Worth, or our own Ends?   150
What good. or better, we may call,
And what, the very best of all?
    Our Friend Dan Prior,[1] told, (you know)
A Tale extremely *à propos :*
Name a Town Life, and in a trice,   155
He had a Story of two Mice.
Once on a time (so runs the Fable)
A Country Mouse, right hospitable,
Receiv'd a Town Mouse at his Board,
Just as a Farmer might a Lord.   160
A frugal Mouse upon the whole,
Yet lov'd his Friend, and had a Soul,
Knew what was handsome, and would do't,
On just occasion, *coute qui coute.*
He brought him Bacon (nothing lean),   165
Pudding, that might have pleas'd a Dean ;
Cheese, such as men in Suffolk make,
But wish'd it Stilton for his sake ;
Yet, to his Guest tho' no way sparing,
He ate himself the rind and paring.   170
Our Courtier scarce could touch a bit,
But show'd his Breeding and his Wit ;
He did his best to seem to eat,
And cry'd, "I vow you 're mighty neat.
"But Lord, my Friend, this savage Scene!   175
"For God's sake, come, and live with Men :
"Consider, Mice, like Men, must die,
"Both small and great, both you and I :
"Then spend your life in Joy and Sport,
"(This Doctrine, Friend, I learnt at Court)."   180
    The veriest Hermit in the Nation
May yield, God knows, to strong temptation.
Away they come, thro' thick and thin,
To a tall house near Lincoln's-Inn ;
('T was on the night of a Debate,   185
When all their Lordships had sat late.)
    Behold the place, where if a Poet
Shin'd in Description, he might show it ;
Tell how the Moon-beam trembling falls,
And tips with Silver all the walls ;   190

[1] [The *City Mouse and Country Mouse* was written by Prior and Charles Montagu (afterwards Earl of Halifax) in 1688, in ridicule of Dryden's *Hind and Panther.* The reason why Pope was so sparing in his praise of Prior, is found by Warton in the satirical epigrams written by Prior on Atterbury. 'Dan' is the old familiar abbreviation for *dominus ;* Douglas speaks of 'Dan Chaucer;' and Prior himself, in his *Alma,* facetiously mentions 'Dan Pope.']

Palladian walls, Venetian doors,
Grotesco roofs, and Stucco floors :
But let it (in a word) be said,
The Moon was up, and Men a-bed,
The Napkins white, the Carpet red :   195
The Guests withdrawn had left the Treat,
And down the Mice sate, *tête-à-tête.*
  Our Courtier walks from dish to dish,
Tastes for his Friend of Fowl and Fish ;
Tells all their names, lays down the law,   200
" *Que ça est bon ! Ah goûtez ça !*
" That Jelly 's rich, this Malmsey healing,
" Pray, dip your Whiskers and your Tail in."
Was ever such a happy Swain ?
He stuffs and swills, and stuffs again.   205
" I 'm quite asham'd — 't is mighty rude
" To eat so much — but all 's so good.
" I have a thousand thanks to give —
" My Lord alone knows how to live."
No sooner said, but from the Hall   210
Rush Chaplain, Butler, Dogs and all :
" A Rat, a Rat ! clap to the door " —
The Cat comes bouncing on the floor.
 O for the heart of Homer's Mice,
Or Gods to save them in a trice !   215
(It was by Providence they think,
For your damn'd Stucco has no chink.)
" An 't please your Honour, quoth the Peasant,
" This same Dessert is not so pleasant :
" Give me again my hollow Tree,   220
" A crust of Bread, and Liberty ! "

BOOK IV. ODE I.

To VENUS.[1]

A GAIN ? new Tumults in my breast ?
   Ah spare me, Venus ! let me, let me rest ?
I am not now, alas ! the man
  As in the gentle Reign of My Queen Anne.
Ah sound no more thy soft alarms,   5
  Nor circle sober fifty with thy Charms.
Mother too fierce of dear Desires !
  Turn, turn to willing hearts your wanton fires.
To *Number five* [2] direct your Doves,
  There spread round MURRAY all your blooming Loves ;   10

---

[1] It may be worth observing, that the measure Pope has here chosen is precisely the same that Ben Jonson used in a translation of this very Ode. *Warton.*

[2] The number of Murray's lodgings in King's Bench Walks. *Bowles.* [See *Imitations of Horace*, Bk. I. *Ep.* VI. 49, *note.*]

Noble and young, who strikes the heart
  With ev'ry sprightly, ev'ry decent part;
Equal, the injur'd to defend,
  To charm the Mistress, or to fix the Friend.
He, with a hundred Arts refin'd,   15
  Shall stretch thy conquests over half the kind:
To him each Rival shall submit,
  Make but his Riches equal to his Wit.[1]
Then shall thy Form the Marble grace,
  (Thy Grecian Form) and Chloe lend the Face: 20
His House, embosom'd in the Grove,
  Sacred to social life and social love,[2]
Shall glitter o'er the pendant green,
  Where Thames reflects the visionary scene:
Thither, the silver-sounding lyres   25
  Shall call the smiling Loves, and young Desires;
There, ev'ry Grace and Muse shall throng,
  Exalt the dance, or animate the song;
There Youths and Nymphs, in concert gay,
  Shall hail the rising, close the parting day.   30
With me, alas! those joys are o'er;
  For me, the vernal garlands bloom no more.
Adieu, fond hope of mutual fire,
  The still-believing, still-renew'd desire;
Adieu, the heart-expanding bowl,   35
  And all the kind Deceivers of the soul!
But why? ah tell me, ah too dear![3]
  Steals down my cheek th' involuntary Tear?
Why words so flowing, thoughts so free,
  Stop, or turn nonsense, at one glance of thee?   40
Thee, drest in Fancy's airy beam,
  Absent I follow thro' th' extended Dream;
Now, now I seize, I clasp thy charms,
  And now you burst (ah cruel!) from my arms;
And swiftly shoot along the Mall,   45
  Or softly glide by the Canal,
Now, shown by Cynthia's silver ray,
  And now, on rolling waters snatch'd away.

PART OF THE NINTH ODE OF THE FOURTH BOOK.[4]

LEST you should think that verse should die,
  Which sounds the Silver Thames along,
Taught, on the wings of Truth to fly
  Above the reach of vulgar song;

---

[1] [Lord Mansfield is reported to have been in embarrassed circumstances during the early part of his career.]

[2] This alludes to Mr. Murray's intention at one time of taking the lease of Pope's house and grounds at Twickenham. *Bowles.*

[3] This was in the original:
  ' But why, my Patty, ah too dear ' —
relating to Martha Blount. *Bowles.*

[4] [Viz. stanzas 1, 2, 3, 7.]

Tho' daring Milton sits sublime,   5
  In Spenser native Muses play;
Nor yet shall Waller yield to time,
  Nor pensive Cowley's moral lay.

Sages and Chiefs long since had birth
  Ere Cæsar was, or Newton nam'd;   10
These rais'd new Empires o'er the Earth,
  And Those, new Heav'ns and Systems fram'd.

Vain was the Chief's, the Sage's pride!
  They had no Poet, and they died.
In vain they schem'd, in vain they bled!   15
  They had no Poet, and are dead.

EPISTLES.

EPISTLE

TO

ROBERT EARL OF OXFORD, AND EARL MORTIMER.[1]

SUCH were the notes thy once-lov'd Poet sung,
  'Till Death untimely stopp'd his tuneful tongue.
Oh just beheld, and lost![2] admir'd and mourn'd!
With softest manners, gentlest Arts adorn'd!
Blest in each science, blest in ev'ry strain!   5
Dear to the Muse! to HARLEY dear — in vain!
  For him, thou oft hast bid the World attend,
Fond to forget the statesman in the friend;
For SWIFT and him despis'd the farce of state,
The sober follies of the wise and great;   10

---

[1] *Epist. to Robert Earl of Oxford,*] This Epistle was sent to the Earl of Oxford with Dr. Parnell's Poems published by our Author, after the said Earl's Imprisonment in the Tower, and Retreat into the Country, in the Year 1721. P. [As to Parnell v. ante p. 455. Robert Harley, though descended from a Puritan family and in the early part of his career an extreme Whig, had, by a transition not unparalleled in political history, become the leader of the Country Party; and was chosen Speaker of the House of Commons in 1701. In 1704 he became Secretary of State in the Godolphin Ministry, and after being expelled from office succeeded in obtaining the Chancellorship of the Exchequer by employing ' female intrigue and raising the cry of the Church in danger.' (*Macknight.*) He subsequently was created Earl of Oxford and made Lord Treasurer; and it was at this time that he principally availed himself of the services of Swift and his friends. The rivalry between himself and Bolingbroke ended in his downfall immediately after the death of Queen Anne; in 1716, he was impeached for treasonable intrigues with the Jacobites during his tenure of power; and confined in the Tower. In 1717 the trial was abandoned; and he died in retirement in 1724.]

[2] [Verg. *Æn.* vi. 870.]

Dext'rous the craving, fawning crowd to quit,
And pleas'd to 'scape from Flattery to Wit.
Absent or dead, still let a friend be dear
(A sigh the absent claims, the dead a tear) ;
Recall those nights that clos'd thy toilsome days ;　　15
Still hear thy Parnell in his living lays,
Who, careless now of Int'rest, Fame, or Fate,
Perhaps forgets that OXFORD e'er was great ;
Or, deeming meanest what we greatest call,
Beholds thee glorious only in thy Fall.　　20
And sure, if aught below the seats divine
Can touch Immortals, 't is a Soul like thine :
A Soul supreme in each hard instance try'd,
Above all Pain, all Passion, and all Pride,
The rage of Pow'r, the blast of public breath,　　25
The lust of Lucre, and the dread of Death.
In vain to Deserts thy retreat is made ;
The Muse attends thee to thy silent shade :
'T is hers, the brave man's latest steps to trace,
Rejudge his acts, and dignify disgrace.　　30
When Int'rest calls off all her sneaking train,
And all th' oblig'd desert, and all the vain ;
She waits, or to the scaffold, or the cell,
When the last ling'ring friend has bid farewell.
Ev'n now, she shades thy Ev'ning-walk with bays　　35
(No hireling she, no prostitute to praise) ;
Ev'n now, observant of the parting Ray,
Eyes the calm Sun-set of thy various Day,
Thro' Fortune's cloud one truly great can see,
Nor fears to tell, that MORTIMER is he.　　40

EPISTLE TO JAMES CRAGGS,[1] ESQ.

SECRETARY OF STATE.[2]

A SOUL as full of Worth, as void of Pride,
　Which nothing seeks to shew, or needs to hide,
Which nor to Guilt nor Fear, its Caution owes,
And boasts a Warmth that from no Passion flows.
A Face untaught to feign ; a judging Eye,　}　　5
That darts severe upon a rising Lie,　　　　}
And strikes a blush thro' frontless Flattery.　}

[1] James Craggs was made Secretary at War in 1717, when the Earl of Sunderland and Mr. Addison were appointed Secretaries of State. *Bowles.* [He succeeded Addison in the latter office in 1720, and to him Addison dedicated his works in the last letter which he ever composed. Craggs was afterwards involved in the South Sea speculations (concerning which he advised Pope) ; but his death in 1721 saved him from the exposure with which he was threatened. He was a frequent correspondent of Pope's during the years from 1711 to 1719 ; and is celebrated by Gay as 'bold generous Craggs whose heart was ne'er disguised.' Compare *Epitaph* IV. *infra.*]

[2] *Secretary of State.*] In the year 1720. P.

All this thou wert, and being this before,
Know, Kings and Fortune cannot make thee more.
Then scorn to gain a Friend by servile ways,   10
Nor wish to lose a Foe these Virtues raise;
But candid, free, sincere, as you began,
Proceed, — a Minister, but still a Man.
Be not, exalted to whate'er degree,
Asham'd of any Friend, not ev'n of Me: 15
The Patriot's plain, but untrod, path pursue;
If not, 't is I must be asham'd of You.

EPISTLE TO MR. JERVAS,[1] WITH MR. DRYDEN'S TRANSLATION OF FRESNOY'S ART OF PAINTING.

THIS Verse be thine, my friend, nor thou refuse
   This, from no venal or ungrateful Muse.
Whether thy hand strike out some free design,
Where Life awakes, and dawns at ev'ry line;
Or blend in beauteous tints the colour'd mass,   5
And from the canvas call the mimic face:
Read these instructive leaves, in which conspire
Fresnoy's close Art, and Dryden's native Fire:[2]
And reading wish, like theirs, our fate and fame,
So mix'd our studies, and so join'd our name;   10
Like them to shine thro' long succeeding age,
So just thy skill, so regular my rage.
  Smit with the love of Sister-Arts we came,
And met congenial, mingling flame with flame;
Like friendly colours found them both unite,   15
And each from each contract new strength and light.
How oft in pleasing tasks we wear the day,
While summer-suns roll unperceiv'd away;
How oft our slowly-growing works impart,
While Images reflect from art to art;   20
How oft review; each finding like a friend
Something to blame, and something to commend!
  What flatt'ring scenes our wand'ring fancy wrought,
Rome's pompous glories rising to our thought!
Together o'er the Alps methinks we fly,   25
Fir'd with Ideas of fair Italy.

---

[1] *Epist. to Mr. Jervas.*] This Epistle, and the two following, were written some years before the rest, and originally printed in 1717. P. [Charles Jervas was an early and intimate friend of Pope's, and instructed him in painting about the year 1713. Three years later we find Pope occupying the painter's house during the absence of the latter from London. As a painter, Jervas is spoken slightingly of by Horace Walpole. He is also, says Roscoe, well known by his excellent translation of Don Quixote.]

[2] [Du Fresnoy's *Art of Painting*, hastily turned into English by Dryden as a piece of hack work, was afterwards more elaborately translated by Mason, who was himself a proficient in the art.]

With thee, on Raphael's Monument I mourn,
Or wait inspiring Dreams at Maro's Urn:
With thee repose, where Tully once was laid,
Or seek some Ruin's formidable shade: 30
While fancy brings the vanished piles to view,
And builds imaginary Rome anew;
Here thy well-study'd marbles fix our eye;
A fading Fresco here demands a sigh:
Each heav'nly piece unwearied we compare,   35
Match Raphael's grace with thy lov'd Guido's[1] air,
Caracci's strength,[2] Correggio's softer line,
Paulo's[3] free stroke, and Titian's warmth divine.
  How finish'd with illustrious toil appears
This small, well-polish'd Gem, the work of years![4]   40
Yet still how faint by precept is exprest
The living image in the painter's breast!
Thence endless streams of fair Ideas flow,
Strike in the sketch, or in the picture glow;
Thence Beauty, waking all her forms, supplies   45
An Angel's sweetness, or Bridgewater's eyes.[5]
  Muse! at that Name thy sacred sorrows shed,
Those tears eternal, that embalm the dead:
Call round her Tomb each object of desire,
Each purer frame inform'd with purer fire: 50
Bid her be all that cheers or softens life,
The tender sister, daughter, friend, and wife:
Bid her be all that makes mankind adore;
Then view this Marble, and be vain no more!
  Yet still her charms in breathing paint engage;   55
Her modest cheek shall warm a future age.
Beauty, frail flow'r that ev'ry season fears,
Blooms in thy colours for a thousand years.
Thus Churchill's race shall other hearts surprise,[6]
And other Beauties envy Worsley's eyes;[7]   60

---

[1] [Guido Reni.]

[2] By Caracci's strength, Pope probably meant to refer to Annibale Caracci only; the most distinguished of the three brothers (A., Agostino and Ludovico) for his knowledge of the human figure. *Roscoe.*

[3] [Paola Veronese.]

[4] Fresnoy employed about twenty Years in finishing his Poem. P.

[5] [See next note.]

[6] Churchill's race were the four beautiful daughters of John the great Duke of Marlborough: Henrietta, Countess of Godolphin, afterwards duchess of Marlborough; Anne Countess of Sunderland; Elizabeth Countess of Bridgewater; and Mary, Duchess of Montagu. Their portraits are at Blenheim. Lady Bridgewater, whom Jervas affected to be in love with, and who accused herself at his expense, was the most beautiful of the four sisters. She died March 1714, aged 27. *Bowles.* [Pope in a letter to Gay, August 23rd, 1713, quoted in Carruthers' *Life*, speaking of his own attempts, says that he has thrown away among other portraits, 'two Lady Bridgewaters and a Duchess of Montagu.' In a fragment of Pope's published in Roscoe's *Supplement* (1825) the fair Bridgewater and Jervas are compared to Campaspe and Apelles.]

[7] Frances Lady Worsley, wife of Sir Robert Worsley, Bart., mother of Lady Carteret, wife of John Lord Carteret, afterwards Earl Granville. *Warton.* This name originally stood Wortley; but the compliment was transferred from her after her quarrel with Pope by the alteration of a single letter. *Carruthers.*

Each pleasant Blount shall endless smiles bestow,[1]
And soft Belinda's blush for ever glow.[2]
  Oh lasting as those Colours may they shine,
Free as thy stroke, yet faultless as thy line;
New graces yearly like thy works display,   65
Soft without weakness, without glaring gay;
Led by some rule, that guides, but not constrains;
And finish'd more thro' happiness than pains.
The kindred Arts shall in their praise conspire;
One dip the pencil, and one string the lyre.   70
Yet should the Graces all thy figures place,
And breathe an air divine on ev'ry face;
Yet should the Muses bid my numbers roll
Strong as their charms, and gentle as their soul;
With Zeuxis' Helen thy Bridgewater vie,   75
And these be sung 'till Granville's Mira die;[3]
Alas! how little from the grave we claim!
Thou but preserv'st a Face, and I a Name.

EPISTLE TO MISS BLOUNT,[4] WITH THE WORKS OF VOITURE.[5]

IN these gay thoughts the Loves and Graces shine,
  And all the Writer lives in ev'ry line;
His easy Art may happy Nature seem,
Trifles themselves are elegant in him.
Sure to charm all was his peculiar fate,   5
Who without flatt'ry pleas'd the fair and great;
Still with esteem no less convers'd than read;
With wit well-natur'd, and with books well-bred:
His heart, his mistress, and his friend did share,
His time, the Muse, the witty, and the fair.   10
Thus wisely careless, innocently gay,
Cheerful he play'd the trifle, Life, away;
Till fate scarce felt his gentle breath supprest,
As smiling Infants sport themselves to rest.
Ev'n rival Wits did Voiture's death deplore,   15
And the gay mourn'd who never mourn'd before;
The truest hearts for Voiture heav'd with sighs,
Voiture was wept by all the brightest Eyes:

---

[1] [Martha Blount.]

[2] [Miss Arabella Fermor, the heroine of the *Rape of the Lock*.]

[3] [See *Windsor Forest*, v. 298.]

[4] [Miss Teresa Blount. See *Introductory Memoir*, p. xxx. This Epistle was first published in *Lintot's Miscellany* in 1712; so that Pope's note (*ante*, p. 462) is not accurate.]

[5] [Vincent Voiture (1598–1648), one of the chief ornaments of the Hotel Rambouillet (the centre of the society of the so-called *précieux* and *précieuses* at Paris under the regency of Mary de' Medici). 'His great merit,' says a modern French critic (M. Masson), 'consists in the inexhaustible variety of forms which he applies to a monotonous sterility of ideas.']

The Smiles and Loves had died in Voiture's death,
But that for ever in his lines they breathe.   20
  Let the strict life of graver mortals be
A long, exact, and serious Comedy;
In ev'ry scene some Moral let it teach,
And, if it can, at once both please and preach.
Let mine, an innocent gay farce appear,[1]   25
And more diverting still than regular,
Have Humour, Wit, a native Ease and Grace,
Tho' not too strictly bound to Time and Place:
Critics in Wit, or Life, are hard to please,
Few write to those, and none can live to these.   30
  Too much your Sex is by their forms confin'd,
Severe to all, but most to Womankind;
Custom, grown blind with Age, must be your guide;
Your pleasure is a vice, but not your pride;
By Nature yielding, stubborn but for fame;   35
Made Slaves by honour, and made Fools by shame,
Marriage may all those petty Tyrants chase,
But sets up one, a greater, in their place;
Well might you wish for change by those accurst,
But the last Tyrant ever proves the worst.   40
Still in constraint your suff'ring Sex remains,
Or bound in formal, or in real chains:
Whole years neglected, for some months ador'd,
The fawning Servant turns a haughty Lord.
Ah quit not the free innocence of life,   45
For the dull glory of a virtuous Wife;
Nor let false Shows, or empty Titles please:
Aim not at Joy, but rest content with Ease.
  The Gods, to curse Pamela with her pray'rs,
Gave the gilt Coach and dappled Flanders Mares,   50
The shining robes, rich jewels, beds of state,
And, to complete her bliss, a Fool for Mate.
She glares in Balls, front Boxes, and the Ring,
A vain, unquiet, glitt'ring, wretched Thing!
Pride, Pomp, and State but reach her outward part;   55
She sighs, and is no Duchess at her heart.
  But, Madam, if the fates withstand, and you
Are destin'd Hymen's willing Victim too;
Trust not too much your now resistless charms,
These, Age or Sickness, soon or late disarms: 60
Good humour only teaches charms to last,
Still makes new conquests, and maintains the past;
Love, rais'd on Beauty, will like that decay,
Our hearts may bear its slender chain a day;

---

[1] [*Antonio.* I hold the world but as the world, Gratiano;
A stage where every man must play a part,
And mine a sad one.
    Gratiano. Let me play the fool, &c.
    Merchant of Venice, Act I. Sc. I.]

2 H

As flow'ry bands in wantonness are worn, 65
A morning's pleasure, and at evening torn;
This binds in ties more easy, yet more strong,
The willing heart, and only holds it long.
Thus Voiture's [1] early care still shone the same,
And Montausier [2] was only chang'd in name: 70
By this, ev'n now they live, ev'n now they charm,
Their Wit still sparkling, and their flames still warm.
Now crown'd with Myrtle, on th' Elysian coast,
Amid those Lovers, joys his gentle Ghost:
Pleas'd, while with smiles his happy lines you view, 75
And finds a fairer Rambouillet in you.
The brightest eyes of France inspir'd his Muse;
The brightest eyes of Britain now peruse;
And dead, as living, 't is our Author's pride
Still to charm those who charm the world beside. 80

EPISTLE [3] TO THE SAME, ON HER LEAVING THE TOWN AFTER THE CORONATION. [4]

A S some fond Virgin, whom her mother's care
Drags from the Town to wholesome Country air,
Just when she learns to roll a melting eye,
And hear a spark, yet think no danger nigh;
From the dear man unwilling she must sever, 5
Yet takes one kiss before she parts for ever:
Thus from the world fair Zephalinda [5] flew,
Saw others happy, and with sighs withdrew;
Not that their Pleasures caus'd her discontent,
She sigh'd not that they stay'd, but that she went. 10
She went, to plain-work, and to purling brooks,
Old fashion'd halls, dull Aunts, and croaking rooks:
She went from Op'ra, Park, Assembly, Play,
To morning-walks, and pray'rs three hours a day;
To part her time 'twixt reading and bohea; 15
To muse, and spill her solitary tea;
Or o'er cold coffee trifle with the spoon,
Count the slow clock, and dine exact at noon;
Divert her eyes with pictures in the fire,

---

[1] Mademoiselle Paulet. P.

[2] [The Duke of Montausier, governor to the Dauphin son of Louis xiv., married Mdlle. de Rambouillet. He was believed to have been the original of Molière's *Misanthrope.*]

[3] [This Epistle is cited by M. Taine (*Lit. Angl.* iv. c. 7) to exemplify the realistic element which, according to his theory, was no more absent from Pope than from any of the contemporary English poets.]

[4] *Coronation.*] Of King George the first, 1715. P. [Really, Oct. 20, 1714. *Am. Ed.*]

[5] The assumed name of Teresa Blount, under which she corresponded for many years with a Mr. Moore, under the feigned name of Alexis. *Bowles.* [James Moore Smythe.] Originally, according to Warburton (cited from Ruffhead by Carruthers):

' So fair Teresa gave the town a view.'

Hum half a tune, tell stories to the squire;   20
Up to her godly garret after sev'n,
There starve and pray, for that 's the way to heav'n.[1]
  Some Squire, perhaps you take delight to rack;
Whose game is Whisk,[2] whose treat a toast in sack;
Who visits with a Gun, presents you birds,   25
Then gives a smacking buss, and cries, — ' No words ! '
Or with his hound comes hollowing from the stable,
Makes love with nods, and knees beneath a table;
Whose laughs are hearty, tho' his jests are coarse,
And loves you best of all things — but his horse.   30
  In some fair ev'ning, on your elbow laid,
You dream of Triumphs in the rural shade;
In pensive thought recall the fancy'd scene,
See Coronations rise on ev'ry green;
Before you pass th' imaginary sights   35
Of Lords, and Earls, and Dukes, and garter'd Knights,
While the spread fan o'ershades your closing eyes;
Then give one flirt, and all the vision flies.
Thus vanish sceptres, coronets, and balls,
And leave you in lone woods, or empty walls!   40
  So when your Slave, at some dear idle time,
(Not plagu'd with head-aches, or the want of rhyme,)
Stands in the streets, abstracted from the crew,
And while he seems to study, thinks of you;
Just when his fancy points your sprightly eyes,   45
Or sees the blush of soft Parthenia[3] rise,
Gay pats my shoulder, and you vanish quite,
Streets, Chairs, and Coxcombs, rush upon my sight;
Vex'd to be still in town, I knit my brow,
Look sour, and hum a Tune, as you may now.   50

ON RECEIVING FROM THE

RIGHT HON. THE LADY FRANCES SHIRLEY

A STANDISH AND TWO PENS.[4]

YES, I beheld th' Athenian Queen[5]
   Descend in all her sober charms;
" And take," (she said, and smil'd serene,)
  " Take at this hand celestial arms:

---

[1] [Sheridan may have remembered this passage, when writing the famous scene between Sir Peter and Lady Teazle, *School for Scandal*, Act II. Sc. I.]

[2] [According to Dr. Johnson, the word *whist* was vulgarly pronounced *whisk*.]

[3] In the first edition it is ' the blush of Parthenissa,' which was the principal designation of Martha Blount in the correspondence of the sisters with James Moore. *Carruthers*.

[4] To enter into the spirit of this address, it is necessary to premise, that the Poet was threat-

[5] [Pallas Athene.]

"Secure the radiant weapons wield;   5
  "This golden lance shall guard Desert,
"And if a Vice dares keep the field,
  "This steel shall stab it to the heart."

Aw'd, on my bended knees I fell,
  Receiv'd the weapons of the sky;   10
And dipt them in the sable Well,
  The fount of Fame or Infamy.

'What *well?* what *weapons?*' (Flavia cries,)
  'A standish, steel and golden pen!
'It came from Bertrand's,[1] not the skies;   15
  'I gave it you to write again.

'But, Friend, take heed whom you attack;
  'You 'll bring a House (I mean of Peers)
'Red, Blue, and Green, nay white and black,
  'L...... and all about your ears.[2]   20

'You 'd write as smooth again on glass,
  'And run, on ivory, so glib,
'As not to stick at fool or ass,
  'Nor stop at Flattery or Fib.[3]

'*Athenian Queen!* and *sober charms!*   25
  'I tell ye, fool, there 's nothing in 't:
'"T is Venus, Venus gives these arms;
  'In Dryden's Virgil see the print.[4]

'Come, if you 'll be a quiet soul,
  'That dares tell neither Truth nor Lies,[5]   30
'I 'll lift you in the harmless roll
  'Of those that sing of these poor eyes.'

ened with a prosecution in the House of Lords, for the two poems entitled the *Epilogue to the Satires.* On which with great resentment against his enemies, for not being willing to distinguish between

  'Grave epistles bringing vice to light'

and licentious libels, he began a *Third Dialogue,* more severe and sublime than the first and second; which being no secret, matters were soon compromised. His enemies agreed to drop the prosecution, and he promised to leave the third Dialogue unfinished and suppressed. This affair occasioned this little beautiful poem, to which it alludes throughout, but more especially in the four last stanzas. *Warburton.* Lady Frances Shirley was fourth daughter of Earl Ferrers, who had at that time a house at Twickenham. Notwith-

standing her numerous admirers, she died at Bath, *unmarried,* in the year 1762. *Bowles.* [Bowles thinks the *Third Dialogue* alluded to by Warburton to be the fragment '1740' discovered after Pope's death among his papers by Bolingbroke; but there is no evidence to support this plausible conjecture.]

  [1] A famous toy-shop at Bath. *Warburton.*
  [2] Lambeth; alluding to the Scandal hinted at in *Epil. to Satires,* Dial. I. v. 120. *Carruthers.*
  [3] The *Dunciad. Warburton.*
  [4] *The Epistle to Arbuthnot. Warburton.*
  [5] i.e. If you have neither the courage to write *Satire,* nor the application to attempt an *Epic* poem. He was then meditating on such a work. *Warburton.*

EPITAPHS.

'His saltem accumulem donis, et fungar inani
Munere!'   VIRG. [*Æn.* VII. vv. 885, 6.]

[No observations would be called for upon these *Epitaphs*, composed at different periods of Pope's life, were it not that they were subjected to a minute, and indeed a petty, criticism by Dr. Johnson, in his *Dissertation on the Epitaphs written by Pope* (contributed to a paper called the *Universal Visitor* in 1756, and afterwards thought worthy of republication in the *Idler*). Johnson's criticisms, though occasionally just, are in this instance too thoroughly in the Ricardus Aristarchus style to need quotation. Perhaps the most pointed is that on the *Epitaph on Rowe*, concerning which Johnson remarks that 'its chief fault is that it belongs less to Rowe than to Dryden, and indeed gives very little information concerning either.' The *Epitaph on Newton*, (which he afterwards declared to Mrs. Piozzi to be little less than profane, as designed for the tomb of a Christian in a Christian Church,) the *Dissertation* condemned because 'the thought is obvious, and the words *night* and *light* too nearly allied!' Johnson afterwards remembered (Hayward's *Autobiography, &c. of Mrs. Piozzi*, II. p. 159) 'that something like this was said of Aristotle,' but 'he forgot by whom.' Pope's *Epitaphs* — with the exception of the charming lines on Gay — only rise above the ordinary level of this class of composition, because that level is so extremely low.]

I.

ON CHARLES EARL OF DORSET,

In the Church of Withyam in Sussex.[1]

(1706.)

DORSET, the Grace of the Courts, the Muses' Pride,
  Patron of Arts, and Judge of Nature, died.
The scourge of Pride, tho' sanctify'd or great,
Of Fops in Learning, and of Knaves in State:
Yet soft his Nature, tho' severe his Lay;   5
His Anger moral, and his Wisdom gay.
Blest Satirist! who touch'd the Mean so true,
As show'd, Vice had his hate and pity too.
Blest Courtier! who could King and Country please,
Yet sacred keep his Friendships, and his Ease.   10
Blest Peer! his great Forefathers' ev'ry grace
Reflecting, and reflected in his Race;
Where other BUCKHURSTS,[2] other DORSETS shine,
And Patriots still, or Poets, deck the Line.

---

[1] [As to Dorset, cf. *Imitations of English Poets in Juvenile Poems*, p. 186.

[2] [Thomas Sackville, first Lord Buckhurst and first Earl of Dorset, author of the *Mirror for Magistrates*, and *Gorboduc*, the first English tragedy, died in 1608. Edward, Earl of Dorset, was a prominent Royalist in the first part of the Civil war, and was, according to Clarendon, distinguished for his wit and learning. His grandson is the subject of Pope's epitaph.]

II.

ON SIR WILLIAM TRUMBAL,

One of the Principal Secretaries of State to King WILLIAM III. who having resigned
his Place, died in his Retirement at Easthamstead in Berkshire, 1716.[1]

A PLEASING Form; a firm, yet cautious Mind;
  Sincere, tho' prudent; constant, yet resign'd:
Honour unchang'd, a Principle profest,
Fix'd to one side, but mod'rate to the rest:
An honest Courtier, yet a Patriot too;   5
Just to his Prince, and to his Country true:
Fill'd with the Sense of Age, the Fire of Youth,
A Scorn of wrangling, yet a Zeal for Truth;
A gen'rous Faith, from superstition free;
A love to Peace, and hate of Tyranny;   10
Such this Man was; who now, from earth remov'd,
At length enjoys that Liberty he lov'd.

III.

ON THE HON. SIMON HARCOURT,

Only Son of the Lord Chancellor HARCOURT; at the Church of Stanton-Harcourt in
Oxfordshire, 1720.

TO this sad shrine, whoe'er thou art! draw near;
  Here lies the Friend most lov'd, the Son most dear;
Who ne'er knew Joy, but Friendship might divide,
Or gave his Father Grief but when he died.[2]
  How vain is Reason, Eloquence how weak!   5
If *Pope* must tell what HARCOURT cannot speak.
Oh let thy once-lov'd Friend inscribe thy Stone,
And, with a Father's sorrows, mix his own!

---

[1] [As to Sir William Trumball, see note to p. 10.] The first six lines of this epitaph were originally written for John Lord Caryll, afterwards Secretary of State to the exiled king James II.; the remainder of the same epitaph on Caryll being inserted in the *Epistle to Jervas. Athenæum,* July 15th, 1854.

[2] These were the very words used by Louis XIV., when his Queen died, 1683; though it is not to be imagined they were copied by Pope. *Warton.*

IV.

ON JAMES CRAGGS, ESQ.

In Westminster Abbey.[1]

JACOBUS CRAGGS
REGI MAGNÆ BRITANNIÆ A SECRETIS
ET CONSILIIS SANCTIORIBUS,
PRINCIPIS PARITER AC POPULI AMOR ET DELICIÆ:
VIXIT TITULIS ET INVIDIA MAJOR
ANNOS, HEU PAUCOS, XXXV.
OB. FEB. XVI. MDCCXX.

Statesman, yet Friend to Truth! of Soul sincere,
In Action faithful, and in Honour clear!
Who broke no Promise, serv'd no private End;
Who gain'd no Title, and who lost no Friend;
Ennobled by Himself, by All approv'd;
Prais'd, wept, and honour'd, by the Muse he lov'd.[2]

V.

INTENDED FOR MR. ROWE,

In Westminster Abbey.[3]

THY relics, ROWE, to this fair Urn we trust,
And sacred, place by DRYDEN'S awful dust:
Beneath a rude[4] and nameless stone he lies,
To which thy Tomb shall guide enquiring eyes.[5]

[1] [As to Craggs, v. *ante*, p. 453. Horace Walpole sent to Sir Horace Mann a very ill-natured epitaph on the same Craggs, whose father had been a footman; 'Here lies the last, who died before the first of his family.' (*Jesse.*) As Craggs's death alone arrested the enquiry into the charge of peculation brought against him in connexion with the South Sea frauds (his father committing suicide shortly afterwards) the praise in the third line of Pope's *Epitaph* is singularly bold.]

[2] These verses were originally the conclusion of the *Epistle to Mr. Addison on his Dialogue on Medals*, and were adopted as an Epitaph by an alteration in the last line, which in the *Epistle* stood —

'And prais'd unenvied by the Muse he lov'd.'
Roscoe [cf. p. 271].

[3] [As to Rowe, see note to *Epil. to Jane Shore*, p. 97.]

[4] *Beneath a rude*] The Tomb of Mr. Dryden was erected upon this hint by the Duke of Buckingham; to which was originally intended this Epitaph,

This SHEFFIELD *rais'd. The sacred Dust below*
Was DRYDEN *once: The rest who does not know?*

which the Author since changed into the plain inscription now upon it, being only the name of that great Poet.

J. DRYDEN.

Natus Aug. 9, 1631. Mortuus Maij. 1, 1700.
JOANNES SHEFFIELD DUX BUCKINGHAMIENSIS
POSUIT.   P.

[5] [The above epitaph was subsequently altered by Pope, the following lines being added:

'Peace to thy gentle shade, and endless rest!
Blest in thy Genius, in thy Love too blest!
One grateful Woman to thy fame supplies
What a whole thankless land to his denies.'

But further alterations and additions were made in the inscription, until it read as it now stands on the monument in Westminster Abbey to Rowe and his daughter.]

VI.

ON MRS. CORBET,

Who died of a Cancer in her Breast.[1]

HERE rests a Woman, good without pretence,
  Blest with plain Reason and with sober Sense:
No Conquests she, but o'er herself, desir'd,
No Arts essay'd, but not to be admir'd.
Passion and Pride were to her soul unknown,   5
Convinc'd that Virtue only is our own.
So unaffected, so compos'd a mind;
So firm, yet soft; so strong, yet so refin'd;
Heav'n, as its purest gold, by Tortures try'd;
The Saint sustain'd it, but the Woman died.   10

VII.

ON THE MONUMENT OF THE HONOURABLE ROBERT DIGBY, AND OF HIS SISTER MARY,

Erected by their Father, the Lord DIGBY, in the Church of Sherborne in Dorsetshire, 1727.[2]

GO! fair Example of untainted youth,
  Of modest wisdom, and pacific truth:
Compos'd in suff'rings, and in joy sedate,
Good without noise, without pretension great.
Just of thy Word, in ev'ry thought sincere,   5
Who knew no wish but what the world might hear:
Of softest manners, unaffected mind,
Lover of peace, and friend of human kind:
Go live! for Heav'n's Eternal year is thine,
Go, and exalt thy Moral to Divine.   10
  And thou, blest Maid! attendant on his doom,
Pensive hast follow'd to the silent tomb,
Steer'd the same course to the same quiet shore,
Not parted long, and now to part no more!
Go then, where only bliss sincere is known!   15
Go, where to love and to enjoy are one!
  Yet take these Tears, Mortality's relief,
And till we share your joys, forgive our grief:
These little rites, a Stone, a Verse, receive;
'T is all a Father, all a Friend can give!   20

---

[1] This epitaph is on a monument in St. Margaret's Church, Westminster, where the date of Mrs. Elizabeth Corbet's death is recorded as March 1st, 1724. Mr. Hunter conceives that she was the Mrs. Corbet who was a sister of Pope's mother. *Carruthers.* [Hunter enumerates Mrs. Corbet among the Roman Catholic members of the Turner family; and as the notice preceding the epitaph on the monument speaks of her as the daughter of Sir Uvedale Corbett, Bart., it is irreconcileable with Hunter's statement.]

[2] [Robert Digby was a frequent correspondent of Pope's during the years 1717 to 1724. He died in 1726; and Pope laments his death in a letter to his brother Edward Digby.]

VIII.

ON SIR GODFREY KNELLER,

In Westminster Abbey, 1723.[1]

KNELLER, by Heav'n, and not a Master, taught,
Whose Art was Nature, and whose Pictures Thought;
Now for two ages having snatch'd from fate
Whate'er was beauteous, or whate'er was great,
Lies crown'd with Princes' honours, Poets' lays,   5
Due to his Merit, and brave Thirst of praise.
Living, great Nature fear'd he might outvie[2]
Her works; and dying, fears herself may die.

IX.

ON GENERAL HENRY WITHERS,

In Westminster Abbey, 1729.[3]

HERE, WITHERS, rest! thou bravest, gentlest mind,
Thy Country's friend, but more of human kind.
Oh born to Arms! O Worth in Youth approv'd!
O soft Humanity, in Age belov'd!
For thee the hardy Vet'ran drops a tear, ·   5
And the gay Courtier feels the sigh sincere.
WITHERS, adieu! yet not with thee remove
Thy Martial spirit, or thy Social love!
Amidst Corruption, Luxury, and Rage,
Still leave some ancient Virtues to our age: 10
Nor let us say (those English glories gone)
The last true Briton lies beneath this stone.

---

[1] Pope had made Sir Godfrey Kneller, on his death-bed, a promise to write his epitaph, which he seems to have performed with reluctance. He thought it 'the worse thing he ever wrote in his life.' (*Spence.*) *Roscoe.* Sir Godfrey Kneller was born at Lübeck in 1648, and after being introduced by the Duke of Monmouth to King Charles II., filled the office of State-painter under that monarch and his successors up to George I., in whose reign (in 1726) he died.]

[2] Imitated from the famous Epitaph on Raphael.

*Raphael, timuit, quo sospite, vinci
Rerum magna parens, et moriente, mori.* P.
Much better translated by Mr. W. Harrison, of New College, Oxford, a favourite of Swift:

'Here Raphael lies, by whose untimely end
Nature both lost a rival and a friend.'
Warton.

[3] [The following is the prose inscription on General Withers's monument in Westminster Abbey, which is also believed to be by Pope:

'Henry Withers, Lieutenant-General, descended from a military stock, and bred in arms in Britain, Dunkirk, and Tangier. Through the whole course of the two last wars of England with France, he served in Ireland, in the Low Countries, and in Germany: was present in every battle and at every siege, and distinguished in all by an activity, a valour and a zeal which nature gave and honour improved. A love of glory and of his country animated and raised him above that spirit which the trade of war inspires—a desire of acquiring riches and honours by the miseries of mankind. His temper was humane, his benevolence universal, and among all those ancient virtues which he preserved in practice and in credit none was more remarkable than his hospitality. He died at the age of 78, on the 11th of November, 1729, to whom this monument is erected by his companion in the wars and his friend through life, HENRY DISNEY.'

Both Withers and Disney (who rests beside his comrade) are mentioned among Pope's friends by Gay, who alludes to the hospitality panegyrized in the above epitaph.]

X.

ON MR. ELIJAH FENTON,

At Easthamstead in Berks, 1730.[1]

THIS modest Stone, what few vain Marbles can,[2]
  May truly say, Here lies an honest Man:
A Poet, blest beyond the Poet's fate,
Whom Heav'n kept sacred from the Proud and Great:
Foe to loud Praise, and Friend to learned Ease,   5
Content with Science in the Vale of Peace.
Calmly he look'd on either Life, and here
Saw nothing to regret, or there to fear;
From Nature's temp'rate feast rose satisfy'd,[3]
Thank'd Heav'n that he had liv'd, and that he died.   10

XI.

ON MR. GAY,

In Westminster Abbey, 1732.

OF Manners gentle, of Affections mild;
  In Wit, a Man; Simplicity, a Child:
With native Humour temp'ring virtuous Rage,
Form'd to delight at once and lash the age:
Above Temptation, in a low Estate,   5
And uncorrupted, ev'n among the Great:
A safe Companion, and an easy Friend,
Unblam'd thro' Life, lamented in thy End.
These are Thy Honours! not that here thy Bust
Is mix'd with Heroes, or with Kings thy dust;   10
But that the Worthy and the Good shall say,
Striking their pensive bosoms — *Here* lies GAY.[4]

[1] [Elijah Fenton was born in 1683. Fenton, together with Broome, wrote part of the translation of the *Odyssey* in a style so similar to Pope's that most readers would fail to distinguish between the work of the latter and that of his coadjutors. A survey of Fenton's works shows a striking reproduction on his part of most of the species of poetry cultivated by Pope. Fenton has a pastoral (*Florelio*) to correspond to Pope's fourth and favourite Pastoral; a paraphrase of the 14th chapter of Isaiah to correspond to Pope's *Messiah;* an epistle from *Sappho to Phæon,* Epistles, Prologues, and Translations and Imitations of Horace. Fenton was a thorough master of versification, and excelled Pope in his command of a variety of metres. His *Ode to Lord Gower* (which Pope placed next in merit to Dryden's *St. Cecilia*) avoids the faults committed by Pope in his own 'Pindaric' essay; and his blank verse translation of the 11th book of the *Odyssey* is dignified without heaviness. Fenton's tragedy of *Mariamne* seems to have owed its success in part to the judicious suggestions of the author of *Oroonoko.*]

[2] The modest front of this small floor
  Believe me, reader, can say more
  Than many a braver marble can:
  Here lies a truly honest man.
Crashaw, *Epitaph upon Mr. Ashton. Johnson.*

[3] Cf. Hor. *Sat.* Lib. I. I. 117–119. *Wakefield.*

[4] [There is a very striking coincidence between these four lines and the following in the *Epitaph* recently published by Prof. H. Morley, and believed by him to be Milton's:

'In this little bed my dust
  Incurtained round I here entrust,
  While my more pure and noble part
  Lies entomb'd in every heart.'

This parallel passage at once explains the meaning of Pope's last line, which he complained to Warburton 'was not generally understood.']

XII.

INTENDED FOR SIR ISAAC NEWTON,

In Westminster Abbey.[1]

ISAACUS NEWTONUS:

Quem Immortalem
Testartur *Tempus, Natura, Cœlum:*
Mortalem
Hoc marmor fatetur.

Nature and Nature's Laws lay hid in Night:
GOD said, *Let Newton be!* and all was Light.[2]

XIII.

ON DR. FRANCIS ATTERBURY,

Bishop of Rochester,

Who died in Exile at Paris, 1732 (his only Daughter having expired in his arms, immediately after she arrived in France to see him).[3]

DIALOGUE.[4]

SHE.

YES, we have liv'd — one pang, and then we part!
May Heav'n, dear Father! now have all thy Heart.
Yet ah! how once we lov'd, remember still,
Till you are dust like me.

HE.

Dear Shade! I will:
Then mix this dust with thine — O spotless Ghost!   5
O more than Fortune, Friends, or Country lost!
Is there on Earth one care, one. wish beside?
Yes — SAVE MY COUNTRY, HEAV'N,

He said, and died.[5]

---

[1] [Died, 1727.]

[2] *and all was Light.*] It had been better — *and there was Light,* — as more conformable to the reality of the *fact,* and to the *allusion* whereby it is celebrated. *Warburton.*

[3] [As to Atterbury, see *Epis. to Satires,* Dial. II. v. 82.] Macaulay, in his essay on *Francis Atterbury,* in relating that after his death his body was brought to England and privately buried under the nave of Westminster Abbey, observes: 'That the epitaph with which Pope honoured the memory of his friend does not appear on the walls of the great national cemetery, is no subject of regret; for nothing worse was ever written by Colley Cibber.']

[4] [Bowles has pointed out that many of our old epitaphs are written *in dialogue.*]

[5] [Cf. *Moral Essays,* Ep. I. v. 265. Atterbury's letter to the Pretender, 'almost the last expressions of this most eloquent man' (*Lord Stanhope*), may be compared with Pope's poetic version, which was sarcastically annotated by Warburton, a safer kind of prelate.]

XIV.

ON EDMUND D. OF BUCKINGHAM,

Who died in the Nineteenth Year of his Age, 1735.[1]

IF modest Youth, with cool Reflection crown'd,
  And ev'ry op'ning Virtue blooming round,
Could save a Parent's justest Pride from fate,
Or add one Patriot to a sinking state;
This weeping marble had not ask'd thy Tear,   5
Or sadly told, how many Hopes lie here!
The living Virtue now had shone approv'd,
The Senate heard him, and his Country lov'd.
Yet softer Honours, and less noisy Fame
Attend the shade of gentle BUCKINGHAM :   10
In whom a Race, for Courage fam'd and Art,
Ends in the milder Merit of the Heart;
And Chiefs or Sages long to Britain giv'n,
Pays the last Tribute of a Saint to Heav'n.

XV.

FOR ONE WHO WOULD NOT BE BURIED IN WESTMINSTER ABBEY.[2]

HEROES, and KINGS! your distance keep :
  In peace let one poor Poet sleep,
Who never flatter'd Folks like you :
Let Horace blush, and Virgil too.

ANOTHER, ON THE SAME.[3]

UNDER this Marble, or under this Sill,
  Or under this Turf, or e'en what they will;
Whatever an Heir, or a Friend in his stead,
Or any good creature shall lay o'er my head,
Lies one who ne'er car'd, and still cares not a pin   5
What they said, or may say of the mortal within :
But, who living and dying, serene still and free,
Trusts in GOD, that as well as he was, he shall be.

---

[1] Only son of John Sheffield, Duke of Buckinghamshire, by Katharine Darnley, natural daughter of James II. *Roscoe.*

[2] [These lines were placed by Warburton on the monument erected by him to Pope in Twickenham Church, seventeen years after his death. Mr. Carruthers points out that this execrable piece of bad taste was in contravention of Pope's own desire as expressed in his will, where he directs that *only* the date of his death, and his age, should be inscribed on his tomb.]

[3] [Imitated from Ariosto's epitaph on himself.]

MISCELLANEOUS.

A PARAPHRASE

(ON THOMAS À KEMPIS, l. III. c. 2).

[Done by the Author at twelve years old; and first published from the Caryll Papers in the *Athenæum*, July 15th, 1854.]

SPEAK, Gracious Lord, oh, speak; thy Servant hears:
For I 'm thy Servant and I 'll still be so:
Speak words of Comfort in my willing Ears;
   And since my Tongue is in thy praises slow,
And since that thine all Rhetoric exceeds: 5
Speak thou in words, but let me speak in deeds!

Nor speak alone, but give me grace to hear
   What thy celestial Sweetness does impart;
Let it not stop when entered at the Ear,
   But sink, and take deep rooting in my heart.   10
As the parch'd Earth drinks Rain (but grace afford)
With such a Gust[1] will I receive thy word.

Nor with the Israelites shall I desire
   Thy heav'nly word by Moses to receive,
Lest I should die: but Thou who didst inspire   15
   Moses himself, speak Thou, that I may live.
Rather with Samuel I beseech with tears,
Speak, gracious Lord, oh, speak, thy servant hears.

Moses, indeed, may say the words, but Thou
   Must give the Spirit, and the Life inspire;   20
Our Love to thee his fervent Breath may blow,
   But 't is thyself alone can give the fire:
Thou without them may'st speak and profit too;
But without thee what could the Prophets do?

They preach the Doctrine, but thou mak'st us do 't;   25
   They teach the mysteries thou dost open lay;
The trees they water, but thou giv'st the fruit;
   They to Salvation show the arduous way,
But none but you can give us Strength to walk;
You give the Practice, they but give the Talk.   30

[1] [i.e. taste.]

477

Let them be Silent then; and thou alone,
  My God! speak comfort to my ravish'd ears;
Light of my eyes, my Consolation,
  Speak when thou wilt, for still thy Servant hears.
Whate'er thou speak'st, let this be understood: 35
Thy greater Glory, and my greater Good!

TO THE AUTHOR OF A POEM

ENTITLED

SUCCESSIO.

[First published in Lintot's *Miscellanies;* avowed by Pope as written by him when fourteen years of age, in note to *Dunciad,* Bk. I. v. 181. Elkanah Settle, the city poet, and the Doeg of *Absalom and Achitophel,* had written a poem in celebration of the settlement of the crown on the house of Brunswick. Of this poem vv. 4 and 17–18 were afterwards, with slight alterations, inserted in the *Dunciad* as vv. 183–4 and 181–2 of Bk. I.]

BEGONE, ye Critics, and restrain your spite,
  CODRUS writes on, and will for ever write.
The heaviest Muse the swiftest course has gone,
As clocks run fastest when most lead is on;
What tho' no bees around your cradle flew,   5
Nor on your lips distill'd their golden dew;
Yet have we oft discover'd in their stead
A swarm of drones that buzz'd about your head.
When you, like Orpheus, strike the warbling lyre,
Attentive blocks stand round you and admire.   10
Wit pass'd through thee no longer is the same,
As meat digested takes a diff'rent name;
But sense must sure thy safest plunder be,
Since no reprisals can be made on thee.
Thus thou may'st rise, and in thy daring flight   15
(Though ne'er so weighty) reach a wondrous height.
So, forced from engines, lead itself can fly,
And pond'rous slugs move nimbly through the sky.
Sure BAVIUS copied MÆVIUS to the full,
And CHÆRILUS[1] taught CODRUS to be dull;   20
Therefore, dear friend, at my advice give o'er
This needless labour; and contend no more
To prove a *dull succession* to be true,
Since 't is enough we find it so in you.

---

[1] Perhaps by *Chærilus*, the juvenile satirist designed *Flecknoe* or *Shadwell*, who had received their immortality of Dulness from his master Catholic in poetry and opinions: *Dry-den. D'Israeli*, cited by *Roscoe*.

ARGUS.

'HOMER'S account of Ulysses's dog Argus is the most pathetic imaginable, all the circumstances consider'd, and an excellent proof of the old bard's good-nature. Ulysses had left him at Ithaca when he embark'd for Troy, and found him at his return after twenty years (which by the way is not unnatural, as some critics have said, since I remember the dam of my dog was twenty-two years old when she died. May the omen of longevity prove fortunate to her successors!) You shall have it in verse.' *Pope to H. Cromwell, Oct.* 19, 1709.

WHEN wise Ulysses, from his native coast
    Long kept by wars, and long by tempests toss'd,
Arriv'd at last, poor, old, disguis'd, alone,
To all his friends and ev'n his Queen unknown;
Chang'd as he was, with age, and toils, and cares,   5
Furrow'd his rev'rend face, and white his hairs,
In his own palace forc'd to ask his bread,
Scorn'd by those slaves his former bounty fed,
Forgot of all his own domestic crew:
The faithful dog alone his rightful master knew!   10
Unfed, unhous'd, neglected, on the clay,
Like an old servant, now cashier'd, he lay;
Touch'd with resentment of ungrateful man,
And longing to behold his ancient Lord again.
Him when he saw — he rose, and crawl'd to meet,   15
('T was all he could) and fawn'd, and kiss'd his feet,
· Seiz'd with dumb joy — then falling by his side,
Own'd his returning lord, look'd up, and died!

IMITATION OF MARTIAL.

[Lib. x. Epigr. XXIII. Mentioned as Pope's 'imitation of Martin's epigram on *Antonius Primus*,' by Sir William Trumball, in a letter to Pope, Jan. 19, 1716.]

AT length, my Friend, (while Time, with still career
    Wafts on his gentle wing his eightieth year,[1])
Sees his past days safe out of Fortune's pow'r,
Nor dreads approaching Fate's uncertain hour;
Reviews his life, and in the strict survey   ⎫   5
Finds not one moment he could wish away,   ⎬·
Pleas'd with the series at each happy day.   ⎭
Such, such a man extends his life's short space,
And from the goal again renews the race;
For he lives twice, who can at once employ   10
The present well, and ev'n the past enjoy.

[1] How soon hath Time, the subtle thief of youth,
  Stol'n on his wing my three-and-twentieth year!
    Milton's Sonnets. Carruthers.

OCCASIONED BY SOME VERSES OF HIS GRACE THE DUKE OF BUCKINGHAM.[1]

MUSE, 't is enough: at length thy labour ends,
  And thou shalt live, for Buckingham commends.
Let Crowds of Critics now my verse assail,
Let Dennis write, and nameless numbers rail:
This more than pays whole years of thankless pain;   5
Time, health, and fortune are not lost in vain.
Sheffield approves, consenting Phœbus bends,
And I and Malice from this hour are friends.

ON MRS. TOFTS,

A CELEBRATED OPERA-SINGER.[2]

SO bright is thy Beauty, so charming thy Song,
  As had drawn both the Beasts and their Orpheus along;
But such is thy Av'rice, and such is thy Pride,
That the Beasts must have starv'd, and the Poet have died.

EPIGRAM ON THE FEUDS ABOUT HANDEL AND BONONCINI.[3]

[Sometimes, but incorrectly, attributed to Swift.]

STRANGE! all this Difference should be
  'Twixt Tweedle-*dum* and Tweedle-*dee!*

EPIGRAM.

YOU beat your Pate, and fancy Wit will come:
  Knock as you please, there 's nobody at home.

EPITAPH.

[Imitated by Goldsmith in his Epitaph on Edward Purdon, 'a bookseller's hack.']

WELL then, poor G—— lies under Ground!
  So there 's an End of honest Jack.
So little Justice here he found,
  'T is ten to one he 'll ne'er come back.

---

[1] The verses referred to are the commendatory lines prefixed to Pope's poem by B. *Roscoe*. [As to Sheffield, Duke of Buckinghamshire, see note to *Essay on Criticism*, v. 724.]

[2] [Katharine Tofts first came before the public in 1703, as a singer of Italian and English, at the theatre in Lincoln's Inn Fields. Subsequently her rivalry with Margherita de l'Epine divided the public into an English and an Italian party. Hughes celebrated her as 'the British Tofts.' She retired from the stage in 1709, being then under the influence of a mental malady. See the *Tatler*, No. 20, where her insanity (which led her to identify herself with Camilla, one of her operatic characters, is described. She was married to a Mr. Smith; and died in Italy in 1760. See Hogarth's *Memoirs of the Musical Drama.*]

[3] [Giovanni Battista Bononcini's first English opera appeared in 1720; but he was at that time already well-known as the composer of *Camilla.*]

EPITAPH.

[From the Latin on Joannes Mirandula.[1] The lines were afterwards applied by Pope to Lord Coningsby; as to whom cf. *Moral Essays*, Ep. III. v. 397.]

HERE Francis C——[2] lies. Be civil;
The rest God knows — perhaps the Devil!

THE BALANCE OF EUROPE.[3]

NOW Europe 's balanc'd, neither Side prevails;
For nothing 's left in either of the Scales.

TO A LADY WITH "THE TEMPLE OF FAME."

["I send you my Temple of Fame, which is just come out; but my sentiments about it you will see better by this epigram." — *Pope to Martha Blount*, 1714.]

WHAT 'S Fame with Men, by Custom of the Nation,
Is call'd in Women only Reputation;
About them both why keep we such a pother?
Part you with one, and I 'll renounce the other.

IMPROMPTU TO LADY WINCHILSEA.

OCCASIONED BY FOUR SATIRICAL VERSES ON WOMEN-WITS, IN THE "RAPE OF THE LOCK."

[The four verses are apparently Canto IV. vv. 59–62. The Countess of Winchilsea, a poetess whom Rowe hailed as inspired by ' more than Delphic ardour,' replied by some pretty lines, where she declares that, ' disarmed with so genteel an air,' she gives over the contest. Her reply will be found in Roscoe's *Supplement*, pp. 183–6.]

IN vain you boast Poetic Names of yore,
And cite those Sapphos we admire no more:
Fate doom'd the Fall of every Female Wit;
But doom'd it then, when first Ardelia writ.
Of all Examples by the World confess'd,   5
I knew Ardelia could not quote the best;
Who, like her Mistress on Britannia's Throne,[4]
Fights and subdues in Quarrels not her own.
To write their Praise you but in vain essay;
E'en while you write, you take that Praise away: 10
Light to the Stars the Sun does thus restore,
But shines himself till they are seen no more.

---

[1] Joannes jacet hic Mirandula; cætera norunt Et Tagus et Ganges — forsan et Antipodes.

[2] [Chartres.]

[3] [' The Balance of Europe ' is a term of which the origin belongs to the times of Henry IV. of France. Pope's epigram refers to the state of Europe after the peace of Utrecht in 1715, as a peace resulting (which was not in truth the case) from general exhaustion.]

[4] [Alluding to the wars concerning the Spanish succession, in which England certainly had no direct interest, under Queen Anne.]

2 I

EPIGRAM

ON THE TOASTS OF THE KIT-CAT CLUB, ANNO 1716.

[The Kit-Cat Club was so named from Christopher Katt, a famous pastry-cook. Steele, Addison, and many other wits were members, and Tonson secretary. It was customary to write verses in honour of the ' Toasts,' and engrave them upon the glasses. Each member gave his picture to the club.]

WHENCE deathless *Kit-Cat* took its Name,
  Few Critics can unriddle;
Some say from Pastry-cook it came,
  And some from Cat and Fiddle.
From no trim Beaux its Name it boasts,
  Gray statesmen or green wits;
But from this Pell-mell Pack of Toasts
  Of old " Cats " and young " Kits."

A DIALOGUE.

1717.

POPE. — SINCE my old friend is grown so great
  As to be Minister of State,
I 'm told, but 't is not true, I hope,
That Craggs [1] will be ashamed of Pope.

CRAGGS. — Alas! if I am such a creature
  To grow the worse for growing greater;
Why, faith, in spite of all my brags,
'T is Pope must be ashamed of Craggs.

ON DRAWINGS OF THE STATUES OF APOLLO, VENUS, AND HERCULES,

MADE FOR POPE BY SIR GODFREY KNELLER.

WHAT god, what genius, did the pencil move,
  When Kneller painted these?
'T was friendship warm as Phœbus, kind as love,
  And strong as Hercules.

PROLOGUE TO THE "THREE HOURS AFTER MARRIAGE."

[From the *Miscellanies* of Pope, Swift, Arbuthnot, and Gay.]

[Though I am not aware on what evidence Roscoe and Carruthers agree in ascribing the Prologue of this farce to Pope, instead of leaving its joint honours like those of the farce itself to Gay and Arbuthnot (for both contributed to the volume of *Miscellanies* in which it was published) as well as him; yet the following has been inserted on account of the interest attaching to the piece, as the origin of Pope's quarrel with Cibber. A brief notice of the play, which was produced at Drury-Lane on Jan. 16th, 1717, will be found in the *Introductory Memoir :* and the play itself in most editions of Gay, and in Bowles's edition of Pope, vol. X.]

[1] [See p. 461.]

AUTHORS are judg'd by strange capricious Rules;
　The great ones are thought mad, the small ones Fools:
Yet sure the best are most severely fated,
For Fools are only laugh'd at, Wits are hated.
Blockheads with Reason Men of Sense abhor;　　　　5
But Fool 'gainst Fool is barb'rous Civil War.
Why on all Authors then should Critics fall,
Since some have writ, and shown no Wit at all?
Condemn a Play of theirs, and they evade it,
Cry, " Damn not us, but damn the *French* who made it."　　10
By running Goods, these graceless Owlers[1] gain;
These are the *Rules* of *France*, the *Plots* of *Spain*:
But Wit, like Wine, from happier climates brought,
Dash'd by these Rogues, turns *English* common Draught.
They pall *Molière's* and *Lopez'*[2] sprightly strain,　　　15
And teach dull *Harlequins* to grin in vain.
　How shall our Author hope a gentler Fate,
Who dares most impudently not translate?
It had been civil in these ticklish times,
To fetch his Fools and Knaves from foreign Climes,　　20
Spaniards and *French* abuse to the World's End,
But spare old *England*, lest you hurt a Friend.
If any Fool is by our Satire bit,
Let him hiss loud, to show you all, he 's hit.
Poets make Characters, as *Salesmen* Clothes,　　　25
We take no Measure of your Fops and Beaus,
But here all Sizes and all Shapes you meet,
And fit yourselves, like Chaps[3] in *Monmouth-street*.
　Gallants! look here, this *Fools-cap* has an Air, 　*[Shows a cap*
Goodly and smart, with Ears of *Issachar*.　　　 *with ears.*
Let no one Fool engross it, or confine,
A common Blessing! now 't is yours, now mine.
But Poets in all Ages had the Care
To keep this Cap, for such as will, to wear,
Our Author has it now, (for every Wit　　　　　35
Of Course resign'd it to the next that writ:)　 *[Flings down*
And thus upon the Stage 't is fairly[4] thrown;　 *the cap, and*
Let him that takes it, wear it as his own.　　　 *exit.*

---

[1] [i.e. smugglers: prop. woollers.]

[2] [Lopez de Vega, the most prolific of Spanish dramatists.]

[3] [Cheap salesmen.]

[4] [C. Johnson, in the Prologue to his *Sultaness*, thus referred to this exit and the farce:
' Some wags have been, who boldly durst adventure

To club a Farce by Tripartite-Indenture
But let them share their dividend of praise
And their own *Fools-cap* wear, instead of
　　　　Bays.'
Which attack procured him a place in the *Dunciad*. Geneste's *Account of the Stage*, &c. II.
p. 598.]

PROLOGUE DESIGNED FOR MR. D'URFEY'S[1]
LAST PLAY.

[First published in Pope and Swift's *Miscellanies.*]

GROWN old in Rhyme, 't were barbarous to discard
 Your persevering, unexhausted Bard:
Damnation follows Death in other men ;
But your damn'd Poet lives, and writes again.
Th' adventurous Lover is successful still,   5
Who strives to please the Fair *against* her *Will:*
Be kind, and make him in his Wishes easy,
Who in your own *Despite* has strove to please ye.
He scorn'd to borrow from the Wits of yore ;
But ever writ, as none e'er writ before.   10
You Modern Wits, should each man bring his Claim,
Have desperate Debentures on your Fame ;
And little would be left you, I 'm afraid,
If all your Debts to *Greece* and *Rome* were paid.
From his deep Fund our Author largely draws ;   15
Nor sinks his Credit lower than it was.
Though Plays for Honour in old time he made,
'T is now for better Reasons — to be paid.
Believe him, he has known the World too long,
And seen the Death of much immortal Song.   20
He says, poor Poets lost, while Players won,
As Pimps grow rich, while Gallants are undone.
Though *Tom* the Poet writ with ease and pleasure,
The Comic *Tom* abounds in other treasure.
Fame is at best an unperforming Cheat ;   25
But 't is substantial Happiness, *to eat.*
Let Ease, his last Request, be of your giving,
Nor force him to be damn'd to get his Living.

A PROLOGUE BY MR. POPE,

To a Play for Mr. DENNIS'S Benefit, in 1733, when he was old, blind, and in great
Distress, a little before his Death.[2]

AS when that Hero, who in each Campaign,
 Had brav'd the *Goth,* and many a *Vandal* slain,

---

[1] [As to D'Urfey or Durfey, see p. 67.]

[2] Dennis being much distressed very near the close of his life, it was proposed to act a play for his benefit ; and Thomson, Mallet, Benjamin Martin and Pope took the lead upon the occasion. The play, which was the *Provoked Husband* (by Vanbrugh and Cibber), was represented at the Haymarket, Dec. 18th, 1733; and Pope condescended so far as to lay aside his resentment against his former antagonist as to write a Prologue, which was spoken by Theophilus Cibber (the Laureate's son). Geneste, *English Stage,* Vol. III. p. 318. [The annalist adds, with much truth, that Pope's benevolence was not so pure as could be wished ; for his Prologue was throughout a sneer at the poor old critic, who happily, either from vanity or the decay of his intellects, failed to perceive its tendency. He died twenty days afterwards. As to the general character of the

Lay Fortune-struck, a spectacle of Woe!
Wept by each Friend, forgiv'n by ev'ry Foe:
Was there a gen'rous, a reflecting mind,   5
But pitied BELISARIUS old and blind?
Was there a Chief but melted at the Sight?[1]
A common Soldier, but who clubb'd his Mite?
Such, such emotions should in *Britons* rise,
When press'd by want and weakness DENNIS lies;   10
Dennis, who long had warr'd with modern *Huns*,
Their Quibbles routed, and defy'd their Puns;
A desp'rate *Bulwark*, sturdy, firm, and fierce
Against the *Gothic* Sons of frozen verse:
How chang'd from him who made the boxes groan,   15
And shook the Stage with Thunders all his own!
Stood up to dash each vain PRETENDER's hope,
Maul the French Tyrant, or pull down the POPE!
If there 's a *Briton* then, true bred and born,
Who holds Dragoons and wooden shoes in scorn: 20
If there 's a Critic of distinguished rage;
If there 's a Senior, who contemns this age;
Let him to night his just assistance lend,
And be the *Critic's*, *Briton's*, *Old Man's* Friend.

MACER: A CHARACTER.

[First printed in the *Miscellanies* of Swift and Pope (1727), and interpreted by Warton to mean James Moore-Smythe (see *Dunciad*, Bk. II. v. 50). But Bowles thinks it more likely that the character was intended for Ambrose Philips, called 'lean Philips' by Pope (see *Farewell to London*, p. 496); who 'borrowed' a play from the French, and 'translated' the Persian tales. Mr. Carruthers completes the identification by showing a note prefixed to this character on its first publication and speaking of Macer's advertisements for a *Miscellany* in 1713, to refer to such an advertisement actually issued by Philips in the *London Gazette* in 1715. As to Philips, see *Dunciad*, Bk. III. v. 326, *et al.*

WHEN simple *Macer*, now of high renown,
    First fought a Poet's Fortune in the Town,
'T was all th' Ambition his high soul could feel,
To wear red stockings, and to dine with *Steele*.
Some Ends of verse his Betters might afford,   5
And gave the harmless fellow a good word.
Set up with these he ventur'd on the Town,
And with a borrow'd Play,[2] out-did poor *Crown*.[3]

relations between Pope and Dennis, see *Introductory Memoir*, p. xxiv.] The furious patriotism of Dennis is of course alluded to in the appeal for 'British' sympathy.

[1] *Was there a Chief, etc.*] The fine figure of the Commander in that capital Picture of Belisarius at Chiswick, supplied the Poet with this beautiful idea. *Warburton.*

[2] [The borrowed play, *The Distrest Mother*, was, as Carruthers says, from Racine, not, as Bowles says, from Voltaire. It is the *Andromaque*, and the epilogue was ascribed to Addison.]

[3] [John Crown, who wrote 12 tragedies, 6 comedies, and a masque, in little more than a quarter of a century, died about 1698. As a

There he stopp'd short, nor since has writ a tittle,
But has the wit to make the most of little;　　　　　　10
Like stunted hide-bound Trees, that just have got
Sufficient sap at once to bear and rot.
Now he begs Verse, and what he gets commends,
Not of the Wits his foes, but Fools his friends.
　　So some coarse Country Wench, almost decay'd,　　15
Trudges to town, and first turns Chambermaid;
Awkward and supple, each devoir to pay;
She flatters her good Lady twice a day;
Thought wond'rous honest, tho' of mean degree,
And strangely lik'd for her *Simplicity:*　　　　　　20
In a translated Suit, then tries the Town,
With borrow'd Pins, and Patches not her own:
But just endur'd the winter she began,
And in four months a batter'd Harridan.
Now nothing left, but wither'd, pale, and shrunk,　　25
To bawd for others, and go shares with Punk.

UMBRA.

[From the *Miscellanies.* The original of the character has been variously sought in Walter Carey (a F. R. S. and Whig official), Charles Johnson and Ambrose Philips. 'Umbra' must in no case be confounded with the 'Lord Umbra' of the Satires.]

CLOSE to the best known Author Umbra sits,
　　The constant Index to all Button's Wits.[1]
"Who's here?" cries Umbra: "only Johnson,"[2] — "Oh!
Your Slave," and *exit;* but returns with Rowe:
"Dear Rowe, let's sit and talk of tragedies:"　　　　5
Ere long *Pope enters*, and to Pope he flies.
Then up comes Steele: he turns upon his Heel,
And in a Moment fastens upon Steele;
But cries as soon, "Dear Dick, I must be gone,
For, if I know his Tread, here's Addison."　　　　　10
Says Addison to Steele, "'T is Time to go;"
Pope to the Closet steps aside with Rowe.
Poor Umbra left in this abandoned Pickle,
E'en sets him down and writes to honest T—.[3]
Fool! 't is in vain from Wit to Wit to roam;　　　　15
Know, Sense, like Charity, begins at Home.

sample of a borrow'd play, see Geneste's account of Crown's version of *Part I. of Henry VI.*]

[1] [Button's coffee-house in Covent Garden was the resort of Addison's circle.]

[2] [Charles Johnson, a second-rate dramatist. *Bowles.*]

[3] [Tickell. See *Introductory Memoir*, p. xxix.]

TO MR. JOHN MOORE, Author of the celebrated Worm-Powder.

[From the *Miscellanies*.]

HOW much, egregious *Moore*, are we
　　Deceiv'd by Shows and Forms!
Whate'er we think, whate'er we see,
　　All Humankind are Worms.

Man is a very Worm by birth,　　　　　　　　5
　　Vile, Reptile, weak, and vain!
A While he crawls upon the Earth,
　　Then shrinks to Earth again.

That Woman is a Worm, we find
　　E'er since our Grandam's evil;
She first convers'd with her own Kind,
　　That ancient Worm, the Devil.

The Learn'd themselves we Book-worms name,
　　The Blockhead is a Slow-worm;
The Nymph whose Tail is all on Flame,　　　15
　　Is aptly term'd a Glow-worm:

The Fops are painted Butterflies,
　　That flutter for a Day;
First from a Worm they take their Rise,
　　And in a Worm decay.　　　　　　　　　20

The Flatterer an Ear-wig grows;
　　Thus Worms suit all Conditions;
Misers are Muck-worms, Silk-worms Beaux,
　　And Death-watches Physicians.

That Statesmen have the Worm, is seen,　　25
　　By all their winding Play;
Their Conscience is a Worm within,
　　That gnaws them Night and Day.

Ah *Moore!* thy Skill were well employ'd,
　　And greater Gain would rise,　　　　　　30
If thou couldst make the Courtier void
　　The Worm that never dies!

O learned Friend of *Abchurch-Lane*,[1]
　　Who sett'st our entrails free,
Vain is thy Art, thy Powder vain,　　　　　35
　　Since Worms shall eat ev'n thee.

[1] [Abchurch (properly Upchurch) Lane, Lombard Street.]

> Our Fate thou only canst adjourn
> 　　Some few short years, no more!
> Ev'n *Button's* Wits to Worms shall turn,
> 　　Who Maggots were before.　　　　　　40

SANDYS' GHOST;

OR

A PROPER NEW BALLAD ON THE NEW OVID'S METAMORPHOSES.

AS IT WAS INTENDED TO BE TRANSLATED BY PERSONS OF QUALITY.

[From the *Miscellanies*. It is obviously not by Gay (see St. 13). Sir Walter Scott, quoted by Roscoe, explains the ballad to refer to a translation of the *Metamorphoses* published by Sir Samuel Garth (and written by several hands, of which Pope's was one), to supersede the old translation of George Sandys, who died in 1643.]

> YE Lords and Commons, Men of Wit,
> 　　And Pleasure about Town;
> Read this ere you translate one Bit
> 　　Of Books of high Renown.

> Beware of *Latin* Authors all!　　　　　　5
> 　　Nor think your Verses Sterling,
> Though with a Golden Pen you scrawl,
> 　　And scribble in a *Berlin:*

> For not the Desk with silver Nails,
> 　　Nor *Bureau* of Expense,　　　　　　10
> Nor Standish well japann'd avails
> 　　To writing of good Sense.

> Hear how a Ghost in dead of Night,
> 　　With saucer Eyes of Fire,
> In woeful wise did sore affright　　　　　　15
> 　　A Wit and courtly 'Squire.

> Rare Imp of Phœbus, hopeful Youth
> 　　Like Puppy tame that uses
> To fetch and carry, in his Mouth,
> 　　The Works of all the Muses.　　　　　　20

> Ah! why did he write Poetry,
> 　　That hereto was so civil;
> And sell his soul for vanity,
> 　　To Rhyming and the Devil?

> A Desk he had of curious Work,　　　　　　25
> 　　With glittering Studs about;
> Within the same did *Sandys* lurk,
> 　　Though *Ovid* lay without.

Now as he scratch'd to fetch up Thought,
    Forth popp'd the Sprite so thin ;
And from the Key-hole bolted out,
    All upright as a Pin.
30

With Whiskers, Band, and Pantaloon,
    And Ruff composed most duly ;
This 'Squire he dropp'd his Pen full soon,
    While as the Light burnt bluely.
35

"Ho! Master Sam," quoth Sandys' sprite,
    "Write on, nor let me scare ye ;
Forsooth, if Rhymes fall in not right,
    To Budgell [1] seek, or Carey.[2]
40

"I hear the Beat of Jacob's Drums,[3]
    Poor Ovid finds no Quarter!
See first the merry P—— comes [4]
    In Haste, without his Garter.

"Then Lords and Lordlings, 'Squires and Knights,
    Wits, Witlings, Prigs, and Peers!
Garth at St. James's, and at White's,
    Beats up for Volunteers.
45

"What Fenton will not do, nor Gay,
    Nor Congreve, Rowe, nor Stanyan,
Tom B——t [5] or Tom D'Urfey may,
    John Dunton, Steele, or any one.
50

"If Justice Philips' costive head
    Some frigid Rhymes disburses ;
They shall like *Persian Tales* [6] be read,
    And glad both Babes and Nurses.
55

"Let W—rw—k's Muse with Ash—t join,[7]
    And Ozell's with Lord Hervey's :
Tickell and Addison combine,
    And P—pe translate with Jervas.
60

"L—— himself, that lively Lord,[8]
    Who bows to every Lady,
Shall join with F——[9] in one Accord,
    And be like Tate and Brady.

---

[1] [See *Dunciad*, Bk. II. v. 397.]
[2] [John Carey. See note 5 on pag. 490.]
[3] [Jacob Tonson.]
[4] The Earl of Pembroke, probably. *Roscoe.*
[5] [Tom Burnet, the bishop's son. See *Dunciad*, Bk. III. v. 179. John Dunton: see *Dunciad*, Bk. II. v. 144.]
[6] [Ambrose Philips (among whose translated pieces were the *Persian Tales*) was appointed (by his patron Archbp. Boulter) Judge of the Prerogative Court in Ireland.]
[7] Lord Warwick and Dr. Ashurst. *Carruthers.*
[8] Lord Lansdowne. *Id.*
[9] Philip Frowde, a dramatic writer and fine scholar, a friend of Addison's. *Id.*

"Ye Ladies too draw forth your pen,   65
  I pray where can the hurt lie?
Since you have Brains as well as Men,
  As witness Lady W—l—y.[1]

"Now, Tonson, list thy Forces all,
  Review them, and tell Noses;   70
For to poor Ovid shall befal
  A strange *Metamorphosis.*

"A *Metamorphosis* more strange
  Than all his Books can vapour;"
'To what' (quoth 'squire) 'shall Ovid change?'   75
  Quoth Sandys: " *To waste paper.*"

THE TRANSLATOR.

EGBERT SANGER served his apprenticeship with Jacob Tonson, and succeeded Bernard Lintot in his shop at Middle Temple Gate, Fleet Street. Lintot printed Ozell's translation of Perrault's *Characters,* and Sanger his translation of Boileau's *Lutrin,* recommended by Rowe, in 1709. *Warton.*

OZELL,[2] at Sanger's call, invoked his Muse —
  For who to sing for Sanger could refuse?
His numbers such as Sanger's self might use.
Reviving Perrault, murdering Boileau, he
Slander'd the ancients first, then Wycherley;   5
Which yet not much that old bard's anger raised,
Since those were slander'd most, whom Ozell praised
Nor had the gentle satire caus'd complaining,
Had not sage Rowe pronounc'd it entertaining:
How great must be the judgment of that writer   10
Who the *Plain-dealer*[3] damns, and prints the *Biter!*[4]

THE THREE GENTLE SHEPHERDS.

OF gentle Philips will I ever sing,
  With gentle Philips shall the valleys ring.
My numbers too for ever will I vary,
With gentle Budgell and with gentle Carey.[5]
Or if in ranging of the names I judge ill,   5
With gentle Carey and with gentle Budgell:[6]
Oh! may all gentle bards together place ye,

---

[1] [Lady Mary Wortley Montagu.]
[2] [See *Dunciad,* Bk. i. v. 286.]
[3] [By Wycherley.]
[4] [By Rowe.]
[5] Henry Carey. *Roscoe.* The author of 'Sally in our alley' and a dramatist. But

there was also a John Carey, a contributor to the *Tatler* and *Spectator,* and Walter Carey. *Carruthers.*
[6] [These four lines seem to have suggested Canning's well-known epigram on Hiley and Bragge.]

Men of good hearts, and men of delicacy
May satire ne'er befool ye, or beknave ye,
And from all wits that have a knack, God save ye.[1]   10

LINES

WRITTEN IN WINDSOR FOREST.

[Letter to a Lady (Martha Blount) in Bowles, dated by Carruthers, September, 1717.]

ALL hail, once pleasing, once inspiring shade!
   Scene of my youthful loves and happier hours!
Where the kind Muses met me as I stray'd,
   And gently press'd my hand, and said " Be ours!—
Take all thou e'er shalt have, a constant Muse :   5
   At Court thou may'st be liked, but nothing gain :
Stock thou may'st buy and sell, but always lose,
   And love the brightest eyes, but love in vain."

TO MRS. M. B. ON HER BIRTH-DAY.[2]

[1723.]

OH be thou blest with all that Heav'n can send,
   Long Health, long Youth, long Pleasure, and a Friend:
Not with those Toys the female world admire,
Riches that vex, and Vanities that tire.
With added years if Life bring nothing new,   5
But, like a Sieve, let ev'ry blessing thro',
Some joy still lost, as each vain year runs o'er,
And all we gain some sad Reflection more ;
Is that a Birth-Day? 't is alas! too clear,
'T is but the Fun'ral of the former year.   10
   Let Joy or Ease, let Affluence or Content,
And the gay Conscience of a life well spent,
Calm ev'ry thought, inspirit ev'ry grace,
Glow in thy heart, and smile upon thy face.
Let day improve on day, and year on year,   15

---

[1] Curll said, that in prose he was equal to Pope; but that in verse Pope had merely a particular knack. *Bowles.*

[2] [Martha Blount. Lines 5-10 occur as a reflection on the poet's own birthday in a letter to Gay of the year 1722, and they were also adapted for him to a kind of epitaph on Henry Mordaunt, the nephew of Lord Peterborough, who committed suicide in 1724. On this occasion the following lines were added:

' If there's no hope with kind, though fainter ray
To gild the ev'ning of our future day;
If ev'ry page of life's long volume tell
The same dull story — MORDAUNT, thou didst well.'

The lines concerning which the charge of plagiarism was mutually made between Pope and James Moore-Smythe were omitted by Pope on reprinting the poem, but introduced (slightly altered) in the *Characters of Women* (*Moral Essays*, Ep. II. vv. 243-248).]

Without a Pain, a Trouble, or a Fear;
Till Death unfelt that tender frame destroy,
In some soft Dream, or Extasy of joy,
Peaceful sleep out the Sabbath of the Tomb,
And wake to Raptures in a Life to come.   20

THE CHALLENGE.[1]

A COURT BALLAD.

To the Tune of ' To all you Ladies now at Land,' &c. [By Dorset.]

Written anno 1717. *Warton.*

[This delightful trifle is addressed to Pope's charming friends at the Court of the Prince and Princess of Wales (afterwards King George II. and Queen Caroline), and is full of *petits mots* alluding to the ladies and gentlemen of their society.]

I.

TO one fair lady out of Court,
  And two fair ladies in,
Who think the Turk[2] and Pope[3] a sport,
  And wit and love no sin!
Come, these soft lines, with nothing stiff in,   5
To Bellenden,[4] Lepell,[5] and Griffin.[6]
    With a fa, la, la.

II.

What passes in the dark third row,
  And what behind the scene,
Couches and crippled chairs I know,   10
  And garrets hung with green;
I know the swing of sinful hack,
Where many damsels cry alack.
    With a fa, la, la.

III.

Then why to Courts should I repair,   15
  Where 's such ado with Townshend?[7]

---

[1] [This delightful trifle is addressed to Pope's charming friends at the Court of the Prince and Princess of Wales (afterwards King George II. and Queen Caroline), and is full of *petits mots* alluding to the ladies and gentlemen of their society.]

[2] Ulrick, the little Turk. P.

[3] The author. P.

[4] [Mary, youngest daughter of the second Lord Bellenden, was afterwards married to Colonel Campbell, who became after her death fifth Duke of Argyll. Lord Hervey (*Memoirs*, Vol. I. p. 54) speaks of her as ' incontestably the most agreeable, the most insinuating, and the most likeable woman of her time; made up of every ingredient likely to engage or attach a lover.']

[5] [The beautiful Miss Mary Lepell, Maid of Honour to the Princess Caroline, and afterwards married to Lord Hervey. Born 1700; married 1720; died 1768.]

[6] [Sister to the Lady Rich mentioned below.]

[7] [Lord Townshend was dismissed from office in 1616, the King being jealous of his supposed subserviency to the Prince of Wales.]

To hear each mortal stamp and swear,
  And every speech with "Zounds" end;
To hear them rail at honest Sunderland,[1]
And rashly blame the realm of Blunderland.   20
    With a fa, la, la.

IV.

Alas! like Schutz[2] I cannot pun,
  Like Grafton[3] court the Germans;
Tell Pickenbourg how slim she's grown,
  Like Meadows run to sermons;   25
To court ambitious men may roam,
But I and Marlbro'[4] stay at home.
    With a fa, la, la.

V.

In truth, by what I can discern,
  Of courtiers, 'twixt you three,   30
Some wit you have, and more may learn
  From Court, than Gay or Me:
Perhaps, in time, you'll leave high diet,
To sup with us on milk and quiet.
    With a fa, la, la.   35

VI.

At Leicester Fields,[5] a house full high,
  With door all painted green,
Where ribbons wave upon the tie,
  (A Milliner, I mean;)
There may you meet us three to three,   40
For Gay[6] can well make two of Me.
    With a fa, la, la.

VII.

But should you catch the prudish itch,
  And each become a coward,
Bring sometimes with you lady Rich,[7]   45
  And sometimes mistress Howard;[8]
For virgins, to keep chaste, must go
Abroad with such as are not so.
    With a fa, la, la.

[1] [The Earl of Sunderland, Lord-Lieutenant of Ireland.]

[2] [See *Imit. of Horace* Bk. i. Ep. i. v. 112.]

[3] [Charles second Duke of Grafton, born in 1683; afterwards Lord Chamberlain.]

[4] [Henrietta Duchess of Marlborough, whom Pope is believed to have so cruelly satirised as the 'Flavia' of *Moral Essays, Ep.* ii. vv. 87 ff.]

[5] [Now Leicester Square, where Leicester House, the town residence of the Prince of Wales, was situate.]

[6] [Alluding to Gay's rotundity of person.]

[7] [Lady Rich, daughter of Col. Griffin and wife of Sir Robert Rich. Many of Lady M. W. Montagu's letters are addressed to her.]

[8] [See *On a Certain Lady at Court*, p. 495.]

VIII.

And thus, fair maids, my ballad ends ;   50
  God send the king safe landing ;
And make all honest ladies friends
  To armies that are standing ;
Preserve the limits of those nations,
And take off ladies' limitations.   55
    With a fa, la, la.

ANSWER TO THE FOLLOWING QUESTION OF MRS. HOWE.[1]

WHAT is PRUDERY?
                'T is a Beldam,
Seen with Wit and Beauty seldom.
'T is a fear that starts at shadows.
'T is (no, 't is n't) like Miss *Meadows*.
'T is a Virgin hard of Feature,   5
Old, and void of all good-nature ;
Lean and fretful ; would seem wise ;
Yet plays the fool before she dies.
'T is an ugly envious Shrew,
That rails at dear *Lepell* and You.   10

SONG, BY A PERSON OF QUALITY.

Written in the Year 1733.

I.

FLUTT'RING spread thy purple Pinions,
  Gentle *Cupid*, o'er my Heart ;
I a Slave in thy Dominions ;
  Nature must give Way to Art.

II.

Mild *Arcadians*, ever blooming,   5
  Nightly nodding o'er your Flocks,
See my weary Days consuming,
  All beneath yon flow'ry Rocks.

III.

Thus the *Cyprian* Goddess weeping,
  Mourn'd *Adonis*, darling Youth :   10
Him the Boar in Silence creeping,
  Gor'd with unrelenting Tooth.

---

[1] Mary, daughter of Viscount Howe, Maid of Honour to Queen Caroline, married Lord Pembroke, and after his death Colonel Mordaunt, brother to the Earl of Peterborough. *Croker ;* note to Lord Hervey's *Memoirs.*

IV.

Cynthia, tune harmonious Numbers;
 Fair *Discretion*, string the Lyre;
Sooth my ever-waking Slumbers: 15
 Bright *Apollo*, lend thy Choir.

V.

Gloomy *Pluto*, King of Terrors,
 Arm'd in adamantine Chains,
Lead me to the Crystal Mirrors,
 Wat'ring soft Elysian Plains.   20

VI.

Mournful Cypress, verdant Willow,
 Gilding my *Aurelia's* Brows,
Morpheus hov'ring o'er my Pillow,
 Hear me pay my dying Vows.

VII.

Melancholy smooth *Mæander*,   25
 Swiftly purling in a Round,
On thy Margin Lovers wander,
 With thy flow'ry Chaplets crown'd.

VIII.

Thus when *Philomela* drooping,
 Softly seeks her silent Mate,   30
See the Bird of *Juno* stooping;
 Melody resigns to Fate.

ON A CERTAIN LADY AT COURT.[1]

I KNOW the thing that's most uncommon;
 (Envy, be silent, and attend!)
I know a reasonable Woman,
 Handsome and witty, yet a Friend.

Not warp'd by Passion, aw'd by Rumour,   5
 Not grave thro' Pride, or gay through Folly,
An equal Mixture of good Humour,
 And sensible soft Melancholy.

"Has she no faults then (Envy says), Sir?"
 Yes, she has one, I must aver;   10
When all the World conspires to praise her,
 The Woman's deaf, and does not hear.

---

[1] The lady addressed was Mrs. Howard, bed-chamber woman to Queen Caroline, and afterwards Countess of Suffolk. *Warton.* [Mistress of George II., who, according to Horace Wal-pole, quoted by Carruthers, granted the reprieve of a condemned malefactor, in order that an experiment might be made on his ears for her benefit.]

A FAREWELL TO LONDON.

IN THE YEAR 1715.

[The second stanza of this has been omitted.]

DEAR, damn'd distracting town, farewell!
  Thy fools no more I 'll tease :
This year in peace, ye critics, dwell,
  Ye harlots, sleep at ease !

Soft B—— and rough C——s adieu,   5
  Earl Warwick make your moan,
The lively H——k and you
  May knock up whores alone.[1]

To drink and droll be Rowe allow'd
  Till the third watchman's toll ;   10
Let Jervas gratis paint, and Frowde
  Save three-pence and his soul.

Farewell, Arbuthnot's raillery
  On every learned sot ;
And Garth, the best good Christian he,   15
  Although he knows it not.

Lintot, farewell ! thy bard must go ;
  Farewell, unhappy Tonson !
Heaven gives thee for thy loss of Rowe,[2]
  Lean Philips, and fat Johnson.[3]   20

Why should I stay ? Both parties rage ;
  My vixen mistress squalls ;
The wits in envious feuds engage :
  And Homer (damn him !) calls.[4]

The love of arts lies cold and dead   25
  In Halifax's urn :
And not one Muse of all he fed
  Has yet the grace to mourn.[5]

My friends, by turns, my friends confound,
  Betray, and are betrayed :   30
Poor Y——r 's sold for fifty pound,
  And B——ll is a jade.[6]

---

[1] [C—s is evidently Craggs ; and H—k, as Carruthers interprets the hiatus, Lord Hinchinbrook, a young nobleman of spirit and fashion.]

[2] Rowe had the year before, on the accession of George I., been made Poet Laureate, one of the land-surveyors of the port of London, Clerk of the Closet to the Prince of Wales, and Secretary of Presentations under the Lord Chancellor. Such an accumulation of offices might well suspend for a season the poetical and publishing pursuits of Rowe. *Carruthers.*

[3] Cf. *Umbra*, v. 3.]

[4] [The first four books of the *Iliad* were published in this year.]

[5] [Lord Halifax, who offered a pension to Pope died in this year.]

[6] [Most likely Miss Younger and Mrs. Bicknell, sisters, both actresses. *Carruthers.* [Mrs. Bicknell acted Phœbe Clinket in Pope's farce.]

Why make I friendships with the great,
   When I no favour seek?
Or follow girls, seven hours in eight?   35
   I us'd but once a week.

Still idle, with a busy air,
   Deep whimsies to contrive;
The gayest valetudinaire,
   Most thinking rake, alive.   40

Solicitous for others' ends,
   Though fond of dear repose;
Careless or drowsy with my friends,
   And frolic with my foes.

Luxurious lobster-nights, farewell,   45
   For sober, studious days!
And Burlington's delicious meal,
   For salads, tarts, and pease!

Adieu to all, but Gay alone,
   Whose soul, sincere and free,   50
Loves all mankind, but flatters none,
   And so may starve with me.

THE BASSET–TABLE.

AN ECLOGUE.

ONLY this of all the *Town Eclogues* was Mr. Pope's; and is here printed from a copy corrected by his own hand. — The humour of it consists in this, that the one is in love with the *Game*, and the other with the *Sharper*. *Warburton.* [The original edition of the *Town Eclogues* was published in 1716 anonymously, and consisted of three eclogues, written to parody the Pastorals of Pope and Philips, entitled respectively the *Basset-Table*, the *Drawing-Room*, and *The Toilet.* They were first ascribed to Gay, to whose mock pastorals they bear much resemblance. Three others were added by the same hand which had written all the *Town Eclogues* except the *Basset-Table*, viz. that of Lady M. W. Montagu.]

CARDELIA. SMILINDA.

CARDELIA.

THE *Basset-Table* spread, the *Tallier* come;[1]
   Why stays SMILINDA in the Dressing-Room?
Rise, pensive Nymph, the *Tallier* waits for you:

[1] [*Basset* was a game commonly played in England at the period after the Restoration; and in France in the reign of Louis XIV., who issued an ordinance prohibiting it and similar games. *Chatto.*]

2 K

SMILINDA.

Ah, Madam, since my SHARPER is untrue,
I joyless make my once ador'd *Alpeu*.   5
I saw him stand behind OMBRELIA'S Chair,
And whisper with that soft, deluding air, ⎫
And those feign'd sighs which cheat the list'ning Fair. ⎭

CARDELIA.

Is this the cause of your Romantic strains?
A mightier grief my heavy heart sustains.   10
As You by Love, so I by Fortune cross'd;
One, one bad *Deal*, Three *Septleva's* have lost.

SMILINDA.

Is that the grief, which you compare with mine?
With ease, the smiles of Fortune I resign:
Would all my gold in one bad *Deal* were gone;   15
Were lovely SHARPER mine, and mine alone.

CARDELIA.

A Lover lost, is but a common care;
And prudent Nymphs against that change prepare:
The KNAVE OF CLUBS thrice lost: Oh! who could guess
This fatal stroke, this unforeseen Distress?   20

SMILINDA.

See BETTY LOVET! very *à propos*,
She all the cares of *Love* and *Play* does know:
Dear BETTY shall th' important point decide;
BETTY, who oft the pain of each has try'd;
Impartial, she shall say who suffers most,   25
By *Cards' Ill Usage*, or by *Lovers lost*.

LOVET.

Tell, tell your griefs; attentive will I stay,
Tho' Time is precious, and I want some Tea.

CARDELIA.

Behold this *Equipage*, by *Mathers* wrought,
With Fifty Guineas (a great Pen'worth) bought.   30
See, on the Tooth-pick, Mars and Cupid strive;
And both the struggling figures seem alive.
Upon the bottom shines the Queen's bright Face;
A Myrtle Foliage round the Thimble-Case.
Jove, Jove himself, does on the Scissors shine;   35
The Metal, and the Workmanship, divine!

SMILINDA.

This *Snuff-Box,* — once the pledge of SHARPER's love,
When rival beauties for the Present strove;
At *Corticelli's* he the Raffle won;
Then first his Passion was in public shown: 40
HAZARDIA blush'd, and turn'd her Head aside,
A Rival's envy (all in vain) to hide.
This *Snuff-Box,* — on the Hinge see Brilliants shine:
This *Snuff-Box* will I stake; the Prize is mine.

CARDELIA.

Alas! far lesser losses than I bear,   45
Have made a Soldier sigh, a Lover swear.
And Oh! what makes the disappointment hard,
'T was my own Lord that drew the *fatal Card.*
In complaisance, I took the *Queen* he gave;
Tho' my own secret wish was for the *Knave.*   50
The *Knave* won *Sonica,* which I had chose;
And, the next *Pull,* my *Septleva* I lose.

SMILINDA.

But ah! what aggravates the killing smart,
The cruel thought, that stabs me to the heart;
This curs'd OMBRELIA, this undoing Fair,   55
By whose vile arts this heavy grief I bear;
She, at whose name I shed these spiteful tears,
She owes to me the very charms she wears.
An awkward Thing, when first she came to Town;
Her Shape unfashion'd, and her Face unknown: 60
She was my friend; I taught her first to spread
Upon her sallow cheeks enliv'ning red:
I introduc'd her to the Park and Plays;
And, by my int'rest, *Cozens* made her Stays.
Ungrateful wretch, with mimic airs grown pert,   65
She dares to steal my Fav'rite Lover's heart.

CARDELIA.

Wretch that I was, how often have I swore,
When WINNALL *tally'd,* I would *punt* no more?
I know the Bite, yet to my Ruin run;
And see the Folly, which I cannot shun.   70

SMILINDA.

How many Maids have SHARPER's vows deceiv'd?
How many curs'd the moment they believ'd?
Yet his known Falsehoods could no Warning prove:
Ah! what is warning to a Maid in Love?

CARDELIA.

But of what marble must that breast be form'd, 75
To gaze on *Basset*, and remain unwarm'd?
When *Kings*, *Queens*, *Knaves*, are set in decent rank;
Expos'd in glorious heaps the tempting Bank,
Guineas, Half-Guineas, all the shining train;
The Winner's pleasure, and the Loser's pain: 80
In bright Confusion open *Rouleaux* lie,
They strike the Soul, and glitter in the Eye.
Fir'd by the sight, all Reason I disdain;
My Passions rise, and will not bear the rein.
Look upon *Basset*, you who Reason boast; 85
And see if Reason must not *there* be lost.

SMILINDA.

What more than marble must that heart compose,
Can hearken coldly to my SHARPER'S Vows?
Then, when he trembles! when his Blushes rise!
When awful Love seems melting in his Eyes! 90
With eager beats his Mechlin Cravat moves:
'*He Loves*,' — I whisper to myself, '*He Loves!*'
Such unfeign'd Passion in his Looks appears,
I lose all Mem'ry of my former Fears;
My panting heart confesses all his charms, 95
I yield at once, and sink into his arms:
Think of that moment, you who Prudence boast;
For such a moment, Prudence well were lost.

CARDELIA.

At the *Groom-Porter's*, batter'd Bullies play,
Some DUKES at *Mary-Bone* bowl Time away.[1] 100
But who the Bowl, or ratt'ling Dice compares
To *Basset's* heav'nly Joys, and pleasing Cares?

SMILINDA.

Soft SIMPLICETTA doats upon a Beau;
PRUDINA likes a Man, and laughs at Show.
Their several graces in my SHARPER meet; 105
Strong as the Footman, as the Master sweet.

LOVET.

Cease your contention, which has been too long;
I grow impatient, and the Tea's too strong.
Attend, and yield to what I now decide;

---

[1] [The Duke of Buckinghamshire (Sheffield) was in the habit of frequenting the bowling-alley behind the manor-house of Marylebone parish. Cunningham's *London*. As to the Groom-Porter's, cf. note to *Dunciad*, Bk. 1. v. 309.]

The *Equipage* shall grace SMILINDA'S Side: 110
The *Snuff-Box* to CARDELIA I decree,
Now leave complaining, and begin your *Tea*.

TO LADY MARY WORTLEY MONTAGU.

[Originally published in a Miscellany of the year 1720.]

I.

IN beauty, or wit,
   No mortal as yet
To question your empire has dared:
   But men of discerning
   Have thought that in learning,   5
To yield to a lady was hard.

II.

Impertinent schools,
   With musty dull rules,
Have reading to females denied;
   So Papists refuse   10
   The Bible to use,
Lest Locks should be wise as their guide.

III.

'T was a woman at first
   (Indeed she was curst)
In knowledge that tasted delight,   15
   And sages agree
   The laws should decree
To the first possessor the right.

IV.

Then bravely, fair dame,
   Resume the old claim,   20
Which to your whole sex does belong;
   And let men receive,
   From a second bright Eve,
The knowledge of right and of wrong.

V.

But if the first Eve   25
   Hard doom did receive,
When only one apple had she,
   What a punishment new
   Shall be found out for you,
Who tasting, have robb'd the whole tree?   30

EXTEMPORANEOUS LINES,

ON THE PICTURE OF LADY MARY W. MONTAGU,

BY KNELLER.

[Bowles, from Dallaway's *Life of Lady M. W. M.*]

THE playful smiles around the dimpled mouth,
   That happy air of majesty and truth;
So would I draw (but oh! 't is vain to try,
My narrow genius does the power deny;)
The equal lustre of the heav'nly mind,   5
Where ev'ry grace with every virtue 's join'd;
Learning not vain, and wisdom not severe,
With greatness easy, and with wit sincere;
With just description show the work divine,
And the whole princess in my work should shine.   10

IMITATION OF TIBULLUS.

POPE, in his letters to Lady Mary Wortley Montagu in the East, expresses a desire, real or fanciful, to meet her. 'But if my fate be such,' he says, 'that this body of mine (which is as ill matched to my mind as any wife to her husband) be left behind in the journey, let the epitaph of Tibullus be set over it.' *Carruthers.* [The letter is in Bowles, Vol. VIII. The original is Tibull. *Lib.* I. *Eleg.* IV. 55–6.]

HERE, stopt by hasty death, Alexis lies,
   Who crossed half Europe, led by Wortley's eyes.

EPITAPHS

ON JOHN HUGHES AND SARAH DREW.

[Pope, in a letter to Lady M. W. Montagu, Sept. 1st, 1718, written from Stanton-Harcourt, Lord Harcourt's seat in Oxfordshire, relates the anecdote of the death of two lovers 'as constant as ever were found in romance,' by name John Hewet and Sarah Drew, who were simultaneously struck by lightning at a harvest-home; and sends her two epitaphs composed by him, 'of which the critics have chosen the godly one.' (See Lord Wharncliffe's *Letters,* &c. II. 100.) Lady Mary (Nov. 1st, *ejusd. ann.*) returned a decidedly cynical answer, with an epitaph of her own, commencing,

> 'Here lie John Hughes and Sarah Drew;
> Perhaps you 'll say, What 's that to you?'

and concluding, after a doubt whether perchance ' 't was not kindly done,' considering the chances of married life,

> 'Now they are happy in their doom,
> For Pope has wrote upon their tomb.'

According to Gay's letter to Mr. F—— (Aug. 9th, 1718), Lord Harcourt, apprehensive that the country people would not understand even the godly epitaph, determined to substitute one 'with something of Scripture in it, and with as little of poetry as Hopkins and Sternhold.' This prose epitaph was also written by Pope.]

WHEN Eastern lovers feed the fun'ral fire,
　On the same pile the faithful fair expire :
Here pitying Heav'n that virtue mutual found,
And blasted both, that it might neither wound.
Hearts so sincere th' Almighty saw well pleas'd,　　5
Sent his own ligt.tning, and the victims seiz'd.

I.

THINK not, by rig'rous judgment seiz'd,
　A pair so faithful could expire ;
Victims so pure Heav'n saw well pleas'd,
　And snatch'd them in celestial fire.　　10

II.

LIVE well, and fear no sudden fate ;
　When God calls virtue to the grave,
Alike 't is justice, soon or late,
　Mercy alike to kill or save.
Virtue unmov'd can hear the call,　　15
And face the flash that melts the ball.

ON THE COUNTESS OF BURLINGTON CUTTING PAPER.

[The lady of Pope's friend, to whom Ep. IV. of the *Moral Essays* is addressed. Her maiden name was Lady Dorothy Saville.]

PALLAS grew vapourish once, and odd,
　She would not do the least right thing,
Either for goddess, or for god,
　Nor work, nor play, nor paint, nor sing.

Jove frown'd, and, " Use," he cried, "those eyes　　5
　So skilful, and those hands so taper ;
Do something exquisite and wise — "
　She bow'd, obey'd him, — and cut paper.

This vexing him who gave her birth,
　Thought by all heaven a burning shame ;　　10
What does she next, but bids, on earth,
　Her Burlington do just the same.

Pallas, you give yourself strange airs ;
　But sure you 'll find it hard to spoil
The sense and taste of one that bears　　15
　The name of Saville and of Boyle.

Alas! one bad example shown ;
　How quickly all the sex pursue!
See, madam, see the arts o'erthrown,
　Between John Overton and you!　　20

ON A PICTURE OF QUEEN CAROLINE,

DRAWN BY LADY BURLINGTON.

PEACE, flattering Bishop ![1] lying Dean![2]
This portrait only paints the Queen!

THE LOOKING–GLASS.

ON MRS. PULTENEY.[3]

WITH scornful mien, and various toss of air,
Fantastic, vain, and insolently fair,
Grandeur intoxicates her giddy brain,
She looks ambition, and she moves disdain.
Far other carriage grac'd her virgin life,5
But charming G——y's lost in P——y's wife.
Not greater arrogance in him we find,
And this conjunction swells at least her mind:
O could the sire renown'd in glass, produce
One faithful mirror for his daughter's use!10
Wherein she might her haughty errors trace,
And by reflection learn to mend her face:
The wonted sweetness to her form restore,
Be what she was, and charm mankind once more!

ON CERTAIN LADIES.

WHEN other fair ones to the shades go down,
Still Chloe, Flavia, Delia, stay in town:
Those ghosts of beauty wandering here reside,
And haunt the places where their honour died.

CELIA.

CELIA, we know, is sixty-five,
Yet Celia's face is seventeen;
Thus winter in her breast must live,
While summer in her face is seen.

How cruel Celia's fate, who hence5
Our heart's devotion cannot try;
Too pretty for our reverence,
Too ancient for our gallantry!

[1] Dr. Gilbert. *Carruthers.* [Or it might be Hoadley.]

[2] Dr. Alured Clarke. *Id.*

[3] [Anna Maria Gumley, daughter of John Gumley of Isleworth, who had gained his fortune by a glass manufactory, was married to Pulteney, afterwards Earl of Bath.]

EPIGRAM.

ENGRAVED ON THE COLLAR OF A DOG WHICH I GAVE TO HIS ROYAL HIGHNESS.[1]

I AM his Highness' dog at Kew;
Pray tell me, sir, whose dog are you?

LINES SUNG BY DURASTANTI[2] WHEN SHE TOOK LEAVE OF THE ENGLISH STAGE.

THE WORDS WERE IN HASTE PUT TOGETHER BY MR. POPE, AT THE REQUEST OF THE EARL OF PETERBOROUGH.

GEN'ROUS, gay, and gallant nation,
  Bold in arms, and bright in arts;
Land secure from all invasion,
  All but Cupid's gentle darts!
From your charms, oh who would run?   5
Who would leave you for the sun?
  Happy soil, adieu, adieu!

Let old charmers yield to new;
  In arms, in arts, be still more shining;
All your joys be still increasing;   10
  All your tastes be still refining;
All your jars for ever ceasing:
  But let old charmers yield to new.
  Happy soil, adieu, adieu!

ON HIS GROTTO AT TWICKENHAM,

COMPOSED OF

MARBLES, SPARS, GEMS, ORES, AND MINERALS.[3]

THOU who shalt stop, where *Thames*' translucent wave
  Shines a broad Mirror thro' the shadowy Cave;
Where ling'ring drops from min'ral Roofs distill,
And pointed Crystals break the sparkling Rill,

---

[1] [Frederick, Prince of Wales. Roscoe traces the idea of this epigram to Sir W. Temple's *Heads designed for an Essay on Conversation.*]

[2] [Margherita Durastanti was brought out at the English Opera-house by Handel, and sang in his operas and those of Boronisni from 1719 to 1723. She then retired, finding herself unable to contend with the superior powers of Cuzzoni.

She took a formal leave of the English stage, for which occasion the above lines were composed by Pope, at her patron's desire. Arbuthnot wrote a burlesque version of them, which is not remarkably witty. See Hogarth's *Memoirs of the Musical Drama.*]

[3] [As to Pope's grotto, see *Introductory Memoir*, p. xxxiv.]

Unpolish'd Gems no ray on Pride bestow,　　　　5
And latent Metals innocently glow:
Approach!　Great NATURE studiously behold;
And eye the Mine without a wish for Gold.
Approach; but awful! Lo! th' Egerian Grot,
Where, nobly-pensive, ST. JOHN sate and thought;　　10
Where *British* sighs from dying WYNDHAM stole,[1]
And the bright flame was shot thro' MARCHMONT'S[2] Soul.
Let such, such only tread this sacred Floor,
Who dare to love their Country, and be poor.

VERSES TO MR. C.[3]

ST. JAMES'S PALACE. LONDON, OCT. 22.

FEW words are best; I wish you well;
　BETHEL, I 'm told, will soon be here;
Some morning walks along the Mall,
　And ev'ning friends, will end the year.

If, in this interval, between　　　　　　　　　5
　The falling leaf and coming frost,
You please to see, on Twit'nam green,
　Your friend, your poet, and your host:

For three whole days you here may rest
　From Office bus'ness, news and strife;　　　　10
And (what most folks would think a jest)
　Want nothing else, except your wife.

TO MR. GAY,

WHO HAD CONGRATULATED MR. POPE ON FINISHING HIS HOUSE AND GARDENS.

AH, friend! 't is true — this truth you lovers know —
　In vain my structures rise, my gardens grow;
In vain fair Thames reflects the double scenes
Of hanging mountains, and of sloping greens:
Joy lives not here, — to happier seats it flies,　　　　5
And only dwells where WORTLEY casts her eyes.
What are the gay parterre, the chequer'd shade,
The morning bower, the ev'ning colonnade,
But soft recesses of uneasy minds,
To sigh unheard in, to the passing winds?　　　　10
So the struck deer in some sequester'd part
Lies down to die, the arrow at his heart;
He, stretch'd unseen in coverts hid from day,
Bleeds drop by drop, and pants his life away.

---

[1] [See *Epil. to Satires.* Dial. II. v. 88.]
[2] [The Earl of Marchmont, afterwards one of Pope's executors.]
[3] [Probably Craggs, who was in office at the time when Pope established himself at Twickenham.]

UPON THE DUKE OF MARLBOROUGH'S HOUSE AT WOODSTOCK.

'Atria longa patent; sed nec cœnantibus usquam,
Nec somno, locus est: quam bene non habitas.'
MARTIAL, *Epigr.* [XII. 50. vv. 7, 8.]

[Blenheim, built by Vanbrugh. 'In his buildings,' says Sir Joshua Reynolds, 'there is a greater display of imagination than we shall find perhaps in any other.' At the same time the heaviness of his style of architecture was the subject of the constant ridicule of Horace Walpole and others.]

SEE, sir, here's the grand approach;
   This way is for his Grace's coach:
There lies the bridge, and here's the clock,
Observe the lion and the cock,
The spacious court, the colonnade,   5
And mark how wide the hall is made!
The chimneys are so well design'd,
They never smoke in any wind.
This gallery's contrived for walking,
The windows to retire and talk in;   10
The council chamber for debate,
And all the rest are rooms of state.
   Thanks, sir, cried I, 't is very fine,
But where d' ye sleep, or where d' ye dine?
I find, by all you have been telling,   15
That 't is a house, but not a dwelling.[1]

ON BEAUFORT HOUSE GATE AT CHISWICK.

[The Lord Treasurer Middlesex's house at Chelsea, after passing to the Duke of Beaufort, was called Beaufort House. It was afterwards sold to Sir Hans Sloane. When the House was taken down in 1740, its gateway, built by Inigo Jones, was given by Sir Hans Sloane to the Earl of Burlington, who removed it with the greatest care to his garden at Chiswick, where it may be still seen. See Cunningham's *London.*]

I WAS brought from Chelsea last year,
   Batter'd with wind and weather;
   Inigo Jones put me together;
Sir Hans Sloane let me alone;
   Burlington brought me hither.

---

[1] The same idea is used by Lord Chesterfield in his *Epigram on Burlington House:*

'How will you *build*, let flatt'ry tell,
And all mankind, how ill you dwell.'
        Bowles.

LINES TO LORD BATHURST.

[In illustration Mitford refers to Pope's letter to Lord Bathurst of September 13, 1732, where 'Mr. L.' is spoken of as 'more inclined to admire God in his greater works, the tall timber.' From Mr. Mitford's notes to his edition of *Gray's Correspondence with the Rev. Norton Nichols.* As to Lord Bathurst's improvements at Cirencester, to which these lines allude, see *Moral Essays,* Ep. IV. vv. 186 ff.]

" A WOOD!" quoth Lewis, and with that
   He laugh'd, and shook his sides of fat.
His tongue, with eye that mark'd his cunning,
Thus fell a-reasoning, not a-running:
"Woods are — not to be too prolix —   5
Collective bodies of straight sticks.
It is, my lord, a mere conundrum
To call things woods for what grows under 'em.
For shrubs, when nothing else at top is,
Can only constitute a coppice.   10
But if you will not take my word,
See anno quint. of Richard Third;
And that's a coppice call'd, when dock'd,
Witness an. prim. of Harry Oct.
If this a wood you will maintain,   15
Merely because it is no plain,
Holland, for all that I can see,
May e'en as well be term'd the sea,
Or C——by [1] be fair harangued
An honest man, because not hang'd."   20

INSCRIPTION ON A PUNCH–BOWL,

IN THE SOUTH-SEA YEAR [1720], FOR A CLUB, CHASED WITH JUPITER PLACING
CALLISTO IN THE SKIES, AND EUROPA WITH THE BULL.

C OME, fill the South Sea goblet full;
   The gods shall of our stock take care;
Europa pleas'd accepts the *Bull,*
And Jove with joy puts off the *Bear.* [2]

VERBATIM FROM BOILEAU.

Un Jour dit un Auteur, etc. [3]

O NCE (says an Author; where, I need not say)
   Two Trav'lers found an Oyster in their way;
Both fierce, both hungry; the dispute grew strong,

[1] Thomas, first Lord Coningsby, a zealous promoter of the Revolution of 1688. *Carruthers.*

[2] [There seems no doubt that these terms originated in the South-Sea year; and that they gradually came into general use. See a lively discussion of the subject, and of the meaning of the terms, in *Notes and Queries* for 1859.]

[3] [This famous fable is narrated at the close

While Scale in hard Dame *Justice* past along.
Before her each with clamour pleads the Laws, 5
Explain'd the matter, and would win the cause.
Dame *Justice* weighing long the doubtful Right,
Takes, opens, swallows it, before their sight.
The cause of strife remov'd so rarely well,
"There take" (says *Justice*) "take ye each a *Shell*. 10
We thrive at *Westminster* on Fools like you:
'T was a fat Oyster — Live in peace — Adieu."

EPIGRAM.

MY Lord[1] complains that Pope, stark mad with gardens,
Has cut three trees, the value of three farthings.
"But he 's my neighbour," cries the peer polite:
"And if he visit me, I 'll waive the right."
What! on compulsion, and against my will, 5
A lord's acquaintance? Let him file his bill!

EPIGRAM.

[Explained by Carruthers to refer to the large sums of money given in charity on
account of the severity of the weather about the year 1740.]

YES! 't is the time, (I cried,) impose the chain,
Destined and due to wretches self-enslaved;
But when I saw such charity remain,
I half could wish this people should be saved.

Faith lost, and Hope, our Charity begins; 5
And 't is a wise design in pitying Heaven,
If this can cover multitude of sins,
To take the *only* way to be forgiven.

OCCASIONED BY READING THE TRAVELS OF CAPTAIN LEMUEL GULLIVER.

ON the publication of *Gulliver's Travels* Pope wrote several pieces of humour
intended to accompany the work, which he sent to Swift; and they were printed in
1727 under the title of *Poems occasioned by reading the Travels of Captain Lemuel Gul-
liver explanatory and commendatory. Roscoe.* [I. II. IV. were also published in the
joint *Miscellanies.*]

of Boileau's *Second Epistle;* and is said to be
originally derived from an old Italian comedy.
La Fontaine, who also versified the fable, sub-
stituted a judge (named Perrin Dandin) for ' Jus-
tice'; wherein, according to Boileau's opinion,
he erred; inasmuch as it is not the judges only,
but all the officers of justice, who empty the pock-
ets of litigants. From a note to Amsterdam edi-
tion (1735) of *Œuvres de Boileau.*]

[1] Lord Radnor. *Warton.*

I.

TO QUINBUS FLESTRIN, THE MAN–MOUNTAIN.

An Ode by Tilly-Tit, Poet Laureate to His Majesty of Lilliput. Translated into English.

IN amaze,
Lost I gaze,
Can our eyes
Reach thy size?
May my lays
Swell with praise,
Worthy thee!
Worthy me!
Muse, inspire,
All thy fire!
Bards of old
Of him told,
When they said
Atlas' head
Propp'd the skies:
See! and believe your eyes!
See him stride
Valleys wide,
Over woods,
Over floods!
When he treads,
Mountains' heads
Groan and shake:
Armies quake:
Lest his spurn

Overturn
Man and steed:
Troops, take heed!
Left and right,
Speed your flight!
Lest an host
Beneath his foot be lost.
Turn'd aside,
From his hide,
Safe from wound,
Darts rebound.
From his nose
Clouds he blows:
When he speaks,
Thunder breaks!
When he eats,
Famine threats!
When he drinks,
Neptune shrinks!
Nigh thy ear,
In mid air,
On thy hand
Let me stand;
So shall I,
Lofty Poet, touch the sky.

II.

THE LAMENTATION OF GLUMDALCLITCH FOR THE LOSS OF GRILDRIG.

A PASTORAL.

SOON as *Glumdalclitch* miss'd her pleasing care,
She wept, she blubber'd, and she tore her hair.
No *British* miss sincerer grief has known,
Her squirrel missing, or her sparrow flown.
She furl'd her sampler, and haul'd in her thread,
And stuck her needle into *Grildrig's* bed;
Then spread her hands, and with a bounce let fall
Her baby, like the giant in *Guildhall*.
In peals of thunder now she roars, and now

5

She gently whimpers like a lowing cow: 10
Yet lovely in her sorrow still appears,
Her locks dishevell'd, and her flood of tears
Seem like the lofty barn of some rich swain,
When from the thatch drips fast a shower of rain.
    In vain she search'd each cranny of the house,   15
Each gaping chink impervious to a mouse.
"Was it for this" (she cry'd) "with daily care
Within thy reach I set the vinegar!
And fill'd the cruet with the acid tide,
While pepper-water worms thy bait supply'd;   20
Where twined the silver eel around thy hook,
And all the little monsters of the brook.
Sure in that lake he dropp'd; my *Grilly's* drown'd."
She dragg'd the cruet, but no *Grildrig* found.
    "Vain is thy courage, *Grilly*, vain thy boast;   25
But little creatures enterprise the most.
Trembling, I 've seen thee dare the kitten's paw,
Nay, mix with children, as they play'd at taw,
Nor fear the marbles, as they bounding flew;
Marbles to them, but rolling rocks to you.   30
    "Why did I trust thee with that giddy youth?
Who from a *Page* can ever learn the truth?
Versed in Court tricks, that money-loving boy
To some Lord's daughter sold the living toy;
Or rent him limb from limb in cruel play,   35
As children tear the wings of flies away.
From place to place o'er *Brobdingnag* I 'll roam,
And never will return or bring thee home.
But who hath eyes to trace the passing wind?
How, then, thy fairy footsteps can I find?   40
Dost thou bewilder'd wander all alone,
In the green thicket of a mossy stone;
Or tumbled from the toadstool's slippery round,
Perhaps all maim'd, lie grov'lling on the ground?
Dost thou, embosom'd in the lovely rose,   45
Or sunk within the peach's down, repose?
Within the king-cup if thy limbs are spread,
Or in the golden cowslip's velvet head:
O show me, *Flora*, midst those sweets, the flower
Where sleeps my *Grildrig* in his fragrant bower.   50
    "But ah! I fear thy little fancy roves
On little females, and on little loves;
Thy pygmy children, and thy tiny spouse,
Thy baby playthings that adorn thy house,
Doors, windows, chimneys, and the spacious rooms,   55
Equal in size to cells of honeycombs.
Hast thou for these now ventured from the shore,
Thy bark a bean-shell, and a straw thy oar?
Or in thy box, now bounding on the main,

Shall I ne'er bear thyself and house again?　　　　　　60
And shall I set thee on my hand no more,
To see thee leap the lines, and traverse o'er
My spacious palm?　Of stature scarce a span,
Mimic the actions of a real man?
No more behold thee turn my watch's key,　　　　　　65
As seamen at a capstern anchors weigh?
How wert thou wont to walk with cautious tread,
A dish of tea like milk-pail on thy head?
How chase the mite that bore thy cheese away,
And keep the rolling maggot at a bay?"　　　　　　70
　　She said, but broken accents stopp'd her voice,
Soft as the speaking-trumpet's mellow noise:
She sobb'd a storm, and wip'd her flowing eyes,
Which seem'd *like* two broad suns in misty skies.
O squander not thy grief;　those tears command　　　　75
To weep upon our cod in *Newfoundland:*
The plenteous pickle shall preserve the fish,
And *Europe* taste thy sorrows in a dish.

III.

TO MR. LEMUEL GULLIVER,

THE GRATEFUL ADDRESS OF THE UNHAPPY HOUYHNHNMS, NOW
IN SLAVERY AND BONDAGE IN ENGLAND.

TO thee, we wretches of the *Houyhnhnm* band,
　　Condemn'd to labour in a barbarous land,
Return our thanks.　Accept our humble lays,
And let each grateful *Houyhnhnm* neigh thy praise.

O happy *Yahoo*, purg'd from human crimes,　　　　　5
By thy sweet sojourn in those virtuous climes,
Where reign our sires;　there, to thy country's shame,
Reason, you found, and virtue were the same.
Their precepts raz'd the prejudice of youth,
And even a *Yahoo* learn'd the love of truth.　　　　10

Art thou the first who did the coast explore;
Did never *Yahoo* tread that ground before?
Yes, thousands!　But in pity to their kind,
Or sway'd by envy, or through pride of mind,
They hid their knowledge of a nobler race,　　　　　15
Which own'd, would all their sires and sons disgrace.

You, like the *Samian*, visit lands unknown,
And by their wiser morals mend your own.
Thus *Orpheus* travell'd to reform his kind,
Came back, and tamed the brutes he left behind.　　　20

You went, you saw, you heard: with virtue fought,
Then spread these morals which the *Houyhnhnms* taught.
Our labours here must touch thy generous heart,
To see us strain before the coach and cart;
Compell'd to run each knavish jockey's heat!   25
Subservient to *Newmarket's* annual cheat!

With what reluctance do we lawyers bear,
To fleece their country clients twice a year?
Or managed in your schools, for fops to ride,
How foam, how fret beneath a load of pride!   30
Yes, we are slaves — but yet, by reason's force,
Have learn'd to bear misfortune, like a Horse.

O would the stars, to ease my bonds, ordain,
That gentle *Gulliver* might guide my rein!
Safe would I bear him to his journey's end,   35
For 't is a pleasure to support a friend.
But if my life be doom'd to serve the bad,
O! may'st thou never want an easy pad!

                                                  HOUYHNHNM.

IV.

MARY GULLIVER TO CAPTAIN LEMUEL GULLIVER.

AN EPISTLE.

ARGUMENT.

THE Captain, some time after his return, being retired to Mr. Sympson's in the country, Mrs. Gulliver, apprehending from his late behaviour some estrangement of his affections, writes him the following expostulating, soothing, and tenderly complaining epistle.

WELCOME, thrice welcome, to thy native place!
    — What, touch me not? what, shun a wife's embrace?
Have I for this thy tedious absence borne,
And wak'd, and wish'd whole nights for thy return?
In five long years I took no second spouse;   5
What *Redriff* wife so long hath kept her vows?
Your eyes, your nose, inconstancy betray;
Your nose you stop; your eyes you turn away.
'T is said, that thou should'st *cleave unto thy Wife*;
Once *thou* didst cleave, and I could cleave for life.   10
Hear, and relent! hark how thy children moan;
Be kind at least to these: they are thy own;
Be bold, and count them all; secure to find
The honest number that you left behind.
See how they pat thee with their pretty paws: 15
Why start you? are they snakes? or have they claws?

2 L

Thy Christian seed, our mutual flesh and bone:
Be kind at least to these, they are thy own.
  Biddel, like thee, might farthest *India* rove;
He changed his country, but retain'd his love.   20
There 's Captain *Pennell,* absent half his life,
Comes back, and is the kinder to his wife.
Yet *Pennell's* wife is brown, compared to me;
And Mrs. *Biddel* sure is fifty-three.
  Not touch me! never neighbour call'd me slut: 25
Was *Flimnap's* dame more sweet in *Lilliput?*
I 've no red hair to breathe an odious fume;
At least thy consort 's cleaner than thy *Groom.*
Why then that dirty stable-boy thy care?
What mean those visits to the *Sorrel Mare?*   30
Say, by what witchcraft, or what demon led, —
Preferr'st thou *Litter* to the marriage bed!
  Some say the devil himself is in that *Mare:*
If so, our *Dean* shall drive him forth by prayer.
Some think you mad, some think you are possess'd;   35
That *Bedlam* and clean straw will suit you best.
Vain means, alas! this frenzy to appease,
That straw, that straw, would heighten the disease.
  My bed (the scene of all our former joys,
Witness two lovely girls, two lovely boys,)   40
Alone I press; in dreams I call my dear,
I stretch my hand, no *Gulliver* is there!
I wake, I rise, and, shivering with the frost,
Search all the house, — my *Gulliver* is lost!
Forth in the street I rush with frantic cries;   45
The windows open, all the neighbours rise:
"Where sleeps my Gulliver? O tell me where!"
The neighbours answer, "With the *Sorrel Mare.*"
  At early morn, I to the market haste,
(Studious in everything to please thy taste;)   50
A curious *Fowl* and *Sparagrass* I chose
(For I remember you were fond of those);
Three shillings cost the first, the last seven groats;
Sullen you turn from both, and call for *Oats.*
  Others bring goods and treasure to their houses,   55
Something to deck their pretty babes and spouses;
My *only* token was a cup like horn,
That 's made of nothing but a lady's corn.
'T is not for that I grieve; no, 't is to see
The *Groom* and *Sorrel Mare* preferr'd to me!   60
  These, for some moments when you deign to quit,
And (at due distance) sweet discourse admit,
'T is all my pleasure thy past toil to know,
For pleased remembrance builds delight on woe.
At every danger pants thy consort's breast,   65
And gaping infants squall to hear the rest.

How did I tremble, when, by thousands bound,
I saw thee stretch'd on *Lilliputian* ground?
When scaling armies climb'd up every part,
Each step they trod, I felt upon my heart. 70
But when thy torrent quench'd the dreadful blaze,
King, queen, and nation, staring with amaze,
Full in my view how all my husband came,
And what extinguish'd theirs, increas'd my flame.
Those *Spectacles*, ordain'd thine eyes to save, 75
Were once my present; *Love* that armour gave.
How did I mourn at *Bolgolam's* decree!
For when he sign'd thy death, he sentenc'd me.

   When folks might see thee all the country round
For sixpence, I 'd have giv'n a thousand pound. 80
Lord! when the *Giant-babe* that head of thine
Got in his mouth, my heart was up in mine!
When in the *Marrow-bone* I see thee ramm'd;
Or on the house-top by the *Monkey* cramm'd,
The piteous images renew my pain, 85
And all thy dangers I weep o'er again.
But on the *Maiden's Nipple* when you rid,
Pray Heav'n, 't was all a wanton maiden did!
Glumdalclitch too — with thee I mourn her case:
Heav'n guard the gentle girl from all disgrace! 90
O may the king that one neglect forgive,
And pardon her the fault by which I live!
Was there no other way to set him free?
My life, alas! I fear proved death to thee.

   O teach me, dear, new words to speak my flame! 95
Teach me to woo thee by thy best-loved name!
Whether the style of *Grildrig* please the most,
So call'd on *Brobdingnag's* stupendous coast,
When on the Monarch's ample hand you sate,
And halloo'd in his ear intrigues of state; 100
Or *Quinbus Flestrin* more endearment brings;
When like a Mountain you looked down on kings:
If ducal *Nardac, Lilliputian* peer,
Or *Glumglum's* humbler title soothe thy ear:
Nay, would kind *Jove* my organs so dispose, 105
To hymn harmonious *Houyhnhnm* through the nose,
I 'd call thee *Houyhnhnm*, that high-sounding name;
Thy children's noses all should twang the same.
So might I find my loving spouse of course .
Endu'd with all the *Virtues* of a *Horse*. 110

LINES ON SWIFT'S ANCESTORS.

[Swift set up a plain monument to his grandfather, and also presented a cup to the church of Goodrich, or Gotheridge (in Herefordshire). He sent a pencilled elevation of the monument (a simple tablet) to Mrs. Howard, who returned it with the following lines, inscribed on the drawing by Pope. The paper is endorsed, in Swift's hand: 'Model of a monument for my grandfather, with Pope's roguery.'

Scott's *Life of Swift*.]

JONATHAN SWIFT
  Had the gift,
By fatherige, motherige,
And by brotherige,
To come from Gotherige,[1]
But now is spoil'd clean,
And an Irish dean:

In this church he has put
A stone of two foot,
With a cup and a can, sir,
In respect to his grandsire ;
So, Ireland, change thy tone,
And cry, O hone! O hone!
For England hath its own.

FROM THE GRUB-STREET JOURNAL.

[This Journal was established in January, 1730, and carried on for eight years by Pope and his friends, in answer to the attacks provoked by the *Dunciad*. It corresponds in some measure to the *Xenien* of Goethe and Schiller. Only such pieces are here inserted as bear Pope's distinguishing signature A.; several others are probably his.]

I.

EPIGRAM

Occasioned by seeing some sheets of Dr. Bentley's edition of Milton's *Paradise Lost*.[2]

DID Milton's prose, O Charles, thy death defend?
  A furious foe unconscious proves a friend.
On Milton's verse does Bentley comment? — Know
A weak officious friend becomes a foe.
While he but sought his Author's fame to further,   5
The murderous critic has aveng'd thy murder.

II.

EPIGRAM.

SHOULD D——s [3] print, how once you robb'd your brother,
Traduc'd your monarch, and debauch'd your mother ;
Say, what revenge on D——s can be had ;
Too dull for laughter, for reply too mad?
Of one so poor you cannot take the law ;   5
On one so old your sword you scorn to draw.
Uncag'd then let the harmless monster rage,
Secure in dulness, madness, want, and age.

---

[1] Goodrich, or Gotheridge, in Herefordshire, where Swift had erected a monument to his grandfather, presenting a cup to the church at the same time. *Scott.*

[2] [Cf. *Dunciad*, Bk. IV. v. 212. 'Milton's prose' is the *Defensio pro populo Anglicano* &c. of 1649; and the *Defensio Secunda* of 1654.]

[3] [Dennis.]

III.

MR. J. M. S——E.[1]

Catechised on his One Epistle to Mr. Pope.

WHAT makes you write at this odd rate?
Why, Sir, it is to imitate.
What makes you steal and trifle so?
Why, 't is to do as others do.
But there 's no meaning to be seen.   5
Why, that 's the very thing I mean.

IV.

EPIGRAM.

On Mr. M——re's going to law with Mr. Gilliver: inscribed to Attorney Tibbald.

ONCE in his life M——re judges right:
  His sword and pen not worth a straw,
An author that could never write,
A gentleman that dares not fight,
  Has but one way to tease — by law.
This suit, dear Tibbald, kindly hatch;
  Thus thou may'st help the sneaking elf;
And sure a printer is his match,
  Who 's but a publisher himself.

V.

EPIGRAM.

A GOLD watch found on cinder whore,
Or a good verse on J——y M——e,
Proves but what either should conceal,
Not that they 're rich, but that they steal.

VI.

EPITAPH.

[On James Moore-Smythe.]

HERE lies what had nor birth, nor shape, nor fame;
No gentleman! no man! no-thing! no name!
For Jamie ne'er grew James; and what they call
More, shrunk to Smith — and Smith 's no name at all.
Yet die thou can'st not, phantom, oddly fated: 5
For how can no-thing be annihilated?[2]
        Ex nihilo nihil fit.

[1] [James Moore-Smythe.]   [2] [Cf. *Dunciad*, Bk. II. v. 50.]

VII.

A QUESTION BY ANONYMOUS.

TELL, if you can, which did the worse,
    Caligula or Gr——n's[1] Gr—ce?
That made a Consul of a horse,
    And *this* a Laureate of an ass.

VIII.

EPIGRAM.

GREAT G——,[2] such servants since thou well can'st lack,
Oh! save the salary, and drink the sack.

IX.

EPIGRAM.

BEHOLD! ambitious of the British bays,
Cibber and Duck[3] contend in rival lays.
But, gentle Colley, should thy verse prevail,
Thou hast no fence, alas! against his flail:
Therefore thy claim resign, allow his right: 5
For Duck can thresh, you know, as well as write.

ON SEEING THE LADIES AT CRUX–EASTON WALK IN THE WOODS BY THE GROTTO.

EXTEMPORE BY MR. POPE.

AUTHORS the world and their dull brains have traced
    To fix the ground where Paradise was placed;
Mind not their learned whims and idle talk;
Here, here's the place where these bright angels walk.

INSCRIPTION ON A GROTTO, THE WORK OF NINE LADIES.

[Carruthers, from *Dodsley's Miscellany*.]

HERE, shunning idleness at once and praise,
    This radiant pile nine rural sisters raise;
The glittering emblem of each spotless dame,
Clear as her soul and shining as her frame;

---

[1] [The Duke of Grafton.]
[2] [King George II. The epigram is of course on the Laureate Cibber.]
[3] [Stephen Duck, originally a thresher, concerning whom there are other verses in the Journal, probably written by Pope. Cf. *Imitations of Horace*, Bk. II. Ep. II. v. 140.]

Beauty which nature only can impart, 5
And such a polish as disgraces art;
But Fate disposed them in this humble sort,
And hid in deserts what would charm a Court.

VERSES LEFT BY MR. POPE,

ON HIS LYING IN THE SAME BED WHICH WILMOT, THE CELEBRATED EARL OF ROCHESTER, SLEPT IN AT ADDERBURY, THEN BELONGING TO THE DUKE OF ARGYLE,[1] JULY 9TH, 1739.

WITH no poetic ardour fir'd
   I press the bed where Wilmot lay;
That here he lov'd, or here expir'd,
   Begets no numbers grave or gay.

Beneath thy roof, Argyle, are bred 5
   Such thoughts as prompt the brave to lie
Stretch'd out in honour's nobler bed,
   Beneath a nobler roof — the sky.

Such flames as high in patriots burn,
   Yet stoop to bless a child or wife; 10
And such as wicked kings may mourn,
   When freedom is more dear than life.

TO THE RIGHT HON. THE EARL OF OXFORD,

UPON A PIECE OF NEWS IN MIST [MIST'S JOURNAL], THAT THE REV. MR. W. REFUS'D TO WRITE AGAINST MR. POPE BECAUSE HIS BEST PATRON HAD A FRIENDSHIP FOR THE SAID P.

[From Nichols's *Literary Anecdotes*, where it is given in facsimile; accompanied by the statement that ' W.' alluded to was Samuel Wesley, and ' Father Francis,' the then exiled Bishop of Rochester (Atterbury).]

WESLEY, if Wesley 't is they mean,
   They say on Pope would fall,
Would his best Patron let his Pen
   Discharge his inward Gall.

What Patron this, a doubt must be, 5
   Which none but you can clear,
Or father Francis, cross the sea,
   Or else Earl Edward here.

That both were good must be confess'd,
   And much to both he owes; 10
But which to Him will be the best
   The Lord of Oxford knows.

[1] [As to the Duke of Argyle, cf. *Epilogue to Satires, Dial.* II. v. 82.]

TRANSLATION OF A PRAYER OF BRUTUS.

THE Rev. Aaron Thompson, of Queen's College, Oxon., translated the *Chronicle of Geoffrey of Monmouth.* He submitted the translation to Pope, 1717, who gave him the following lines, being a translation of a prayer of Brutus. *Carruthers.*

GODDESS of woods, tremendous in the chase,
To mountain wolves and all the savage race,
Wide o'er the aërial vault extend thy sway, .
And o'er the infernal regions void of day.
On thy third reign look down ; disclose our fate,   5
In what new station shall we fix our seat?
When shall we next thy hallow'd altars raise,
And choirs of virgins celebrate thy praise?

LINES WRITTEN IN EVELYN'S BOOK ON COINS.[1]

[" Wrote by Mr. P. in a Volume of *Evelyn on Coins* presented to a painter by a parson." *Gentleman's Magazine* for 1735. " Wrote in Evelyn's *Book of Coins* given by Mr. Wood to Kent." *Notes and Queries*, March 13, 1851, from a copy by Mason.]

TOM WOOD of Chiswick, deep divine,
To painter Kent gave all this coin.
'T is the first coin, I 'm bold to say,
That ever churchman gave to lay.

TO MR. THOMAS SOUTHERN,

On his Birth-day, 1742.[2]

RESIGN'D to live, prepar'd to die,
With not one sin, but poetry,
This day TOM'S fair account has run
(Without a blot) to eighty-one.
Kind Boyle, before his poet, lays   5
A table,[3] with a cloth of bays ;
And Ireland, mother of sweet singers,
Presents her harp [4] still to his fingers.

---

[1] [*Numismata: a Discourse on Medals ;* published at London in 1697.]

[2] [Southern, the author of *Oroonoko*, according to Warton's expression, ' lived the longest and died one of the richest of all our poets.' He was born in 1660, and died in 1746. The date of the first production of *Oroonoko* is 1696, and it kept the stage till the third decade of the present century, a rare example of popularity attaching to a drama founded on a sensation novel ; for Mrs. Aphra Behn's *Oroonoko* was the *Uncle Tom's Cabin* of her day.]

[3] *A table*] He was invited to dine on his birth-day with this Nobleman (Lord Orrery), who had prepared for him the entertainment of which the bill of fare is here set down. *Warburton.* [John Earl of Cork and Orrery was a friend of Swift, Pope, and Bolingbroke, and in earlier days a member of the Brothers' Club. He died in 1762.]

[4] *Presents her harp*] The Harp is generally wove on the Irish Linen ; such as Table-cloths, &c. *Warburton.*

The feast, his tow'ring genius marks
In yonder wild goose and the larks!   10
The mushrooms shew his wit was sudden!
And for his judgment, lo a pudden!
Roast beef, tho' old, proclaims him stout,
And grace, altho' a bard, devout.
May TOM, whom heav'n sent down to raise   15
The price of prologues and of plays,[1]
Be ev'ry birth-day more a winner,
Digest his thirty thousandth dinner;
Walk to his grave without reproach,
And scorn a rascal and a coach.   20

BISHOP HOUGH.[2]

A BISHOP, by his neighbours hated,
  Has cause to wish himself translated;
But why should HOUGH desire translation,
Loved and esteemed by all the nation?
Yet if it be the old man's case,   5
I 'll lay my life I know the place:
'T is where God sent some that adore him,
And whither Enoch went before him.

PRAYER OF ST. FRANCIS XAVIER.

[Translated from an *Oratio a Sancto Xavierio composita*, at the desire of a Catholic priest named Brown. *Gentleman's Magazine*, October, 1791, where the original is given commencing '*O Deus ego amo te.*']

THOU art my God, sole object of my love;
  Not for the hope of endless joys above;
Not for the fear of endless pains below,
Which they who love thee not must undergo.

For me, and such as me, thou deign'st to bear   5
An ignominious cross, the nails, the spear:
A thorny crown transpierc'd thy sacred brow,
While bloody sweats from ev'ry member flow.

---

[1] *The price of prologues and of plays,*] This alludes to a story Mr. Southern told about the same, to Mr. P. and Mr. W. of Dryden; who, when Southern first wrote for the stage, was so famous for his Prologues, that the players would act nothing without that decoration. His usual price till then had been four guineas: but when Southern came to him for the Prologue he had bespoke, Dryden told him he must have six guineas for it; "which (said he) young man, is out of no disrespect to you, but the Players have had my goods too cheap." *Warburton.* [This was the regular tariff for prologues and epilogues. Later, Southern could tell Dryden (according to Warton) that he had cleared £700 by a single play, while Dryden never made more than a seventh of that sum by one drama.]

[2] [Bishop of Worcester. Deprived by James II. of the Presidentship of Magdalene College, Oxford; he afterwards successively held several sees, and died in 1743.]

For me in tortures thou resignd'st thy breath,
Embrac'd me on the cross, and sav'd me by thy death.   10
And can these sufferings fail my heart to move?
What but thyself can now deserve my love?

Such as then was, and is, thy love to me,
Such is, and shall be still, my love to thee —
To thee, Redeemer! mercy's sacred spring!   15
My God, my Father, Maker, and my King!

APPENDIX.

I.

1740.

A POEM.

[This unfinished piece was communicated to Warton by Dr. Wilson, formerly Fellow and Librarian of Trinity College, Dublin, to whom it had been lent by a grandson of Lord Chetwynd, 'an intimate friend of the famous Lord Bolingbroke, who gratified his curiosity by a box full of the rubbish and sweepings of Pope's study, whose executor he was, in conjunction with Lord Marchmont.' It is possible that Bowles's conjecture may be correct, according to which '1740' was to grow into the third Dialogue which Pope at one time intended to add to the *Epilogue to the Satires.* See the *Verses on receiving from Lady Frances Shirley a Standish,* &c. *ante,* p. 467]. Roscoe doubts whether so mediocre a production be Pope's: Carruthers also hesitates on the subject; and the piece is at most to be taken as a few rough jottings accidentally discovered.]

O WRETCHED B——![1] jealous now of all,
   What God, what mortal, shall prevent thy fall?
Turn, turn thy eyes from wicked men in place,
And see what succour from the Patriot Race.
C——,[2] his own proud dupe, thinks Monarchs things   5
Made just for him, as other fools for Kings;
Controls, decides, insults thee every hour,
And antedates the hatred due to Pow'r.
   Through Clouds of Passion P——'s[3] views are clear,
He foams a Patriot to subside a peer;   10
Impatient sees his country bought and sold,
And damns the market where he takes no gold.
   Grave, righteous S——[4] jogs on till, past belief,
He finds himself companion with a thief.
   To purge and let thee blood, with fire and sword,   15
Is all the help stern S——[5] would afford.
   That those who bind and rob thee, would not kill,
Good C——[6] hopes, and candidly sits still.
   Of Ch——s W——[7] who speaks at all,
No more than of Sir Har—y[8] or Sir P——?[9]   20
Whose names once up, they thought it was not wrong
To lie in bed, but sure they lay too long.

[1] Britain. *Bowles.*

[2] Cobham. *Bowles.* This is impossible. *Roscoe.* Campbell (Argyle), or Cholmondely. *Carruthers.*

[3] Pulteney. *Carruthers.*

[4] Sandys. *Bowles.* [Afterwards Lord Sandys.]

[5] Shippen. *Bowles, Carruthers.* Impossible. *Roscoe.*

[6] Carlisle? *Bowles.* Cornbury. *Carruthers.*

[7] Sir Charles Hanbury Williams. *Bowles.*

[8] Sir Henry Oxenden. *Bowles.*

[9] Sir Paul Methuen. *Bowles.*

G——r,[1] C——m,[2] B——t,[3] pay thee due **regards**,
Unless the ladies bid them mind their cards.
with wit that must

And C——d,[4] who speaks so well and writes,   25
Whom (saving W.[5]) every S.[6] harper bites.
must needs

Whose wit and   equally provoke one,
Finds thee, at best, the butt to crack his joke on.
As for the rest, each winter up they run,
And all are clear, that something must be done,   30
Then, urged by C——t,[7] or by C——t stopp'd,
Inflam'd by P——,[8] and by P—— dropp'd;
They follow rev'rently each wondrous wight,
Amaz'd that one can read, that one can write:
So geese to gander prone obedience keep,   35
Hiss, if he hiss, and if he slumber, sleep.
Till having done whate'er was fit or fine,
Utter'd a speech, and ask'd their friends to dine;
Each hurries back to his paternal ground,
Content but for five shillings in the pound;   40
Yearly defeated, yearly hopes they give,
And all agree, Sir Robert cannot live.
Rise, rise, great W——,[9] fated to appear,
Spite of thyself, a glorious minister!
Speak the loud language Princes   45
And treat with half the . . . .
At length to B—— [10] kind, as to thy . . . .
Espouse the nation, you . . . .
What can thy H [11] . . . .
Dress in Dutch   50
Tho' sfill he travels on no bad pretence,
To show . . . .
Or those foul copies of thy face and tongue,
Veracious W——,[12] and frontless Young;[13]
Sagacious Bubb,[14] so late a friend, and there   55
So late a foe, yet more sagacious H——?[15]
Hervey and Hervey's school, F—, H——y, H——n,[16]
Yea, moral Ebor, or religious Winton.[17]
How! what can O——w, what can D——,[18]

[1][2][3] Lords Gower, Cobham and Bathurst. *Bowles.*

[4] Lord Chesterfield. *Bowles.*

[5] Peter Walter? *Carruthers?*

[6] ['The Earl of Chesterfield was . . . fond of play, and was partial to the company of Mr. Lookup, one of the most noted professional gamesters of the day.' Chatto's *History of Playing-Cards*, p. 173.]

[7] Lord Carteret. *Bowles.* [Afterwards Lord Granville.]

[8] Pulteney. *Bowles.*

[9] Sir Robert Walpole. *Bowles.*

[10] Britain. *Carruthers.*

[11] Horace Walpole, brother of Sir Robert, who had just quitted his embassy at the Hague. *Bowles.*

[12][13] W. Winnington. *Bowles.* [A member of the ministry.] Sir William Yonge. *Bowles.*

[14] Doddington [afterwards Lord Melcombe].

[15] Probably Hare, Bp. of Chichester. *Bowles.*

[16] Fox, Henley, Hinton. *Bowles.*

[17] Blackburn, Archbishop of York, and Hoadley, Bishop of Winchester. *Bowles.*

[18] Speaker Onslow and Lord Delaware, chairmen of committees of House of Lords. *Bowles.*

The wisdom of the one and other chair, 60
N——,[1] laugh, or D——s[2] sager,
Or the dread truncheon, M.'s mighty peer?[3]
What help from J——'s[4] opiates canst thou draw,
Or H——k's quibbles voted into law?[5]
C. that Roman in his nose alone,[6] 65
Who hears all causes, B——,[7] but thy own,
Or those proud fools whom nature, rank, and fate
Made fit companions for the Sword of State.
  Can the light packhorse, or the heavy steer,
The sousing Prelate,[8] or the sweating Peer, 70
Drag out, with all its dirt and all its weight,
The lumb'ring carriage of thy broken State?
Alas! the people curse, the carman swears,
The drivers quarrel, and the master stares.
  The plague is on thee, Britain, and who tries 75
To save thee, in th' infectious office, *dies.*
The first firm P——y,[9] soon resign'd his breath.
Brave S——[10] lov'd thee, and was lied to death.
Good M—m—t's fate tore P——th from thy side,[11]
And thy last sigh was heard, when W——m died.[12] 80
  Thy nobles Sl—s, thy Se—s bought with gold,
Thy Clergy perjur'd, thy whole people sold.
An Atheist ☽ a ⊕''''s ad . . . . . .
Blotch thee all o'er, and sink . . . . .
  Alas! on one alone our all relies,[13] 85
Let him be honest, and he must be wise;
Let him no trifler from his   school,
Nor like his . . . . still a . . . .
Be but a man! unminister'd, alone,
And free at once the Senate and the Throne; 90
Esteem the public love his best supply,
A ☉'s true glory his integrity;
Rich *with* his . . . . *in* . . . his strong,
Affect no conquest, but endure no wrong.
Whatever his religion or his blood, 95
His public virtue makes his title good.
Europe's just balance and our own may stand,
And one man's honesty redeem the land.

---

[1] Duke of Newcastle. *Bowles.*

[2] Duke of Dorset. *Bowles.*

[3] The (second) Duke of Marlborough. *Bowles.*

[4] Sir Joseph Jekyll. *Bowles.* Probably; but he died in 1738. *Carruthers.*

[5] Lord Chancellor Hardwicke. *Bowles.*

[6] Probably Sir John Cummins, C. J. of the Common Pleas. *Bowles.* Or Spencer Compton, Lord Wilmington, President of the Council. *Carruthers.*

[7] Britain. *Bowles.*

[8] Sherlock. *Carruthers.* [Cf. *Dunciad*, Bk.

II. v. 323, where 'his pond'rous grace' may correspond to 'the sweating peer' in this passage.]

[9] Pulteney. *Carruthers.*

[10] Earl of Scarborough (*ow*). *Bowles.*

[11] Earl of Marchmont and his son, Lord Polwarth. *Bowles.* The former died in Jan. 1740. *Carruthers.*

[12] Sir William Wyndham. *Bowles.* He died in June, 1740. *Carruthers.*

[13] [Obviously the Pretender, concerning the intrigues with whom in this year see Chap. xxi. of Lord Stanhope's *Hist. of Engl.*]

APPENDIX.

II.

SYLVIA. A FRAGMENT.[1]

SYLVIA, my heart in wondrous wise alarmed,
   Awed without sense, and without beauty charmed:
But some odd graces and some flights she had,
Was just not ugly, and was just not mad:
Her tongue still ran on credit from her eyes,   5
More pert than witty, more a wit than wise:
Good nature, she declared it, was her scorn:
Though 'twas by that alone she could be borne:
Affronting all, yet fond of a good name;
A fool to pleasure, yet a slave to fame: 10
Now coy, now studious in no point to fall,
Now all agog for D—y at a ball:[2]
Now deep in Taylor and the Book of Martyrs,
Now drinking citron with his Grace and Chartres.[3]
   Men, some to business, some to pleasure take,   15
But every woman is at heart a rake,
Frail feverish sex; their fit now chills, now burns:
Atheism and superstition rule by turns;
And a mere heathen in her carnal part,
Is still a sad good Christian in her heart.   20

---

[1] First published in the Miscellanies, 1727. It will be seen by comparing these lines with verses 45-68 of the Second Moral Essay [see p. 242], that the poet afterwards divided the character into two, and developed into the portraits of Calypso and Narcissa.

[2] *i.e.*, Durfey.

[3] The Duke of Wharton and Francis Chartres, for whom see Moral Essay iii. 20.

APPENDIX.

III.

THE RAPE OF THE LOCK.

Nolueram, Belinda, tuos violare capillos
 Sed juvat, hæc precibus me tribuisse tuis. — MART.

FIRST EDITION.

THE RAPE OF THE LOCK.

CANTO I.

WHAT dire offence from am'rous causes springs,
    What mighty quarrels rise from trivial things,
I sing — This verse to C—l, Muse! is due:
This, ev'n Belinda may vouchsafe to view:
Slight is the subject, but not so the praise,   5
If she inspire, and he approve my lays.
    Say what strange motive, goddess! could compel
A well-bred lord t' assault a gentle belle?
O say what stranger cause, yet unexplored,
Could make a gentle belle reject a lord?   10
And dwells such rage in softest bosoms then,
And lodge such daring souls in little men?
    Sol through white curtains did his beams display,
And ope'd those eyes which brighter shine than they,
Shock just had giv'n himself the rousing shake,   15
And nymphs prepared their chocolate to take;
Thrice the wrought slipper knocked against the ground,
And striking watches the tenth hour resound.
Belinda rose, and midst attending dames,
Launched on the bosom of the silver Thames: 20
A train of well-dressed youths around her shone,
And ev'ry eye was fixed on her alone:
On her white breast a sparkling cross she wore
Which Jews might kiss and infidels adore.
Her lively looks a sprightly mind disclose,   25
Quick as her eyes, and as unfixed as those:
Favours to none, to all she smiles extends;
Oft she rejects, but never once offends.
Bright as the sun, her eyes the gazers strike,
And, like the sun, they shine on all alike.   30
Yet graceful ease, and sweetness void of pride,
Might hide her faults, if belles had faults to hide:
If to her share some female errors fall,
Look on her face, and you 'll forgive 'em all.
    This nymph, to the destruction of mankind,   35
Nourished two locks, which graceful hung behind
In equal curls, and well conspired to deck
With shining ringlets her smooth iv'ry neck.
Love in these labyrinths his slaves detains,

And mighty hearts are held in slender chains.   40
With hairy springes we the birds betray,
Slight lines of hair surprise the finny prey,
Fair tresses man's imperial race insnare,
And beauty draws us with a single hair.
   Th' adventurous baron the bright locks admired;   45
He saw, he wished, and to the prize aspired.
Resolved to win, he meditates the way,
By force to ravish, or by fraud betray;
For when success a lover's toil attends,
Few ask if fraud or force attained his ends.   50
   For this, ere Phœbus rose, he had implored
Propitious heav'n, and every pow'r adored,
But chiefly Love — to Love an altar built,
Of twelve vast French romances, neatly gilt.
There lay the sword-knot Sylvia's hands had sewn   55
With Flavia's busk that oft had wrapped his own:
A fan, a garter, half a pair of gloves,
And all the trophies of his former loves.
With tender billets-doux he lights the pire,
And breathes three am'rous sighs to raise the fire.   60
Then prostrate falls, and begs with ardent eyes
Soon to obtain, and long possess the prize:
The pow'rs gave ear, and granted half his pray'r,
The rest the winds dispersed in empty air.
   Close by those meads, for ever crowned with flow'rs,   65
Where Thames with pride surveys his rising tow'rs,
There stands a structure of majestic frame,
Which from the neighb'ring Hampton takes its name.
Here Britain's statesmen oft the fall foredoom
Of foreign tyrants, and of nymphs at home;   70
Here thou, great Anna! whom three realms obey,
Dost sometimes counsel take — and sometimes tea.
   Hither our nymphs and heroes did resort,
To taste awhile the pleasures of a court,
In various talk the cheerful hours they passed,   75
Of who was bit, or who capotted last;
This speaks the glory of the British queen,
And that describes a charming Indian screen;
A third interprets motions, looks, and eyes;
At ev'ry word a reputation dies.   80
Snuff, or the fan, supply each pause of chat,
With singing, laughing, ogling, and all that.
   Now when, declining from the noon of day,
The sun obliquely shoots his burning ray;
When hungry judges soon the sentence sign,   85
And wretches hang that jurymen may dine;
When merchants from th' Exchange return in peace,
And the long labours of the toilet cease,
The board 's with cups and spoons, alternate, crowned,

The berries crackle, and the mill turns round;   90
On shining altars of Japan they raise
The silver lamp, and fiery spirits blaze:
From silver spouts the grateful liquors glide,
While China's earth receives the smoking tide.
At once they gratify their smell and taste,   95
While frequent cups prolong the rich repast.
Coffee (which makes the politician wise,
And see through all things with his half-shut eyes)
Sent up in vapours to the baron's brain
New stratagems, the radiant lock to gain.   100
Ah cease, rash youth! desist ere 't is too late,
Fear the just gods, and think of Scylla's fate!
Changed to a bird, and sent to flit in air,
She dearly pays for Nisus' injured hair!
But when to mischief mortals bend their mind,   105
How soon fit instruments of ill they find!
Just then, Clarissa drew with tempting grace
A two-edged weapon from her shining case:
So ladies, in romance, assist their knight,
Present the spear, and arm him for the fight;   110
He takes the gift with rev'rence, and extends
The little engine on his fingers' ends;
This just behind Belinda's neck he spread,
As o'er the fragrant steams she bends her head.
He first expands the glitt'ring forfex wide   115
T' enclose the lock; then joins it, to divide;
One fatal stroke the sacred hair does sever
From the fair head, for ever, and for ever!
The living fires come flashing from her eyes,
And screams of horror rend th' affrighted skies.   120
Not louder shrieks by dames to heav'n are cast,
When husbands die, or lapdogs breathe their last;
Or when rich china vessels, fall'n from high,
In glitt'ring dust and painted fragments lie!
"Let wreaths of triumph now my temples twine,"   125
The victor cried, "the glorious prize is mine!
While fish in streams, or birds delight in air,
Or in a coach and six the British fair,
As long as Atalantis shall be read,
Or the small pillow grace a lady's bed,   130
While visits shall be paid on solemn days,
When num'rous wax-lights in bright order blaze,
While nymphs take treats, or assignations give,
So long my honour, name, and praise shall live!"
What time would spare, from steel receives its date,   135
And monuments, like men, submit to fate!
Steel did the labour of the gods destroy,
And strike to dust th' aspiring tow'rs of Troy;
Steel could the works of mortal pride confound,

And hew triumphal arches to the ground.   140
What wonder then, fair nymph! thy hairs should feel
The conqu'ring force of unresisted steel?

‾ CANTO II.

BUT anxious cares the pensive nymph oppressed,
And secret passions laboured in her breast.
Not youthful kings in battle seized alive,
Not scornful virgins who their charms survive,
Not ardent lover robbed of all his bliss,   5
Not ancient lady when refused a kiss,
Not tyrants fierce that unrepenting die,
Not Cynthia when her manteau's pinned awry,
E'er felt such rage, resentment, and despair,
As thou, sad virgin! for thy ravished hair.   10
   While her racked soul repose and peace requires,
The fierce Thalestris fans the rising fires.
"O wretched maid!" she spread her hands, and cried,
(And Hampton's echoes, "Wretched maid!" replied)
"Was it for this you took such constant care   15
Combs, bodkins, leads, pomatums to prepare?
For this your locks in paper durance bound?
For this with tort'ring irons wreathed around?
Oh had the youth been but content to seize
Hairs less in sight, or any hairs but these!   20
Gods! shall the ravisher display this hair,
While the fops envy, and the ladies stare!
Honour forbid! at whose unrivalled shrine
Ease, pleasure, virtue, all, our sex resign.
Methinks already I your tears survey,   25
Already hear the horrid things they say,
Already see you a degraded toast,
And all your honour in a whisper lost!
How shall I, then, your helpless fame defend?
'T will then be infamy to seem your friend!   30
And shall this prize, th' inestimable prize,
Exposed through crystal to the gazing eyes,
And heightened by the diamond's circling rays,
On that rapacious hand for ever blaze?
Sooner shall grass in Hyde Park Circus grow,   35
And wits take lodgings in the sound of Bow;
Sooner let earth, air, sea, to chaos fall,
Men, monkeys, lapdogs, parrots, perish all!"
   She said; then raging to Sir Plume repairs,
And bids her beau demand the precious hairs: 40
Sir Plume, of amber snuff-box justly vain,
And the nice conduct of a clouded cane,
With earnest eyes, and round unthinking face,

He first the snuff-box opened, then the case,
And thus broke out — " My lord, why, what the devil!   45
Zounds! damn the lock! 'fore Gad, you must be civil!
Plague on 't! 't is past a jest — nay, prithee, pox!
Give her the hair." — He spoke, and rapped his box.
    " It grieves me much," replied the peer again,
" Who speaks so well should ever speak in vain: 50
But by this lock, this sacred lock, I swear,
(Which never more shall join its parted hair;
Which never more its honours shall renew,
Clipped from the lovely head where once it grew)
That, while my nostrils draw the vital air,   55
This hand, which won it, shall for ever wear."
He spoke, and speaking, in proud triumph spread
The long-contended honours of her head.
    But see! the nymph in sorrow's pomp appears,
Her eyes half-languishing, half drowned in tears;   60
Now livid pale her cheeks, now glowing red ⎫
On her heaved bosom hung her drooping head, ⎬
Which with a sigh she raised, and thus she said: ⎭
" For ever cursed be this detested day,
Which snatched my best, my fav'rite curl away;   65
Happy! ah ten times happy had I been,
If Hampton Court these eyes had never seen!
Yet am not I the first mistaken maid,
By love of courts to num'rous ills betrayed.
O had I rather unadmired remained   70
In some lone isle, or distant northern land,
Where the gilt chariot never marked the way,
Where none learn ombre, none e'er taste bohea!
There kept my charms concealed from mortal eye,
Like roses, that in deserts bloom and die.   75
What moved my mind with youthful lords to roam?
O had I stayed, and said my pray'rs at home!
'T was this the morning omens did foretell,
Thrice from my trembling hand the patchbox fell;
The tott'ring china shook without a wind,   80
Nay, Poll sat mute, and Shock was most unkind!
See the poor remnants of this slighted hair!
My hands shall rend what ev'n thy own did spare:
This in two sable ringlets taught to break,
Once gave new beauties to the snowy neck;   85
The sister-lock now sits uncouth, alone,
And in its fellow's fate foresees its own;
Uncurled it hangs, the fatal shears demands,
And tempts once more thy sacrilegious hands."
    She said: the pitying audience melt in tears;   90
But fate and Jove had stopped the baron's ears.
In vain Thalestris with reproach assails,
For who can move when fair Belinda fails?

Not half so fixed the Trojan could remain,
While Anna begged and Dido raged in vain.   95
" To arms, to arms! " the bold Thalestris cries,
And swift as lightning to the combat flies.
All side in parties, and begin th' attack ;
Fans clap, silks rustle, and tough whalebones crack ;
Heroes' and heroines' shouts confus'dly rise,   100
And bass and treble voices strike the skies ;
No common weapons in their hands are found,
Like gods they fight, nor dread a mortal wound.
  So when bold Homer makes the gods engage,
And heav'nly breasts with human passions rage,   105
'Gainst Pallas, Mars ; Latona, Hermes arms,
And all Olympus rings with loud alarms ;
Jove's thunder roars, heav'n trembles all around,
Blue Neptune storms, the bellowing deeps resound :
Earth shakes her nodding tow'rs, the ground gives way,   110
And the pale ghosts start at the flash of day!
  While through the press enraged Thalestris flies,
And scatters death around from both her eyes,
A beau and witling perished in the throng,
One died in metaphor, and one in song.   115
" O cruel nymph ; a living death I bear,"
Cried Dapperwit, and sunk beside his chair.
A mournful glance Sir Fopling upwards cast,
" Those eyes are made so killing " — was his last.
Thus on Mæander's flow'ry margin lies   120
Th' expiring swan, and as he sings he dies.
  As bold Sir Plume had drawn Clarissa down,
Chloe stepped in, and killed him with a frown ;
She smiled to see the doughty hero slain,
But at her smile the beau revived again.   125
  Now Jove suspends his golden scales in air,
Weighs the men's wits against the lady's hair ;
The doubtful beam long nods from side to side ;
At length the wits mount up, the hairs subside.
  See fierce Belinda on the baron flies,   130
With more than usual lightning in her eyes :
Nor feared the chief th' unequal fight to try,
Who sought no more than on his foe to die.
But this bold lord, with manly strength endued,
She with one finger and a thumb subdued :   135
Just where the breath of life his nostrils drew,
A charge of snuff the wily virgin threw ;
Sudden, with starting tears each eye o'erflows,
And the high dome re-echoes to his nose.
  " Now meet thy fate," th' incensed virago cried,   140
And drew a deadly bodkin from her side.
  " Boast not my fall," he said, " insulting foe!
Thou by some other shalt be laid as low ;

Nor think to die dejects my lofty mind;
All that I dread is leaving you behind!   145
Rather than so, ah let me still survive,
And still burn on, in Cupid's flames, alive."
  "Restore the lock!" she cries; and all around
"Restore the lock!" the vaulted roofs rebound.
Not fierce Othello in so loud a strain   150
Roared for the handkerchief that caused his pain.
But see how oft ambitious aims are crossed,
And chiefs contend till all the prize is lost!
The lock, obtained with guilt, and kept with pain,
In ev'ry place is sought, but sought in vain: 155
With such a prize no mortal must be blessed,
So heav'n decrees! with heav'n who can contest?
Some thought it mounted to the lunar sphere,
Since all that man e'er lost is treasured there.
There heroes' wits are kept in pond'rous vases,   160
And beaux' in snuff-boxes and tweezer-cases.
There broken vows, and death-bed alms are found,
And lovers' hearts with ends of ribbon bound,
The courtier's promises, and sick man's pray'rs,
The smiles of harlots, and the tears of heirs,   165
Cages for gnats, and chains to yoke a flea,
Dried butterflies, and tomes of casuistry.
But trust the muse — she saw it upward rise,
Though marked by none but quick poetic eyes:
(Thus Rome's great founder to the heav'ns withdrew,   170
To Proculus alone confessed in view)
A sudden star, it shot through liquid air,
And drew behind a radiant trail of hair,
Not Berenice's locks first rose so bright,
The skies bespankling with dishevelled light.   175
This the beau monde shall from the Mall survey,   ⎫
As through the moonlight shade they nightly stray, ⎬
And hail with music its propitious ray;   ⎭
This Partridge soon shall view in cloudless skies,
When next he looks through Galileo's eyes;   180
And hence th' egregious wizard shall foredoom
The fate of Louis, and the fall of Rome.
  Then cease, bright nymph! to mourn thy ravished hair,
Which adds new glory to the shining sphere!
Not all the tresses that fair head can boast,   185
Shall draw such envy as the lock you lost.
For after all the murders of your eye,
When, after millions slain, yourself shall die;
When those fair suns shall set, as set they must,
And all those tresses shall be laid in dust,   190
This lock the muse shall consecrate to fame,
And 'midst the stars inscribe Belinda's name.

APPENDIX.

IV.

REPRINT OF THE FIRST EDITION

OF

THE DUNCIAD.

THE

D U N C I A D.

AN

Heroic Poem.

IN

THREE BOOKS.

DUBLIN, Printed, LONDON, Re-
printed for A. DODD. 1728.

THE PUBLISHER TO THE READER.

IT will be found a true observation, tho' somewhat surprising, that when any scandal is vented against a man of the highest distinction and character either in the State or in Literature, the publick in general afford it a most quiet reception, and the larger part accept it as favourably as if it were some kindness done to themselves: Whereas if a known scoundrel or blockhead chance to be but touch'd upon, a whole legion is up in Arms, and it becomes the common Cause of all Scriblers, Booksellers, and Printers whatsoever.

Not to search too deeply into the reason hereof, I will only observe as a *Fact*, that every week for these two Months past, the town has been persecuted with Pamphlets, Advertisements, Letters, and weekly Essays, not only against the Wit and Writings, but against the Character and Person, of Mr. Pope. And that of all those men who have received pleasure from his Writings (which by modest computation may be about a hundred thousand in these Kingdoms of England and Ireland, not to mention Jersey, Guernsey, the Orcades, those in the New World, and Foreigners who have translated him into their languages) of all this number, not a man hath stood up to say one word in his defence.

The only exception is the Author of the following Poem, who doubtless had either a better insight into the grounds of this clamour, or a better opinion of Mr. Pope's integrity, join'd with a greater personal love for him, than any other of his numerous friends and admirers.

Further, that he was in his peculiar intimacy, appears from the knowledge he manifests of the most *private* Authors of all the *anonymous* pieces against him, and from his having in this Poem attacked no man living, who had not before printed and published against this particular Gentleman.

How I became possest of it, is of no concern to the Reader; but it would have been a wrong to him, had I detain'd this publication: since those *Names* which are its chief ornaments, die off daily so fast, as must render it too soon unintelligible. If it provoke the Author to give us a more perfect edition, I have my end.

Who he is, I cannot say, and (which is great pity) there is certainly nothing in his style and manner of writing, which can distinguish, or discover him. For if it bears any resemblance to that of Mr. P. 't is not improbable but it might be done on purpose, with a view to have it pass for his. But by the frequency of his allusions to Virgil, and a *labour'd*, (not to say *affected*,) *shortness*, in imitation of him, I should think him more an admirer of the Roman Poet than of the Grecian, and in that, not of the same taste with his Friend.

I have been well inform'd, that this work was the labour of full six years of his life, and that he retired himself entirely from all the avocations and pleasures of the world, to attend diligently to its correction and perfection; and six years

541

more he intended to bestow upon it, as it should seem by this verse of Statius, which was cited at the head of his manuscript.

> Oh mihi bissenos multum vigilata per annos,
> Duncia! ——

Hence also we learn the true *Title* of the Poem; which with the same certainty as we call that of Homer the Iliad, of Virgil the Æneid, of Camoens the Lusiad, of Voltaire the Henriad, we may pronounce could have been, and can be no other, than

The Dunciad.

It is styled *Heroic,* as being *doubly* so; not only with respect to its nature, which according to the best Rules of the Ancients and strictest ideas of the Moderns, is critically such; but also with regard to the Heroical disposition and high courage of the Writer, who dar'd to stir up such a formidable, irritable, and implacable race of mortals.

The time and date of the Action is evidently in the last reign, when the office of City Poet expir'd upon the death of Elkanah Settle, and he has fix'd it to the Mayoralty of Sir Geo. Tho——ld. But there may arise some obscurity in Chronology from the *Names* in the Poem, by the inevitable removal of some Authors, and insertion of others, in their Niches. For whoever will consider the unity of the whole design, will be sensible, that the *Poem was not made for these Authors, but these Authors for the Poem.* And I should judge they were clapp'd in as they rose, fresh and fresh, and chang'd from day to day, in like manner as when the old boughs wither, we thrust new ones into a chimney.

I would not have the reader too much troubled or anxious, if he cannot decypher them; since when he shall have found them out, he will probably know no more of the Persons than before.

Yet we judg'd it better to preserve them as they are, than to change them for fictitious names, by which the Satyr would only be multiplied; and applied to many instead of one. Had the Hero, for instance, been called Codrus, how many would have affirm'd him to be Mr. W——, Mr. D——, Sir R—— B—, &c., but now, all that unjust scandal is saved, by calling him Theobald, which by good luck happens to be the name of a real person.

I am indeed aware, that this name may to some appear too mean, for the Hero of an Epic Poem? But it is hoped, they will alter that opinion, when they find, that an Author no less eminent than La Bruyere, has thought him worthy a place in his Characters.

Voudriez vous, THEOBALDE, que je crusse que vous êtes baisse? que vous n'êtes plus Poete, ni bel esprit? que vous êtes présentement aussi *Mauvais juge* de *tout genre d'Ouvrage,* que *Méchant Auteur?* Votre air libre & presumptueux me rassure, & me persuade tout le contraire, &c. *Characteres,* Vol. I, de la Société & de la Conversation, p. 176, *Edit. Amst.* 1720.

THE DUNCIAD.

BOOK THE FIRST.

BOOK and the man I sing, the first who brings
The *Smithfield* muses to the ears of kings ;
Say great *Patricians!* (since yourselves inspire
These wond'rous works ; so *Jove* and fate require!)
Say from what cause, in vain decry'd and curst,   5
Still [1] *Dunce the second reigns like Dunce the first ?* [2]

In eldest time, e'er mortals writ or read,
E'er *Pallas* issued from the Thund'rer's head,
Dulness o'er all possess'd her antient right,
Daughter of *Chaos* and eternal *Night :*   10
Fate in their dotage this fair idiot gave,
Gross as her sire, and as her mother grave,
Laborious, heavy, busy, bold, and blind,
She rul'd, in native anarchy, the mind.

Still her old empire to confirm, she tries, [3]   15
For born a Goddess, *Dulness* never dies.

Where wave the tatter'd ensigns of *Rag-Fair*,
A yawning ruin hangs and nods [4] in air ;
Keen, hollow [5] winds howl thro' the bleak recess,
Emblem of music caus'd by emptiness :   20
Here in one bed two shiv'ring sisters lye,
The cave of *Poverty* and *Poetry*.
This, the *Great Mother* dearer held than all
The clubs of *Quidnuncs*, or her own *Guild-hall :*
Here stood her Opium, here she nurs'd [6] her Owls,   25
And destin'd here th' imperial seat of fools.
Hence springs each weekly muse, the living boast
Of *C—l's* chaste press, and *L—t's* rubric post ;
Hence hymning [7] *Tyburn's* elegiac lay,
Hence the soft sing-song [8] on *Cecilia's* day,   30
Sepulchral lyes our holy [9] walls to grace,
And *New-year-Odes*, and all the *Grubstreet* race.

---

[1] *Dryd.*

[2] Jonathan Richardson corrected the first edition of the 'Dunciad' from what he calls 'the first Broglio MS.' His corrections have been transcribed by Mr. Elwin, and are here preserved. In the MS. the first six lines ran :
" Books and the Man who first from Grub Street
    brings
The Smithfield Muses to the Courts of Kings
I sing : Say, great ones, (you these works inspire

Since thus Jove's will $\left\{ \begin{matrix} or \\ and \end{matrix} \right\}$ Britain's fate require,
Say what the cause that still this taste remains,
And when a Settle falls a Tibbald reigns."

[3] In the MS.: " Still her lost empire to restore she tries."

[4] In the MS.: " Seems to nod."

[5] In the MS.: " Eternal."

[6] In the MS.: " Kept."

[7] In the MS.: " Weeping."

[8] In the MS.: " Nothings."

[9] In the MS.: " Hallowed."

'Twas here in clouded majesty she shone;
Four guardian *Virtues*, round, support her throne;[1]
Fierce[2] champion *Fortitude*, that knows no fears[3]   35
Of hisses, blows, or want, or loss of ears:
Calm *Temperance*, whose blessings those partake[4]
Who hunger, and who thirst for scribling sake:
Prudence, whose glass presents th' approaching jayl;
Poetic *Justice*, with her lifted scale;[5]   40
Where in nice balance, truth with gold she weighs,
And solid pudding against empty praise.

Here she beholds the Chaos dark and deep,
Where nameless *somethings* in their causes sleep,
'Till genial *Jacob*, or a warm *third-day*   45
Calls forth each mass, a poem or a play.
How hints, like spawn, scarce quick in embryo lie;[6]
How new-born nonsense first is taught to cry;
Maggots half-form'd, in rhyme exactly meet,
And learn to crawl upon poetic feet.   50
Here one poor *Word* a hundred clenches makes,
And ductile dulness new meanders takes;
There motley[7] *Images* her fancy strike,
Figures ill-pair'd,[8] and *Similes* unlike.
She sees a mob of[9] *Metaphors* advance,   55
Pleas'd with the madness of the mazy dance:
How[10] *Tragedy* and *Comedy* embrace;
How[11] *Farce* and *Epic* get a jumbled race:
How[12] *Time* himself stands still at her command,
Realms shift their place, and Ocean turns to land.   60
Here gay *Description Ægypt* glads[13] with showers,
Or gives to *Zembla* fruits, to *Barca* flowers;
Glitt'ring with ice here hoary hills are seen,
Fast by, fair[14] vallies of eternal green,
On cold *December* fragrant[15] chaplets blow,   65
And heavy harvests nod beneath the snow.

All these and more, the cloud-compelling Queen
Beholds thro' fogs, that magnify the scene;
She, tinsel'd o'er[16] in robes of varying hues,

---

[1] In the MS.: " With every Virtue that upheld her throne."
[2] In the MS.: " First."
[3] In the MS.: " Nothing fears."
[4] In the MS.: " Next Vestal Temperance that blest can make."
[5] In the MS.:
" Here P. . . . with a patron for her bail,
And there poetic Justice holds her scale."
[6] In the MS.: " Here she beholds how hints in embryo lie."
[7] In the MS.: " Now two-shaped."
[8] In the MS.: " Ill-joined."

[9] In the MS.: " Now sees contending."
[10] In the MS.: " Now."
[11] In the MS.: " Now."
[12] In the MS.: " Now."
[13] In the MS.: " Here unconfined description paints."
[14] In the MS.: " There smiling." In edition of 1729: " There painted."
[15] In the MS.: { " Flow'ry. Rosy." }
[16] In the MS.: " She high enthroned Refulgent she."

With self-applause her wild creation views,   70
Sees momentary monsters rise and fall,
And with her own fools-colours gilds them all.

   'T was on the day,[1] when [2] *Tho—d*, rich and grave,
Like [3] *Cimon* triumph'd both on land and wave,
(Pomps without guilt, of bloodless swords and maces,   75
Glad chains, warm furs, broad banners,[4] and broad faces)
Now night descending, the proud scene was o'er,
Yet [5] liv'd, in *Settle's* numbers, one day more.
Now *May'rs* and *Shrieves* in pleasing slumbers lay,
And eat in dreams the custard of the day :   80
But pensive poets painful vigils keep ;
Sleepless themselves, to give their readers sleep.
Much to her mind the solemn feast recalls,
What city-*Swans* once sung within the walls,
Much she revolves their arts, their antient [6] praise,   85
And sure succession down from [7] *Heywood's* days.
She saw with joy the line immortal run,
Each sire imprest and glaring in his son ;
So watchful *Brain* forms with plastic care
Each growing lump, and brings it to a Bear.   90
She saw in *N—n* all his father shine,
And *E—n* eke out *Bl—'s* endless line ;
She saw slow *P—s* creep like *T—te's* poor page,
And furious *D—n* foam in *Wh—'s* rage.[8]

   In each, she marks her image full exprest,   95
But chief, in *Tibbald's* monster-breeding breast,
Sees Gods with Dæmons in strange league ingage,
And [9] earth, and heav'n, and hell, her battels wage ![10]

   She ey'd the Bard where supperless he sate,
And pin'd, unconscious of his rising [11] fate ;   100
Studious he sate, with all his books around,
Sinking from thought to thought, a vast profound !
Plung'd for his sense, but found no bottom there :
Then writ, and flounder'd on, in mere despair.
He roll'd his eyes that witness'd huge dismay,   105

---

[1] " 'T was that great day."

[2] Sir *Geo. Tho——*. — POPE.

[3] *Cimon*, the famous *Athenian* general who obtained a victory by sea, and another by land, on the same day, over the *Persians* and *Barbarians*. — POPE.

[4] In the MS.: " Streamers."

[5] In edition of 1729: " But."

[6] In the MS.: " Former."

[7] *John Heywood*, whose Interludes were printed in *Hen.* VIIIth's time. — POPE.

[8] In the MS.:

" And all the mighty mad in Dennis rage,
And Dunton foaming still in { Whatley's / Welsted's } rage."

[9] This, I presume, alludes to the extravagancies of the Farces of this author. See Book III. ver. 170, &c. — POPE.

[10] In the MS. these four lines ran:
" But chief her darling Tibbald filled her thought
With rising worlds, and monsters yet unwrought,
Fiends, monsters, gods amazing leagues prepare,
And in her cause engage Hell, Earth, and Air."

[11] In the MS.: " The birth of."

Where yet unpawn'd, much learned lumber[1] lay,
Volumes, whose size the space exactly fill'd;
Or which fond authors were so good to gild;
Or where, by Sculpture made for ever known,
The page admires new beauties, not its own.[2]   110
Here swells the shelf[3] with *Ogleby* the *great*,
There, stamp'd with arms, *Newcastle* shines compleat,
Here all his suff'ring brotherhood retire,
And 'scape the martyrdom of jakes and fire;[4]
A *Gothic* Vatican! of *Greece* and *Rome*   115
Well-purg'd, and worthy *W—y*, *W—s*, and *Bl—*.[5]

But high above, more solid Learning shone,[6]
The *Classicks* of an age that heard of none;
There *Caxton* slept, with *Wynkin* at his side,
One clasp'd in wood, and one in strong cow-hide: 120
There sav'd by spice, like mummies, many a year,
Old Bodies of Philosophy appear:
De Lyra there a dreadful front extends,
And there, the groaning Shelves *Philemon* bends.

Of these twelve volumes, twelve of amplest size,   125
Redeem'd from tapers[7] and defrauded pyes,
Inspir'd he seizes: These an altar raise:
An hecatomb of pure, unsully'd lays
That altar crowns; a folio Common-place
Founds the whole pyle, of all his works the base: 130
Quarto's, octavo's, shape the lessening pyre,
And last, a[8] *little Ajax* tips the spire.

Then he. Great Tamer of all human art![9]
First in my care, and nearest at my heart!
Dulness! whose good old cause I yet defend,[10]   135
With whom my muse began, with whom shall end!
Oh thou! of business the directing soul,
To human heads like byass to the bowl,
Which as more pond'rous makes their aim more true,
Obliquely wadling to the mark in view.   140

[1] In the MS.:
    " The spoils of Sturbridge, }
    Philemon's labours."   }
[2] In the MS.:
" Or where the pictures for the piece atone,
Saved by the graver's work and not their own."
    [3] In the MS.: " Here bends a shelf."
    [4] After v. 114 in the MS.:
" Here Christian Quarles thy pictured works are
    thrown,
And all who Benlowes as Mæcenas own."
    Or,
" Polemics huge of strength to fortifie,
The feeble band-box, or uphold the pie."

[5] In the MS.:
    " Withers, { Quarles } and Bloom."
               { Watts   }
In editions of 1729, 1736, " Withers, Quarles,
and Bloom."
In 1743, " Settle, Banks, and Broome."
    [6] In the MS.: " But far above in Time's old
tarnish shone."
    [7] In the MS.: " Spices."
    [8] In duodecimo, translated from *Sophocles*. —
POPE.
    [9] In the MS.: " Then thus, O Dulness, victor
of all art."
    [10] In the MS.: " Whose good old cause un-
prosperous I defend."

O ever gracious to perplex'd mankind!
Who spread a healing mist before the mind,
And, lest we err by wit's wild, dancing [1] light,
Secure us kindly in our native *night*.
Ah! still o'er *Britain* stretch that peaceful wand,[2]   145
Which lulls th' *Helvetian* and *Batavian* land,
Where 'gainst thy throne if rebel Science rise,[3]
She does but show her coward face and dies :
There, thy good *scholiasts* with unweary'd pains
Make *Horace* flat, and humble *Maro's* strains ;   150
Here studious I unlucky Moderns save,
Nor sleeps one error in its father's grave,
Old puns restore, lost blunders nicely seek,
And crucify poor *Shakespear* once a week.[4]
For thee I dim these eyes, and stuff this head,   155
With all such reading as was never[5] read ;
For thee supplying, in the worst of days,
Notes to dull books, and Prologues to dull plays ;
For thee explain a thing 'till all men doubt it,
And write about it, Goddess, and about it ;   160
So spins the silkworm small its slender store,
And labours, 'till it clouds itself all o'er.
Not that my pen to criticks[6] was confin'd,
My verse gave ampler lessons to mankind ;
So written[7] precepts may successless prove,   165
But sad examples never fail to move.
As forc'd from wind-guns, lead itself can fly,
And pond'rous slugs cut swiftly thro' the sky :
As clocks to weight their nimble motion owe,
The wheels above urg'd by the load below ;   170
Me, Emptiness and Dulness could inspire,
And were my Elasticity, and Fire.
Had heav'n decreed such works a longer date,
Heav'n had decreed to spare the *Grubstreet*-state.
But see[8] great *Settle* to the dust descend,   175
And all thy cause and empire at an end,
Cou'd *Troy* be sav'd by any single hand,
His gray-goose-weapon must have made her stand.
But what can I! *my Flaccus* cast aside,
Take up th' *Attorney's* (once my better) *guide ?*[9]   180

---

[1] In the MS.: " Reason's wandering."

[2] In the MS.: " And may'st thou yet o'er Britain stretch that wand."

[3] In the edition of 1729: " Where rebel to thy throne if Science rise."

[4] In the MS.:
" Lost puns or blunders to each line restore,
And crucify poor Shakespeare o'er and o'er."

[5] In the MS.: " No man e'er."

[6] In the MS. and edition of 1729 : " Not that my quill."

[7] In edition of 1729: " Gravest."

[8] This was the last year of *Elkanah Settle's* life. He was poet to the city of *London*, whose business was to compose yearly panegyricks on the Lord Mayor, and verses for the Pageants; but since the abolition of that part of the shows, the employment ceas'd, so that *Settle* had no successor to that place. — POPE.

[9] In the MS.:
" But what can I! Thus, thus at least I show
My zeal, thy long-tried confessor below."

Or rob the *Roman* geese of all their glories,
And save the state by cackling to the Tories?
Yes, to my country I my pen consign,[1]
Yes,[2] from this moment, mighty *Mist!* am thine,
A rival, *Curtius!* of thy fame and zeal,   185
O'er head and ears plunge for the public weal.
Adieu my children! better thus expire
Un-stall'd, unsold; thus glorious mount in fire
Fair without spot; than greas'd by grocer's hands,
Or shipp'd with *W*— to ape and monkey lands,   190
Or wafting ginger, round the streets to go,[3]
And visit alehouse where ye first did grow.[4]

With that, he lifted thrice the sparkling brand,
And thrice he dropt it from his quiv'ring hand:
Then lights the structure, with averted eyes;   195
The rowling smokes involve the sacrifice.
The opening clouds disclose each work by turns,
Now flames old [5] *Memnon*, now *Rodrigo* burns,
In one quick flash see *Proserpine* expire,
And last, his own cold *Æschylus* took fire.   200
Then gush'd the tears, as from the *Trojan's* eyes
When the last blaze sent *Ilion* to the skies.

Rowz'd by the light, old *Dulness* heav'd the head,
Then snatch'd a sheet of *Thulè* from her Bed,
Sudden she flies, and whelms it o'er the pyre;   205
Down sink the flames, and with a hiss expire.

Her ample presence fills up all the place;
A veil of fogs dilates her awful face,
Great in her charms! as when on Shrieves and May'rs
She looks, and breathes herself into their airs.   210
She bids him wait her to the sacred Dome;
Well-pleas'd he enter'd, and confess'd his home:
So spirits, ending their terrestrial race,
Ascend, and recognise their native place:
Raptur'd, he gazes round the dear retreat,   215
And [6] in sweet numbers celebrates the feat.

Here to her Chosen all her works she shows; [7]
Prose swell'd to verse, Verse loit'ring into prose:
How random thoughts now meaning chance to find,[8]
Now leave all memory of sense behind;   220
How Prologues into Prefaces decay,

---

[1] In the MS.: "Let Pryn and Withers now their wreaths resign."
[2] In the MS.: "I."
[3] In the MS.: "Run."
[4] In the MS.: "Begun."
[5] Plays and Farces of *T——d*.

[6] He writ a poem called the *Cave of Poverty*, printed in 1715.
[7] In the MS.: "Here the whole process of her art she shows."
[8] In the MS.: "How unideal thoughts now meaning find."

And those [1] to Notes are fritter'd quite away:
How Index-learning turns no student pale,
Yet holds the eel of science by the Tail:
How, with less reading than makes felons 'scape,   225
Less human genius [2] than God gives an ape,
Small thanks to *France*, and none to *Rome* or *Greece*,
A past, vamp'd, future, old, reviv'd, new piece,
'Twixt *Plautus*, *Fletcher*, *Congreve*, and *Corneille*,
Can make a *C——r*, *Jo——n*, or *O——ll*. [3]   230

The Goddess then, o'er his anointed head,
With mystic words the sacred Opium shed;
And lo! her *Bird* (a monster of a fowl!
Something betwixt a *H—* and Owl)
Perch'd on his crown. All hail! and hail again,   235
My son! the promis'd land expects thy reign. [4]
Know [5] *Settle*, cloy'd with custard and with praise,
Is gather'd to the Dull [6] of antient days,
Safe, where no [7] criticks damn, no duns molest,
Where *G—n*, *B—*, and high-born *H—* rest! [8]   240
I see a King! who leads my chosen sons [9]
To [10] lands that flow with clenches and with puns:
Till each fam'd theatre [11] my empire own,
Till *Albion*, as *Hibernia*, bless my throne. [12]
I see! I see! — Then rapt, she spoke no more.   245
God save King Tibbald! *Grubstreet* alleys roar.

So when *Jove's* block descended from on high,
(As sings thy great fore-father, *Ogilby*,)
Hoarse thunder to its bottom shook [13] the bog,
And the loud nation croak'd, *God save King* Log!   250

[1] In the edition of 1729: "These."
[2] In the MS.: "Science."
[3] In the MS.:
  "Cibber, Bladen } or Ozell."
  Shadwell, Welsted }
[4] In the MS.:
"Behold, she cried, the day,
The promised nation now expects thy sway."
[5] In the MS.: "Since."
[6] In the MS.: "Now sleeps among the dull."
[7] In the MS.: "Where neither."
[8] In the MS.: "Where Dunton, Babor, Gildon, Howard rest."
[9] In the MS.: "Take thou the sceptre, rule thy chosen sons."
[10] In the MS.: "In."
[11] In the MS.: "Rule till both theatres."
[12] In the MS.: "And near our Monarch's dulness fix her throne."
[13] In the MS.: "Shook the bottom of."

END OF THE FIRST BOOK.

THE DUNCIAD.

BOOK THE SECOND.

THE sons of *Dulness* meet:[1] an endless band
Pours forth, and leaves unpeopled half the land,
A motley mixture! in long wigs, in bags,
In silks, in crapes, in garters, and in rags;
From drawing rooms, from colleges, from garrets,   5
On horse, on foot, in hacks, and gilded chariots,
All who true Dunces in her cause appear'd,
And all who knew those Dunces to reward.[2]

Now herald hawker's rusty voice proclaims
Heroic prizes, and advent'rous Games;   10
In that wide space the Goddess took her stand
Where the tall May-pole once o'erlook'd the *Strand;*
But now (so *ANNE* and Piety ordain)
A Church collects the saints of *Drury-lane.*
With authors, stationers obey'd the call;[3]   15
The field of glory is a field for all;
Glory, and gain, th' industrious tribe provoke,
And gentle *Dulness* ever loves a joke.
A Poet's Form she sets before their eyes,
And bids the nimblest racer seize the prize.   20
No meagre, muse-rid mope, adust and thin,
In a dun night-gown of his own loose skin;[4]
But such a bulk as no twelve bards could raise,
Twelve starving[5] bards of these degen'rate days.
All as a partridge plump, full-fed, and fair,   25

---

[1] In the MS.: "She summons all her sons."
In the edition of 1729 the opening lines ran:
"High on a gorgeous seat that far outshone
Henley's gilt tub, or Fleckno's Irish throne,
Or that where on her Curlls the Public pours
All bounteous, fragrant grains and golden showers,
Great Tibbald nods: The proud Parnassian sneer,
The conscious simper and the jealous leer,
Mix on his look. All eyes direct their rays
On him, and crowds grow foolish as they gaze."

[2] After this verse in the MS.:
"Ranked side by side the Patron and the Scrub,
Each Quarles his Benlowes, and each Tibbald B——"
For which couplet see note to v. 250 of Epistle to Arbuthnot. Then follow these lines:
"High on a bed of state that far outshone
Flecno's proud seat, or Querno's nobler throne
—— Exalted sat: around him bows

The Laureat band, and breathe poetic vows.
With kingly joy he hears their loyal lies ⎫
With kingly pride the general joy he spies ⎭
And sees his subjects' transport in their eyes.
His strut, his grin, and his dead stare they praise,
And gaping crowds grow foolish as they gaze."
It will be observed that the name of the monarch is left blank in the MS., as if this part of the poem had been written before the first book, and before the poet had fixed on any particular hero. On this point see Introduction.

[3] In the MS.:
"Ev'n booksellers obeyed the Hawker's call."

[4] These four lines in the MS. run:
"To these in sport she first proposed the prize
And raised a poet's phantom in their eyes;
Not such as garrets lodge, of visage thin,
Who like a night-gown round him wraps his skin."

[5] In the MS. and edition of 1729: "Starveling."

She form'd this image of well-bodied air,
With pert flat eyes she window'd well its head,[1]
A brain of feathers, and a heart of lead,
And empty words she gave, and sounding strain;[2]
But senseless, lifeless! Idol void and vain!   30
Never was dasht out, at one lucky hit,
A fool, so just a copy of a wit;
So like, that criticks said and courtiers swore,
A wit it was, and call'd the phantom, *M*—.

All gaze with ardour; some, a Poet's name,   35
Others, a sword-knot and lac'd suit inflame:
But lofty *L—t*[3] in the circle rose;
"This prize is mine; who tempt it, are my foes:
"With me began this genius, and shall end:"
He spoke, and who with *L—t*[4] shall contend?   40

Fear held them mute. Alone, untaught to fear,
Stood dauntless *C—l.* "Behold that rival here!
"The race by vigor, not by vaunts is won;
"So take the hindmost, Hell." — He said, and run.
Swift as a bard the bailiff leaves behind,   45
He left huge *L—t*,[5] and out-stript the wind.
As when a dab-chick waddles thro' the copse,
On legs and wings, and flies, and wades, and hops;
So lab'ring on, with shoulders, hands, and head,
Wide as a windmill all his figure spread,   50
With steps unequal *L—t* urg'd the race,
And seem'd to emulate great *Jacob's* pace.[6]
Full in the middle way there stood a lake,
Which *Cl—'s Corinna* chanc'd that morn to make,
(Such was her wont, at early dawn to drop   55
Her evening cates before his neighbour's shop,)
Here fortun'd *C—l* to slide: loud shout the band,[7]
And *L—t*, *L—t*,[8] rings thro' all the Strand.
Obscene with filth the varlet lies bewray'd,
Fal'n in the plash his wickedness had lay'd: 60
Then first (if Poets aught of truth declare)
The caitiff *Vaticide* conceiv'd a prayer.

---

[1] In the MS.:
"With laughing eyes that twinkled in his head,
Well-looked, well-turned, well-natured and well-
    fed,
So wondrous like that Wotton's self might say,
And Kent would swear, by G—d, it must be
    Gay."

[2] The next eight lines are not in the MS., another indication that this part of the poem was composed before the Dunciad in its present form was designed. The passage in the MS. was clearly not intended to apply to James Moore.

[3] In the MS.: "Awful Tryphon."

[4] In the MS.: { "Tryphon, / Tonson."

[5] In the MS.: "Fat Tonson."

[6] In the MS.:
"With arms expanded Tryphon rows his state,
And left-legged Jacob seems to emulate."
This shows that by Tryphon he meant the younger Tonson.

[7] In the MS.:
"Here sliddered Curll: loud shout the laughing band."

[8] In the MS.: "Jacob, Jacob."

Hear *Jove!* whose name my bards and I adore,
As much at least as any Gods, or more ;
And him and his, if more devotion warms,   65
Down with the [1] *Bible,* up with the [2] *Pope's Arms.*[3]

[4] A place there is, betwixt earth, air and seas,
Where from *Ambrosia, Jove* retires for ease.[5]
There in his seat two spacious Vents appear,
On this he sits, to that he leans his ear,   70
There hears the various vows of fond mankind,
Some beg an eastern, some a western wind : [6]
All vain petitions, sent by winds on high,
With reams abundant this abode supply ;
Amus'd he reads, and then returns the bills   75
Sign'd with that *Ichor* which from Gods distills.[7]

In office here fair [8] *Cloacina* stands,
And ministers to *Jove* with purest hands ;
Forth from the heap she pick'd her vot'ry's pray'r,
And plac'd it next him, a distinction rare!   80
Oft, as he fish'd her nether realms for wit,
The Goddess favour'd him, and favours yet.
Renew'd by ordure's sympathetic force,
As oil'd with magic juices for the course,
Vig'rous he rises ; from th' effluvia strong   85
Imbibes new life, and scours and stinks along.
Re-passes *L—t,*[9] vindicates the race,
Nor heeds the brown dishonours of his face.

And now the victor stretch'd his eager hand,[10]
Where the tall Nothing stood, or seem'd to stand ;   90
A shapeless shade, it melted from his sight,
Like forms in clouds, or visions of the night! [11]

[1] The *Bible C——l's* sign. — POPE.
[2] The *Cross-keys L——t's.* — POPE.
[3] In the MS.:
" In him and his if greater grace abound,
Then let mine host of Shakespeare's Head be
    crowned."
In a note, " Shakespear's Head, Tonson's
sign."
[4] See *Lucian's Icaro-Menippus.* — POPE.
[5] In the MS.:
" Called by the Gods the Thunderer's House of
    Ease."
[6] In the MS.:
" There lists delighted to the jests unclean
Of link-boys vile and watermen obscene."
This couplet first appears in print in the edi-
tion of 1743.
[7] In the MS.:
" Then with Mist's Journals and with Tanner's
    Bills

Wipes that rich ichor which a God distills."
[8] In the MS.: " Black."
[9] In the MS.: " Tonson."
[10] In the MS. there is the following variation
of this passage.:
" How Jove still just, defeats man's erring aim!
How Hope deludes, how Fortune shifts the
    game!
As Curll rapacious spreads his eager hand
And the plump phantom stands, or seems to
    stand,
His frustrate arms the impassive air confess,
All of the idol vanished but the dress.
Unhappy stationer! his author gone,
He grasps an empty Joseph for a John."
[11] In the MS.:
" The impassive form from his embraces flies
And melts to air: loud laughter shakes the
    skies."

Baffled, yet present ev'n amidst despair,
To seize his papers, *C—l*, was next thy care;
His papers all, the sportive winds up-lift,[1]
And whisk 'em back to *G—*, to *Y—*, to *S—*.[2]   95
Th' embroider'd suit, at least, he deem'd his prey;
That suit, an unpay'd Taylor snatch'd away!
No rag, no scrap, of all the beau, or wit,
That once so flutter'd, and that once so writ.   100

Heav'n rings with laughter: Of the laughter vain,[3]
Dulness, good Queen, repeats the jest again.
Three wicked imps of her own *Grubstreet* Choir
She deck'd like *Congreve, Addison*, and *Prior;*
Mears, Warner, Wilkins run: Delusive thought!   105
* * * *, and * *.[4] the wretches caught.
C—l stretches after *Gay*, but *Gay* is gone,
He grasps an empty[5] *Joseph* for a *John.*
So *Proteus*, hunted in a nobler shape,
Became, when seiz'd, a Puppy or an Ape.   110

To him the Goddess. Son, thy grief lay down,
And turn this whole illusion on the town.
As the sage dame experienc'd in her trade,
By names of Toasts retails each batter'd jade,
(Whence hapless Monsieur much complains at *Paris*   115
Of wrongs from Duchesses and Lady *Marys*)
Be thine, my stationer! this magic gift;
C— shall be *Prior*, and *C—n, Swift;*
So shall each hostile name become our own,
And we too boast our *Garth* and *Addison.*   120

With that the Goddess (piteous of his case,[6]
Yet smiling at his ruful length of face)
Gives him a cov'ring, worthy to be spread
On *Codrus'* old, or * * 's[7] modern bed;
Instructive work! whose wry-mouth'd portraiture   125
Display'd the fates her confessors endure.[8]

---

[1] In the MS.:
"Songs, sonnets, epigrams the winds uplift."
  [2] In the MS.: "To Evans and to S——"
  [3] In the MS. there was the following variation:
"Pleased at her wit, and of applauses vain,
Dulness, good Queen! repeats the jest again.
Another Poet and another rise,
Curll not discouraged at each quarry flies."
  For this last couplet he substituted:
"Forthwith she dressed like Addison and Prior,
Two wicked imps of her own Grub Street choir."
Or,
"A wicked sprite she dressed like Pope and
    Prior,

The same their voice, their mien, and their
    attire."
  [4] In 1729 and 1736, " Breval, Besaleel, Bond."
In 1743, " Breval, Bond, Besaleel."
  [5] *Joseph Gay*, a fictitious name put by *C——l*
before several Pamphlets. — POPE.
  [6] The edition of 1729 gives the reading of the
existing text.
  [7] In the MS.: " Durfey's." The edition of
1729 first reads " Dunton's."
  [8] In the MS.:
" There Dulness traced in wry-mouthed por-
    traiture,
The fates her martyrs militant endure."

Ear-less [1] on high, stood pillory'd *D——* [2]
And *T——* flagrant from the lash, below:
There kick'd and cudgel'd *R—* might ye view,
The very worstead still look'd black and blue:⠀⠀⠀⠀⠀⠀⠀⠀130
Himself among the storied chiefs he spies,
As from the blanket high in air he flies,
And oh! (he cry'd) what street, what lane but knows
Our purgings, pumpings, blanketings and blows?
In ev'ry loom our labors shall be seen,⠀⠀⠀⠀⠀⠀⠀⠀135
And the fresh vomit run for ever green!

⠀⠀See in the circle next, *Eliza* plac'd;
Two babes of love close clinging to her waist;
Fair as before her works she stands confess'd
In flow'r'd brocade by bounteous *Kirkall* dress'd,⠀⠀⠀140
Pearls on her neck, and roses in her hair,
And her fore-buttocks to the navel bare.
The Goddess then: "Who best can send on high
"The salient spout, fair-streaming to the sky;
"His be yon *Juno* of majestic size,⠀⠀⠀⠀⠀⠀⠀145
"With cow-like udders, and with ox-like eyes.
"This *China*-Jordan, let the chief o'ercome
"Replenish, not ingloriously, at home."

⠀⠀*Ch——d* [3] and *C——l* accept this glorious strife,
(Tho' one his Son dissuades, and one his Wife)⠀⠀⠀150
This on his manly confidence relies,
That on his vigor and superior size.
First *C——d* lean'd against his letter'd post;
It rose, and labor'd to a curve [4] at most:
So *Jove's* bright bow displays its wat'ry round,⠀⠀⠀155
(Sure sign, that no spectator shall be drown'd)
A second effort brought but new disgrace,
For straining more, it flies in his own face; [5]
Thus the small jett which hasty hands unlock,
Spirts in the gard'ner's eyes who turns the cock.⠀⠀⠀160
Not so from shameless *C——l*: Impetuous spread
The stream, and smoaking, flourish'd o'er his head.
So, (fam'd like thee for turbulence and horns,)
Eridanus his humble fountain scorns,
Thro' half the heav'ns he pours th' exalted urn;⠀⠀⠀165
His rapid waters in their passage burn.

---

[1] In the MS.: "Dauntless."

[2] In a MS. note to this line Pope says: "Daniel Defoe stood in the pillory for certain papers called the Reviews. He thereupon, no whit abashed, published A Hymn to the Pillory, a Pindaric Ode. It appears from hence that this poem was writ before Mr. Curll himself stood in the pillory, which happened not till February, 1727-8." — Pope.

[3] In the edition of 1729, "Chetwood"; in 1735 and 1736, "Chapman"; in 1743, "Osborne."

[4] In the MS.: "An arch."

[5] In the MS.:
"The wild mæander washed the artist's face."
⠀⠀This line of the MS. was inserted in the text in the edition of 1736.

Swift as it mounts, all follow with their eyes;
Still happy, Impudence obtains the prize.
Thou triumph'st. Victor of the high-wrought [1] day
And the pleas'd dame soft-smiling leads [2] away.   170
Ch——d, through perfect modesty o'ercome,
Crown'd with the Jordan, walks contented home.

But now for *Authors* nobler palms [3] remain:
Room for my Lord! three Jockeys [4] in his train;
Six huntsmen with a shout precede his chair;   175
He grins, and looks broad nonsense with a stare.[5]
His honour'd [6] meaning, *Dulness* thus exprest.
" He wins this Patron who can tickle best."

He chinks his purse, and takes his seat of state,
With ready quills the Dedicators [7] wait,   180
Now at his head the dext'rous task commence,
And instant, fancy feels th' imputed sense; [8]
Now gentle touches wanton o'er his face,
He struts *Adonis,* and affects grimace:
R—— the feather to his ear conveys,   185
Then his nice taste directs our *Operas:* [9]
* * his mouth with *Classic* flatt'ry opes,[10]
And the puft *Orator* bursts out in tropes.
But *O——* the *Poet's* healing balm [11]
Strives to extract from his soft, giving palm;   190
Unlucky *O——!* thy lordly master [12]
The more thou ticklest, gripes his fist the faster.

While thus each hand promotes the pleasing pain,
And quick sensations skip from vein to vein,
A youth unknown to *Phœbus,* in despair,   195
Puts his last refuge all in Heav'n in Pray'r.
What force have pious vows? the *Queen* of *Love*

[1] In the MS.: " Well p—t."

[2] In the MS.: " Moves."

[3] In the MS.: " Tasks."

[4] In the MS.: " Six huntsmen."

[5] In the MS.:
" In the blue string a jockey leads the Bear,
Who silent looks broad nonsense with a stare."

[6] In the MS.: { " Worship's,
          { " Secret."

[7] In the MS.: " Listening authors."

[8] In the MS.:
" Tindal and Gordon at his head commence,
The quickening numskull feels the fancied sense."

[9] In the MS.:
" He turns subscriber to all Operas."

[10] In the MS.:
" Bentley his mouth with classic flattery opes."

" His mouth now Bentley's kind instruction opes."

In 1729 Welsted's name was inserted in the place of the asterisks. In 1736 " Welsted " was replaced by " Bentley."

[11] In the MS.: " Oldmixon," and so in edition of 1729. In the edition of 1736:
" But Welsted most the poet's healing balm."
There is also another variation in the MS. which helps to explain the passage that follows, about " the youth unknown to Phœbus":
" Concanen from his soft and giving palm
Strives to extract the poet's healing balm.
A nicer part sly W——r chose to probe," &c.

[12] In the MS.:
" Unhappy Oldmixon, thy lord and master."
In 1736:
" Unlucky Welsted, thy unfeeling master."

His Sister sends, her vot'ress, from above.
As taught by *Venus*, *Paris* learnt the art
To touch *Achilles'* only tender part,[1]   200
Secure, thro' her,[2] the noble prize to carry,
He marches off, his Grace's *Secretary*.

Now turn to diff'rent sports (the Goddess cries)
And learn, my sons, the wond'rous pow'r of *Noise*.
To move, to raise, to ravish ev'ry heart,   205
With *Shakespear's* nature, or with *Johnson's* art,
Let others aim: 'T is yours to shake the soul
With *Thunder* rumbling from the mustard-bowl,[3]
With *horns* and *trumpets* now to madness swell,
Now sink in sorrows with a tolling *Bell*.   210
Such happy arts attention can command,
When fancy flags, and sense is at a stand:
Improve we these.[4]   Three *Cat-calls* be the bribe
Of him, whose chatt'ring shames the *Monkey* tribe;
And his this *Drum*, whose hoarse heroic base   215
Drowns the loud Clarion of the braying *Ass*.

Now thousand tongues are heard in one loud din,
The Monkey-mimicks rush discordant in;[5]
'T was chatt'ring, grinning, mouthing, jabb'ring all,
And *R*———, and railing, Brangling, and *B*———,[6]   220
D——*s* and Dissonance;[7] And captious art,
And snip-snap short, and interruption smart.
Hold (cry'd the Queen) ye all alike shall win,
Equal your merits, equal is your din;
But that this well-disputed game may end,   225
Sound forth my *Brayers*, and the welkin rend.

As when the long-ear'd, milky mothers wait[8]
At some sick miser's triple-bolted gate,[9]
For their[10] defrauded, absent foals they make[11]

---

[1] In the MS.:
"So great Achilles! Paris learnt the art
To touch thy only penetrable part."
[2] In the MS.: "By Venus taught."
[3] In the MS. the above passage runs:
"For noise and nonsense next behold the prize,
Whose voice stentorian loudest shakes the skies;
Who fails to ravish or command the heart
With Shakespeare's nature, or with Jonson's art,
Shall wake the sense and terrify the soul
With rolling thunder } from the mustard-bowl."
    thunders rattling }
[4] In the MS. the next four lines are:
"Now try we first who cat-like growl and whine,
The next who chattering match the monkey line.
Who emulates an owl shall these surpass,
But he the chief whose braying shames an ass."
Or,

"Try then new arts whose feebly plaining lines,
Match the thin music of the cat who whines:"
    &c.
[5] In the MS.:
"Welstead and Wickstead at each other grin."
[6] In the MS.:
"Welsted at Wickstead, Budgell at Breval."
In 1729:
"And Noise and Norton, Brangling and
    Breval."
[7] In the MS.: "And loud-tongued Disso-
nance."
[8] In the MS.: "Mother milked before."
[9] In the MS.:
"The gouty miser's triple-bolted door."
[10] In the MS.: "her."
[11] In the MS.: "foal she makes."

A moan [1] so loud, that all the *Guild* awake: [2]   230
So sighs Sir *G———t*, starting at the bray
From dreams of millions, and three groats [8] to pay.
So swells each Windpipe; [4] Ass intones to Ass,
Harmonic twang! [5] of leather, horn, and brass:
Such as from lab'ring [6] lungs th' Enthusiast blows,   235
High sounds, attemp'red to the vocal nose.
But far o'er all sonorous *Bl—'s* strain,
Walls, steeples, skies, bray back to him again:
In *Tot'nham* [7] fields, the brethren [8] with amaze
Prick all their ears up, and forget to graze; [9]   240
Long *Chanc'ry-lane* retentive rolls the sound,
And courts to courts return it round and round;
Thames wafts it thence to *Rufus'* roaring hall,
And *H———d* re-echoes, bawl for bawl.
All hail him victor in both gifts of Song,   245
Who sings so *loudly*, and who sings so *long*. [10]

    This labor past, by *Bridewell* all descend, ⟡
(As morning [11] pray'r and flagellation end).
To where *Fleet-ditch* with disemboguing streams
Rolls the large tribute of dead dogs to *Thames*,   250
The king of Dykes! than whom, no sluice of mud
With deeper sable blots the silver flood.
'Here strip, my children! here at once leap in!
'Here prove who best can dash thro' thick and thin,
'And who the most in love of dirt excel,   255
'Or dark dexterity of groping well. [12]
'Who flings most mud, and wide pollutes around
'The stream, be his the * * * [13] *Journals*, bound.
'A pig of lead to him who dives the best;
'A peck of coals a-piece shall glad the rest.'   260

    In naked majesty great *D———* [14] stands,
And *Milo*-like surveys his arms and hands:
Then sighing, thus. "And am I now *threescore?*
"Ah why, ye Gods! should two and two make four?"
He said, and climb'd a stranded Lighter's height,   265

---

[1] In the MS.: "cry."
[2] In the MS.: "awakes."
[8] In the MS.: "a groat."
[4] In the MS.: "such chatter rises."
[5] In the MS.: "Dry sound that twangs."
[6] In the MS.: "groaning."
[7] In the MS.: "Tothill."
[8] In the MS.: "asses."
[9] In the MS.:
"Prick all their ears, and wondering cease to graze."
[10] In the MS.:

"Confessed supreme in both the powers of song,
None sings so loudly, and none sings so long."
Or:
"And 'Blackmore, Blackmore,' shouts the applauding throng,
Who sings so *loudly*, and who sings so *long*."
[11] In the MS.: "Evening."
[12] In the MS.:
    "And whose the alacrity of sinking well."
[13] In the MS.: { "The London. / All Hoadley's."
[14] In the MS.: "Great Dennis"; and so in the edition of 1729. In 1736: "Oldmixon."

Shot to the black abyss, and plung'd down-right.
The senior's judgment all the crowd admire,
Who but to sink the deeper, rose the higher.

Next *E*—[1] div'd; slow circles dimpled o'er
The quaking mud, that clos'd and op'd no more:[2]   270
All look, all sigh, and call on *E*— lost;
E——— in vain resounds thro' all the coast.

H— try'd the next,[3] but hardly snatch'd from sight,
Instant buoys up, and rises into light;
He bears no token of the sabler streams,   275
And mounts far off, among the swans of *Thames*.

Far worse unhappy *D*——*r*[4] succeeds,
He search'd for coral, but he gather'd weeds.

True to the bottom * * * and * * * creep,[5]
Long-winded both, as natives of the deep,   280
This only merit pleading for the prize,[6]
Nor everlasting *Bl*— this denies.[7]

But nimbler *W*——*d* reaches at the ground,[8]
Circles in mud, and darkness all around,
No crab more active, in the dirty dance,   285
Downward to climb, and backward to advance;
He brings up half the bottom on his head,
And boldly claims the *Journals*[9] and the *Lead*.

Sudden, a burst of thunder shook the flood,
Lo *E*—[10] rose, tremendous all in mud![11]   290
Shaking the horrors of his sable brows,
And each ferocious feature grim with ooze.
Greater he looks, and more than mortal stares;
Then thus the wonders of the deep declares.

First he relates, how sinking to the chin,   295
Smit with his mien, the *Mudnymphs* suck'd him in,
How young *Lutetia* softer than the down,

[1] In the MS.: "Eusden." In the edition of 1729: "Smedley."
[2] In the MS.:
"Just where he sunk that closing oped no more."
[3] In the edition of 1729: "Then * * tried." In 1735: "Then P * * essayed." In 1736: "Then * essayed."
[4] In the MS.: "Diaper."
[5] In the MS.: "Roome and Whatley." In 1729: "See Concanen creep."
[6] In edition of 1729:
"If perseverance gain the Diver's prize."
[7] In the MS.: "Blackmore."

[8] In the edition of 1729 this and the next three lines run:
"Not Welsted so: drawn endlong by his skull, Furious he sinks, precipitately dull.
Whirlpools and storms his circling arms invest With all the might of gravitation blest."
In 1735 the opening of the passage was altered to: "Not so bold Arnall."
[9] In the MS.: "H—d—y."
[10] In the MS.: "Dennis." In the edition of 1729: "Smedley."
[11] In the edition of 1729: "In majesty of mud."

'*grina* black, and *Merdamante* brown,
'd for his love in jetty bow'rs below;
Hylas fair was ravish'd long ago.   300
en sung how, shown him by the nutbrown maids,
branch of *Styx* here rises from the *Shades*,
at tinctur'd as it runs with *Lethe's* streams,
d wafting vapors from the *Land* of *Dreams*,
s under seas *Alphœus'* sacred sluice [1]   305
ars *Pisa's* offerings to his *Arethuse*)
urs into *Thames*: Each City-bowl is full
the mixt wave, and all who drink grow dull.
w to the banks where bards departed doze,
ey led him soft; how all the bards arose;   310
ylor, sweet bird of *Thames*, majestic bows,
And *Sh*— nods the poppy [2] on his brows;
While *M—n* there, deputed by the rest,
Gave him the cassock, surcingle, and vest;
And "Take (he said) these robes which once were mine, 315
"Dulness is sacred in a sound Divine."

He ceas'd, and show'd the robe; the crowd confess
The rev'rend *Flamen* in his lengthen'd dress.
Slow mov'd the Goddess from the silver flood,[3]
(Her Priest preceding) thro' the gates of *Lud*.   320
Her *Criticks* there she summons, and proclaims
A gentler exercise to close the games.

Hear you! in whose grave heads,[4] as equal scales,
I weigh what author's heaviness prevails,
Which most conduce to sooth the soul in slumbers,[5]   325
My *H—'s* [6] periods, or my *Bl—'s* [7] numbers?
Attend the trial we propose to make:
If there be man who o'er such works can wake,
Sleep's all-subduing pow'r who dares defy,
And boasts *Ulysses'* ear with *Argus'* eye; [8]   330
To him we grant our amplest pow'rs to sit
Judge of all present, past, and future wit,
To cavil, censure, dictate, right or wrong,
Full, and eternal privilege of tongue.

[1] In the MS.:
" As Alpheus under seas by secret sluice."
[2] In the MS.: " Poppies."
[3] In the MS. this and the three next lines run:
" This done, the goddess from the sable flood
Moves to her quarters in the walls of Lud.
The tribes pursue, and now, to close the games,
A gentler exercise the Queen proclaims."
[4] In the MS.:
      " My critics! in whose heads."
[5] In the MS.: " To indolence and slumbers."
[6] In the MS.: " Hoadley."

[7] In the MS.: " Blackmore."
[8] After ver. 328 in the MS.:
" His be the license which shall ever last
On all my authors, present, future, past.
Yet, not to drive well-willers to despair,
Who haply slumber some reward shall share.
To him who nodding steals a transient nap,
We give Tate's Ovid, and thy Virgil, Trap.
Unable heads, that sleep and wake by fits,
Win Steel well sifted from all alien wits.
Nay, who successless quite but gape and wish,
Shall gain the whole Poetic Art of Bysshe."

Three *Cambridge Sophs* and three pert *Templars* came, 335
The same their talents, and their tastes the same;
Each prompt to query, answer, and debate,
And smit with love of poesie and prate.
The pond'rous books two *gentle Readers* bring;
The heroes sit; the vulgar form a ring.[1] 340
The clam'rous crowd is hush'd with mugs of *Mum*,
'Till all tun'd equal, send a general hum.
Then mount the Clerks; and in one lazy tone,[2]
Thro' the long, heavy, painful page,[3] drawl on,
Soft creeping words on words the sense[4] compose, 345
At ev'ry line, they stretch, they yawn, they doze.
As to soft gales top-heavy pines bow low
Their heads, and lift them as they cease to blow,
Thus oft they rear, and oft the head decline,
As breathe, or pause, by fits, the airs divine,[5] 350
And now to this side, now to that, they nod,
As verse, or prose, infuse the drowzy God.
Thrice *B—l*[6] aim'd to speak, but thrice supprest
By potent *Arthur*, knock'd his chin and breast.[7]
C—s and *T—d*,[8] prompt at Priests to jeer, 355
Yet silent bow'd to *Christ's no kingdom* here.
Who sate the nearest, by the words o'ercome
Slept first, the distant nodded to the hum.
Then down are roll'd the books; stretch'd o'er 'em lies .
Each gentle clerk, and mutt'ring seals his eyes. 360
As what a *Dutchman* plumps into the lakes,[9]
One circle first, and then a second makes,[10]
What Dulness dropt among her sons imprest
Like motion, from one circle to the rest;
So from the mid-most the nutation spreads 365
Round, and more round, o'er all the sea of heads.[11]
At last *C—re*[12] felt her voice to fail,
And * * *[13] himself unfinish'd left his Tale.
T—s and *T—* the church and state gave o'er,
Nor * * * talk'd, nor S—— whisper'd more.[14] 370

[1] After ver. 338 in the MS.:
" And first a Laureate youth in gentlest lays
Preludes a lullaby in Brunswick's praise."
[2] In the MS.: "In one low equal tone."
[3] In the MS.: "Line."
[4] In the MS.: "Each restless sense."
[5] In the MS.:
" As less or more are breathed the airs divine."
[6] In the MS.: "Budgell."
[7] After ver. 352, in the MS.:
" Next, Philips dropt, and Thule left half sung;
Next, Collins, ceased thy turbulence of tongue."
[8] In the MS.: "Collins and Toland." In
1729: "Toland and Tindal."
[9] In the MS.: "A lake."
[10] In the MS.:

" Will first one circle, then a hundred make."
[11] In the MS.: "A waving sea of heads."
And after this verse in the MS.:
" Not more, when winds succeed some heavy
rain,
Unnumbered nod the poppies on the plain."
[12] In the MS.: "Centlivre."
[13] In the MS.: "Bruce." In edition of
1729: "Old James." In 1736: "Motteux
himself."
[14] In the MS.: "Travers and Trapp." In
edition of 1729:
" Boyer the State, and Law the Stage gave
o'er,
Nor Motteux talked, nor Naso whispered more."
In the MS. the second line is:

Ev'n *N———n*, gifted with his mother's tongue,
Tho' born at *Wapping*, and from *Daniel* sprung,[1]
Ceas'd his loud bawling breath, and dropt the head;[2]
And all was hush'd, as *Folly's* self lay dead.

Thus the soft gifts of *Sleep* conclude the day,   375
And stretch'd on bulks, as usual, Poets lay.
Why should I sing what bards the Nightly Muse
Did slumb'ring visit, and convey to stews?
Or prouder march'd, with magistrates in state,
To some fam'd round-house, ever open gate!   380
How *E———* lay inspir'd beside a sink,
And to mere mortals seem'd a Priest in drink?
All others timely to the neighbouring *Fleet*
(Haunt of the Muses) made their safe retreat.

" Nor Kelsal talked, nor $\left\{ \begin{array}{c} \text{Loughton} \\ \text{Selkirk} \end{array} \right\}$ whispered
    more."
In 1736:
" Nor Kelsey talked, nor Naso whispered more."
In 1743:
" Morgan and Mandeville could prate no more."
   [1] In the MS.:
" Norton himself, untired in foul debate,
Sprung from Defoe, and born at Billingsgate."

In the edition of 1729:
" Norton from Daniel and Ostræa sprung,
Blest with his father's front, and mother's
    tongue."
   [2] In the MS.:
" Even he sat mute: on critics critics spread."
In edition of 1729:
" Hang silent down his never-blushing head."

2 O

END OF THE SECOND BOOK.

THE DUNCIAD.

BOOK THE THIRD.

BUT in her *Temple's* last recess inclos'd,
On *Dulness'* lap th' Anointed head repos'd.[1]
Him close she curtain'd round with vapors blue,
And soft besprinkled with *Cimmerian* dew.[2]
Then Raptures high the seat of sense o'erflow,[3]   5
Which only heads refin'd[4] from reason know :
Hence from the straw where *Bedlam's* Prophet nods,
He hears loud[5] Oracles, and talks with Gods ;
Hence the Fool's paradise, the Statesman's scheme,
The air-built Castle, and the golden Dream,   10
The Maid's romantic wish,[6] the Chymist's flame
And Poet's vision of eternal fame.

And now, on Fancy's easy wing convey'd,[7]
The King[8] descended to th' *Elyzian* shade.
There in a dusky vale where *Lethe* rolls,   15
Old *Bavius* sits, to dip poetic souls,
And blunt the sense, and fit it for a skull[9]
Of solid proof, impenetrably dull.
Instant when dipt, away they wing their flight,
Where[10] *Brown* and *Mears* unbar the gates of Light,   20
Demand new bodies, and in Calf's array
Rush to the world, impatient for the day.
Millions and millions on these banks he views,
Thick as the Stars of night, or morning dews,[11]
As thick as bees o'er vernal blossoms fly,   25
As thick as eggs at *W——d* in pillory.

Wond'ring he gaz'd : When lo! a Sage appears,
By his broad shoulders known, and length of ears,
Known by the band and suit which *Settle* wore,
(His only suit) for twice three years before.   30
All as the Vest, appear'd the wearer's frame,

[1] In the MS.:
" But in the Temple's holiest holy spread,
On Dulness' lap was laid the anointed head."
[2] In MS.:
" And sprinkled o'er his lids Lethæan dew."
[3] In MS.:
" O'er all his brain ecstatic raptures flow."
[4] In MS.: " Well-purged."
[5] In the MS.: " high."
[6] In the MS.: " The maiden's reverie."
[7] In the MS.:
" In the soft arms of Sleep and Death con-
veyed."

[8] In the MS.: " He seems."
[9] In the MS. this and the next five lines stand:
" And proof to sense, impenetrably dull,
With Achillean thickness arm the skull.
Instant away they scud, just shake their ears,
Knock at the gate of Life (which Curll and Mears
Let wide to all), assume a calf-skin dress
Demanding birth, impatient for the press."
[10] Booksellers. — POPE.
[11] In the MS.:
" As thick as stars, as thick as morning dews."

Old in new state, another, yet the same.
Bland and familiar as in life, begun
Thus the great Father to the greater Son.

Oh! born to see what none can see awake!   35
Behold the wonders of th' *Oblivious Lake.*
Thou, yet unborn, hast touch'd this sacred shore,
The hand of *Bavius* [1] drench'd thee o'er and o'er.
But blind to former, as to future, *Fate,*
What mortal knows his [2] pre-existent state?   40
Who knows how long,[3] thy transmigrating soul
Did from *Bœotian* to *Bœotian* roll? [4]
How many *Dutchmen* she vouchsaf'd to thrid?
How many stages thro' old *Monks* she rid?
And all who since, in mild benighted days,   45
Mix'd the Owl's ivy with the Poet's bays?
As Man's mæanders to the vital spring
Roll all their tydes, then back their circles bring;
Or whirligigs, twirl'd round by skilful swain,
Suck the thread in, then yield it out again: 50
All nonsense thus, of old or modern date,
Shall in thee centre, from thee circulate.
For this, our Queen unfolds [5] to vision true
Thy mental eye, far thou hast much to view:
Old scenes of glory, times long cast behind,   55
Shall first recall'd, rush forward to thy mind;
Then stretch thy sight o'er all her rising reign,
And let the past and future fire thy brain.[6]

Ascend this hill, whose cloudy point commands
Her boundless [7] Empire over seas and lands.   60
See round the poles where keener spangles [8] shine,
Where spices smoke beneath the burning Line,

[1] In the MS.: "The sacred Bavius."
There is also the following variation of this passage:
"These arms my T—d drenched thee o'er and o'er,
I made thee proof to all the points of sense,
Impenetrable dulness thy defence.
Know, unremembering of thy former fate,
What dulness graced thy pre-existent state.
Thou wert Ap Rice, Van-Dunk, and numbers more,
Who Cambrian leek or High-Dutch laurel wore.
What though no bees around thy cradle flew,
Nor on thy lips distilled their golden dew,
Yet have I oft —— in their stead
A swarm of drones have buzzed about thy head
When you, like Orpheus, strike the warbling lyre,
Attentive blocks stand round thee and admire.
Come then (for Dulness sure accords this grace),
Come and survey the wonders of the place,
Survey thy progeny, the illustrious throng,
In Nature's order as they move along.
Ascend this mount from whence thy eye commands," &c.

[2] In the MS.:
"Thou know'st not, son, thy."
[3] In the MS.: "Thou know'st not how."
[4] In the MS.:
"Did long from Dutchman down to Dutchman roll?"
[5] In the MS.: "Has purged."
[6] In the MS.:
"Let scenes of glory past inflame thy mind,
How wide her empire once and unconfined."
Or:
"Scenes of old glory, all her ancient reign,
Shall, thus recalled, rush forward on thy brain."
[7] In the MS.: "Spacious."
[8] In the MS.: "Freezing planets."

(Earth's wide extreams) her sable flag display'd;
And all the nations cover'd in [1] her shade!

Far Eastward cast thy eye, from whence the *Sun*   65
And orient *Science* at a birth begun.
One man immortal all that pride confounds,
He, whose long *Wall* the wand'ring *Tartar* bounds.[2]

[3]Heav'ns! what a pyle? whole ages perish there:
And one bright blaze turns Learning into air.   70

Thence to the South as far extend thy eyes;
Their rival flames with equal glory rise,
From shelves to shelves [4] see greedy *Vulcan* roll,
And lick up [5] all their *Physick* of the *Soul.*

How little, see! that portion of the ball,   75
Where faint at best the beams of science fall!
Against her throne, from *Hyperborean* skies,
In dulness strong, th' avenging *Vandals* rise; [6]
Lo where *Mæotis* sleeps, and hardly flows
The freezing [7] *Tanais* thro' a waste of snows,   80
The North by myriads [8] pours her mighty sons,
Great nurse of *Goths*, of *Alans*, and of *Huns.*
See *Alaric's* stern port, the martial [9] frame
Of *Genseric*, and *Attila's* dread name!
See! the bold *Ostrogoths* on *Latium* fall;   85
See! the fierce *Visigoths* on *Spain* and *Gaul.*
See! where the morning gilds the palmy shore,
(The soil that arts and infant letters bore)
His conq'ring tribes th' *Arabian* prophet draws,
And saving Ignorance enthrones by Laws.   90
See *Christians*, *Jews*, one heavy sabbath keep,
And all the Western World believe and sleep.

Lo *Rome* herself, proud mistress now no more
Of arts, but thund'ring against *Heathen* lore;
Her gray-hair'd Synods damning books unread,   95
And *Bacon* trembling for his brazen Head.
Lo statues, temples, theatres o'erturn'd,
Oh glorious ruin! and * * *[10] burn'd.

---

[1] In the MS.: " Safe beneath."

[2] In the MS.:
" That early dawn which sudden night surrounds."

[3] *Ho-am-ti*, Emperor of *China*, the same who built the great wall between *China* and *Tartary*, destroyed all the books and learned men of that empire. — POPE.

[4] The *Caliph, Omar I.* having conquer'd *Ægypt*, caused his General to burn the *Ptole-* *mæan* library, on the gates of which was this inscription, *Medicina Animæ.* — POPE.

[5] In the MS.: " swallow."

[6] In the MS.:
" Southward behold from Libya's torrid skies,
Against her throne the glorious Vandal rise."

[7] In the MS.: " The streams of."

[8] In the MS.: " Millions."

[9] In the MS.: " God-like."

[10] In the MS.: { " Virgilius."
                   { " A Varius."

See'st thou an *Isle*, by Palmers, Pilgrims trod,
Men bearded, bald. cowl'd, uncowl'd, shod, unshod,[1]   100
Peel'd, patch'd, and pieball'd, linsey-woolsey brothers
Grave mummers, sleeveless some, and shirtless others.
That once was *Britain* — Happy! had she seen
No fiercer sons, had[2] *Easter* never been.[3]
In peace, great Goddess! ever be ador'd;   105
How keen the war, if dulness draw the sword?
Thus visit not thy own![4] on this blest age
Oh spread thy Influence, but restrain thy Rage!

And see my son, the hour is on its way
That lifts our Goddess to imperial sway:[5]   110
This fav'rite Isle, long sever'd from her reign,
Dove-like, she gathers to her wings again.
Now look thro' Fate! behold the scene she draws!
What aids, what armies, to assert her cause!
See all her progeny, illustrious sight!   115
Behold, and count them[6] as they rise to light:
As *Berecynthia*,[7] while her offspring vye
In homage, to the mother of the sky,
Surveys around her in the blest abode
A hundred sons, and ev'ry son a God.   120
Not with less glory[8] mighty *Dulness* crown'd,
Shall take thro' *Grubstreet* her triumphant round,
And all *Parnassus* glancing o'er at once,
Behold a hundred sons, and each a dunce.

Mark first the youth who takes the foremost place   125
And thrusts his person full into your face.
With all thy Father's virtues blest, be born!
And a new *C———r* shall the stage adorn.

See yet a younger, by his blushes known,
And modest as the maid who sips alone.   130
From the strong fate of drams if thou get free,
Another *Durfey*, * * * shall sing in thee.
For thee each Ale-house, and each Gill-house mourn,
And answ'ring Gin-shops sowrer sights return.

Behold yon pair, in strict embraces join'd;   135
How like their manners, and how like their mind!

Fam'd for good nature, *B*——[1] and for truth,
D———[2] for pious passion to the youth.
Equal in wit, and equally polite,
Shall this a *Pasquin*, that a *Grumbler* write;   140
Like are their merits, like rewards they share,
That shines a Consul, this Commissioner.

Ah *D*———, *G*———[3] ah! what ill-starr'd rage
Divides a friendship long confirm'd by age?
Blockheads with reason wicked wits abhor,   145
But fool with fool is barb'rous, civil war.
Embrace, embrace, my Sons! be foes no more!
Nor glad vile Poets with true Criticks' gore.

See next two slip-shod *Muses* traipse along,
In lofty madness meditating song,[4]   150
With tresses staring from poetic dreams,
And never wash'd, but in *Castalia's* streams.
H——— and *T*———,[5] glories of their race!
Lo *H*——*ck's*[6] fierce, and *M*——*'s*[7] rueful face!
W——*n*, the scourge[8] of Scripture, mark with awe!   155
And mighty *J*———*b*,[9] Blunderbus of Law!
Lo thousand thousand, ev'ry nameless name,
All crowd, who foremost shall be damn'd to fame;
How proud! how pale! how earnest all appear!
How rhymes eternal gingle in their ear!   160

Pass these to nobler sights: Lo *H*— stands
Tuning his voice, and balancing his hands,[10]
How honey'd nonsense trickles from his tongue!
How sweet the periods, neither said nor sung!
Still break the benches, *H*— with thy strain,   165
While *K*———, *Br*———, *W*———[11] preach in vain
Round him, each *Science* by its modern type
Stands known; *Divinity* with box and pipe,
And proud *Philosophy* with breeches tore,
And *English Musick* with a dismal score:[12]   170
While happier *Hist'ry* with her comrade *Ale*,
Sooths the sad series of her tedious tale.[13]

[1] In the MS.: "Burnet."
[2] In the MS.: "Ducket."
[3] In the MS.: "Ah Dennis, Gildon."
[4] In the MS.:
"See Pix and slip-shod W—— traipse along,
With heads unpinned and meditating song."
[5] In the MS.: "Heywood and T——;" doubtless Thomas, the Corinna of Book ii. In 1729: "Heywood, Centlivre."
[6] In the MS.: "Horneck."
[7] In the MS.: "Mitchell."
[8] In the MS.: "Dull Woolston, scourge."
[9] In the MS.: "Jacob." In edition of 1729, the couplet was altered to the present reading.

[10] In the MS.:
"But lo, amidst yon crowd where Henley stands,
And tunes his voice, and balances his hands."
[11] Perhaps "Kennet, Bramston, Warren." In the edition of 1736: "Kennet, Hare, and Gibson." In the edition of 1743: "Sherlock, Hare, and Gibson."
[12] In the MS.:
"Music with crotchets and a tedious score."
[13] In the MS.:
"More happy History with her pots of ale,
Consoles } by fits her { long disastrous } tale."
Relieves }   { melancholy }

Fast by, in darkness palpable inshrin'd
W—s, B—r, M—n,[1] all the poring kind,
A lumberhouse of Books in every head,   175
Are ever reading, and are never read.

But who is he, in closet close y-pent,
With visage from his shelves with dust besprent?
Right well mine eyes arede that myster wight,
That wonnes in haulkes and hernes, and *H—* he hight.   180
To future ages may thy dulness last,
As thou preserv'st the dulness of the past!

But oh! what scenes, what miracles behind?
Now stretch thy view, and open all thy mind.

He look'd and saw a sable seer[2] arise,   185
Swift to whose hand a winged volume flies.
All sudden, gorgons hiss, and dragons glare,
And ten-horn'd fiends, and giants, threaten war.
Hell rises, heav'n descends, to dance on earth:
Gods, monsters, furies, musick, rage and mirth;   190
A fire, a jig, a battel, and a ball,
'Till one wide conflagration swallows all.

Then a new world to nature's laws unknown,
Refulgent rises, with a heav'n its own:
Another *Cynthia* her new journey runs,   195
And other planets circle other suns:
The forests dance, the rivers upward rise,
Whales sport in woods, and dolphins in the skies;
And last, to give the whole creation grace,
Lo! one vast *Egg* produces human race.   200

Silent the monarch gaz'd;[3] yet ask'd in thought
What God or Dæmon all these wonders wrought?
To whom the Sire: In yonder cloud, behold,
Whose sarcenet skirts are edg'd with flamy gold,
A godlike youth: See *Jove's* own bolts he flings,   205
Rolls the loud thunder, and the light'ning wings!
Angel of *Dulness*, sent to scatter round
Her magic charms on all unclassic ground:
Yon stars, yon suns, he rears at pleasure higher,
Illumes their light, and sets their flames on fire.[4]   210
Immortal *R——ch!* how calm he sits at ease,
Mid snows of paper, and fierce hail of pease?
And proud his mistress' orders to perform,
Rides in the whirlwind, and directs the storm.

---

[1] Perhaps " Watts, Baker, Milbourn."

[2] In 1729: " A sable sorcerer."

[3] In the MS.: " No word the king could speak."

[4] After this verse in the MS.:
" His lightnings flash, his mimic thunders roll,
Like Jove's own delegate from bowl to bowl."

But lo! to dark encounter in mid air[1]   215
New wizards rise: here *B——th,* and *C——r* there.
B——th in his cloudy tabernacle shrin'd,
On grinning dragons *C———r* mounts the wind:
Dire is the conflict, dismal is the din,
Here shouts all *Drury,* there all *Lincoln's-Inn;*   220
Contending Theatres our empire raise,
Alike their labours, and alike their praise.

And are these wonders, Son, to thee unknown?
Unknown to thee? These wonders are thy own.
These Fate reserv'd to grace thy reign divine,   225
Foreseen by me, but ah! withheld from mine.
In *Lud's* old walls tho' long I rul'd renown'd,
Far as loud *Bow's* stupendous bells resound;
Tho' my own Aldermen conferr'd my bays,
To me committing their eternal[2] praise,   230
Their full-fed Heroes, their pacific May'rs,
Their annual trophies, and their monthly wars:
Tho'[3] long my Party built on me their hopes,
For writing Pamphlets, and for roasting *Popes*
(Different our parties, but with equal grace   235
Our Goddess smiles on *Whig* and *Tory* race,
'T is the same rope at sev'ral ends they twist,
To *Dulness, Ridpath* is as dear as *Mist*).
Yet lo! in me what Authors have to brag on!
Reduc'd at last to hiss in my own dragon.   240
Avert it, heav'n! that thou or *C———r* e'er
Should wag two serpent tails in *Smithfield* fair.
Like the vile straw that's blown about the streets,
The needy Poet sticks to all he meets,
Coach'd, carted, trod upon, now loose, now fast,   245
In the Dog's tail his progress ends at last.
Happier thy fortunes! like a rolling stone
Thy giddy dulness still shall lumber on,
Safe in its heaviness, can never stray,
And licks up every blockhead in the way.   250
Thy dragons * * and * *[4] shall taste,
And from each show rise duller than the last:
'Till rais'd from Booths to Theatre, to Court,
Her seat imperial Dulness shall transport.

[1] In the MS., this and the next three lines stand:
"See opposite, with Cibber at his side,
Booth, in his cloudy tabernacle ride;
On flaming dragons in the fields of air,
Seer wars with seer here, Rich and Cibber there."

[2] In the MS.: "Immortal."

[3] *Settle* was once famous for party papers, but very uncertain in his political principles.

He was employ'd to hold the pen in the *Character of a popish successor,* but afterwards printed his *Narrative* on the contrary side.

He managed the ceremony and pageants at the burning of a famous *Pope,* and was at length employ'd in making the machinery at *Bartholomew* fair, where in his old age he acted in a dragon of leather of his own invention. — POPE.

[4] In MS.:
"Peers and Potentates," or, "Up— and L—."

(Already, *Opera* prepares the way,   255
The sure fore-runner of her gentle sway.)
To aid her cause, if heav'n thou canst not bend,
Hell thou shalt move; for *Faustus* is thy friend:
Pluto with *Cato* thou for her shalt join,
And link the *Mourning-Bride* to *Proserpine*.   260
Grubstreet! thy fall should men and Gods conspire,
Thy stage shall stand, ensure it but from Fire.
Another *Æschylus* appears! prepare
For new [1] Abortions, all ye pregnant fair!
In flames like *Semele's* be brought to bed,   265
While opening Hell spouts wild-fire at your head.

Now *Bavius* take the poppy from thy brow,
And place it here! here all ye Heroes bow!
This, this is He, foretold by ancient rhymes,
Th' *Augustus*, born to bring *Saturnian* times!   270
Beneath his reign, shall *E———n* wear the bays,
C———r preside, Lord Chancellor of Plays,
B——— sole judge of Architecture sit,
And *A—e P—s* be preferr'd for Wit!
I see th' unfinish'd *Dormitory* wall!   275
I see the *Savoy* totter to her fall!
The sons of *Isis* reel! the towns-men sport;
And *Alma Mater* all dissolv'd in *Port!*

Then, when these signs declare the mighty Year,
When the dull Stars roll round, and re-appear;   280
Let there be darkness! (the dread pow'r shall say)
All shall be darkness, as it ne'er were Day;
To their first Chaos Wit's vain works shall fall,
And universal Dulness cover all!

No more the Monarch could such raptures bear;   285
He wak'd, and all the Vision mix'd with air.

---

[1] It is reported of *Æschylus* that when his Tragedy of the *Eumenides* was acted, the audience were so terrified that the children fell into fits, and the bigbelly'd women miscarry'd. *T———d* is translating this Author. — POPE.

FINIS.

INDEX TO FIRST LINES.